Titles in the Series

THE
NEW BRITISH
HISTORY

Founding a Modern State
1603–1715

Edited by

Glenn Burgess

I.B.Tauris *Publishers*
LONDON • NEW YORK

Published in 1999 by I.B.Tauris & Co Ltd
Victoria House, Bloomsbury Square, London WC1B 4DZ
175 Fifth Avenue, New York NY 10010

In the United States and Canada distributed by St. Martin's Press
175 Fifth Avenue, New York NY 10010

ISBN 1 86064 190 3

A full CIP record for this book is available from the British Library
A full CIP record for this book is available from the Library of
Congress

Library of Congress catalog card: available

Typeset in 10/12pt New Baskerville by the Midlands Book Typesetting
Company, Loughborough
Printed and bound in Great Britain by WBC Ltd, Bridgend

Contents

PREFACE

This collection of essays takes stock of the ways in which 'the new British history' has illuminated the history of Britain and Ireland in the seventeenth century. There are now many collections of essays in which early modern 'British' history is practised. There are also essays in the present collection that are exercises in 'British' history; but the collection as a whole aims to be critical. Critical, that is, in the sense that it tries to stand back from the subject and provide some reflection on it. That reflection takes various forms, from mild scepticism to convinced advocacy. There are essays that respond to critics of the new British history, and essays that add to the criticisms. There are essays that are substantive examples of British history, and others that are historiographical analyses. The book has no overall thesis to argue (and it should be emphasised, therefore, that the arguments of its introduction reflect the views only of its editor and not of the other contributors); and the contributors have been allowed to choose an approach and direction with which they feel comfortable. Nonetheless, the book as a whole has a shape and purpose that transcends the variety of opinions contained within it. I hope that it will enable readers, especially students, to approach the new British history with intelligent caution – but also with an expectation that it might suggest some new approaches to some seemingly familiar subjects.

Attempts to find authors for proposed chapters on sixteenth-century developments in 'British' history, and on the theme of Gaelic responses to Anglicisation, sadly failed. Both chapters would have added to the book's range; but I remain grateful, indeed, to the team of contributors who signed up for the project. They have produced, with speed and efficency, a set of essays that covers much ground and raises many questions. If readers learn as much from reading them as I did from editing them, then we can all be well pleased. Special thanks is owed to Dr Lester Crook at I.B. Tauris for his enthusiastic support of the project, and for his advice.

Glenn Burgess

Introduction:
The New British History

(1) WHAT IS 'BRITISH HISTORY'?[1]

The discovery of something that can be called a 'British history' has been to some historians of England a revelation of hitherto obscured and unsuspected truths. Historians of Scotland, Ireland and Wales have possibly been less amazed by the knowledge that the history of 'the triple-crowned islands' is more than just the history of England writ large.[2] 'British history' has its critics, as we shall see, but it has both captured the mood of historians in the 1990s, and provided insights into the past that have been widely, if not universally, welcomed. We are now beginning to see the publication of textbooks and student summaries of the findings of the new British history,[3] a sure sign that the development of the field is putting down deep roots. In spite of this, it is still rightly asked whether it will prove possible to 'sustain "new British" history as a legitimate and definable field of study'.[4] This collection explores ways of answering that question.

What is this 'new' British history? How does it differ from what we must assume to have been an 'old' British history? What value does it have for historians of Ireland, Scotland, Wales or England? What limitations does it have? These are the questions that this introduction raises and discusses; and to which a variety of answers can be found in the essays that follow. The book is intentionally multi-vocal. It focuses on the seventeenth century, trying to take stock of what we have so far learnt about the period from the new British history, but trying as well to ask whether there might not be ways in which the value of British history has been exaggerated. In the pages that follow themes and topics will be addressed from a variety of angles. I hope that the result encourages readers of the book, whether teachers, students or the interested general reader, to reach their own verdicts on the value of the new British history. The essays in part one attempt to survey what has so far been done in the field, and they cover both chronological periods and themes. The authors have been given the space to perform this task in a variety of ways. The essays in the second part attempt some critical assessment of 'British history' from several different perspectives.

The first question to confront is the obvious one. What, exactly, is the new British history? Oddly, one answer might be that whatever it is, it is not *British*. That word refers to the largest island of what some historians now call the 'Atlantic archipelago', that is to England, Wales and Scotland. It does not include the island of Ireland. It is no doubt a fact of some significance that there is in ordinary usage no single name that embraces all of the Atlantic archipleago – Britain, Ireland, and the outlying islands. The first person to rule over the entire group of islands, King James VI & I, carefully and correctly styled himself 'King of Great Britain, France and Ireland, Defender of the Faith, &c.'. The claim to the French crown was, by this time, of course no more than nostalgic wishful thinking; the distinction between Britain and Ireland, though, reflected James's own belief that his accession to the English throne had resulted in the 'Reuniting of these two mightie, famous, and ancient Kingdomes of England and Scotland, under one Imperiall Crowne'. Uniting 'the whole Island' of Britain still left Ireland out on a limb, a separate appendage of the English crown, notwithstanding the fact that it had been raised to the status of a kingdom by Henry VIII in 1541.[5]

Historians are left with a problem. How do we refer to a history that embraces England, Wales, Scotland *and* Ireland? Many alternatives have been tried: none combines inclusiveness with euphony. It may be that the best solution is not to try too hard. From different directions, perhaps, Toby Barnard [below] and Nicholas Canny (both of them, significantly, historians of Ireland) give us reason to think that we might wisely rest content with a terminology that itself embodies the problematic or 'enigmatic' nature of the relationship between Ireland and Britain.[6] In this collection, therefore, the term 'British history' has generally been used in historiographical discussion,[7] in good part because there is no easy alternative, and the fact that it only ambiguously and imperfectly includes Ireland reflects the fact that the history itself only imperfectly and ambiguously included Ireland. There is no point looking for a word to describe an entity which has scarcely ever existed, and may never have existed beyond all reasonable doubt. British history *aspires* to include Ireland – then and now; in writing and in reality. There is a politics as well as a history to this aspiration. And British history is about both the effort to include Ireland and the Irish resistance to inclusion.[8]

There are also problems with the place of Welsh history within a broader British history. The constitutional incorporation of Wales into the Tudor state over the years 1536–43, and the lack of protest that that union brought about, have together led to the subsumption of Welsh history into English. This is perhaps ending, with a vigorously-publishing generation of Welsh historians now writing about early-modern Wales; but it remains the case that Welsh history has probably been affected by the new British history least of all, if only because its history has been written so much with reference to England anyway. As one recent account put it, '[t]he so called Acts of Union (1536–43) are convenient pegs on which to hang virtually all developments and trends in Wales for the remainder of the period covered in this volume'.[9]

The geographical range of 'British history' is one area of ambiguity. Another is exactly what *sort* of history it is. There seem to be three possibilities, and I will refer to them as the *holistic* approach; the *episodic* approach; and the *comparative* approach. Although proponents of one of these approaches are likely to reject the others, I shall suggest that we do not need to choose between them. Each approach is appropriate to a particular purpose or in a particular field.

The *holistic* approach, of which the leading proponent is John Morrill, suggests that there is a continuous British history, embracing England and Wales, Scotland and Ireland. It does not replace the separate histories of those places, but is a higher-level history of their interrelationships and interraction. For Morrill, at least, this history is a history of two things, state-building and the mingling of peoples.[10] British history is, for a start, the story of 'the formation of a British federated and composite state', and Morrill is careful to affirm that it 'is a story about a process of state formation if not the formation of a single state'. But it is also the story of the way in which 'four or more peoples' have been caught up in this often traumatic political development, interacting, adapting and evolving in complex processes of 'refashioning'.[11] The two processes combined to produce peoples aware of their own particular identity; but only in some cases and only intermittently were (and are) these peoples fully aware of their joint Britishness. Defining the subject in this way avoids an excessive reliance upon a one-way process, the acculturation of Scots, Irish and Welsh to English norms. All peoples of the Atlantic archipelago, the English included, became involved in historical interactions that altered the particular and joint identities of them all.

Morrill has in part defined this approach through a critique of the *episodic* approach practised by Conrad Russell.[12] Russell stands accused of writing not British history, but an 'enriched English history'.[13] His concern is – to use the title of his Ford lectures – the causes of the *English* Civil War; and he pursues British history only insofar as it helps to throw light on that subject. Thus, it is suggested, Russell's books contain no full explanation of the Scottish and Irish rebellions; both are treated primarily for their impact on English politics. However, leaving aside the question of how well Russell has in fact carried out his tasks, there seems in principle no reason to object to the sort of history he has written. All history is – as Collingwood might put it – written in answer to particular questions;[14] and content is determined by how well something serves to answer that question.[15] Provided that the question, what caused the English Civil War? is a legitimate question, then any attempt to answer it can legitimately limit itself to those aspects of a British history that directly contribute to its answer. If we do not accept this principle, there is no way of preventing a history of anything from becoming a history of everything. A history that is holistic in that sense would be a history that could not be written.

Accepting the legitimacy of an episodic approach, we are still left with the need to define it. It consists in the view that at certain points, but not continuously, the histories of the component parts of the British Isles intersect. These episodes – perhaps 1603–8, 1638–51, 1688–90, 1707 – need to be understood in pan-British terms. So much so that it might be argued that at these points a history confined to England, Scotland or Ireland is in principle invalid. It might remain true that at other times, the 1620s perhaps is an example, there is no reason why the history of England cannot be written substantially without reference to a wider British context. Methodologically, as I have suggested, this episodic approach might be based on the logic of question and answer: for some periods and not others historians pose questions that require British answers.

The *comparative* approach to British history might seem less problematic. Comparative history is not a new thing. Nonetheless, I fear that comparative history is in itself a problematic enterprise. It suffers too readily from the fault of 'arbitrary connectedness' (to appropriate a handy phrase that has been used in a different context, against the literary-critical movement known as the 'New Historicism'). One can compare any two things, given sufficient ingenuity; but why are some comparisons more valid and more enlightening than others? Is a comparison of England and Scotland any more significant than one of Scotland and France, or England and China, or Ireland and Brazil, or Wales and Lichtenstein? The questions suggest the difficulty of defending the *especial* validity of British history by pointing out the benefits of comparing the histories of the component parts of the British Isles.

Jack Goldstone has suggested that, if it is to be intellectually defensible, comparative history has to do more than just compare whatever might be at hand. It should concentrate either on uncovering and exploring what he calls 'robust processes'; or on examining *causes*, through a consideration of the significant similarities and differences between the causes of events deemed to be of the same type.[16] In the latter sense, comparative history explores historical causation in much the same way that 'virtual history' does, the only difference being that counterfactual comparisons involve imaginary scenarios, while comparative history examines two actual causal sequences side-by-side.[17] In both, one attempts to illuminate causes by comparing one set of events with another that may be either real or imagined.

It is apparent that Conrad Russell's examination of the causes of the English civil war is not just episodic, but in places also an exercise in the comparative history of the causes of rebellion. He has suggested that '[w]hen three kingdoms under one ruler all take to armed resistance within three years, it seems sensible to investigate the possiblility that their actions may have had some common causes'.[18] The natural result of obeying that injunction would be neither *The Causes of the English Civil War*, nor *The Fall of the British Monarchies*. It would be a comparative study of the Scottish, Irish and English rebellions, in which both similarity and difference might be discerned. (Russell's work is, of course, explicitly comparative in another sense: his understanding of the British and Irish 'multiple monarchy' is rooted in a comparative history of European multiple monarchies and composite states,[19] as we shall see later; but this is separate from the question of whether British history should in itself be seen as a form of comparative history.)

Nonetheless, the comparative approach to British history has, so far, been most obviously practised in relation to socio-economic matters. A good number of explicitly comparative essays have appeared in this field,[20] and there is much said in defence of it in Ian Whyte's contribution to the present volume. In defending the legitimacy of this approach, it may be difficult to rely upon the argument that it illuminates causal explanation. Certainly, explaining long-term economic development is an important and intriguing task;[21] but

Scottish, Irish and English socio-economic development might be thought too different to afford a ready basis for comparison. Ian Whyte identifies many important themes that could serve as the basis for a comparative British socio-economic history – most obviously the theme of regional, national and supra-national market integration. But it may also be possible here to identify one of Goldstone's 'robust processes' at work within the various early modern British economies and societies; and the comparative approach can be justified by reference to it. It concerns the changing relationship between lowland and highland societies and economies, which Steven Ellis suggests often underlay what appears superficially to be a conflict between English and Celtic or Welsh social patterns.[22] Examining socio-economic regions, and the problems of governance they created, breaks down a nationalist emphasis. The task was not one of imposing English government or landholding patterns on other peoples; but one of imposing lowland socio-political norms on highlanders, whether in the North of England, beyond the Irish Pale, or in the Scottish Highlands and Western Isles. London and the English South-East was not the only core of lowland society: there was, as well as the Dublin Pale, the Scottish lowlands, to which Edinburgh stood in very approximately the same relationship that London stood to southern England.[23] British history written in these terms might be the exploration of a robust process occurring across and within three kingdoms, and much of its approach would be explicitly comparative (as in the recent work, albeit with a sharply political edge, of Steven Ellis).[24]

Each of these approaches seems to possess some degree of value, provided that we are clear about our purposes in employing them. British history may be no single type of history, but a combination of holistic, episodic and comparative histories that together match the elusive complexity of its subject matter. The final section of John Morrill's contribution to this volume comes to a similar, or at least compatible, conclusion. The new British history is too new to be able to afford any premature closure of this question about its own identity. This is true not least because the critics of British history have generally attributed to it a simple rather than multiple identity. Refusal to accept such an identity enables a flexibility of response to these critics, as we shall see.

(2) ATLANTIC ARCHIPELAGO, MULTIPLE MONARCHY AND THE BRITISH ATLANTIC: A SURVEY OF HISTORIOGRAPHICAL TRENDS

Although the self-conscious effort to study 'British history', in the senses defined above, is relatively new, it nonetheless has an interesting historiography, one that has been developing rapidly over a short space of time.

A number of contributors to the present volume (especially Morrill and Claydon) explore the way in which historians dealt with British subjects before the advent of the 'new' British history with which we are primarily concerned. They show us that a British history did exist before the new British history, at least for some portions of the past; and that it was a history that could be tightly coherent. It was the history of the making of the unions of 1707 and 1800 and of their consequences, told either from the 'unionist' point-of-view as a triumphalist story; or from the 'nationalist' as a story of betrayal and oppression. Clearly, these too were histories with overt political implications, and in many cases the result was a form of 'Whig' history (in the sense that it served to validate a set of present-day political beliefs and goals). Leaving aside the question of whether it is desirable or possible to aspire to write a value-free history, it might nonetheless be thought that history is better written with the sound of axes grinding at a less deafening pitch. Few historians – certainly few *English* historians – wrote British history of this sort before recent times. One honourable exception, uncovered by Morrill, was Dame Veronica Wedgwood. In one of her essays, indeed, she managed deftly to weave a Britsh dimension into an account of the causes of the English Civil War that emphasised foreign and European politics as much as domestic. In the process, Wedgwood anticipated a claim that has been much elaborated by Conrad Russell, that the Irish rebellion 'was greatly stimulated by fear of what the powerful English parliament . . . might perpetrate in Ireland'.[25]

The 'new British history' might, in a sense, count as doubly 'revisionist'. It is, like the revisionism of Tudor-Stuart historiography, a reaction against the Whig view of the English past. That Whig view included, among many other elements, a belief that can be traced back to the seventeenth century, that English history is a self-sufficient thing in which the main patterns of development owe nothing to outside influence, whether European or British. But there may also be discerned within the new British history, as more obviously in Irish 'revisionism',[26] a reaction against an overtly politicised version of *British* history. The anglocentric view is that the new British history restores a forgotten dimension to English history; but there is another view, in which the new British history may be revisionist in the Irish sense, seeking to escape the nationalist-unionist framework of interpretation. In this view, more likely to be accessible to Scottish and Irish historians, the new British history is not so obviously a bolt from the blue. This double character to the new historiography also helps to explain why Irish and Scottish historians are sometimes uncomfortably ambivalent in their attitude to it. In many of its forms it can very readily be *read* as containing a political message, regardless of whether or not that message was intended.

Attempts, like Wedgwood's, to incorporate a British dimension into a history that was not caught in the unionist-nationalist dichotomies were rare. There was British history of sorts in Macaulay and Lecky, in the Oxford History of England, but it tended to be a history, whether pro- or anti-unionist, of the manifest destiny or the equally manifest perfidy behind English hegemony.[27] The 'new British history' seeks to escape a British history written purely and simply in terms of the inexorable growth of English dominance; and for that reason it must recognise the existence of separate English, Scottish, Irish and Welsh histories; as well as their particular patterns of interaction. For that reason, then, the new British history can be 'holistic'; but it can never coherently claim completely to replace the separate national histories. Their separateness and individual identites constitute the necessary basis for constructing a British history that pays attention to difference and mutuality as much as to English preponderance. For that reason, the connections between the emergence of the new British history, and the politics of the world that followed the United Kingdom's entry into the EEC or the revival of Scottish and Welsh political particularism is more complex than many commentators allow. It is as true to say that both in politics and in scholarship the trends reflect a revival of the viability of nationalism even for very small states as it is to say that they reflect a world in which the nation has been superseded by larger entities (whether they are built from nation-states, like the European Union, or built across them, like so many modern mega-corporations).

Whatever its political roots, there is no denying the sense of newness that has accompanied the turn to a particular brand of British history. When John Pocock, addressing the New Zealand Historical Association in 1973, called for something more, he did so in the form of 'a plea for a new subject'. As recently as 1982, he followed up this unheeded plea with a further account of his 'search for the new subject'.[28] The British history for which Pocock called was a long time in coming. When it did come, it bore only partial resemblance to the vision that Pocock's wizardry had so beguilingly conjured from nothing.[29]

The British history of which Pocock wrote – indeed, for which he still calls – was a history of the English and British cultural and demographic diasporas; Atlantic, later global and oceanic, in focus. British history 'should start with what I have called the Atlantic archipelago', Pocock tells us; and in that context British history is for the medieval period 'the history of contacts and penetrations between three *loci* of Anglo-Norman power – one might use the term "Scotto-Anglian" of one of them, for distinction's sake – a variety of predominantly Celtic societies based on kinship rather than administration, and a diversity of marcher and marginal societies brought into being by these interactions'. But it is, at least by the eighteenth century, a drama that comes to be performed on the Atlantic as well as the archipelagic stage; and then as it translates to the Pacific and elsewhere, it remains still a drama about 'the conflict between, and creation of, societies and cultures, which it has been since the beginning'.[30] There seems a sense in which – and this is not said in criticism – Pocock's vision here is one integrally related to the 'culture-contact' studies of European overseas expansion. In his second approach to the theme, Pocock was even more emphatic: '[w]hatever "British history" may be, it has not been confined to the island that the cartographers have named "Britain"'. It extends, first to Ireland, then 'into oceanic, American, and global dimensions'.[31] The 'new British history' actually written has not, on the whole, been like this. When it moves from its archipelagic core, it has tended to become, not Atlantic and oceanic, but European, terrestrial and continental. It is worth exploring the reasons behind this.

When Pocock first issued his plea there was already coming into existence work by Irish historians that could form a basis for his proposed new British history. Nicholas Canny, building on earlier work, especially by D.B. Quinn,[32] had been exploring the ways in which Tudor and Stuart Ireland was treated as a colony.[33] Ireland was the laboratory in which the ideologies and techniques of colonialism and imperialism were tested; and the reduction of Ireland to colonial status, symbolised especially by the Elizabethan, Jacobean and (later) Cromwellian plantations, was the prelude to the construction of a colonial empire in north America. The new British history, as in Pocock's vision, was thus a history that pointed to the British Atlantic. Canny's work has not surprisingly, therefore, been taken up by and published in connection with those (mostly American) historians who have been interested in developing a British Atlantic history. Some of the work done in this field quite explicitly incorporates a British dimension. The collection edited by Bernard Bailyn and Philip D. Morgan, *Strangers in the Realm: Cultural Margins of the First British Empire*,[34] includes (for example) chapters on Ireland (Canny) and Scotland (Eric Richards), alongside accounts of the roles played by various peoples (Native American, African, Dutch, German, 'Scotch-Irish') in British America and an account of the impact that the colonies had on British society and politics. The relations within 'Britain' become subsumed in an account of the relations within an Atlantic Empire. Several distinguished historians have, from very different perspectives, contributed to this trend, which has even (in work by J.C.D. Clark and Jack P. Greene) led to attempts to create new constitutional histories of the British-Atlantic empire.[35] In recent work, Pocock himself has explored the intellectual connections between the Anglo-Scottish union of 1707 and the American Revolution viewed, as he puts it, as a crisis within a 'multiple monarchy'.[36]

That last term reveals Pocock drawing upon historiographical trends that do not seem to have been at the forefront of his mind when he first issued his plea for a new subject. But the concept of 'multiple monarchy' certainly reflects Pocock's awareness of the way in which the 'new British history' had in fact developed and progressed. A key influence on these developments has been the work of an historian of early modern Spain, J.H. Elliott. Elliott explored the collapse of the Spanish monarchies in the 1640s, examining in the process the internal dynamics of a multiple monarchy. His work also became caught up in debates of the 1960s about the 'General Crisis of the Seventeenth Century', the simultaneous crisis of governmental authority afflicting many European states in the 1640s (i.e. towards the end of the Thirty Years War). That crisis had many faces – as many as there were historians to write about it, it seemed – but it served also to bring into the picture discussion of the financial and adminstrative burden imposed on states by the growing scale and cost of warfare (the so-called military revolution). Those pressures could be used to explain the rebelllions that followed the Thirty Years War. Except, of course, for England, largely uninvolved in the continental war.[37] Nonetheless, these developments in continental historiography have had a discernible impact on the revisionist historians of seventeenth century England. They have provided, at the least, a mine of comparative material on the financial and administrative weaknesses of early modern governments, and on the fragility of the control those governments could exercise over their peoples. Echoes of that might be visible in revisionist accounts of the difficulties of central administration in controlling the English counties, and in Russell's account of the politics of the 1620s, in which the pressures of England's brief involvment in war are used to explain much of the political turbulence evident during the decade.[38] It as against such a background that Elliott's analysis of composite states and multiple monarchies, generalised in an important article of 1992,[39] becomes significant. Those English historians most closely identified with the new British history – Morrill and Russell especially[40] – have been very ready to acknowledge the lessons imbibed from Elliott's work.

Seeing Britain and Ireland as a multiple monarchy has been a way of achieving one of the central tasks of revisionist writing on seventeenth century England. That task has been to overthrow 'Whiggish' emphases on the long-term destiny of the English state, to cast away such anachronisms, and to place England's, Britain's and Ireland's early modern history back in to the past to which it belongs. In doing this it may be necessary to avoid a proleptic identification of an English nation-state as the central unit of study. The British multiple monarchy is an early modern creature, not a modern one, and is at home in waters well stocked with its kindred. A multiple monarchy is, amongst other things, a form of composite state in which several units, otherwise almost completely independent of one another, come through dynastic accident or war to be ruled by a single family. They are multi-ethnic multistates, and need to be analysed in appropriate ways. (One of the obvious questions, figuring largely in the historiography, is how institutions and policies can be devised to keep the components of these states in some sort of balance.) Even those kingdoms not, except perhaps at the margins, multiple monarches were composite monarchies, in the sense that strong regional identities and institutions, reflecting in part the complex historical process of territorial acquisition and consolidation, rendered them much less than the simple coherent states that they appear to be (and, especially, as they appear with hindsight). Even England itself was, in origin at least, a composite monarchy; and its remaining regional particularisms were still a vehicle for some sort of deep memory of this fact.

The gap between these two versions of British history – the Atlantic and oceanic, with the 'Atlantic archipelago' at its core; and the 'multiple monarchy' approach founded on an implicit comparative history of early modern European state structures – is interestingly revealed in a debate between Nicholas Canny and Hiram Morgan. Canny, whom we shall later encounter as an important critic of much of what has recently been done in the name of British history, has emphasised the colonial character of early modern Ireland. In response, Morgan has pointed to the dimensions of Irish history that do not fit the colonial model. He complains that Ireland 'has been dragged into mid-Atlantic, cut off from Europe and left an English stepping-stone to America'. The English sought to reform Ireland, as the Habsburgs did the margins of their empire, not to conquer it.[41] The English did not treat Ireland as they treated their American colonies because Ireland was in the last resort part of European Christendom in ways that the colonies were not. While it is true that the Gaelic Irish could be seen by the English as barbarians – as could the Scottish Highlanders and (especially) the inhabitants of the Western Isles, even by lowlander Scots – that did not seem to place Ireland in quite the same category as the 'wilderness' encountered beyond the seas.

This debate serves as a useful fulcrum for the see-saw relationship between oceanic and continental views of British history, views which perhaps have their political counterparts in the idea that Britain's destiny lies in the European Union and the idea that it lies instead in the 'special relationship' with the United States (or even, perhaps, in a revivified no-longer-'British' Commonwealth). Historiographically, and perhaps politically, it is the continental and European view that has the upper hand, at least within the British historical community. But we need to remain aware that this is not the only way of doing British history. Nor should we assume that the two approaches that have been identified are mutually exclusive. Although they have, by and large, developed along separate trajectories, it may be that the future of the subject lies in their combination (something that is already visible in the work of Pocock, and in the activities that he has organised at the Folger Library). It may indeed be that there is important variation over time: for the seventeenth century, British history may be largely continental; for the eighteenth it must become increasingly oceanic.

(3) FOR AND AGAINST THE NEW BRITISH HISTORY

Not everyone has welcomed the development of the new British history. Among its most forceful and effective critics has been Nicholas Canny. He has suggested that the new British history exaggerates the unity of Britain and Ireland, that it improperly stresses the things that England, Scotland, Ireland and Wales have in common at the expense of 'fundamental diversities', and that it adopts a 'high politics' perspective that widens further the unhelpful gap that already exists between political and socio-economic history.[42]

In these and other comments by Canny, the most far-reaching critique that the new British history has received, we might discern four battlefronts. (1) There is the charge that British history detracts attention from the comparative perspectives, both European and colonial, that are most enlightening. Canny's emphasis on the colonial context has been discussed above, and my comments on this first line of criticism will concentrate on the question of whether British history is not better replaced by a European or – to use John Reeve's term – an Anglo-European history. (2) British history, it is claimed, exaggerates the things that were most similar about England, Scotland, Wales and Ireland, and draws attention away from the differences between those places. It thus emphasises *convergence* over *divergence*, better terms, perhaps, than unionism and nationalism. (3) It might be suggested that the construction of British history undermines the significance of the particular histories of England, Scotland, Ireland and Wales. More particularly, it might be argued by those hostile to British history that most things in the histories of the component parts of 'Britain' are primarily explicable without reference to British dimension. There might remain, on this view, some place for British history; but it could scarcely be central to the study of English, Welsh, Scottish or Irish history. And (4) there remains the charge of Anglocentrism. British history, some suggest, is dominated by perspectives, periodisation, problem-framing and so on largely derived from English history. All of this is imposed onto Irish, Scottish or Welsh history, which then ends up doing little more than serving the explanatory needs of English historians. British history is thus a covert form of Anglocentrism.

I shall elaborate upon each of these claims in turn, and suggest some lines of response to them. It should not be forgotten, though, that each of these battlefronts is likely to remain active for some time to come.

Britain or Europe

The most forceful argument for rejecting the new British history because of its neglect of the European context has come from Jonathan Scott.[43] In historians' concern with the British context, Scott detects 'the anachronistic shadow of the modern British nation state'. But this state did not exist in the seventeenth century. The British context is being used in such a way 'that the territories which later became Britain are being taken to provide an explanatory context for (one part of) the history of seventeenth-century England'. But it is a context that does not explain much at all. Scott does not deny that the three kingdoms of Britain and Ireland were tied together dynastically and suffered a joint 'crisis' in 1637–42; but he stresses that the only adequate explanatory context for this crisis was European: the religious polarisation and conflict of the Thirty Years' War (1618–48). 'I am claiming,' he writes, 'not only that from 1618 to 1648–9 developments in England, Scotland and Ireland had this European context, but that they were a part of this single European conflict.'[44]

There are a number of things that could be asked in reply. Is it really true that a historiography concerned with composite states and multiple monarchies foreshadows the existence of a British *nation*-state? Indeed, has there ever been such a thing as a British nation or nation-state? Can we plausibly see the British conflicts as *part of* the Thirty Years' War, when the British kingdoms were at peace during the 1630s, only involved directly in European warfare in the 1620s, not subject to the same financial and administrative burdens as those powers at war, and where the most damaging religious conflicts were as much intra-protestant as protestant-catholic? Of course, European confessional conflict was a context within which British crisis developed; but Scott's claims require more than that. They require European events to have a direct role in causing the British conflicts. While it *is* true that Ship Money can be seen as a diplomatic bargaining tool designed to give England leverage in the European conflicts; that the Thirty Years War was itself confessionally more complex than a simple Protestant-Catholic conflict; and in general that European warfare was an important source of both the fears and the military experience of many British people, all of this falls well short of suggesting the British wars were part of the Thirty Years War. It still does not make Europe the crucial contextual framework within which to understand the sequence of events triggered off by the imposition of a new Prayer Book on the Scottish kirk in 1637.[45]

However these questions may be answered, there is a more important and more direct line of response to Scott's arguments. It consists in reminding ourselves of what was shown above: that the new British history as it has actually developed has been *rooted in* a comparative European history. It has been a way of restoring the

British multiple monarchy to a Europe of 'composite monarchies', and removing it from anachronistic focus on the *nation* state, a focus which automatically converts British history into the history of the growing hegemony and self-consciousness of the English state. British history is European history, and has been practised as such. It is as much European history as French, German or Spanish history – or as the history of the Holy Roman Empire, and of the kingdoms of Castile, Aragon, Naples, Portugal, and so on. Any European history must – like British history – be a mixture of the holistic, the episodic and the comparative; and it must be a history that respects the particular identities, often fiercely defended, of the component parts of Europe. To practice British history is not a denial that British history is a part of European history; it is a reminder of that fact.

In this regard, it is especially important to revisit the subject of comparative history. Canny has advocated, as an alternative to the new British history a comparative history that begins with the history of one part of Britain and Ireland and 'compares developments there with happenings in the other societies within the same jurisdiction, and compares developments in this larger entity with those in apparently analogous circumstances throughout Europe and in Europe's overseas colonies'.[46] In his chapter in the present volume, John Reeve, with a core focus on England, gives a broad picture of what a comparative (and relational) 'Anglo-European' history might achieve. It should not be forgotten that, although much of Reeve's ambitious agenda remains to be achieved, the new British history has been a comparative European history for much of its existence. It seems, in fact, to provide a path to exactly the destination that Canny recommends.

Convergence and Divergence

There may be truth in the claim that historians interested in British 'unification' have shown a tendency to identify elements of convergence within the British kingdoms and to ignore elements of divergence. But it is precisely this fact that should encourage us to forge an identity for British history that escapes from the unionist-nationalist alternatives, and this the new British history has – albeit not always and only intermittently – tried to do. The alternatives of convergence-divergence and unionism-nationalism map too easily onto one another; and the best way of defending the new British history against Canny's strictures might be to show that it has on occasion been able to escape from this framework.

Certainly, it must first be acknowledged that there is justice in Canny's claims. Historians, especially those interested in the Anglo-Scottish unions of 1603 and 1707, have been inclined to look for and list items of convergence to demonstrate a stable basis for union. This approach predates the new British history.[47] But no doubt recent trends in British history have encouraged more of this, and we have seen, for example, work by Jane Dawson on Anglo-Scottish religious convergence and by Roger Emerson on later seventeenth century Anglo-Scottish cultural convergence.[48] These essays can be read as providing a backdrop for the unions of 1603 and 1707 (the latter is explicit about this); and together they might give some substance to Canny's worries. Other work might be fitted into the same mould, including even Keith Brown's studies of British elite integration (notwithstanding the fact that a key message is the slow hesitancy with which the process occurred),[49] or Jane Ohlmeyer's study of a genuinely British nobleman, Randal MacDonnell, Marquis of Antrim. Such work, even though sceptical of some aspects of the new British history, draws attention to the process of convergence or linkage.[50]

It is apparent, though, that the matter does not end here (none of what follows should be taken as a direct criticism of any of the work just referred to). Other writers for each of these periods have, in fact, emphasised divergence rather than convergence (for the Restoration period this theme is also raised in the essay by Clare Jackson below). Jenny Wormald has, indeed, stated emphatically, with regard to England and Scotland in 1603, that 'Historians have tended to follow the lead which King James gave, in looking for similarities. The differences are what matter'.[51] And her accounts of the 1603 union have come increasingly to stress the enormous gulf dividing the two kingdoms from one another – a perspective from which the achievements of James VI & I seem even more remarkable.[52] At the least, this suggests that a concern with British themes does not compel historians to over-emphasise similarities. So one response to the criticism advanced by Canny is to suggest that whatever fault there is has lain not in the assumptions inherent in the concept of British history, but in the actual way that historians have chosen to pursue the subject. The criticism will probably prove enough in itself to ensure that it is falsified, because British historians will have been alerted by it to the dangers they run.

A second line of response is also possible. In his account of the background to the union of 1707, Mark Goldie – in contrast with Emerson – has emphasised the growing difference between the two kingdoms.[53] This, as well as Wormald's work on 1603, should make us aware that it is at least *possible* that the new British history will develop frameworks that will make it possible to do full justice to *di*vergence, precisely because they will make a sharp separation between the politics of union and the question of cultural, religious or social similarity and difference. If the union of 1707 occurred in a context of divergence – and, of course, the point is contestable – then we immediately find ourselves in a very complex world in which political contingencies and underlying structures do not mesh at all well. This is a world in which Britishness is forged, created, imposed – an act of deliberation and will – not part of the destiny of the peoples of Britain and Ireland. Britain was made even against the odds. It seems, though I have developed the point in relation to Scotland, that a historiography of this sort ought to be more rather than less capable of embracing the Irish experience. In particular, it ought to provide a framework within which to explore a theme that Canny has accused the new British history of ignoring – Anglicisation.[54] The Anglicisation of Ireland was an unsuccessful attempt to overcome structural difference. The fact that it did not produce convergence did not prevent over the long-term the development of a United Kingdom of Britain and Ireland, however brief and troubled its existence.

Thus, British history should learn from the criticisms of Canny and others. Faults of practice have been developed; but it should not be impossible to construct a new British history that does not perpetuate them. We did indeed see in the first section of this introduction that British history, given its nature, must be based on an acceptance of the separateness of the histories of England, Scotland, Wales and Ireland.

The Autonomy of English, Irish, Scottish and Welsh History

There are some scholars willing to suggest that the methods and approaches of the new British history have only very limited purchase over the histories of the component peoples of Britain and Ireland. Some historians who believe that may do so because they believe that the history of, say Scotland, needs to be seen in many contexts and that there is no particular privilege to be attached to the *British* context. Others may take the view that the history of England or Scotland – the view is less plausible for and less encountered with regard to Ireland and Wales – can very largely (not entirely) be studied 'internally', without reference to much outside itself. British history is then, at best, a rather peripheral matter, to which English or Scottish historians need to give but passing attention.[55]

A series of essays later in this book (by Toby Barnard, Tim Harris and Keith Brown) explores some of the questions raised by this latter argument, so rather less needs to be said about it here. It is notable that all of them reach a guardedly positive verdict about British history – even Keith Brown, in modification of his earlier scepticism – though all are aware (as are many of the practitioners of the new British history) that it cannot replace fully the separate histories of Ireland, Scotland, England or Wales.

Is there anything to be said for the view that English or Scottish history is largely 'autonomous'? Not much, perhaps. The question ought to force us back into reflecting upon the nature of British history, its mixture of the holistic, the episodic and the comparative. It is only if it were entirely holistic, *and*, in addition, claimed to be exhaustive, that British history would be a threat to the separate identities of English and Scottish, Irish and Welsh history. It has already been suggested that this is not the case. Furthermore, it has also been suggested that British history must respect the differences between the component parts of Britain, and is predicated upon such separateness. Given this, we can afford to see the fears of those who defend the autonomy of 'national' histories as groundless because based on an inadequate view of what British history is and aspires to become. To claim, as Ronald Hutton has done, that because Scotland and Ireland were very different from one another 'to consider them together involves an Anglocentricity as crass as that which the recent change in perspective has been intended to remove' seems itself crass in its assumption that a common history must be built on similarity.[56] Wormald and Goldie show us otherwise. Real historical processes help to make British history, or British-Irish history, a sensible unit of study, even though it is a history built as much upon difference and comparison as upon convergence and similarity. We still need to do much more thinking about the exact nature of the new British history, but it seems unnecessarily harsh to suppose that it is doomed *ab initio* to be the history of happy convergence.

Anglocentricity

Like some of the previous criticisms, the charge of Anglocentricity levelled against British history – one version of which we have just heard from Ronald Hutton – seems largely to be aimed at shortcomings in the way the subject has actually been done rather than at the principle of British history itself. As both Canny and Peter Lake have shown, these criticisms can achieve considerable force and general significance, though in Lake's case much of the latter is aimed at English revisionist historiography and the place of British history in that.[57]

Before looking at Lake's argument, though, it might be better to stay with the claim that one reason for the Anglocentricity of the subject is that it will in practice deflect attention away from the peculiarly unEnglish dynamics of Scottish, Irish or Welsh history. The historiographies of those places will become ever tied to an agenda that originates in the explanatory needs of English historians. The histories of Scotland, Wales and Ireland will dance along to an English rhythm, to which they will now have been even more firmly yoked than before. This fear seems to have underlain Keith Brown's sceptical comment of 1993.[58] Is it justified? Brown's more optimistic view, in the chapter below, perhaps suggests that early fears have not been fully realised. I have said before that there seems no reason to object in principle to an enriched English history – or to put it another way, to English-centred British history – provided that we are very clear about exactly what such a thing is and what purposes it can fulfil. But it follows that equally legitimate would be Scottish-centred British history, Welsh-centred British history, and Irish-centred British history. We have perhaps had such histories for early modern Wales and for modern Ireland. What should give cause for some optimism that the new British history will harm the historiographies of Ireland, Wales and Scotland is the fact that we see emerging already, especially amongst younger scholars, British history that is not centred on England, much of it showcased in a recent collection edited by John Young.[59] Of its contributors, one has produced a major monograph that is an exercise in Scottish-centred British history.[60] Work such as this might suggest that early fears that in practice the development of a new British history was but a process of Anglicisation are not being fulfilled, and that its impact will be broader than some expected. And there is other work suggesting the possibilities of fruitful interaction between 'British' historians, and historians of Scotland or Ireland, including Jane Ohlmeyer's collection on Ireland in the 1640s and 1650s, and Keith Brown's Scottish-centred survey of the union of crowns (1603–1707).[61] Arthur Williamson has long been building a Scottish-centred contribution to the exploration of British identity; and his essay and others in Roger Mason's *Scots and Britons* form a Scottish-centred account of the political thought surrounding the union of crowns in 1603.[62] There seems more than a little reason to hope that, while the new British history may not have the same impact on the non-English historiographies of Britain and Ireland, it can avoid simply imposing an English historical agenda on them.

Peter Lake, in endorsing the charge of Anglocentricity, has given eloquent expression to a claim often voiced by English anti-revisionists. In its crude form – another of those claims encountered in conversation rather than in print – this consists in the argument that revisionist historians, desperate at having denuded English history of all sources of conflict, had to look to exogenous causes to find the origins of the Civil War. These they found in Scotland and Ireland. The new British history thus charges to the rescue of an intellectually bankrupt revisionism. In Lake's infinitely more sophisticated version, the claim is rather that English revisionism has appropriated an unconvincing picture of Scottish and Irish history – has indeed failed to learn from recent work on Scottish and Irish history. Drawing especially on Allan Macinnes's account of the birth of the covenanting movement,[63] it can be argued that Scottish history reveals a picture of Charles I's government – ruthlessly authoritarian from the beginning, and every bit the aspiring absolutist monarchy – that revisionist historians of England have seemed reluctant to accept.[64] If revisionists *really* took Scottish (or Irish) history seriously, they could not be revisionists.

It is possible to think of answers – that Charles's own Anglocentricity made him a different king outside England from the one he was within it; that the argument could be turned on its head, to suggest that Scottish or Irish history themselves need a dose of revisionist interpretation (in the English rather than Irish sense); that not all revisionists have denied that Charles was authoritarian and high-handed even in ruling England. All of these points would be highly debatable. And in the present context it is more important to suggest that, whatever verdict we reach on the uses made by English revisionist historians of British history, this is another case where the warning and the awareness it gives us can prevent historians from falling into traps. It may be true that some – even much – of the earlier work in British history, because it worked outwards from an English base, did not learn as much as it might have from the histories of Wales, Scotland and Ireland. But that need not remain true.

With this criticism, as with some of the others, we have seen that the answer lies in two things; and it might be that the best place to conclude is with a restatement of them. They seem to point in directions that the new British history needs to develop. First, it needs to be complexly understood, as a mixture of the holistic, the episodic and the comparative. Exactly what mixture we need is still an open question, and one worth discussing. Second, it needs to become – and is becoming – multi-perspectival. We have had an English-centred British history (nothing wrong with that, for certain purposes); but a broader British history will emerge only when there are fully-developed Irish-, Welsh- and Scottish-centred British histories. There is a place for multivocality and for a multiperspectival history. The new British history has the chance to offer something like that – an account of the construction of a British, later British-Irish state and society, that does justice to difference as well as similarity and is able to avoid privileging the experience of any one of the British and Irish peoples, while still recognising and exploring the central role in the processes that concern it of the English state and its culture. Conceived in this way, the new British history is less a research field and more a higher-level integrative framework. That, it seems to me, is why Nicholas Canny's objection that genuine British history exceeds the research skills of any individual is both true and yet not a real objection.[65] The tasks of contextualisation, synthesis and generalisation always push to the outer edges of a scholar's knowledge. Most of those who have written about British history must be aware of their own incomplete preparation for the subject; but I cannot see that it is proper that such awareness should inhibit historians from attempting to construct the big picture. They won't lack for critics to point out where they go astray. Someone has to build integrative perspectives if history is not to fragment into tiny specialised areas. That may be a useful way in which to consider the importance of British history. But, alone, it is not enough: British history remains a real subject in so far as the effort to create a British state, and to resist that creation, were real efforts.

If that last phrase suggests too much that the new British history is a form of *political* history, then it must be emphasised that this too remains an open question. The nature of any British polity may have received the lion's share of attention, but this is unlikely to continue. For one of the great achievments of British history has been the way in which it makes us more aware of the way in which political institutions both shape and are shaped by broader social institutions. In particular, an important dimension of the subject is the way in which any putative British state was compelled to negotiate the complex confessional differences within kingdoms and between them. These differences were part of the complex legacy left by the very different patterns of Reformation in England, Scotland and Ireland, legacies that served for much of the seventeenth-century (and beyond, to our own day) to lend a powerfully, perhaps dangerously, religious edge to the emerging ethnic identities within the Atlantic archipelago. It is arguable that this problem, the negotiation of religious difference at every level from the village, manor or parish to the archipelago as a whole (and beyond it, to the world of western Christendom) is what provides a distinctive identity to the post-Reformation period. The new British history provides at least one set of tools for understanding this problem, and an approach that can bring into the same frame both the polities (from which came in time the construction of a British state) and the peoples (from which, on the whole, did not come the construction of a British people) of the Atlantic archipelago.

In the long term, assessment of the contribution made by the new British history will depend on the exact nature of its own ambitions. The more it aspires to replace separate 'national' histories, the less defensible it becomes. Yet, clearly, if its claims become too modest, it may cease to look as if it has much to offer at all. Can a working balance between ambition and plausibility be achieved? The collection of essays that follows is intended to help the reader to answer this question for her or himself. The contributors have different verdicts, and write from different perspectives; and the reader will no doubt, have her or his own perspective to bring to the material here presented. Unlike some postmodernist historians, I do hope that from the experience of discord, disagreement and debate we edge a little closer to apprehending some truths about the past, a little closer to an objective attitude to the complex, sometimes violently unjust, sometimes inspiring, past of the Atlantic archipelago.

Notes on Chapter 1

1   I am not in general a believer in the principle famously enunciated by E.H. Carr that one should study historians before history. But this introduction is in part a plea for a multi-perspectival British history; and in the spirit of that I ought to declare at the outset the historical perspective from which I write. Like many of the new British historians, I have been initially a historian of seventeenth-century England, and that remains the primary focus of my own research work. I am currently completing a work of British history, an account of English and Scottish political thought 1500–1690, the work for which has given me some research competence in the history of Scottish political thought – or so it is to be hoped. I have no research competence at all in Welsh or Irish history. It is perhaps worth adding that although I work on English and British history, I am neither English nor British but a New Zealander.

2   The phrase is from Ronald Hutton, 'The Triple-Crowned Islands', in Lionel K.J. Glassey (ed.), *The Reigns of Charles II and James VII & II*, (Basingstoke, 1997), ch. 4. Of course, the term rather highlights our terminological problems, since there are only two proper or 'imperial' crowns, notwithstanding the conferral of the title king of Ireland on Henry VIII.

3   See especially Martyn Bennett, *The Civil Wars in Britain and Ireland 1638–1651*, (Oxford, 1997), on which see John Morrill's comments below; Peter Gaunt, *The British Wars 1637–1651*, (London, 1997); and David L. Smith, *A History of the Modern British Isles 1603–1707: The Double Crown*, (Oxford, 1998), which is the first of a projected 6-volume series. A pioneer example, though premature perhaps, was Richard S. Thompson, *The Atlantic Archipelago: A Political History of the British Isles*, (Lewiston NY, 1986); more successful was Ronald Hutton, *The British Republic 1649–1660*, (Basingstoke, 1990), though its central, local and British perspectives were not perfectly integrated. Also intended for student use is the Morrill & Bradshaw collection cited below. And, for a broader general audience, there are fine chapters by Stephen Ellis and Morrill in John Morrill (ed.), *The Oxford Illustrated History of Tudor and Stuart Britain*, (Oxford, 1996); and an important early work of synthesis, Hugh Kearney, *The British Isles: A History of Four Nations*, (Cambridge, 1989).

4   Tony Claydon, 'Problems with the British Problem', *Parliamentary History*, 16 (1997), pp. 221–27, at p. 222.

5   *Stuart Royal Proclamations*, i, pp. 95–7.

6   Cf. Alexander Grant & Keith Stringer, 'Introduction: The Enigma of British History', in Grant & Stringer (eds), *Uniting the Kingdom? The Making of British History*, (London, 1995), ch. 1.

7   'Generally' because contributors have been left free to determine for their own chapters a usage with which they feel happy. I specify the *historiographical* use of the term 'British history' to make it clear that in *geographical* reference I have usually tried to find something more accurate; but again no house style has been imposed.

8   Cf. J.G.A. Pocock, 'Conclusion: Contingency, Identity, Sovereignty', in Grant & Stringer (eds), *Uniting the Kingdom?*, ch. 17, p. 295.

9   J. Gwynfor Jones, *Early Modern Wales, c.1525–1640*, (Basingstoke, 1994), p. ix. Another excellent general summary of the subject is G. Williams, *Recovery, Reorientation and Reformation: Wales c.1415–1642*, (Oxford, 1987).

10 The best summaries of Morrill's view of British history are John Morrill, 'The British Problem. *c*. 1534–1707', in Brendan Bradshaw & John Morrill (eds), *The British Problem, c. 1534–1707: State Formation in the Atlantic Archipelago*, (Basingstoke, 1996), ch. 1; and John Morrill, 'The

Fashioning of Britain', in Steven G. Ellis & Sarah Barber (eds), *Conquest and Union: Fashioning a British State 1485–1725*, (London, 1995), ch. 1.

11   Morrill, 'The British Problem', pp. 1–2.

12   John Morrill, 'The Causes of Britain's Civil Wars', in Morrill, *The Nature of the English Revolution*, (London, 1993), ch. 13.

13   Ibid, p. 260.

14   R.G. Collingwood, *An Autobiography*, (Oxford, 1978 edn), pp. 29–43.

15   Russell's partial admission that he has been guilty as charged seems to contain a hint of the point I am making: Conrad Russell, 'Composite Monarchies in Early Modern Europe: The British and Irish Example', in Grant & Stringer (eds), *Uniting the Kingdom?*, ch. 8, pp. 134–5.

16   See the discussion in Jack Goldstone, *Revolution and Rebellion in the Early Modern World*, (Berkeley CA, 1991), pp. 39–60, and the neat summary on pp. 61–2.

17   Niall Ferguson (ed.), *Virtual History: Alternatives and Counterfactuals*, (London, 1997), introduction.

18   Conrad Russell, 'The British Problem and the English Civil War', in Russell, *Unrevolutionary England, 1603–1642*, (London, 1990), ch. 13, p. 233.

19   See most explicitly Russell, 'Composite Monarchies in Early Modern Europe'; and Conrad Russell, 'The Anglo-Scottish Union 1603–1643: A Success?', in Anthony Fletcher & Peter Roberts (eds), *Religion, Culture and Society in Early Modern Britain: Essays in Honour of Patrick Collinson*, (Cambridge, 1994), ch. 10. Useful material for making the comparisons has been assembled in Mark Greengrass (ed.), *Conquest and Coalescence: The Shaping of the State in Early Modern Europe*, (London, 1991).

20   Many are cited in the chapter by Ian Whyte below (see the Further Reading section). A good example of the approach is Keith Wrightson, '"Kindred and Adjoining Kingdoms": An English Perspective on the Social and Economic History of Early-Modern Scotland', in R.A. Houston & I.D. Whyte, *Scottish Society 1500–1800*, (Cambridge, 1989).

21   J.L.Anderson, *Explaining Long-Term Economic Change*, (Basingstoke, 1991).

22   For a useful summary statement see Steven Ellis, '"Not Mere English": The British Perspective 1400–1650', *History Today*, 38, December 1988, pp. 41–8, at pp. 47–8.

23   Though Scottish government – especially the royal court – was less settled in a capital city than English even in 1603: see the contrasts drawn in Jenny Wormald, 'The High Road from Scotland: One King, Two Kingdoms', in Grant & Stringer (eds), *Uniting the Kingdom?*, ch. 7, pp. 123–32.

24   Steven G. Ellis, *The Pale and the Far North: Government and Society in Two Early Tudor Borderlands*, (National University of Ireland: O'Donnell

Lectures, 1988); Steven G. Ellis, *Tudor Frontiers and Noble Power: The Making of the British State*, (Oxford, 1995).

25 C.V. Wedgwood, 'The Causes of the Civil War', in Wedgwood, *History and Hope: The Collected Essays of C.V. Wedgwood*, (London, 1989), p. 90.

26 On this, see especially Ciaran Brady (ed.), *Interpreting Irish History: The Debate on Historical Revisionism 1938–1994*, (Dublin, 1994). My remarks simplify: Toby Barnard (below) comments briefly on the fact that one recent collection of essays on British history is edited by a Tudor-Stuart revisionist (Morrill) and an Irish *anti*-revisionist (Bradshaw)

27 Cf. David Cannadine, 'British History as a "New Subject": Politics, Perspectives and Prospects', in Grant & Stringer (eds), *Uniting the Kingdom?*, ch. 2, pp. 16–17. See also the survey of the entire span of historical writing since Bede in Thompson, *The Atlantic Archipelago*, pp. 381–427.

28 J.G.A. Pocock, 'British History: A Plea for a New Subject', *New Zealand Journal of History*, 8 (1974); reprinted in *Journal of Modern History*, 47 (1975), pp. 601–28; J.G.A. Pocock, 'The Limits and Divisions of British History: In Search of the Unknown Subject', *American Historical Review*, 87 (1982), pp. 311–336.

29 This point, elaborated below, has also been noted by John Morrill, 'The Fashioning of Britain', in Ellis & Barber (eds), *Conquest and Union*, pp. 14–15.

30 Pocock, 'British History', *Journal of Modern History*, 47 (1975), pp. 606, 608, 619.

31 Pocock, 'Limits and Divisions of British History', *American Historical Review*, p. 318. See also p. 329 for the British Atlantic.

32 Especially D.B. Quinn, 'Sir Thomas Smith (1513–77) and the Beginnings of English Colonial Theory', *Proceedings of the American Philosophical Society*, (1945); Quinn, 'Ireland and Sixteenth Century European Expansion', *Historical Studies: I – Papers Read to the Second Irish Conference of Historians*, (London, 1958), pp. 20–32; and Quinn, *The Elizabethans and the Irish*, (Ithaca NY, 1966).

33 Nicholas Canny, 'The Ideology of English Colonisation: From Ireland to America', *William and Mary Quarterly*, 3rd series, 30 (1973), pp. 575–98; Canny, *The Elizabethan Conquest of Ireland: A Pattern Established, 1565–76*, (Hassocks, 1976); Canny, *Kingdom and Colony: Ireland in the Atlantic World 1560–1800*, (Baltimore MD, 1988); Canny & Anthony Pagden (ed.), *Colonial Identity in the Atlantic World 1500–1800*, (Princeton NJ, 1987). Canny has not been alone: see, for example, Karl Bottigheimer, 'Kingdom and Colony: Ireland in the Westward Enterprise 1536–1660', in K.R. Andrews, N.P. Canny & P.E.H. Blair (eds), *The Westward Enterprise: English Activities in Ireland, the Atlantic and America 1480–1650*, (Liverpool, 1978),

ch. 3; and Aidan Clark, 'Colonial Identity in Early Seventeenth Century Ireland', *Nationality and the Pursuit of National Independence (Historical Studies IX)*, (Belfast, 1978), ch. 3.

34   (Chapel Hill NC, 1991). A pioneering article in this *genre* was John Clive & Bernard Bailyn, 'England's Cultural Provinces: Scotland and America', *William and Mary Quarterly*, series 3, 11 (1954), pp. 200–13.

35   J.C.D. Clark, *The Language of Liberty 1660–1832: Political Discourse and Social Dynamics in the Anglo-American World*, (Cambridge, 1994), see especially ch. 1 for an account of the development of theories of sovereignty in British and American contexts; Jack P. Greene, *Peripheries and Center: Constitutional Development in the Extended Polities of the British Empire and United States 1607–1788*, (New York, 1986), which includes Ireland amongst the colonies. For Clark's earlier writings in British history see J.C.D. Clark, 'English History's Forgotten Context: Scotland, Ireland, Wales', *Historical Journal*, 32 (1989), pp. 211–28; J.C.D. Clark, 'The History of Britain: A Composite State in a *Europe de Patries?*', in Clark (ed.), *Ideas and Politics in Modern Britain*, (London, 1990), pp. 32–49; and J.C.D. Clark, 'Britain as a Composite State – Sovereignty and European Integration', *Culture and History*, 9/10 (1991), pp. 55–83. Clark's work interestingly brings together the 'British-Atlantic' brand of British history, necessary for explaining some of the peculiarities of British state formation, with its more continental version, necessary to his claim that eighteenth century Britain was a composite state typical of the European *ancien régime*, rather than a modern nation state.

36   J.G.A.Pocock, 'Empire, State and Confederation: The War of American Independence as a Crisis in a Multiple Monarchy', in John Robertson (ed.), *A Union for Empire: Political Thought and the Union of 1707*, (Cambridge, 1995), ch. 13. Pocock summarises some of his recent work in his 'Conclusion' to Grant & Stringer, *Uniting the Kingdom?* cited above. Also Pocock, 'States, Republics, and Empires: The American Founding in Early Modern Perspective', *Social Science Quarterly*, 68 (1987), pp. 703–23.

37   J.H. Elliott, 'The King and the Catalans 1621–1640', *Cambridge Historical Journal*, 11 (1955), pp. 253–71; J.H. Elliott, *The Revolt of the Catalans*, (Cambridge, 1963); Trevor Aston (ed.), *Crisis in Europe 1560–1660*, (London, 1965); Geoffrey Parker & Lesley M. Smith, *The General Crisis of the Seventeenth Century*, (London, 1978); Geoffrey Parker, *Europe in Crisis 1598–1648*, (London, 1979).

38   I will not attempt to provide full references to revisionist writing; but one revealing example of the historiographical links I am suggesting here is Conrad Russell, 'Monarchies, Wars and Estates in England, France and Spain, c. 1580–c. 1640', in Russell, *Unrevolutionary England*, ch. 7.

39   J.H. Elliott, 'A World of Composite Monarchies', *Past & Present*, 137 (1992), pp. 48–72.

40   E.g. Morrill, 'The Fashioning of Britain', in Ellis & Barber (eds), *Conquest and Union*, pp. 14–15; Russell, 'Composite Monarchies in Early Modern Europe', in Grant & Stringer (eds), *Uniting the Kingdom?*, ch. 8.

41   Hiram Morgan, review of Canny, *Kingdom and Colony*, in *International History Review*, 13 (1991), pp. 801–6, at pp. 801, 802; also Hiram Morgan, 'Mid-Atlantic Blues', *Irish Review*, Winter 1991, pp. 50–5. The lessons are applied in Morgan, 'British Policies before the British State', in Bradshaw & Morill (eds), *The British Problem*, ch. 3.

42   For a succinct statement see Nicholas Canny, 'Irish, Scottish and Welsh Responses to Centralisation, *c.*1530–*c.*1640', in Grant & Stringer, *Uniting the Kingdom?*, ch. 9, pp. 147–8. Also Canny's review of Russell's *Fall of the British Monarchies* in *Irish Economic and Social History*, xix (1992), pp. 112–15.

43   Jonathan Scott, 'England's Troubles 1603–1702', in Malcolm Smuts (ed.), *The Stuart Court and Europe: Essays in Politics and Political Culture*, (Cambridge, 1996), ch. 2.

44   Ibid, pp. 27–8.

45   See the sensitive and balanced discussion of the European context of the British multiple monarchy in Ann Hughes, *The Causes of the English Civil War*, pp. 57–61. Hughes emphasises, in the end, the things that made the British case different, in order to refocus attention on the peculiar seeds of revolution within the English political and social systems. One need not share the conclusion to agree with its starting point: the British case possessed its unique features as well as being one *species* in a *genus* of multiple-monarchy rebellions. (I am grateful to John Reeve for discussion of the subject dealt with in the previous paragraph).

46   Canny, 'Irish, Scottish and Welsh Responses', p. 148.

47   See especially Gordon Donaldson, 'Foundations of Anglo-Scottish Union', in S.T. Bindoff, J. Hurstfield & C.H. Williams (eds), *Elizabethan Government and Society: Essays Presented to Sir John Neale*, (London, 1961), ch. 10; reprinted in Donaldson, *Scottish Church History*, (Edinburgh, 1985), ch. 12.

48   Jane Dawson, 'Anglo-Scottish Protestant Culture and Integration in Sixteenth-Century Britain', in Ellis & Barber (eds), *Conquest and Union*, ch. 4; Roger L. Emerson, 'Scottish Cultural Change 1660–1710 and the Union of 1707', in Robertson (ed.), *A Union for Empire*, ch. 5.

49   See Keith Brown, 'The Origins of a British Aristocracy: Integration and its Limitations before the Treaty of Union', in Ellis & Barber, *Conquest and Union*, ch. 9; and his earlier essays cited therein. For his scepticism about 'British history' see Brown, 'British History: A Sceptical Comment',

in Ronald G. Asch (ed.), *Three Nations – A Common History? England, Scotland, Ireland and British History c.1600–1920*, (Bochum, 1993), ch. 4, of which a revised and less sceptical version appears below. Its arguments are discussed later in this introduction.

50 Jane Ohlmeyer, *Civil War and Restoration in the Three Stuart Kingdoms: The Career of Randal MacDonnell, Marquis of Antrim, 1609–1683*, (Cambridge, 1993).

51 Wormald, 'High Road from Scotland', in Grant & Stringer, *Uniting the Kingdom?*, p. 123.

52 Jenny Wormald, 'The Creation of Britain: Multiple Kingdoms or Core and Colonies?', *Transactions of the Royal Historical Society*, 6th series, 2 (1992), pp. 175–94; Wormald, 'The Union of 1603', in Roger A. Mason (ed.), *Scots and Britons: Scottish Political Thought and the Union of 1603*, (Cambridge, 1994), ch. 1, in which we find ourselves 'being forcibly reminded of the profound differences between the two countries being pressed into union by dynastic accident' (p. 29). Especially eloquent on James's sagacity is Wormald, 'James VI, James I and the Identity of Britain', in Bradshaw & Morrill (eds), *The British Problem*, ch. 6.

53 Mark Goldie, 'Divergence and Union: Scotland and England, 1660–1707', in Bradshaw & Morrill (eds), *The British Problem*, ch. 9.

54 Nicholas Canny, 'The Attempted Anglicisation of Ireland in the Seventeenth Century: An Exemplar of "British" History', in Asch (ed.), *Three Nations – A Common History?*, ch. 2; reprinted in J.F. Merritt (ed.), *The Political World of Thomas Wentworth, Earl of Strafford 1621–1641*, (Cambridge, 1996), ch. 7.

55 This, clearly, is not a claim made by Canny; and it is in general one of those arguments frequently encountered in conversation, but seldom, at least in any strong form, in print.

56 Hutton, 'Triple-Crowned Islands' in Glassey (ed.), *Reign of Charles II and James VII & II*, pp. 71–2.

57 Peter Lake, 'Retrospective: Wentworth's Political World in Revisionist and Post-Revisionist Perspective', in Merritt (ed.), *Political World of Thomas Wentworth*, ch. 11, pp. 279–83.

58 Brown, 'British History', in Asch (ed.), *Three Nations – A Common History?*, ch. 4.

59 John R. Young, *Celtic Dimensions of the British Civil Wars*, (Edinburgh, 1997).

60 John Coffey, *Politics, Religion and the British Revolutions: The Mind of Samuel Rutherford*, (Cambridge, 1997).

61 Jane Ohlmeyer (ed.), *Ireland from Independence to Occupation 1641–1660*, (Cambridge, 1995); Keith Brown, *Kingdom or Province? Scotland and the Regal Union, 1603–1715*, (Basingstoke, 1992);

62 Arthur Williamson's work can be traced forward from his early *Scottish National Consciousness in the Reign of James VI*, (Edinburgh, 1979), using the references in his chapter below – itself a fine example of the *genre* under discussion; Mason, *Scots and Britons*. It is worth noting that the sister volume to Mason's, Robertson, *A Union for Empire* largely (not entirely) works to Pocock's 'oceanic' agenda rather than the continental one, indicating (perhaps) that this becomes more and more important as we move from the seventeenth to the eighteenth century.

63 Allan I. Macinnes, *Charles I and the Making of the Covenanting Movement 1625–1641*, (Edinburgh, 1991).

64 Witness, for example, the telling use made of Macinnes's work, alongside the exploitation of Wentworth's rule in Ireland, for anti-revisionist purposes in Anthony Milton, 'Thomas Wentworth and the Political Thought of the Personal Rule', in Merritt (ed.), *Political World of Thomas Wentworth*, ch. 6. See also Canny's review of Russell, *Irish Economic and Social History*, xix (1992), pp. 112–15.

65 Canny, 'Irish, Scottish and Welsh Responses', p. 148.

PART ONE:

BRITISH HISTORY –

ACHIEVEMENT AND PROSPECT

CHAPTER 2

Regal Union for Britain, 1603–38

Allan I. Macinnes

INTRODUCTION

Although the move from regal union in 1603 to parliamentary union in 1707 was far from seamless, a cohesive Britishness to the whole of the seventeenth century has been bestowed by the current historiographical agenda with regards to state formation within the three kingdoms.[1] Such a perspective is essentially anglocentric and tends to underwrite a baronial, neo-Whig approach to British history by focusing on the Court, the one pervasive institution of government in all three kingdoms after 1603. Thus, Scotland not only appears to have a unionist destiny, but progressively supports closer ties, if not full integration, with England.[2]

Placing Scotland and Ireland in a British historical context after 1603 is not an end in itself, given both countries' strong ties with Europe and the importance of such continental influences as price inflation, the Thirty Years War and mercantilism. During the first half of the seventeenth century, Scotland was particularly bound to the Dutch by Calvinism and by commerce, to the Swedes by military association and to northern and central Europe by intellectual and confessional linkages. By faith, by trade and by military fortune, the Irish were closely bound to the continental powers espousing the Counter-Reformation, most notably the Habsburgs. The regal union did not mark a decisive British break with the continent in terms of political development. Conversely, the establishment of a composite monarchy for Scotland, England and Ireland in 1603, was a distinctive but not a unique dynastic variant in early modern Europe.[3]

POLITICAL THEOLOGY

The composite shift from a Tudor to a Stuart dynasty was particularly welcomed in Ireland – albeit this dimension to the regal union has been paid little more than lip service.[4] In the same way that Elizabeth had condoned privateering to the detriment of the Spanish Empire, James VI throughout the 1590s had maintained an ambivalent stance towards the employment of Highland mercenaries, the *buannachan* or redshanks, by the Irish Gaels resisting Tudor hegemony. Although he sought the English succession, he was intent on demonstrating that neither was he a supplicating client nor was his native kingdom a satellite state. Only with the impending demise of Elizabeth, had James begun to treat the Irish Gaels and their accomplices as rebels. Nonetheless, he had provided no direct assistance to the English forces that had terminated the rebellion led by Hugh O'Neil, Earl of Tyrone at Kinsale in December 1601.[5]

Indeed, the accession of James to the throne of Ireland at the regal union had not only been welcomed but validated by the Irish Gaels on the grounds of providence, prophecy and genealogy. These traditional ideological mechanisms of legitimacy invested hopes verging on the millennial that James would bring peace, banish strife and produce prosperity. Unlike the Tudors whose rights to Ireland were due to conquest, James could claim direct descent not only from Fergus MacEarc who had arrived from Ulster as first king of the Scottish Gaels in 500, but also from the kings of the other provinces of Munster, Leinster and Connacht. His traditional right to the high kingship of Ireland was endorsed theologically. Under the leadership of Peter Lombard, Archbishop of Armagh, the Roman Catholic Church in Ireland taught that James, despite his Protestantism, was *de iure* king of Ireland and entitled to temporal allegiance.[6] This allegiance was eagerly affirmed by the Irish parliament in 1613, notwithstanding the writings of continental Jesuits that a heretical monarch could be deposed at papal instigation; writings which moved James to a vigorous defence of his composite monarchy as an independent empire to which unequivocal allegiance was owed by all subjects whether Catholic or Protestant.[7]

The hopes of Irish Catholics that allegiance to the Stuart dynasty would be reciprocated by liberty of conscience were to be dashed by plantations in Ulster and Connacht. Nonetheless, the clerical agents of the Counter-Reformation endorsed the aims of the Catholic political elite for an accommodation with the Crown to ensure that Ireland would be treated as an equal partner not as a satellite kingdom.

However, the confessional nationalism which had emerged by the reign of Charles I, remained virulently opposed to a composite British identity for the regal union. At the same time as confessional nationalism struggled to reconcile dual loyalties to Crown and papacy, protagonists of a Catholic Ireland tended to gloss over traditional animosities, as much territorial as racial, between the native Irish and the old English.[8]

Although the Scots were no less wary of England's intrusive hegemony over the three kingdoms being reasserted in a British guise after 1603, their standpoint towards regal union was more ambivalent. On the one hand, the Scottish Estates were much relieved when, after four years of intermittently intense negotiations, the English parliament emphatically rejected the prospect of political and commercial integration.[9] On the other hand, the determination of James VI & I to proclaim himself as King of Great Britain by coinage, seals and flags had firm intellectual roots in his ancient and native kingdom, not least because tangible British harmony enabled the Scots to counter traditional English claims to suzerainty. Aspirations for union, which were given a particular fillip by the Protestant Reformation in both Scotland and England, had a long pedigree founded on the concept of empire that had exclusive sovereignty within the British Isles.[10] At the same time, apocalyptic beliefs that shaped national identity within and beyond the three kingdoms favoured constitutional fundamentalism for which, from a Scottish perspective, the pursuit of British union was but the first eschatological step towards universal reform.[11]

In essence, therefore, the agenda for British union was dominated by considerations of political theology which were, in turn, predicated on organic and contractual constructs for civil society.[12] As a firm advocate of the view that monarchy was divinely interposed between God and civil society, James VI & I viewed dynastic consolidation as the first step towards perfect union under an imperial British monarchy. Such a union opened up the prospect of British leadership in a Protestant Europe battling to resist Anti-Christ in the form of the papacy and the whole panoply of the Counter-Reformation. James's vision for the imperial integration of Scotland and England as two sovereign states was notably supported by Sir Thomas Craig of Riccarton. As well as being one of the joint-commissioners from the Scottish Estates and the English parliament charged to negotiate the actual terms for union from the autumn of 1604, Craig of Riccarton was also the leading Scottish jurist. In support of imperial integration, he drew a fundamental distinction between *lex* and *jus,* a distinction grounded in civil (or Roman) law. Issued usually with the consent of the political nation or sustained by immemorial custom, *lex* was a relative concept that applied to specific law made in different societies by the magistrates or ruler. *Jus* was a universal concept that stemmed from nature and, as the civil bond of human society, was the key to civility. Because close agreement was apparent on the fundamentals of *jus* in both Scotland and England, there need be no insurmountable obstacle to the harmonizing of civil and common laws. Neither country's legal system need be sacrificed in pursuit of perfect union.[13]

Despite the prompting of Craig of Riccarton on the joint-commission, perfect union tended to be interpreted on the English side as the full integration of both government and laws. The more gradualist position in favour of political and commercial integration, which the commissioners had tended to favour from the outset of their discussions, also came under sustained attack from vested legal and mercantile interests in the English parliament of 1606–07. Even although the English had been required, when extending their authority in Ireland, to temper common law with civil law, there was a marked aversion to accept any innovative arrangement for union that neither accorded supremacy nor deferred ultimately to common law.[14] Hence, in order to convince Parliament that the English law would predominate in a united realm, James made a celebrated speech on 31 March 1607. Fundamental law as conceived within the Scottish civil framework posed no threat to the English common law, but was merely restricted to *jus regis* – that is, the laws that ensured the divinely warranted, hereditary succession of the monarchy.[15]

Indeed, the concept of kingship brought by James VI into the realm of James I drew heavily on the notions of divine right which the King of Scots had ardently propagated to counter dissent within the Kirk and State occasioned by the demands for Presbyterian autonomy or by fractiousness among the nobility. Simultaneously, divine right had been deployed to promote his claims to the English throne. In keeping with his successful exercise of kingship in Scotland through equitable management of constituent interests within the body politic, his polemics emphasised his preference to maintain royal supremacy by persuasion rather than by coercion. This distinction between the theoretically absolute powers of an imperial monarch and the empirical exercise of political entente through personal forbearance continued to shape his relationship with the English parliament despite its rejection of union in the autumn of 1607.[16]

James VI, however, had faced an intellectually explicit challenge from within Scotland prior to 1603. Support for imperial union within the British Isles was contested by the ideological alternative of aristocratic republicanism whose main proponent was his erstwhile tutor, George Buchanan, a staunch advocate of a contractual rather than an organic bond between monarchy and civil society.[17] Buchanan's intellectual legacy was manifest in the contractual interpretation of fundamental law favoured by the Scottish Estates when giving their conditional assent to political and commercial integration, in August 1607. Whereas five months earlier for an English audience, James had interpreted the fundamentals of *jus* to apply only to laws governing the untroubled succession to the throne, the Estates insisted *jus* fundamentally related to the whole frame of government for the kingdom, together with the privileges and prerogatives that maintained and defined the structure of society. Thus, fundamental law not only was differentiated from specific acts, statutes or customs that were alterable as required for the common welfare or public good; but was imperative, 'as this Realme could be no more a free Monarchy'. Moreover, with the Court having moved south in 1603, feelings of remoteness from the centre of decision making within the Scottish Estates were heightened by their commissioners' reports about the indifference and arrogance of the their English counterparts in treating for union. These concerns were but partially assuaged by the king's admonition in March to the English Parliament that the civil framework of government in Scotland should not be sacrificed in an integrationist union and 'for want of either magistrate, law or order, they might fall into such a confusion as to become like a native province, without law or liberty, under this kingdom.' However, when James went on to ridicule any supposition that Scotland should be garrisoned like a Spanish province he rather tactlessly made comparisons with Sicily and Naples, comparisons that provoked the Scottish Estates to temper their support for a British imperial monarchy if it resulted in their governance by a viceroy or deputy. For the Scots, the more obvious, albeit implicit, model was not Spain's Italian provinces but the English province of Ireland.[18]

Although James had adopted his mother's Francophile adaptation of Stuart rather than the Scottish Stewart as the founding surname of the first encompassing British dynasty, his hopes for a perfect union as well as the joint-parliamentary commission's proposal for political and commercial integration were effectively terminated by a wrecking motion in the House of Commons in September 1607. Nonetheless, James purposefully established the *jus imperium* of the

Stuarts by grafting his Scottish *jus regis* onto traditional English claims to be an empire free from papal control. In order to demonstrate the sovereign independence of the three kingdoms under the Stuart dynasty, he proceeded to give tangible effect to the regal union as an international example for imperial monarchy in Protestant Europe. The production of the *Authorised Version* of the Bible under the imperial imprimatur of James from 1611 should be viewed positively in this context.[19] James also implemented civilising projects designed to bring order throughout his exclusive British Empire – namely, the cross-Border policing of the Middle Shires, the plantation of Ulster and the military and legislative offensive directed against the clans on the western seaboard. The annexation of Orkney and Shetland was partly an extension of such a frontier policy, but primarily the consolidation of the territorial waters around the British Isles into the Stuarts' *jus imperium*. At the same time, his British agenda was evident in foreign policy through espionage, embassies and military intervention in the Thirty Years War. In continuing this agenda with respect to mercantile as well as frontier and foreign policies, Charles I was significantly influenced by his uncle, Christian IV of Denmark-Norway, a noted exponent of imperial monarchy in Northern Europe.[20]

FRONTIER CIVILITY

Although the British agenda of the imperial monarchy was to produce markedly differing reactions within the three kingdoms, regal union immediately facilitated concerted action in London, Dublin and Edinburgh to civilize frontier areas and rechannell disruptive energies into productive settlements. In addition to the commercial re-orientation of estate management, the promotion of civility necessitated social as well as religious reformation. In this context, the episcopate, which James had fully restored, grafting it on to the Presbyterian framework of the Kirk in Scotland by 1610, served as the Stuarts' imperial agency for the practical application of political theology in all three kingdoms – albeit less attention has been given to frontier bishops in England in comparison to Scotland and Ireland.[21]

As a first step, the Borders of Scotland and England became the Middle Shires of Britain. The main problem in this region had been the riding families or reiving clans. In return for their ready deployment as political muscle, they had enjoyed the protection of powerful Scottish and English nobles. The Borders were not endemically lawless, however. Long before the regal union, noble houses on both sides of the Border had come to recognise the political, social and economic advantages of supporting their respective Crowns in maintaining order. Reiving activities were subject not only to punitive but to preventative measures. Punitive measures, characterised by the imposition of summary justice, varied in scope and effectiveness. Set-piece dauntings, when the respective Crowns separately mobilised military expeditions to overawe and hang incorrigible reivers, were expensive and rare. More usual, though less commemorated in Border ballads, were commissions given to nobles to discipline reivers by fire and sword. Preventative measures tended to concentrate on making heads of families accountable for their followers in the same way that a landlord was held responsible for the conduct of his tenantry. These sureties, which could be exacted comprehensively by the imposition of a general band, also carried fiscal sanctions.[22]

The most glaring weakness of the punitive measures was the capacity of riding families to flit across Scottish and English jurisdictions at will, a weakness seemingly remedied by the establishment of a conjoint Border police commission of five Scottish and five English judicial officers under Sir William Cranston in 1605. Within four years, this police commission was reputed such a pronounced success that the Borders were 'as lawful, peaceable and quiet as any part in any civil kingdom in Christendom'. Such a claim was undoubtedly special British pleading.[23] The general band had to be reimposed in 1612 and selective sureties continued to be exacted over the next three decades. Leading Border families certainly availed themselves of indigenous political muscle in July 1626, to disrupt the endeavours of Scottish privy councillors to carry out directives from Charles I to establish prerogative courts and restructure central government. That the Borders were partially pacified can be attributed less to reformed cultural attitudes than to the selective removal of disruptive elements – to enhance commercialised rather than redistributive approaches to pastoral and arable farming. Social distillation was enforced by migration, either temporarily through military service overseas or permanently as colonists in Ireland.[24]

The plantation of Ulster, which was presaged in the debates on regal union, was not formally launched until 1610, three years after the flight of Tyrone and his allies to the continent and two years after the abortive revolt of Sir Cahir O'Dogherty. The forfeited estates of the exiled Gaelic lords were contracted to undertakers and planters drawn from both England and Scotland. Although this was propagated as a British endeavour, the satellite relationship of Ireland was affirmed by the contractual emphasis on English common law as the determining influence in local government, estate management and conveyancing. The one concession to custom, the retention of the townland as the composite unit defining dispersed farm settlements, was of particular benefit to Scottish migrants from analogous townships of multiple or single tenancies.[25]

Scots were to the fore among the British not only in the forfeited estates, which were extensively located in central and western districts, but in other planted settlements throughout Ulster. As early as 1605, two Scottish adventurers had come to an arrangement with Conn O'Neill that pre-empted the forfeiture of this Gaelic lord. Following a tripartite partition in which O'Neill retained a third of his estates in County Down, Scottish migrants were encouraged by James Hamilton (subsequently Viscount Clandeboye) and William Montgomery of Braidstone (subsequently Viscount Ards) to settle in East Ulster from 1606. At the same time, Randal MacDonnell, the sole Gaelic lord in Ulster untainted by treason at the regal union, was empowered to become a planter. Despite being the Irish branch of the ClanDonald South, the principal contractors of Scottish redshanks, the MacDonnells of Antrim had refrained from irrevocable commitment to the native resistance in Ulster. Subsequently elevated to the peerage – as Viscount Dunluce in 1618, then as Earl of Antrim two years later – Randal, notwithstanding his avowed Roman Catholicism, was noted for his diligence in recruiting Protestant farmers from Lowland Scotland to further his commercial approach to estate management.[26]

Although the plantation of Ulster had been preceded by the substantial colonization of Munster from southern England in the 1580s, the inculcation of civility in Ireland gathered momentum as the showpiece British endeavour of the Stuarts' frontier policy. Despite the polemical promotion of plantation to eradicate barbarity, the task of civilizing the Gaelic frontier placed greater emphasis on relocation than on removal. The paramount need to promote economic recovery after decades of continuous warfare ensured that there was limited displacement of the native Irish outwith the ranks of the landed classes. A minority, but not an insubstantial, stake in the Ulster plantation was allocated to 300 Irishmen on condition they adopted English agrarian practices and abandoned customary Irish exactions from their tenantry. Enthusiasm for British plantation as a civilizing venture also requires differentiation. The City of London had to be cajoled into acting as undertakers for the colonising of County Derry and the commercial development of Londonderry. Scottish undertakers and planters were able to capitalise on growing prosperity that attracted settlers of considerably higher calibre than the disruptive elements distilled from the Borders and other frontier areas. For, it was only by the prior acquisition of funds in Scotland that colonisers were provided with the necessary stake to develop the devastated tracts of Ulster.[27]

While the need for venture capital gave an undoubted advantage to migrants from the commercially developed areas, colonizing by Scots in Ulster should not be regarded as the preserve of Lowlanders. Indeed, the conditions for British undertakers that were issued in 1610 specified inland Scottish as well as English planters. As borne out by the muster-rolls for the 1630s, Gaelic-speaking tenants in Ulster were neither exclusively Irish nor exclusively migrants displaced from the western seaboard as a result of the Crown's associated policy of civilizing Scottish Gaeldom. The imposition of punitive tariffs on grain imports by the Scottish Privy Council during the 1620s had adversely affected the profitability of farming in Ulster and tangibly reduced immigration. But, two bad harvests in successive years in 1635–6 brought a renewed flood of emigrants, mainly from north of the Tay. By the outbreak of the Covenanting Movement, Scottish settlers in the province amounted to no less than a third and probably nearer to half of the 100,000 reputed immigrants.[28]

Demographic ramifications notwithstanding, the efficacy of frontier policy in Scottish as well as Irish Gaeldom must be scrutinised sceptically. Concerted action in the capitals of all three kingdoms was certainly evident in the Crown's endeavours to plant Ulster as a permanent wedge between the Scottish and Irish Gaels. However, the accompanying polemical rhetoric, which castigated the Gael for barbarity and incivility, cannot be dissociated from projected financial gains to the Scottish and English Exchequers, gains which proved more fictitious than factual. In reality, the Stuart dynasty lacked the political commitment as well as the financial resources to effect the wholesale transformation of frontier society within Gaeldom.[29]

Episodic fears of Gaelic rebellion had seemingly warranted continuous surveillance across the North Channel in the opening decades of the seventeenth century. The screening of suitable colonists for Ulster was among the supplementary duties bestowed on the judicial commission charged to "civilize" the western seaboard of Scottish Gaeldom in 1608. The two leading commissioners were Andrew Stewart, Lord Ochiltree and Andrew Knox, Bishop of the Isles. Lord Ochiltree, who had prior experience on the judicial commission for the Borders, subsequently became a colonial undertaker in Ulster and Bishop Knox came to hold the Ulster diocese of Raphoe in conjunction with that of the Isles from 1611 to 1618. Nonetheless, too much should not be made of personal links in the other direction. Certainly, Randal MacDonnell of Antrim secured a temporary lease to the ClanDonald South patrimony of Islay after he proved a successful planter on his Irish estates. However, this lease was abrogated after less than a year by the Scottish Privy Council in 1613, following a petition by the island tenantry against his oppressive imposition of unaccustomed dues according "to the formes and lawis of Yreland".[30]

Concerted British action did not require a uniform policy for 'civilizing' the Gael. The general reluctance of the Gaelic elite in Ireland to comply with frontier reformation resulted not only in the exile of the former Ulster lords, but a vibrant reception being accorded to the Counter-Reformation. In Scottish Gaeldom by contrast, the initial aversion of chiefs and leading clan gentry to collaborate with Ochiltree and Knox was usually remedied after brief spells of imprisonment in the Lowlands. Catholicism, which was largely revived through Franciscan missions from Ireland and from inroads by Jesuits and secular clergy based in landed households on the Lowland peripheries, posed no substantive threat to the gradual spread of Protestantism throughout Scotland since the Reformation in 1560.[31] Despite a shared cultural heritage, Gaelic society in Scotland differed socially and legally from that in Ireland. Whereas clanship can be deemed a product of feudalism, kinship and local association, Gaelic society in Ireland lacked a corresponding feudal dimension. Perhaps the most obnoxious feature of plantation for the Irish Gael, therefore, was the alien imposition of English common law.[32]

Furthermore, the regal priorities of the Crown differed critically with respect to civilizing influences. James I regarded Ulster as a province which, until planted with colonists, was not an acceptable part of his English dominions. Scottish Gaeldom was held not to require such drastic surgery. *Basilikon Doron*, the king's manual for monarchy completed before the regal union, first drew a distinction between the virtually irredeemable islanders and the redeemable Highlanders. James VI subsequently demarcated the western seaboard of Scottish Gaeldom as an 'almost rotten and decayed' member of the body politic which was, nonetheless, capable of recovery through the inculcation of 'civilitie, obedyence and religioun' among the clans. The Scottish Privy Council also exerted a moderating influence by playing on the extravagance and impracticality of colonising along Ulster lines: a case strengthened by the repeated failure of adventurers from Fife to establish a plantation on the island of Lewis in the teeth of repeated native hostility between 1598 and 1609. No less significantly, the prospect of a more fertile area for colonization in Ulster reinforced Lowland reluctance to participate in, or finance, the successive military expeditions which would be required to uproot the clans of the western seaboard.[33]

Accordingly, the essence of frontier policy within Scottish Gaeldom was to seek social and cultural reform rather than promote wholesale displacement: This strategy was to be effected militarily through selective expropriation, but primarily by legislative reform. Three clans, all debilitated by internal dissension among their chiefs and leading gentry, were expropriated between 1607 and 1625 – namely, the MacDonalds of Kintyre, Islay and Jura (the ClanDonald South), the MacLeods of Lewis and the MacIains of Ardnamurchan. A fourth, the ClanGregor, was dispersed and outlawed. The Statutes of Iona of 1609 – reissued piecemeal in the wake of the abortive rising of ClanDonald South in 1615 – professed to educate the clan elite about their responsibilities as members of the Scottish landed classes, not to denigrate their status. Thus, the legislative programme concentrated on the redundancy of the *buannachan*, on the commercial reorientation of customary relationships within the clans and on the imposition of bands of surety to hold the clan elite accountable for the conduct of their followers. Less accommodating measures, such as the promotion of English schooling and the establishment of a Protestant ministry were designed to expedite the pace at which the clan elite on the western seaboard would become assimilated, like chiefs and leading gentry elsewhere in the Highlands, into Scottish landed society.

However, the redeployment of the *buannachan* in order to promote more commercialised estate management was but a gradual accomplishment as evident from the upsurge of banditry in maritime districts between 1609 and 1615 and occasional lapses into piracy by island clans during the 1620s and 1630s. A partial remedy was provided by the commitment of Charles I to a policy of direct intervention in the Thirty Years War. From 1626, the recruitment of clansmen as well as Borderers for military service abroad was linked systematically to the removal of disruptive elements.[34] At the same time, central government's insistence on annual accountability led chiefs and leading clan gentry to spend prolonged and expensive sojourns in the Lowlands. Their accumulating debts severely strained and, in some cases, outstripped their financial resources despite increased rents. These debts were notably exploited by the acquisitive house of Argyll to expand the landed influence of the ClanCampbell, an influence already augmented by their role as leading instigators of and agents for selective military expropriation. In the process, the vernacular poetry of the Scottish Gael, like the strictures of their Irish counterparts against conquest and colonization, afforded a uniquely forceful means of protest against the political, social and commercial ramifications resulting from intrusive British influences since 1603.[35]

Intrusive influences were further evident in the annexation of Orkney and Shetland to the Scottish Crown in 1612. At one level, this accords with the frontier policies pursued elsewhere in the British Isles in that culturally distinctive Norse customs were eradicated in favour of the standardised administration of common laws throughout Scotland. Simultaneously, a social and cultural reformation was promoted, persuasively through the influence of James Law as Bishop of Orkney and, coercively by the forfeiture and subsequent execution of Patrick Stewart, Earl of Orkney. This racketeering earl, whose protectionist behaviour was as oppressive as any Border reiver, had paid as little regard to the directives of the Crown as the expropriated Gaelic elite in Scotland and Ireland.[36] However, there was a wider imperial concern in annexing islands ceded to Scotland by the Danish-Norwegian Crown in the mid-fifteenth century pending redemption of a marriage contract. Residual territorial claims on the northern isles gave Christian IV the opportunity to claim exclusive jurisdiction over fishing in the north-eastern Atlantic and to licence access of English and Scottish whaling ventures to Greenland and Arctic waters. Stuart control over Orkney and Shetland also opened up the prospect of British collaboration to compete effectively with Dutch dominance of the herring fishing in the North Sea. The Stuart dynasty remained acutely conscious of the financial potential from a herring industry which commenced annually off Orkney and Shetland in June and continued along the Scottish and English coasts until late January. Although no plantations were authenticated for the northern isles, migrations from fishing communities in Fife and along the Moray Firth helped assert Scottish control over commercial outposts in the North Sea hitherto regarded as the preserve of the Dutch and the Hanse.[37]

While the financial advantages from the promotion of frontier civility were far from realised by his death in 1625, James VI & I had clearly pointed the way for political advancement in Scotland and Ireland through acceptance of his British vocabulary. The principal beneficiary of the Crown's legislative and military offensive on the western seaboard of Gaeldom was the house of Argyll which, simultaneously, sustained their Gaelic identity and promoted themselves to the first rank of those Scottish landowners prepared to acclimatise to the changing British. From 1607, the house of Argyll was to the fore in using the term "North British" for Scotland and "British" for colonists settling in Ulster. Three years earlier, the British influence at Court of Archibald Campbell, the seventh earl, was actively cultivated by Richard Burke, fourth Earl of Clanricarde, the head of the prominent old English family later acclaimed in both England and Ireland for opposing the plantation of Connacht in his capacity as absentee governor of Galway.[38]

BRITISH INTERNATIONALISM

Despite tensions created by the prominent influx of Scots to the British Court established at the regal union, neither a dominant Scottish presence nor the resultant English antagonism was sustained throughout the reign of James VI & I. That these tensions did not become a constitutional issue can, in part, be attributed to James being weaned away from the familiar readiness of prominent Scottish politicians to criticise royal policies in favour of the more mannered English practice of adulation and flattery from favourites and their clients.[39] Of greater, but understated, significance was the resolve of both James and Charles to promote the Stuarts internationally as a British dynasty. While Ireland was usually tagged on at the end of the royal titles, the Stuarts preferred to represent both Scotland and England as kings of Great Britain when addressing and being addressed by such monarchs as Christian IV of Denmark-Norway, Gustav II Adolphus and Queen Christiana of Sweden, and the Romanov Tsars of Russia; likewise the nobility and elective kings of Poland, the cities of the Hanseatic League and the Germanic Princes within the Holy Roman Empire. Reference to British interests were made not only in a diplomatic, but occasionally in a commercial context as when Charles I, on 27 January 1634, commended the restoration of the commercial privileges between Poland and Britain that had been disrupted by the Thirty Years War.[40] Thus, despite the British ambiguity in the dictum publicly professed by Charles I in 1625, 'that the welfare of England is inseparable from [that of] Scotland', absentee monarchy did not necessarily mean anglicising monarchy.[41]

Once political and commercial integration had been rejected in 1607, the Scottish Estates had reverted to the practice – never abandoned by the English Parliament – of not using the designation Great Britain in its dealings with the Crown on national issues.

Nonetheless, the Scots were foremost amongst the peoples of the three kingdoms in accepting the British internationalism of their native dynasty. Scots played significant roles, covertly and overtly, in the military and diplomatic affairs concerted from the British Court. After Archibald, seventh Earl of Argyll, had fled into self-imposed exile in the Spanish Netherlands during 1618, his continental sojourn, which lasted almost a decade, was monitored by a British espionage network. Not only had he overstretched himself financially in pursuing British influence at Court, but he had come under sustained political attack in Scotland. His far from disinterested suppression of the ClanDonald South rebellion in 1615 was compounded by his conversion to Roman Catholicism. In the early years of his exile, the alliance of Spanish and Austrian Habsburgs was sweeping aside the resistance of the Germanic princes led by Frederick, the Elector Palatine and putative King of Bohemia, who was married to Elizabeth, the daughter of James VI & I. Argyll's inopportune endeavours to find favourable employment with the Spanish Crown were tracked assiduously by William Turnbull, a Scot employed as a royal agent in Brussels.[42]

James and Charles were both prepared to give leading roles to Scottish diplomats, particularly in Northern Europe where the Scottish Crown had hitherto exercised a distinctive influence and enjoyed diplomatic relations no less cordial than that accorded to the English. In essence, Scottish diplomatic expertise was pressed into British service. Most notably, Robert Anstruther, who had served James VI & I extensively in Scandinavia and the Baltic, continued as the foremost British diplomat in the region after the accession of Charles I. Building upon his good standing with the Hanseatic League, Charles gave Anstruther the key responsibility of negotiating with the Germanic princes at the close of 1632, when British backing for Swedish intervention in the Thirty Years War had been checked by the death of Gustavus II Adolphus at Lutzen that September. Another Scot, Sir George Douglas, was appointed legate extraordinary by Charles to facilitate negotiations between Sweden and Poland in the autumn of 1634. For thirteen months from September 1628, Francis Gordon, a Scottish gentleman of the king's bedchamber, had conducted initial British efforts to reconcile mercantile differences in the Baltic.[43]

English expertise continued to prevail in Southern Europe. Nonetheless, Scottish participation did ensure that diplomatic missions after the regal union were British. As legate extraordinary in Italy for Charles I during 1634 and 1635, Lord Basil Fielding was seemingly assisted by one Scot, his deputy, Thomas Rawlandson and advised by another, Oliver Fleming, the king's resident agent among Swiss Protestants. Fielding, whose embassy was directed as much to acquire art treasures as to accumulate intelligence, was controlled from Court by his Scottish brother-in-law, James Hamilton, third Marquis of Hamilton. Simultaneously, Hamilton was the confidant, if not unofficial ambassador, for the king's sister, Queen Elizabeth of Bohemia and broker for the recruitment of mercenaries from the British Isles.[44]

Well in excess of 100,000 people, approximately a tenth of the population, reputedly left Scotland as colonizers or soldiers between 1603 and 1638. In comparison to the plantation of Ulster, at least as many Scots were recruited in levies throughout the three kingdoms for service in the Thirty Years War.[45] Scots featured prominently in successive British expeditionary forces, initially under the command of the German adventurer, Count Ernest von Mansfeld in 1625 and, more substantially, on the side of Christian IV in 1627 and on that of Gustavus II Adolphus four years later. It no doubt helped that these expeditions were directed against Habsburg forces indelibly associated with the Counter-Reformation and that the British troops levied by Charles I were led by two Scottish courtiers: Robert Maxwell, first Earl of Nithsdale commanded the forces assisting Denmark-Norway until 1629 and, for fifteen months, James, Marquis of Hamilton was in charge of the support for Sweden that commenced in 1631.[46]

However, Scots were reluctant participants in the British contingent commanded by another Scottish courtier, William Douglas, sixth Earl of Morton, that was despatched to relieve the Huguenots in La Rochelle after Charles I opened hostilities with France in 1626. Concerns for co-religionists were subordinated to apprehensions about losing favoured nation status in the French wine trade. The French had been sufficiently mindful of the "auld alliance" to set at liberty the 60 Scottish ships among the 120 British vessels impounded while loading claret at Bordeaux. Other major European powers were also prepared to exercise positive discrimination in order to unravel the British packaging the Stuarts gave to traditional English belligerence. When Charles I declared war on Spain in 1625, the Spaniards reciprocated against the three kingdoms. Yet, freedom of trade was maintained with the Scots and the Irish, 'as they coloured not English goods'.[47]

BRITISH UNIFORMITY

Despite their active participation in frontier and foreign policies as British endeavours, the Scots were grudgingly accorded parity of status with the Stuart's imperial subjects in the other two kingdoms. The strained resolution of Colvin's Case under English law in 1608, accorded common nationality to all born within Scotland and England since the accomplishment of regal union. Nonetheless, the abandonment of political and commercial integration had meant that no access to English markets or colonial ventures was freely afforded or guaranteed to Scottish domiciles. Furthermore, Scottish wares were still regarded as foreign imports though Scottish merchants were no longer considered aliens from Christmas 1604, following their exemption from the discriminatory tariffs levied on merchandise imported into England; an exemption that had to be reaffirmed in 1615 owing to the reluctant compliance of English customs officials. Despite the eventual recognition of Scottish settlers in Ulster as naturalised Irishmen in 1632, the Lord-Deputy of Ireland, Thomas Wentworth (later Earl of Strafford), reaffirmed in relation to English and Irish shipping in 1635, that the Scottish carrying trade remained subject to discriminatory tariffs.[48]

Tensions between the Court and Scotland had arisen on the placing of the country in a posture of defence from 1625, especially as Charles I had asserted that the recurrent cost of maintaining British fortifications against Habsburg invasion could better be met from additional imposts on coal rather than by taxation. Not only would these imposts be determined at Court rather than be voted by the Scottish Estates, but the cost differential which notably favoured Scottish over English coal in the lucrative Dutch market would be critically eroded. Faced with such a threat to Scotland's major source of foreign currency and bullion, the Scottish Privy Council reaffirmed the rejection of additional imposts by the Scottish Estates in 1625 and blocked renewed proposals from Court in 1626 and 1627.[49]

These residual tensions from foreign policy paled into insignificance, however, when set against the national outcry against Charles I's scheme for a common fishing. This initiative, fashioned according to English mercantilist aspirations, was intended to open a window of opportunity into Scottish territorial waters at the expense of the native fishing industry as much as the Dutch fleet. On being presented with this proposal in 1630, the Scottish Estates could assert no more than a watching brief over negotiations at Court between commissioners appointed by the Scottish Privy Council and their English counterparts, who were exclusively courtiers and officials appointed by and answerable only to Charles. Determined to promote the common fishing to sustain the king's claim to sovereignty around the British Isles, the English commissioners were prepared to rely on the king's prerogative to secure the proposed association of British adventurers unrestricted and exclusive access to inshore as well as deep-sea fishing off the Scottish coasts. While reluctantly accepting the implementation of the common fishing, the Scottish Privy Council vigorously rebuffed its British promotion. The suppression of the name of Scotland in all authorising warrants was found to be particularly prejudicial. Especially confusing was the generic use of 'the name of great Britane altho ther be no unioun as yit with England'. The Council thus articulated widespread concerns that the common fishing was the thin edge of a wedge designed to relegate Scotland to the provincial status of Ireland. Indeed, Irish interests were not represented directly at the negotiations, but were encompassed with the remit of the English commissioners who exhibited little concern for their advancement.[50]

The common fishing had tellingly signposted the policy of uniformity throughout the three kingdoms notably associated with William Laud, first as Bishop of London and then as Archbishop of Canterbury. His promotion of 'thorough' with respect to fiscal management, local government, economic regulation and, above all, religious polity and observance was conceived at Court as imperial rationalising, but received in Scotland and Ireland as unwarranted anglicising. In particular, the relentless authorisation of uniformity by Charles unleashed pent up Scottish, domestic dissatisfaction with his British agenda that culminated in the termination of his personal rule in all three kingdoms.[51] Religious and constitutional protest, reinforced by economic recession, was propagated as a reaction against the perceived imposition of anglicisation, Counter-Reformation and authoritarianism; a reaction which cannot be explained away by Charles I's regrettable lack of a Scottish Bedchamber at Court.[52]

Of greater significance than the demise of a meddlesome closet, the influence of which had undermined the operation of the Scottish Privy Council, was the Crown's failure to maintain control over the rates at which foreign coin was allowed to circulate within Scotland after 1619. With foreign coin no longer being collated centrally as bullion in exchange for native coin of equivalent value, the Scottish Mint had particular difficulty in acquiring and transporting gold to Scotland. While the official exchange rates of Scots to English pounds remained standardised at 12:1 from the regal union, actual exchange of gold coin in the London money markets pushed up the rate to 16:1 by 1625, 'to the great loss of all the noble and gentlemen and utheris having occasions to repair to the court of Ingland'. Politically, such unfavourable rates made no small contribution to the isolation of the Court from the most influential leaders of the political nation in Scotland – a situation Charles I failed to comprehend, far less correct.[53]

The reassurance of James VI & I to the English Parliament in March 1607 that he now governed Scotland by his pen, 'which others could not do by the sword', has undoubtedly contributed to a somewhat simplified understanding of the government of Scotland after the regal union.[54] Certainly, James retained definite ideas on the ruling of Scotland and implemented them from Court through the prompt establishment of a postal service between London and Edinburgh in 1603. Neither effective decision making nor administrative initiative was totally surrendered by the Scottish Privy Council, however. For the efficacy of royal government in Scotland depended upon the personal initiatives of leading civil servants no less than the maintenance of the postal service. In particular, James was successively well served between 1603 and 1622 by two political managers whom he ennobled – George Hume as Earl of Dunbar and Alexander Seton as Earl of Dunfermline. As well as shuttling regularly between Edinburgh and London, Dunbar and Dunfermline assiduously cultivated British clientage at Court. It was not a coincidence that such political management had lapsed during the troublesome last years of James as King of Scots.[55]

The energetic commitment expended in shuttle diplomacy by William Graham, seventh Earl of Menteith, revived effective liaison between Scotland and the Court from 1628 to 1633. However, the failure of Charles to maintain Menteith in office beyond his coronation parliament demonstrated his manifest lack of understanding about the importance of political management. His capacity to govern Scotland for the rest of his personal rule certainly suffered from his failure to find a successor willing to undertake a similar style of shuttle diplomacy on behalf of absentee monarchy. But, to contend that Menteith's fall from grace transformed the character of Scottish politics, paving the way for revolution, is to overstate the case.[56] Menteith's political eclipse aggravated rather than instigated the growing estrangement between leading officials and the Court. Charles's subsequent delegation of Scottish affairs to Hamilton meant that shuttle diplomacy no longer complemented the assiduous cultivation of British clientage. At the same time, the managerial credibility of the Court was not helped by Hamilton's manifest preference for a policy of benign neglect north of the Border, a policy tantamount to the pursuit of quiescent provincialism. Furthermore, Hamilton's management of Scottish affairs was untrammelled by consultations with the English Privy Council. Ever-conscious if not always responsive to

Scottish fears of provincial relegation, Charles was determined his native kingdom should 'not be dishonoured by a suspicion of having any dependence upon England'.[57]

Despite the nominal but not insubstantial presence of Scottish officials and courtiers on the English Privy Council being reciprocated during the 1630s, Charles was no more mindful than his father to create a British executive for his imperial monarchy. Unlike his more pragmatic father, however, his commitment to uniformity throughout the three kingdoms was relatively inflexible. In this context, although he was informed separately about the state of affairs in each of his three kingdoms, his lack of a British executive to co-ordinate the formulation of imperial policy and act as a central intelligence agency left him an uncounselled king.[58]

Within Scotland, Charles was forced increasingly to rely on the bishops to uphold the managerial interest of the Court which, in turn, reinforced the determination of Archbishop Laud to deploy acolytes among the Scottish episcopate as his Canterburian vanguard for the pursuit of 'thorough' north of the Border. Simultaneously, Wentworth, his close ally at Court, was not only identifying 'thorough' with plantation and conformity to the Church of England, but also associating the process of civilizing with anglicising. In Ireland, as in Scotland, the promotion of uniformity left little room for national diversity.[59]

The promotion of uniformity, though offering token concessions to disparate indigenous practices and customs, can only be sustained as a policy of misunderstood congruity with the benefit of academic detachment.[60] Scotland, like Ireland, was being used as a political laboratory for the perfection of 'thorough' prior to its more rigorous enforcement in England. While the Archbishop of Canterbury made no formal claims to ecclesiastical or political superiority, the British endorsement of uniformity by the Court provoked the Scottish National Covenant of 1638, which offered a tripartite corrective to imperial monarchy. Firstly, it established a written constitution that prioritised parliamentary supremacy within the fundamental context of a religious and constitutional compact between God, king and people. Secondly, it made a clear distinction between the office of the monarch and the person of the king, a further fundamental which sustained loyalty to the house of Stuart but not necessarily to Charles I. Buchanan's notional aristocratic republic was given force by the third, and most radical, aspect of the National Covenant – the oath of allegiance and mutual association. This oath, which was a positive act of defiance in reserving loyalty to a covenanted king, upheld the corporate right of the people to resist a lawful king who threatened to become tyrannical. Such resistance was to be exercised by the natural leaders of society; not the nobles exclusively but the Tables – the revolutionary organisation promoting the Covenanting Movement – as the corporate embodiment of the national interest.[61]

CONCLUSION

The determination of the early Stuarts to promote themselves as Kings of Great Britain had differing resonances throughout the three kingdoms. Given the manifest Protestant commitment of the imperial monarchy, the Irish were effectively left to react to rather than shape this British agenda. The Catholic aversion to plantations was more than compounded by the graceless lack of formal toleration for their faith. The authoritarian disregard at Court towards Irish sensibilities further contributed to a combustible situation that resulted in the rebellion of 1641. Nonetheless, the subsequent emergence of the Catholic Confederacy, as the purported political focus for confessional nationalism and British antagonism, was in no small measure debilitated by ongoing rivalries between the native Irish and the old English.[62]

The working consensus between Crown and Parliament in England was especially threatened after the outbreak of the Thirty Years War in 1618. English concerns, however, were primarily focused on issues of prerogative and property as the Stuarts succeeded more in aggravating than solving inherited difficulties in matters of royal finances, parliamentary privilege and religious dissent. The English parliament undoubtedly acted as though it had exclusive rights to vote supply for foreign as well as domestic policy. In the reported wisdom of Edward Hyde (later Earl of Clarendon), Scotland was rarely given a passing thought at Court where external interest was focused primarily on Germany, Poland and all other parts of Europe. The absence of an imperial executive perpetuated the conflation of British with English interests. Indeed, English attitudes to the Stuarts' British agenda varied from peripheral involvement to downright indifference, attitudes which have continued notwithstanding "New British History".[63]

While absentee kingship was the most enduring legacy of the Stuart dynasty to their "ancient and native kingdom", Scotland was not reduced to the satellite status of an English province.[64] Scots willingly and proactively participated in the Stuarts' frontier and foreign policies. The Scottish Estates successively voted extraordinary taxation to support involvement in the Thirty Years War in 1621, 1625, 1630 and 1633. However, the regal union had a different domestic resonance. Although the regal union was a demonstrable enhancement of his prestige as a monarch, there was a marked decline in James VI's appeal and responsiveness to Scottish public opinion after 1603. Despite promising that he would return to Scotland every three years, he did so only once – in 1617. Charles I repeatedly postponed his Scottish coronation until 1633, eight years later than in England. More critically, despite an express directive to the contrary from his father in 1620 when heir apparent,[65] Charles consistently pushed his prerogative to the limit without convincingly demonstrating the present necessity for authoritarian rule in Scotland. Gathering opposition to his apparent imposition of anglicised uniformity on Scotland led to the emergence of the Covenanting Movement by 1638, which looked back to the defence of fundamental laws by the Scottish Estates in 1604 in order to impose binding limitations on Stuart kingship in Kirk and State. As evident from their negotiations with the Long Parliament that concluded the Treaty of London in 1641 and the Solemn League and Covenant in 1643, the Covenanters were not rejecting but adapting the Stuarts' British agenda. The organic discourse of imperial monarchy was replaced contractually, not so much by aristocratic republicanism as by covenanted confederalism.[66]

The historiography of the negotiations for union between the Scottish Covenanters and the English Parliamentarians has been bedevilled by the anachronistic application of federalism.[67] Confederation for confessional and constitutional purposes had been reinvigorated in early modern Europe, first by the Protestant estates in Moravia, Austria and Hungary against imperial power in 1608, followed by that against territorial integration in Bohemia, Moravia, Silesia and the two Lusatias in 1619.[68] Proposals for an international confederacy also surfaced during negotiations for the Treaty of London as a lasting defensive and offensive league that laid to rest the spectre of provincialism which had haunted Scotland since the regal union. At the same time, the Covenanters were actively promoting a tripartite alliance that would also involve the Estates General of the United Provinces.[69]

Albeit the concept of confederacy was not enhanced among British Protestants by the Irish Catholic establishment of 1642, the association of a solemn league with perpetual confederation was explicitly laid out in New England at the union of the four Puritan plantations of Massachusetts, New Plymouth, Connecticut and New Haven for common defence against the Dutch, the French and the Indians in May

1643.[70] The incorporating articles of the United Colonies of New England were drawn up three months before the Solemn League and Covenant, which constituted a British endeavour to achieve common spiritual and material aims while maintaining distinctive national structures in Church and State. In effect, the Solemn League affirmed the confederal nature of covenanting while exporting Scottish constitutional fundamentalism to England and Ireland.[71] Thus, regal union gave way to confederal union for Britain. The Covenanters reasserted the international identity of the Stuarts in proclaiming Charles II not just as King of Scots, but as King of Great Britain in January 1649. Nonetheless, he was crowned not as the imperial, but as the covenanted, British King on 1 January 1651.[72]

Notes to Chapter 2

1   cf. *Conquest & Union, Fashioning a British State 1485–1725*, S.G. Ellis & S. Barber (eds), (London, 1995); *Three Nations – A Common History? England, Scotland, Ireland & British History c.1660–1920*, R.G. Asch (ed), (Bochum, 1993); *Religion, Culture & Society in Early Modern Britain: essays in honour of Patrick Collinson*, A. Fletcher & P. Roberts (eds), (Cambridge, 1994); *Scotland and the Union*, P.S. Hodge (ed), (Edinburgh, 1994); *Scots and Britons: Scottish Political Thought and the Union of 1603*, R.A. Mason, (Cambridge, 1994); A. Grant & K.J. Stringer (eds), *Uniting the Kingdom? The Making of British History*, R.A. Mason (ed), (London, 1995); *A Union for Empire: Political Thought and the Union of 1707*, J. Robertson (ed), (Cambridge, 1995); *The British Problem c.1534–1707: State Formation in the Atlantic Archipelago*, B. Bradshaw & J. Morrill (eds), (Basingstoke, 1996).

2   A.I. Macinnes, 'Early Modern Scotland: the current state of play', *Scottish Historical Review* [*SHR*], LXXIII (1994), pp 30–46. On the one hand, Scotland and Ireland are brought into play when constitutional controversies appear to admit of no self-contained English solution. This supporting role can be peripheral, as in the application of Scottish precedents to understanding the furore caused by the Crown's assertion of feudal privileges in the Addled Parliament of 1614; or it can be of major significance, as in relation to the Scottish and Irish triggers that brought about the end of Charles I's personal rule in England (C. Russell, *Unrevolutionary England 1603–1642*, (London, 1990) & *The Causes of the English Civil War*, (Oxford, 1990) & *The Fall of the British Monarchies*, (Oxford, 1991). On the other hand, the focusing of British consciousness on the Court has been more holistic (J. Morrill, *The Nature of the English Revolution*, (London, 1993).

3   H.G. Koenigsberger, 'Epilogue: Central and Western Europe' in *Crown, Church and Estates: Central European Politics in the Sixteenth and Seventeenth Centuries*, R.J.W. Evans & T.V. Thomas (eds), (London, 1991), pp 300–10; J.H. Elliot, 'A Europe of composite monarchies', *Past & Present*, 137 (1992), pp 48–71.

4   cf. M. Lee jr, *Great Britain's Solomon: King James VI and I in his Three Kingdoms*, (Urbana, IL, 1990); D.H. Willson, *King James VI and I*, (London, 1956).

5   A.I. Macinnes, 'Crown, clans and fine: The "Civilizing" of Scottish Gaeldom 1587–1638', *Northern Scotland*, 13 (1993), pp 31–55.

6   B. O'Buachalla, *Aisling Ghearr: Na Stiobhartaigh Agus an tAos Leinn 1603–1788*, (Dublin, 1996), pp. 148–94 & 'James Our True King: the Ideology of Irish Royalism in the Seventeenth Century' in *Political Thought in Ireland since the seventeenth century*, G. Boyce, R. Eccleshall & V. Geoghegan (eds), (London, 1993), pp 1–35; J.J. Silke, 'Primate Peter Lombard and Hugh O'Neill', *Irish Theological Quarterly*, XXII (1955), pp 15–30. Archbishop Lombard was a former supporter of O'Neill's rebellion

7   *The Political Works of James I*, C.H. McIlwain (ed), (Cambridge, Mass, 1918), pp 110–268; J.P. Somerville, *Politics and Ideology in England 1603–1640*, (London, 1986), pp 117–20.

8   *Collected songs of Padruic H. Pearse: Songs of the Irish Rebels and Specimens from an Irish Anthology*, (Dublin, 1918), pp 36–49, 62–71, 74–83; *The Poems of David O'Bruadair*, Rev. J.C. MacEarlean (ed), (Irish Texts Society, London), pp 18–9, 28–37, 48–51; A. Clarke, 'Colonial Identity in early seventeenth-century Ireland' in *Nationality and the pursuit of National Independence*, T.W. Moody (ed), pp 57–72.

9   *A Source Book of Scottish History*, vol. III, 1567–1707, W.C. Dickinson & G. Donaldson (eds), (Edinburgh, 1961), pp 456–61; B.P. Levack, *The Formation of the British State: England, Scotland and the Union 1603–1707*, (Edinburgh, 1987), pp. 32–44.

10   B. Galloway, *The Union of England and Scotland 1606–1608*, (Edinburgh, 1986), pp 59–62, 82–4; R.A. Mason, 'Scotching the Brut: Politics, History and National Myth in Sixteenth-century Britain' in *Scotland and England 1286–1815*, R.A. Mason (ed.), (Edinburgh, 1987), pp 6–84 & 'The Scottish Reformation and the Origins of Anglo-British Imperialism' in *Scots and Britons*, pp 161–86.

11   A.H. Williamson, *Scottish National Consciousness in the Reign of James VI*, (Edinburgh, 1979) & 'Scotland, Antichrist and the Invention of Great Britain' in *New Perspectives on the Politics and Culture of Early Modern Scotland*, J. Dwyer, R.A. Mason & A. Murdoch (eds), (Edinburgh, 1982) pp 34–58.

12   J.H. Burns, *The True Law of Kingship: Concepts of Monarchy in Early Modern*

Scotland, (Oxford, 1996), pp 255–81; R.G. Cant, 'Scottish Libertarianism in Theory and Practice 1560–1690', *Proceedings of the Conference of Scottish Studies*, 3 (Norfolk, Va., 1976), pp 20–31; F. Oakley, 'Jacobean Political Theology: The Absolute and Ordinary Powers of the King', *Journal of the History of Ideas*, 29 (1968), pp 323–46.

13 *De Unione Regnorum Britanniae Tractatus by Sir Thomas Craig*, C.S. Terry (ed), (Scottish History Society, Edinburgh, 1909). For a further flavour of the debates on "perfect" and "imperfect" union see *The Jacobean Union: Six Tracts of 1604*, B.R. Galloway & B. Levack (eds), (Scottish History Society, Edinburgh, 1985).

14 G. Burgess, *The Politics of the Ancient Constitution: An Introduction to English Political Thought 1603–1642*, (University Park, PA, 1993), pp 25–8, 102–5, 126–9; B. Levack, 'Law Sovereignty and the Union' in *Scots and Britons*, pp 213–40; C. Russell, 'English Parliaments 1593–1606: One Epoch or Two?' in *The Parliaments of Elizabethan England*, D.M. Dean & N.L. Jones (eds), (Oxford, 1990), 191–213.

15 *The Political Works of James I*, pp 300–02; Galloway, *The Union of England and Scotland*, pp 103–30. In addition to the anticipated trenchant defences from the practitioners of the common law, proponents of English commercial superiority were somewhat apprehensive about the potential impact of the Scottish carrying trade which carried a competitive edge through its association with Dutch shipping (T.M. Devine & S.G.E. Lythe, 'The Economy of Scotland under James VI: a Revision Article', *SHR* L, (1971) pp 91–106).

16 *The Political Works of James I*, pp 307–9, 329–33; J. Wormald, 'James VI and I, Basilikon Doron and The Trew Law of Free Monarchies: The Scottish Context and the English Translation' in *The Mental World of the Jacobean Court*, L.L. Peck (ed), (Cambridge, 1991), pp 36–54; Sommerville, *Politics and Ideology in England 1603–1640*, pp 39–46, 195–9, 303–08; Burgess, *The Politics of the Ancient Constitution*, pp 162–7. Thus, his address of 21 March 1610, distinguished between the absolute powers which served for law at the first establishment of monarchy and the present, settled state of a kingdom governed by its own fundamental laws and orders. In essence, James and the parliamentary upholders of common law did not disagree about the importance of constitutional consensus, but over the priorities for its achievement. Whereas the parliamentary advocates viewed the king's prerogative power as supplementary to statutes grounded in common law, James claimed divine right to suspend or dispense with statutes for which his determination of present necessity was sufficient cause. Despite subsequent encomiums on the omniscient impact of statute when executed, James never fully came to grips with the contractual limitations on monarchy implicit in the English concept of parliamentary sovereignty.

17   R.A. Mason, 'Imagining Scotland: Scottish political thought and the 'problem of Britain, 1560–1650' in *Scots and Britons*, pp 3–16; A.H. Williamson, 'Scots, Indians and Empire: The Scottish Politics of Civilization, 1519–1609', *Past & Present* 150, (1996), pp. 46–83; Burns, *The True Law of Kingship*, pp 283–95.

18   *Acts of the Parliament of Scotland* [*APS*], 12 vols, T. Thomson & C. Innes (eds), (Edinburgh, 1814–72), IV, pp 263–4 c.1, 366–7 c.1; *Registers of the Privy Council of Scotland* [*RPCS*], first series D. Masson (ed), (Edinburgh, 1877–98), VII, pp 534–8; J. Wormald, 'The Union of 1603' in *Scots and Britons*, pp 17–40.

19   In the wake of the Gunpowder Plot of 1605, the eventual imposition of the Oath of Allegiance throughout the English civil and ecclesiastical establishment by 1610, was a negative manifestation of imperial monarchy through denial of papal powers either to depose or to require withdrawal of temporal allegiance following on from spiritual excommunication (Burgess, *The Politics of the Ancient Constitution*, pp 129–30; Burns, *The True Law of Kingship*, pp 267–8).

20   While the full impact of Christian IV's grandiose designs on Charles I awaits investigation, a flavour of his correspondence with the early Stuarts can be gleaned from *Transactions and facsimiles of the original Latin Letters of King James I of England, (VI of Scotland), to his Royal Brother in Law, King Christian IV of Denmark*, R.M. Meldrum (ed), (London, 1977); *The Earl of Stirling's Register of Royal Letters, Relative to the Affairs of Scotland and Nova Scotia from 1615 to 1635*, 2 vols, C. Rogers (ed), (Edinburgh, 1885); *Danske-Norges Traktater 1523–1750, med dertil horende akstykker*, XI binder, C.S. Christiansen (ed), (Copenhagen, 1949).

21   Burns, *The True Law of Kingship*, pp 268–9; Lee jr, *Great Britain's Solomon*, pp 167–71.

22   T.I. Rae, *The Administration of the Scottish Frontier, 1513–1603*, (Edinburgh, 1966); S.J. Watts, *From Border to Middle Shire: Northumberland, 1586–1625* (Leicester, 1975).

23   *A Source Book of Scottish History*, III, pp 275–8; K.M. Brown, *Bloodfeud in Scotland 1573–1625: Violence, Justice and Politics in Early Modern Scotland*, (Edinburgh, 1986), pp 228–9, 243–6; R.T. Spence, 'The Pacification of the Cumberland Borders 1593–1628', *Northern History*, XIII (1977), pp 59–160. Albeit the regal union had also stimulated the cultivation of active Christian communities in Border parishes by the Protestant establishments in both Scotland and England, ecclesiastical courts merely played a supportive role in the disciplining of disruptive elements.

24   National Library of Scotland [NLS], Miscellaneous Charters, Contract for suppression of lawlessness 1612, Ch. 798; Hull University Library [HUL], Maxwell-Constable of Everingham MSS, DDEV/79/H/7; *RPCS*,

second series D. Masson & P.H. Brown (eds), (Edinburgh, 1899–1908), I, pp 359, 361, 402. While some Borderers were directed to plant estates speculatively held by English landowners in the Irish Midlands, the majority were despatched to Ulster to reclaim lands devastated during the Gaelic lords' series of rebellions against Tudor hegemony. The removal of Border reivers to Ulster and to the estates of English landlords in the Irish Midlands should not necessarily be considered as permanent migration, however. There is an apocryphal tradition from the early seventeenth century that the Maharg family in Ayrshire were actually Border Grahams who got out of Ireland by reversing their surname.

Irish Historical Documents 1172–1922, E. Curtis (ed), (London, 1943), pp 128–33.

M. Perceval-Maxwell, *The Scottish Migration to Ulster in the Reign of James I*, (London, 1973), pp 8–10, 29–67, 154–6; J.H. Ohlmeyer, *Civil War and Restoration in the Three Stuart Kingdoms: The career of Randal MacDonnell, Marquis of Antrim 1609–83*, (Cambridge, 1993), pp 24–41, 281–2; Glasgow University Archives, Beith Parish MSS, GU P/CN, vol. II, fo 171.

J.H. Ohlmeyer, '"Civilizing of those Rude Partes": Colonization within Britain and Ireland, 1580s–1640s' in *The Origins of Empire*, N. Canny (ed), (Oxford, 1998), pp 124–46; R. Gillespie, 'Explorers, Exploiters and Entrepreneurs: Early Modern Ireland and its Context 1500–1700' in *An Historical Geography of Ireland*, B.J. Graham & L.J. Proudfoot (eds), (London, 1993), pp 123–57; N. Canny, *Kingdom and Colony: Ireland in the Atlantic World*, (Baltimore & London, 1988), pp 44–59.

British Museum [BM], Muster-Roll of Ulster c.1630–36, Add.MSS. 4770 fos 145–62; A.I. Macinnes, 'Social Mobility in Medieval and Early Modern Scottish Gaeldom: the Controvertible Evidence', *Transactions of the Gaelic Society of Inverness*, LVIII (1992–94), pp 371–405; Maxwell, *Scottish Migration to Ulster*, pp 231–3, 288–9, 294–308, 313–5. For Scotland as a whole, the plantation of Ulster as a British endeavour had particular attractions. Plantation gave an immediate boost to Scottish trade. Not only did the colonisers look to the home market for tools and provisions, but Scottish merchants were the main suppliers of luxuries imported from the continent. In return, Scotland provided a ready market for agricultural produce exported from Ulster, which became a cheaper alternative to the Baltic as an emergency granary. Scottish shipping came to dominate if not monopolise the province's carrying trade, a trade of particular benefit to as many as 26 ports on the western seaboard. However, the Scottish Privy Council did resort to punitive tariffs once the country's balance of trade was adversely affected as imports from Ulster began to outstrip exports thereto.

Advertisements for Ireland, G. O'Brien (ed), (Dublin, 1932); BM, Letters and Papers 1602–c.1711, Add.MSS. 32,476 fos 9–11; D. Gregory, *History of the Western Highlands and Isles of Scotland 1493–1625*, (Edinburgh, 1836 reprinted 1975), pp 275–80, 286–7, 290–4, 313–26, 330–3.

30   *RPCS*, first series, X, pp 13–4; Lee jr, *Great Britain's Solomon*, p 212.

31   A.I. Macinnes, 'Catholic Recusancy and the Penal Laws 1603–1707', *Records of the Scottish Church History Society*, XXIII (1987), pp 27–63; J. Kirk, 'The Jacobean Church in the Highlands 1567–1625' in *The Seventeenth Century Highlands*, L. MacLean (ed), (Inverness, 1985), pp 24–51; N. Canny, 'Irish, Scottish and Welsh Responses to Centralisation, c.1530–c.1640: A Comparative Perspective' in *Uniting the Kingdom? The Making of British History*, pp 148–57.

32   H.S. Pawlisch, *Sir John Davies and the Conquest of Ireland: a study in Legal Imperialism*, (Cambridge, 1985), pp 55–64, 84–100; G. Keating, *The History of Ireland*, (Irish Texts Society, London, 1902), pp 67–71; K.W. Nicholls, *Gaelic and Gaelicised Ireland in the Middle Ages*, (Dublin, 1972), pp 21–44, 57–65. Undoubtedly, James had Scottish precedents for the frontier policy he introduced into Ireland after the regal union. But, his directive of 1594 that clan chiefs and leading gentry produced their charters in order to validate title to their estates led to no substantial land redistribution within Scottish Gaeldom. Yet, his Irish commission to remedy defective titles from 1606 seemingly occasioned extensive redistribution of estates in the Irish Midlands prior to 1620. (*RPCS*, first series, IV, pp 787–92, 802–3, 812–4; M. MacCarthy-Morrogh, 'The English Presence in Early Seventeenth Century Munster' in *Natives and Newcomers: The Making of Irish Colonial Society 1534–1641*, C. Brady & R. Gillespie (eds), (Dublin, 1986) pp 171–90.)

33   *A Source Book of Scottish History*, III, p 261; *RPCS*, first series, VIII, pp 737–61; M. Lee jr, 'James VI's Government of Scotland after 1603', *SHR*, LV (1976), pp 49–53. The demarcation of Hebridean from mainland Gaels was also supported by advice from his Scottish bedchamber after 1603, notably from Lachlan Mackintosh of Dunnachton, chief of ClanChattan, who was knighted but impoverished at his death in 1622 for his services as courtier and companion to the future Charles I.

34   A.I. Macinnes, *Clanship, Commerce and the House of Stuart 1603–1788*, (East Linton, 1996), pp 56–87. The redundancy of a military class as an adjunct of state formation had a contemporaneous parallel in Spain, where the caballeros villanos, the commoner knights of the walled towns who had reclaimed territories from the Arabs in Andalucia, were suppressed in 1619.

35   A.I. Macinnes, 'Gaelic Culture and British Politics in the Seventeenth Century' in *Conquest & Union*, pp 162–94.

36 *A Source Book of Scottish History*, III, pp 273–4; P. Anderson, *Black Patie: The Life and Times of Patrick Stewart, Earl of Orkney*, (Edinburgh, 1986), pp 77–93.

37 H.D. Smith, *Shetland Life and Trade, 1550–1914*, (Edinburgh, 1984), pp 10–45; J.R. Elder, *The Royal Fishery Companies of the Seventeenth Century*, (Glasgow, 1912), pp 7–50; W.R. Scott, *The Constitution and Finance of English, Scottish and Irish Joint-Stock Companies to 1720*, 2 vols, (Cambridge, 1910–12), II, pp 55, 70, 104, 361–3. Unlike his son, James continued to respect the accommodation of 1594, whereby the Dutch had been granted access to Scottish territorial waters providing their busses did not intrude within 28 miles from mainland shores.

38 Inveraray Castle Archives [ICA], bundle 63/3; ICA, Argyll Transcripts, VIII, nos 114, 256; IX, no 163; Scottish Record Office [SRO], Breadalbane Collection, GD 112/1/378. Material collated from ICA was sponsored by successive Major Research Grants from the British Academy to investigate the political and cultural influence of the House of Argyll, 1603–1761.

39 G. Donaldson, *Scotland: James V to James VII*, (Edinburgh & London, 1965), pp 215–6; D. Stevenson, *The Scottish Revolution, 1637–44*, (Newton Abbot, 1973), pp 320–1; K.M. Brown, *Kingdom or Province? Scotland and the Regal Union, 1603–1715*, (London, 1992), pp 9–10.

40 BM, Latin Letters of Charles I, 1627–35, Add.MSS. 38,669 fo 33; Riksarkivet, Copenhagen, TKUA, England, A. 1, 3; Riksarkivet, Stockholm, Anglica, 516, 522, 531/2; *Documenta Bohemica Bellum Tricennale Illustrantia, tomus IV. Der Grosse Kampfe um die Vormacht in Europa 1635–43*, J. Janacek, G. Cechova & J. Koci (eds), (Prague, 1978), pp 253–4. For the Northern European references and considerable persuasion in changing my views on Charles I's unreconstructed anglicisation I have to thank two of my research students, Steve Murdoch and Alexia Grosjean, who are working respectively on Scottish-Danish and Swedish-Scottish relations during the Thirty Years War.

41 *Calendar of State Papers and Manuscripts relating to English Affairs existing in the Archives and Collections of Venice, and in other Libraries of Northern Italy*, [*CSP, Venetian*], A.B. Hinds (ed) (London, 1913–23), XIX, p 294; A.I. Macinnes, *Charles I and the Making of the Covenanting Movement, 1625–41*, (Edinburgh, 1991), p 1.

42 BM, James Hay, Earl of Carlisle. Correspondence, volume I 1602–1619, Egerton 2592 fos 28, 37, 107–8, 127, 132, 195: & volume II 1619–20 fos 59, 69; NLS, Jacobite Papers & Letters, MS. 295, fo 1. Argyll, who had converted to Catholicism following his second marriage, to Anna Cornwallis, a noted English recusant, was allowed to return to Court prior to his death in 1638.

43 BM, Latin Letters of Charles I, Add.MSS. 38,669 fos 1–2, 6–8, 13–9, 27–31. At the same time as Anstruther's mission in Germany, James Wallace led the British mission to Muscovy that also concerned Swedish relations.

44 Ibid., fos 21–2, 24–6; *Historical Manuscripts Commission [HMC], 11th Report, appendix, The Manuscripts of the Duke of Hamilton*, (London, 1887), pp 83, 91, 93; *HMC, Supplementary Report on the Manuscripts of the Duke of Hamilton*, (London, 1932), pp 29, 34–5, 43.

45 T.A. Fischer, *The Scots in Germany*, (Edinburgh, 1902) & *The Scots in Eastern and Western Prussia*, (Edinburgh, 1903) & *The Scots in Sweden*, (Edinburgh, 1907); T. Riis, *Should Auld Acquaintance Be Forgot: Scottish-Danish Relations c.1450–1707*, 2 vols, (Odense, 1988); A.F. Steuart, *Scottish Influences in Russian History, from the end of the 16th to the beginning of the 19th Century*, (Glasgow, 1913); D. Fedesov, *The Caledonian Connection: Scotland-Russia Ties, Middle Ages to Early Twentieth Century. A concise biographical list*, (Aberdeen, 1996); J.A. Fallon, 'Scottish Mercenaries in the Service of Denmark and Sweden, 1626–32 (University of Glasgow, Ph.D. thesis, 1972). Working mainly from these sources, together with original materials from the Danish and Swedish State Archives, Steve Murdoch and Alexia Grosjean have constructed an inter-relation database *SSNE: Scotland, Scandinavia and Northern Europe 1580–1707*, (Aberdeen, 1997). Using the ACCESS program, which is capable of containing some 30,000 entries, they have built upon the earlier datasets of officers in Danish service by Dr Gunnar Lind, University of Copenhagen, to demarcate the involvement of Scots within the British diplomatic, military and intellectual contingents in the seventeenth century. Among their preliminary findings in each category, the following are particularly noteworthy. Of the 30 diplomatic missions sent by James VI and I to the northern states after the regal union, 19 out of the 21 missions to Scandinavia were conducted by Scots and while only two out of the nine missions to Russia were led by Scots, both missions involved conjoint negotiations with Sweden. Around 3000 British officers have been identified, primarily from the mid-seventeenth century. Of these only 54 were Irish and 142 English, the remainder Scottish; an overwhelmingly majority of 94% that was almost replicated in terms of students from the British Isles in Scandinavian and Baltic universities where 204 (90%) of the 227 identified were Scottish.

46 *RPCS*, second series, I, pp 507–8, 524–6, 529–32, 565–8, 604–5, 611, 613, 634–6, 689–93; II, pp 38–9, 55–6, 73, 77–8, 88–91, 313–4, 363, 540, 553–7, 562–4, 580–1, 589, 603–4, 611, 615–6; NLS, Morton Cartulary & Papers, MS.80 fos 55, 65; NLS, Miscellaneous Papers, MS. 10001, fos 12–5; HUL, Maxwell-Constable of Everingham MSS, DDEV/79/G/51, /83, /113; *HMC, The Manuscripts of the Duke of Hamilton*, pp 74–6, 79–81; *Stirling's*

Register of Royal Letters, I, pp 111, 387; G. Burnet, *The Memoirs of the Lives and Actions of James and William, Dukes of Hamilton and Castleherald*, (London, 1838), pp 2–4, 11–3, 21, 25, 28–9, 31.

47 *CSP, Venetian*, XX, pp 26, 77, 143; *Calendar of State Papers Domestic Series, of the reign of Charles I*, [*CSP, Domestic*], 17 vols, J. Bruce & W.D. Hamilton (eds), (London, 1858–82), (1625–49), p 55. Diplomatic dubiety about the Scotland's international status after the regal union had notably benefited its carrying trade. Scottish ships were employed by the English, French and Dutch in waters where warfare imperilled their own nationals (S.G.E. Lythe, *The Economy of Scotland 1550–1625*, (Edinburgh & London, 1960), pp 132–3, 157–8).

48 Levack, *The Formation of the British State*, pp 147–8; Lythe, *The Economy of Scotland*, pp 202–4; *Stirling's Register of Royal Letters*, II, pp 582, 617, 830. The case to secure post-nati equivalency with the English was actually brought by a Scottish courtier, James Colvin, 1st Lord Colville, on behalf of his Edinburgh-born, son Robert whom he hoped to provide with freehold lands in England.

49 *APS*, V, pp 166–76, 181–2, 186; *RPCS*, second series, I, pp 151–6, 269–72, 277–80, 301; II, pp 72–3, 146–7, 561; IV, p 41, 570.

50 *RPCS*, second series, IV, pp 56–7; Macinnes, *Charles I and the Making of the Covenanting Movement*, pp 108–14.

51 Brown, *Kingdom or Province?*, pp 7–8; Macinnes, *Charles I and the Making of the Covenanting Movement*, pp 91–101, 114–54.

52 C. Russell, 'The Anglo-Scottish Union of 1603–43: A Success?' in *Religion, Culture & Society in Early Modern Britain*, pp 238–56.

53 *RPCS*, second series, I, pp 564, 628–31; *Records of the Coinage of Scotland*, 2 vols, R.W. Cochrane-Patrick (ed), (Edinburgh, 1846), II, 73–5, 87, 96, 111–2; K.M. Brown, 'Aristocratic finances and the Origins of the Scottish Revolution', *English Historical Review*, CIV (1989), pp 46–87.

54 *The Political Works of James I*, p 301; Galloway, *The Union of England and Scotland*, pp 116–7.

55 M. Lee jr, 'James VI's government of Scotland after 1603', *SHR*, LV (1976), pp 41–53; Brown, *Kingdom or Province?*, pp 86–94.

56 M. Lee jr, *The Road to Revolution: Scotland under Charles I, 1625–37*, (Urbana & Chicago, 1985), pp 46–8, 69–71, 126.

57 *Diary of Sir Thomas Hope of Craighall 1634–45*, T. Thomson (ed), (Bannatyne Club, Edinburgh, 1843), pp 5, 11–4; E. Hyde, Earl of Clarendon, *The History of the Rebellion and Civil Wars in England*, 6 vols, (Oxford, 1836), I, pp 149, 195.

58 P. Donald, *An Uncounselled King: Charles I and the Scottish Troubles 1637–41*, (Cambridge, 1990), pp 1–42; Brown, *Kingdom or Province?* pp 22–3.

59 J.H. Ohlmeyer, 'Strafford, the "Londonderry Business" and the "New

British History" in *The Political World of Thomas Wentworth, Earl of Strafford 1621–41*, J.F. Merrit (ed), (Cambridge, 1996), pp 209–29.

60   J. Morrill, 'A British patriarchy: Ecclesiastical Imperialism under the Early Stuarts' in *Religion, Culture & Society*, pp 209–37.

61   *APS*, V, pp 272–6.

62   T. O'hAnnrachain, 'Rebels and Confederates: The Stance of the Irish Clergy in the 1640s' in *Celtic Dimensions of the British Civil War*, J.R. Young (ed), (Edinburgh, 1997), pp 96–115; B. Fitzpatrick, *Seventeenth-Century Ireland: The War of Religions*, (Dublin, 1988), pp 28–33, 44–6; N. Canny, 'The Marginal Kingdom: Ireland as a Problem in the First British Empire' in *Strangers within the Realms: Cultural Margins of the First British Empire*, B. Bailyn & P.D. Morgan (eds), (Chappelhill, N.C., 1991), pp 35–66.

63   Clarendon, *The History of the Rebellion*, I, pp 194–5. Probably the most gloriously unreconstructed, recent work in this historiographic vein is K. Sharpe, *The Personal Rule of Charles I*, (New Haven & London, 1992).

64   W. Ferguson, *Scotland's Relations with England*, (Edinburgh, 1977), p 105.

65   Burns, *The True Law of Kingship*, pp 278–81.

66   Williamson, *Scottish National Consciousness in the Age of James VI*, pp 140–1; A.I. Macinnes, 'The Scottish Constitution: The Rise and Fall of Oligarchic Centralism, 1638–1651' in *The Scottish National Covenant in its British Context 1638–51*, J. Morrill (ed), (Edinburgh, 1989), pp 106–33.

67   cf. D. Stevenson, 'The Early Covenanters and the Federal Union of Britain' in *Scotland and England 1286–1815*, pp 163–81; M. Lee jr, 'Scotland, the union and the idea of a General Crisis' in *Scots and Britons*, pp 41–87; Brown, *Kingdom or Province?*, pp 81–3; J. Morrill, 'The Britishness of the English Revolution, 1640–1660' in *Three Nations – A Common History?*, pp 83–115. Federalism did not feature in contemporary British political vocabulary until the eighteenth century (*Oxford English Dictionary*, second edition, J.A. Simpson & E.S.C. Weiner (eds), volume III, (Oxford, 1989), pp 699–700).

68   G. Schramm, 'Armed Conflict in East-Central Europe: Protestant Noble Opposition and Catholic Royalist Factions, 1604–20' & I. Auerbach, 'The Bohemian Opposition, Poland-Lithuania, and the Outbreak of the Thirty Years War' successively in *Crown, Church and Estates*, pp 176–225; J. Robertson, 'Empire and union: two concepts of the early modern European political order' in *A Union for Empire*, pp 3–36. Although Habsburg power peremptorily negated Bohemian endeavours to replace Emperor Ferdinand II by the Elector Palatine, the Central European estates had formed a grand confederation to resist the Turks in 1620.

69   Edinburgh University Library, Instructions of the Committee of Estates, Dc.4.16 fos 101, 105; NLS, Wodrow MSS, folio lxxxiii fo 63; *APS*, V, pp 335–45 c.8; Sir J. Balfour, *Historical Works*, 4 vols, J. Haig (ed),

(Edinburgh, 1824), III, pp 33, 40–1; J. Spalding, *The History of the Troubles and Memorable Transactions in Scotland and England 1624–45*, 2 vols, J. Skene (ed), (Edinburgh, 1828–29), I, pp 293–4.

70 *The Journal of John Winthrop, 1630–1649*, R.S. Dunn, J. Savage & L. Yeandle (eds), (Cambridge, Mass, 1996), pp 429–40; H.M. Ward, *The United Colonies of New England 1643–90*, (New York, 1961), pp 49–59.

71 *APS*, VI(i), pp 47–9; *A Source Book of Scottish History*, III, pp 24–5, 128–31. The creation of a British executive remained problematic. The only institutional innovation under the Treaty of London was to be the appointment of parliamentary commissioners in both kingdoms, charged to conserve the peace and redress any breaches in the intervals between the respective parliaments. The one British institution arising out of the Solemn League and Covenant was the Committee of Both Kingdoms, which was conceived in June 1644 as a confederal body to channel diplomatic dealings between the Covenanters and the Parliamentarians. Although its remit was redefined in November 1645 to include oversight of war in Ireland as well as military collaboration in England, the English Parliament was palpably not prepared to concede that the Committee had an executive role.

72 *The Covenants and the Covenanters*, J. Kerr (ed), (Edinburgh, 1896), pp 348–98; J.R. Young, *The Scottish Parliament 1639–1661: A Political and Constitutional Analysis*, (Edinburgh, 1996) pp 224–5.

CHAPTER 3

The War(s) of the Three Kingdoms

John Morrill

I

In the year 1645 there was a civil war in England, a civil war in Scotland, a civil war in Ireland. At the beginning of the year a Scottish Army stationed in the north Midlands was the largest single army in England; there was a Scottish army in Ireland and the remnants of an English army there too. The army in Scotland upholding the King's interest there was more than half Irish; and the King was actively negotiating for an Irish Catholic army to be shipped to England. Between 1642 and 1652 perhaps one of three of all those subjects of Charles I who bore arms in these wars fought in a kingdom other than their own.

Between 1651 and 1660, there were never less than 30,000 men in the standing armies of the Commonwealth and Protectorate. Indeed at times – as in 1652, in late 1654 and early 1655 and again in 1659 – there were well over 50,000 men in arms. Throughout the period, a majority were serving outside England in either Scotland or Ireland. From early 1652 to the winter of 1659/60 the number of men in England fluctuated between 10,000 and 13,500; the number of men in Scotland and Ireland rose and then fell over the period 1651–60. In Ireland the number peaked at 23,000 in the early part of the Protectorate before falling back to just over 10,000 by early 1659; while in Scotland it rose to almost 19,000 at the height of Glencairn's Rebellion in the winter of 1654/5, but was down to 10,000 by the summer of 1657 and 7,700 in the spring of 1659.[1]

In military terms, it does not make sense to treat the history of England, Scotland and Ireland as three separate histories.

Throughout the 1640s, war in each kingdom went along with proposals for peace. And throughout that time, peace proposals in each kingdom contained terms that sought to redefine the relationship between the kingdoms. As a result of the Anglo-Scottish alliance of 1643 (*The Solemn League and Covenant*), all the terms offered to the King were to include clauses which created a post-war confederation of England and Scotland and which made Ireland an integrated part of the English Kingdom but subject to confederal Anglo-Scottish administration. All proposals for peace in Ireland involved redefinitions of the constitutional relationship of Ireland to the House of Stuart and the English state.[2]

In 1649 the Rump of the Long Parliament abolished monarchy in England and Ireland and set out to absorb Ireland into an enlarged English state, but left Scotland to resume its independence as a free monarchy to the North. The Scots refused to accept independence and declared Charles II to be King of Britain and Ireland and swore to restore him to all his thrones.

In the 1650s, the English Commonwealth completed ruthless military conquests of Ireland and Scotland. More than one third of the land mass of Ireland was confiscated from its existing owners and redistributed to demobilised English soldiers and property speculators mainly from the south of England. The English Commonwealth set out systematically to destroy the power and authority of the Scottish nobility and to create a new substantial yeoman class grateful to the English for their liberation.

In political and constitutional terms, it does not make sense to treat the history of England, Scotland and Ireland as three separate histories.

So far, so uncontentious. But it would be claimed by some historians that Charles I's determination to create a much greater conformity of the churches of England, Ireland and Scotland was the greatest single cause of the collapse of his political authority in first Scotland, then in Ireland and finally in England;[3] that the greatest single outpouring of propaganda in 1642 which helped to shape the resistance to Charles I was the propaganda about the Catholic massacres of Protestants in the early months of the Irish Rebellion;[4] and that amongst the thousands of pamphlets on the future settlement of religion published in the 1640s, were hundreds directed by Scots at an English audience and by Englishmen at a Scottish audience.[5] Certainly, in the 1640s, Parliament was committed by treaty to the establishment of single form of church government, a single confession of faith and catechism, a single form of worship across the three kingdoms.

Scottish attempts to hold the English to their treaty obligation exacerbated divisions with English Puritanism and led to the fateful splits of the later 1640s. Cromwell's determination to 'extirpate popery' in Ireland was a major engine of the harsh conquest of 1649–1650.[6]

In religious terms too, then, it does not make sense to treat the history of England, Scotland and Ireland as three separate histories.

II

This essay reviews the ways in which over the centuries historians have sought to get beyond (or refuse to get beyond) three separate histories which periodically collided and interacted. For to suggest that no account of the mid-seventeenth century which deals only with the events of one kingdom is adequate is not to demonstrate that there was one conflict, one war, one history. For many historians, it is necessary to have a 'British' or 'archipelagic' perspective[7] in order to understand the nature and dynamic of the English Revolution of 1642–60 or the Irish Rebellion of 1641–60, of the Scottish Rebellion of 1637–52; but that is not the same as saying that there was a British Revolution or a single British Civil War. The tension is caught exactly in the fact that some historians speak of the 'war of the three kingdoms' and others of 'the wars of the three kingdoms.'[8] Yet even that fails to reflect the extent to which the European superpowers – the Spanish Habsburgs, the French Bourbons, and to a lesser extent the mercantile Republic of Holland – were active participants in one or more theatres of these internal wars. Their ambassadors promised more than they ever delivered in military and financial aid, but their promises affected the decisions made by the king, his representatives and his enemies.[9] Furthermore, foreign powers released mercenaries for service back home, they and their financiers were willing to grant favourable credit or to allow the purchase of military equipment, and they all offered their services as negotiators and brokers. Too busy and too exhausted to make Britain and Ireland a major theatre of their operations, they still saw the outcome of the British and Irish wars as vital to their own long-term self-interest. The 'War(s) of the Three Kingdoms' are a peripheral but actual part of the Thirty Years War, the greatest of all continental European wars before the era of Bonaparte.[10] And it is clear that they saw the conflicts throughout the archipelago as a complex skein of conflict, not as separable wars.

Insofar as there is a 'war of the five kingdoms' (Jane Ohlmeyer's term, adding the kingdoms of Spain and France to those of England,

Scotland and Ireland), it is a war that reinforces the need to treat the war(s) within the archipelago holistically.[11] Yet three-kingdom narratives have in the past usually been constructed with a view to explaining the causes, course or outcomes in one of them. Since the short-term outcome of the pattern of conflict was the integration of both Scotland and Ireland into an enhanced English state – one Parliament, one law, one religious settlement dictated by the commanders of English armies of conquest and occupation – and since in Ireland between a third and a half of the land was confiscated from Catholic proprietors and allocated to English speculators or demobilised English soldiers, it is not surprising that that the term 'the war of three kingdoms' was coined by a J.C. Beckett, a historian of the Irish war,[12] and that the extent to which internal crises were complicated by archipelagic factors has been most widely accepted by historians of the Covenanting Revolt and the Confederate Rebellion. The task of this chapter is to explore how far it is possible to get beyond a discussion of three interlocking conflicts by the conceptualisation of the period as a single war in several theatres: to work within the tension revealed by the bracket contained in the chapter title: the war (or is it wars?) of the three kingdoms.

The rest of this essay will review the history of historical writing about the way these complex issues have been handled and will suggest that there is good reason not only for prioritising a three-kingdom approach but even for going further than historians have hitherto gone in presenting a holistic approach to events which have important implications for current debates about the constitutional relationships of the component parts of what many inhabitants of the islands of Britain and Ireland call the British Isles and a few scholars call the Atlantic archipelago.

III

The foundation narrative of the crisis of the mid-seventeenth century was provided by Edward Hyde, 1st Earl of Clarendon. Hyde wrote his *History*[13] in the discomfortures of exile, a fugitive from the wreckage of Charles I's cause in the late 1640s, and later during his flight from a parliamentary impeachment after his dismissal from the Lord Chancellorship by Charles II. Hyde had been in the thick of court intrigue and royal political gambling for more than a quarter of a century before his *History* took its definitive form. It is pretty relentlessly anglocentric history, with grudging recognition of Charles I's mistakes in Scotland (restricted to a discussion of the introduction of the Scottish Prayer Book) and of the perfidious role of the Scottish peerage in the 1640s. He writes Hamilton out of the script, does scant justice to Montrose and gives a highly misleading account of the role of the Scots in 1648–51. The *History* is full of pungent sketches of leading actors in the drama: but the courtier Scots and the covenanting Scots are notable by their absence. Yet this scaled down and discontinuous discussion of Scottish affairs is at least a discussion. Clarendon's failure to discuss Irish affairs at all – the deafening silence over the Irish Rebellion and over the movement of British troops to Ireland and the constant attempts to bring Irish troops to England – is eloquent indeed.[14] Clarendon spent much of the 1650s as a principal advisor of Charles II trying to dissuade the exiled King from playing the Scottish card (by adhering to the Covenants) or the Irish card (by showing sympathy with Catholics)[15] and seeking to persuade Charles to wait upon English revulsion at the Rump and at the cuckoo-regime of Cromwell. His polemic that the English would restore the Stuarts without any outside help shaped his historiography. And it helped to shape an anglocentric historiographical tradition.

The second most influential narrative of the period before modern time was David Hume's *History of England* (1754),[16] of which volume 3 covers the period from 1603–88.[17] Never before or since have the histories of England and Scotland been so tightly or cogently woven together. It is possible to identify the different coloured strands, but the effect is a tight weave. Let us take just one short section, covering the winter of 1644/5.[18] Hume's account of the terms discussed between royalist and parliamentarian negotiators at Uxbridge is the only one to give full consideration to the Irish and Scottish articles; the trial of Laud is introduced with an allusion to the Scottish 'bigoted prejudices' that underlay the renewed determination to destroy him; and there follows a linking paragraph that tells us that 'while the king's affairs declined in England, some events happened in Scotland which seemed to promise him a more prosperous issue of the quarrel' [i.e. of the quarrel throughout his kingdoms]. The next page goes on to explore how Montrose's freedom of action was transformed by the downfall of Hamilton at Charles's court which left him (Montrose) as the clear leader of Scottish royalism; and great care is taken to show how Montrose's successes affected the disposition (in all senses) of the Covenanting armies in England. The role played by Irish troops in those Scottish campaigns is fully explored. No-one, before or since has written so skilful an integrated account. And yet, we need to remind ourselves that this was unselfconscious writing.

Hume was a philosopher writing a history for a moral purpose: to denounce Enthusiasm in its political and religious forms and to demonstrate the illegitimacy of rebellion and the perils of priestcraft and of theocratic politics. But as a Scot living within the British state system at its apogee, he wrote naturally and fluently of a single polity at war within itself.

IV

The foundational narrative of all modern historical writing on the period is, of course, the eighteen-volume *History* by S.R. Gardiner which told the History of England and of the Stuart kingdoms from 1603 to 1656.[19] Gardiner was fastidious in correlating events in Scotland and Ireland with those in England, and he was clearly concerned to give them their own narrative integrity and logic. Altogether, some twenty five per cent of Gardiner's account of the years 1638–56 concern the *internal* histories of Scotland and Ireland, quite apart from the discussion of the impact of events in those kingdoms on the progress of events in England. However, he did disintegrate the various histories, so that Scottish and Irish affairs are given their own chapters, often running months or years in arrears behind the strict chronological account of affairs in England. For example, the military subjugation of Ireland after Cromwell's departure is recounted in volume II chapter 19 of *The History of the Commonwealth and Protectorate*; and the post-conquest settlement of 1652–5 follows as volume IV chapter 44, after chapters on the establishment of the Major Generals and on the remodelling of (English) borough corporations in 1655–6. This leads him to miss many of the inter-penetrations of events, such as the frustrations of Irish policy that constituted one layer to the complex background to the dissolution of the Rump Parliament.[20] As a result, we find that the internal histories of Ireland and Scotland are not quite continuous;[21] and if they are intended to be more than a demonstration of how three separate internal wars impinged on one another, they are less than a complete history of how each helped to shape the course of and consequences for the others.

V

From the appearance of the Gardiner and Firth volumes in the decades straddling the turn of the nineteenth century, attempts at a fully developed account of the intimate connection between the war(s) in the three kingdoms went – for reasons we will return to – into inexorable decline. By the 1960s and 1970s they represented an appendix in a rather anatomical sense, an often irritating piece of gristle that was the reminder of a long lost bodily function. In so far there was any account of Irish and Scottish affairs at all, it tended to take one of two forms: it was placed in separate chapters out of sequence with the rest of the book, with no cross reference to affairs in England (or vice versa); or there were brief accounts of particular events, taken out of context as rather obtrusive built-on flying buttresses to bulging walls unable to carry the weight of interpretation that was placed on them.

This decline began dramatically with the publication of what was to be *the* textbook of the period for the first half of the century: G.M. Trevelyan's *England under the Stuarts*. This was first published in 1904 and was one of seven books he published with England or English in the title, as against only one with Britain in the title. And he knew the difference. This was a resolutely English account: the period 1637–1660 is allowed almost exactly 150 pages and there are (usually passing) references to Scotland and Ireland on just twenty three of them. There is a single paragraph on the background to the Irish Rebellion of 1641 ('. . . The general rising of a half-barbarous people, maddened by the loss of tribal lands and rights, and led by an upper class more civilised indeed but goaded to frenzy by religious persecution, could not but result in terrible atrocities . . .'), a single page on the Scottish contribution to the outcome of the English civil war ('Again and again, fear of despotism drove the patriots to restrain their natural sentiments and to hail the Scots as fellow-countrymen, until the repeated process had so far altered public sentiment that the Whigs under Queen Anne carried the Act of Union . . .'). No account is offered of the Cromwellian invasions and settlements of Scotland and Ireland, only imperious judgements rooted in a failure to read Gardiner carefully enough. Yet this deeply influential book set the trend. Published in 1904, it was still in use as the standard authority when I took my Advanced Level History at Grammar School in 1963.

Its influence was reinforced, however, by at least four other historiographical trends. First, from the 1930s onwards, under the influence of a matrix of positivist, christian-socialist and marxist ideas, historians became preoccupied with analysing the underlying economic and social structures within which men (and a few women) operated, on the social-science assumption that people's behaviour is determined, or at any rate shaped, by those structures. Since the economic and social structures of Scotland and Ireland were little studied, or so far as they had been studied were believed to represent a pattern of sharp contrast from the patterns thought to prevail in England (and Wales), the story of how glacial change in English society created fissures in the political and institutional structures that eventuated in civil war in the 1640s became an exclusively *English* story.[22]

Secondly, and related to this, there was a growing fascination – which reached its peak in the late 1960s and early 1970s – with the 'radical' movements spawned by the war and with the print culture associated with these movements. Since these were essentially English movements, there was a resulting de-emphasis on the popular cultural responses to the collapse of royal and noble power in Scotland and Ireland. Neither the 'Whiggamores' of Scotland nor the 'Tories' or 'wood-kerne' of Ireland wrote pamphlets and thus they remained outside the concern of monoglot-English scholars who failed to recognise the potential of these 'brigands' to produce the kind of progressive ideas with which they yearned to identify.[23]

Thirdly, there was a strong tendency – driven as much as anything by the 'PhD industry' – towards atomisation, with fewer and fewer broad research monographs and more and more tightly drawn studies. This created a series of discreet debates, with textbooks and survey books acting as guides to particular debates rather than whole fields. The proliferation of studies of pre civil war and civil war counties and county towns is one obvious example of this. Since Scottish and Irish politics remained clan- or name-driven, with counties that lacked the institutional and cultural strength of early modern English counties, there was no scope for the development of a comparative approach here.

Fourthly, this in turn reinforced the tendency for historians in and of Scotland and Ireland to write within their own separate and rather blinkered historiographical tradition[24] and not to participate in, or – especially to take note of – the blinkered English historiographical discourse.

In 1972, Lawrence Stone published *The causes of the English Revolution*, in many ways the summation of forty years debate and argument on that subject precisely defined. It contains no index entry at all for 'Scotland' or 'Scottish', and just one entry to 'Ireland' under the heading 'Irish Rebellion' which leads the reader to seventeen lines of text unpromisingly prefaced by the words 'tension was enormously increased by *two chance events,* of which the first was the death of the Earl of Bedford . . . [and] the second . . . was the outbreak of the Irish Rebellion.' British History had reached a very low ebb indeed.[25]

The result of these various historiographical trends has been a steady decline in the attempt of the foundational accounts of the seventeenth century to address the three-kingdom dimension.

During the 1950s, 1960s and 1970s a new generation of textbooks for use at A Level and undergraduate level had appeared.[26] Maurice Ashley's *England in the Seventeenth Century* in the Pelican History of England series (1951) begins with four structural chapters on the social, cultural and intellectual background to the century, without any word at all on conditions in Scotland and Ireland or on the relations of their peoples. Three lines are devoted to the failure of James's plans for Anglo-Scottish Union, half a paragraph to the Scottish Revolt of 1638, seven lines to the Irish Rebellion of 1641, four lines to the Scots participation in the English civil war, not a word on the Irish war(s) of the 1640s, then a page on Cromwell's Irish campaigns and rather less to his Scottish campaigns with no mention of the post-conquest settlements or the incorporation of Scotland and Ireland into an enhanced English state. Gerald Aylmer's *The struggle for the constitution: England in the seventeenth century* (1963) in Blandford's *History of England* series has slightly more coverage (four pages on Wentworth in Ireland – 'important because of their bearing on events in England' and two pages on the Scottish crisis of 1637–40, but the summary statement of the causes of the civil war only says less helpfully that 'the war would hardly have come about when it did but for a whole sequence of events partly unrelated in themselves, including the Irish Rebellion' and there is only vestigial reference to the role of the Scots in the 1640s or the nature and consequences of the conquest of Ireland and Scotland in the 1650s. Roger Lockyer's *Tudor and Stuart Britain 1471–1714* (1964), probably the most influential as the first textbook read by most students at A Level and introductory undergraduate level for two, perhaps three, decades, was (by virtue of his title alone) required to be fuller or most systematic. His solution was – in the course of a 470-page book to offer a 15-page chapter on 'Ireland and Scotland in the Sixteenth Century' and a 28-page chapter on 'Ireland, Scotland and Overseas possessions in the seventeenth century.' These are admirably clear but they divorce Irish and Scottish from English history. The abbreviated history of each kingdom at no point indicates the impact of the events in one on the others. The fourth of the textbooks of the 1960s, Christopher Hill's *Century of Revolution* (1961) was perhaps the most widely admired of all: with its emphasis on social and economic analysis and on socio-cultural dynamics within the developed English state in the elusive search for a bourgeois revolution, it marginalised Scotland and Ireland more completely than any other textbook. That a fundamental and un-reversed transformation in the social, cultural and ethnic distribution of land and power in Ireland might constitute a revolution was not considered. The romantic Levellers are treated in depth in about twenty pages; the Irish rebellion, the Solemn League and Covenant and the Cromwellian conquest and settlements less than a paragraph each. By 1980, most historians of England were ignorant of Scottish and Irish history in the mid-seventeenth century and unaware of the inter-penetration or the interaction of those histories.

In the early 1980s, three new textbooks came to form the basis of undergraduate teaching in England: Alan Smith's *The Emergence of a Nation State 1529–1660*, Conrad Russell's *The Crisis of Parliaments 1509–1660* and Barry Coward's *The Stuart Age*. All them devoted paragraphs to the Scottish crisis of 1637–40, the Irish Rebellion of 1641, the Solemn League and Covenant of 1643 and the part played by the Scots at Marston Moor, and Cromwell's brutality in Ireland in 1649–50. All treat them as extrinsic factors which had an impact on English affairs, and none is treated as part of the dialectical process by which affairs in each kingdom shaped events in the others. None of them devoted more than two sentences to the career and death of Montrose or Ormonde; none of them offers any discussion of the Confederation of Kilkenny, the political and religious thought of Samuel Rutherford, the political intrigues of the Earl of Glamorgan to bring Irish Catholic troops to England or the Union of England and Scotland in the 1650s. And all show an insecurity about basic facts with respect to such Irish and Scottish affairs which is not characteristic of them as a whole.[27]

One historian bucked the trend. Shunned by academe if not by literary London, Veronica Wedgwood wrote two wonderfully rich and gripping narratives of the years 1637–47 with the titles *The King's Peace 1637–1641* (1955) and *The King's War 1641–7* (1958). She was greatly assisted by her previous writing, especially by her twice-written biography of Strafford (1938, 1961) and her biography of Montrose. Her narrative is especially strong on showing how events in one kingdom have consequences for the others, and she painstakingly allows the narrative to flow freely across boundaries, rather than abruptly starting new sections (usually with a backwards leap in time to bring the outlying kingdoms up to date since they were last mentioned). Thus, there is a seamless move from a discussion of the recriminations that followed from the failure of the parliamentarians to follow up decisively on the Anglo-Scottish victory at Marston Moor (and the Anglo-Scottish bickering that was *an* aspect of that) to the furrowing of Argyll's brow at that and at the arrival of the Irish Macdonnells in the Highlands. With Huntly dead, Montrose in England, and the Lowlands cowed, it was an irritation he could have done without. From this base, she shows how Montrose's gifts as a guerrilla leader destabilised Scotland and had all kinds of knock-on effects in England. Hers is a distinguished account that is conceptually bolder and more subtle than its successors in the genre of writing that tells the story of the civil wars by interweaving military, logistical and political events.[28] But the reviews of her books, complimentary though they often were, failed to notice or to comment on that aspect of her work.

VI

In the first three quarters of the twentieth century, early modern studies were rather in the doldrums in both Scotland and Ireland. In the universities of Scotland, Scottish, and in the universities of Ireland, Irish History, were hermetically sealed off from other branches of history, and ne'er were the twain encouraged to meet.[29] Furthermore, few of the major figures in Scottish and Irish History specialised in early modern history, most of the Professors being medievalists (or, in the case of Ireland, recent history), and many of those employed to teach early modern history were medievalists by training who were concerned to look for continuities in Scottish or Irish History rather than contiguities within the framework of a British History. The major Scottish exception was Gordon Donaldson, and it is revealing how few textbook writers drew on his work when discussing the crisis of Charles I's reign. It is startling to realise how little new work on mid-seventeenth century Scottish and Irish history was published between 1900 and 1975. When Donaldson published his authoritative textbook on early modern Scotland in 1965,[30] he offered a masterly account of the rise of opposition to Charles I. But he offered no guide to the relationship between Charles's Scottish policies and his policies in England and Ireland – even with respect to the Scottish canons and ordinal of 1636 and the Scottish Prayer Book of 1637 he de-emphasised the extent of anglicisation.[31] And he made no effort to trace any links between the opposition in Scotland and the opposition in England. Although it is less possible for a Scottish historian to chronicle the wars of the 1640s without reference to England than for an English historian to chronicle them without reference to Scotland, Donaldson's account is striking for its lack of discussion of the role of the Scots in English politics: no index entry to the Committee of Both Kingdoms, or to any of the Scots resident in London during the mid 1640s – Robert Baillie, Alexander Henderson etc. This – from the historian who had done so much to show that the Scottish Reformation was a rib from the side of the English Reformation – is as little-Scotlander a history as could be.

Paradoxically, the most important Scottish discussion of the links between the kingdoms was to be found in a book whose purpose was to disown the inevitability or necessity of Anglo-Scottish Union: William Ferguson's defiantly grumpy *Scottish Relations with England: a survey to 1707* (which devotes two chapters, nearly fifty pages to the period from 1603 to 1660). Thus Ferguson minimises the Scottish commitment to union within the Solemn League and Covenant, glossing it to mean that the Scots sought 'accord' not 'organic union' and arguing that the greater part of the explanation for Montrose's brilliant success in the mid 1640s, lies, not in the complexities of a three kingdom grand strategy, but 'deep in the Highlands, which was never as remote and unimportant as the general run of historians, Scottish as well as English, are apt to make out.'[32]

Similarly, apart from a squall of work on Strafford in Ireland and a few popular biographies of leading figures in the Rebellion, little new work had been published on Ireland in the years 1641–60 in the years between the rush of major studies in the closing decades of the nineteenth century and the appearance of the *New History of Ireland* volume covering 1534–1691 in 1976.[33] There had certainly been a robust debate about whether Strafford had sought to use Ireland as a laboratory for policies intended for transfer to England; but the idea that the Irish wars of the 1640s were little more than a drain on English resources and a distraction from the main theatres of war politics was not really challenged.

However, just as rebellion in Scotland in 1638 and Ireland 1641 was to precede rebellion in England in 1642, so a revival of historiographical interest in the connections between the rebellions in three kingdoms was to begin in Ireland and Scotland and to influence the revival of interest in England.

The key figures in this revival were Aidan Clarke in Ireland and David Stevenson in Scotland. Clarke's *The Old English in Ireland 1625–1642* (1965) was a major reappraisal of a group that wanted to be both English and Irish and addressed the denouement of their long-drawn-out crisis of identity in the context of Strafford's Lord Deputyship and its aftermath. In a series of essays influential on both sides of the Irish Sea, Clarke suggested that the Rebellion was not simply a reaction against Strafford's heavy-handed government: rather it was a reaction to the fears of the Catholic population about reprisals planned by the Long Parliament and its Protestant-settler allies, who felt that Strafford had privileged the Catholic population and especially its tacit freedom of worship. This account necessarily involved a close analysis and integration of events in London and in Dublin, and at the way events in the one triggered events in the other.[34] Clarke's aim was to illuminate Irish History, not to construct a broader history, and when he sought to set his work into a broader context he chose a European one, locating the Irish Rebellion within the General Crisis that many historians discerned as the key to mid-seventeenth century government and society.[35]

A later convert was David Stevenson, a prolific writer on the Scottish Covenanters, whose works published as late as 1980 were astonishingly narrow. Thus his *The Scottish Revolution 1637–1644* (Edinburgh, 1973) contains a single, passing reference to John Pym, one passing reference in a footnote to Viscount Saye and Sele and none at all to Oliver St John or the 3rd Earl of Essex. The index contains no entry for the Grand Remonstrance, the Militia Ordinance or the Nineteen Propositions. So this is not British history. It is a study of the perils of absentee kingship and resembles most closely those histories of the Revolt of the Netherlands in the fourth quarter of the sixteenth century which look at the problems created by Philip II and his Spanish advisers without any consideration of the internal dynamics of the Spanish kingdoms. Similarly the sequel volume – *Revolution and Counter-Revolution in Scotland 1644–1651* (1977) – has very little to say about Scottish interference in English political debates (such as Scottish demands relating to the post-war settlement of Ireland, in the establishment of Presbyterianism in London or even in bringing Laud to his death); and it passes over with minimal comment the astonishing decision of the Scots Parliament to proclaim Charles II King of Great Britain, France and Ireland on the death of his father, when the English were already indicating that they believed that the union was severed and Scotland free to resume its historic path as an independent free monarchy.

However, in his later works, he undertook pioneering work on the links between the revolts in Scotland and Ireland, first in a book that examined the role of the Covenanting Armies in Ireland 1642–9,[36] and then in a study of the Irish Catholic troop of Alisdair MacColla who waged clan warfare in Scotland in the mid-1640s as a major component of Montrose's 'royalist' army.[37]

By the mid-1980s, other historians were beginning to look at these events from a more holistically 'British' perspective. A succession of graduate students in Cambridge University were looking at key episodes in a way which sought to be even-handed in their discussion of the English and Scottish sides of particular issues. For example, Peter Donald completed in 1987 a thesis on Anglo-Scottish aspects of the collapse of the Personal Rule (subsequently published as *An uncounselled King* [1990]) and John Scally completed a PhD on the political career of James Hamilton, 3rd Marquis and 1st Duke of Hamilton).[38] By the mid 1980s it was time for the English to catch up.

VII

The clarion call for a return to a British history came in Conrad Russell's inaugural lecture as Astor Professor of British History delivered in University College London on 7 March 1985 and entitled 'The British Problem and the English Civil War'.[39] It was to launch a series of publications concerned with explaining the causes of the collapse of Charles I's government in England by looking at events *outside England*. Russell argued that it required the collapse of Charles' authority in his outlying kingdoms to destabilise a demilitarised England. Russell has not shown any interest in the period beyond 1643, nor in developing a holistic history of the Atlantic archipelago or of the Stuart dynastic agglomerate. It is emblematic that in his inaugural lecture he spoke pointedly about his Chair being in *British* History and then lectured on how a British perspective could assist with the understanding of a central problem of *English* History. That he is interested in more than showing that events outside England affected events inside England can be seen in the insistent sentence early in his inaugural that 'the tendency of dissidents in each kingdom to try to make common cause with sympathisers in the others ensured that that English, Scottish and Irish troubles could not remain three isolated problems: they triggered off a period of repeated interventions by the three kingdoms in each other's affairs . . .'[40]

Russell followed up his pioneering articles with important books. In *The Causes of the English Civil War* (Oxford, 1991) and *The Fall of the British Monarchies 1637–1642* (Oxford, 1992) he offered a masterly account of the rise of opposition to Charles I. Russell's work was cautiously welcomed; but whereas previous attempts to revive an interest in the 'British' dimension had been largely ignored by other scholars, Russell's drew attention to itself and encountered resistance. Some of this criticism comes from fellow historians of England, claiming not to know what all the fuss was about. Many seek to continue the tradition of minimising the importance of British History, believing that events in Ireland and Scotland are epiphenomena to the events in England, happening simultaneously but not any more significant than events in continental Europe or New England, for example. Such historians suggest that the need to keep research and the narratives or units of analysis within manageable parameters impose a self-denying ordinance on a more than contingent discussion of the separate and separable histories of Scotland and Ireland.

Another line of criticism has come from historians of Scotland and Ireland who believe that Russell's work represents some kind of insensitive historiographical imperialism. Keith Brown has suggested that Scottish historiography is too incomplete and immature in relation to English historiography to withstand an intentional or unintentional intellectual imperialism by historians of Britain and Ireland who are approaching the subject from a set of English preoccupations: 'intellectually the case for British history is very persuasive', he suggests but the risk is that the new British History will quickly deteriorate into 'a revitalised history of the English state'.[41]

Rather fiercer criticism has come from Nicholas Canny. Long a proponent of seeing Irish History as a branch of British colonial history, and seeking to explore the place of Ireland within the Atlantic world, he has been extremely suspicious of any attempt to create a British History that is in fact 'nothing but old English History in three-kingdoms clothing' and which both privileges political history which can be made to fit that agenda rather than social, economic and cultural history which cannot and which 'implies an integrity for "these islands" probably in excess of any that ever existed". Canny argues that a *comparative* approach is fruitful and needs doing; but that a holistic approach is not helpful.[42]

However, there is a very different line of criticism of Russell's work, that it fails to locate it adequately as a *European-wide* phenomenon: that it was one of the many theatres of the 'Thirty Years War'; that it was part of a 'General Crisis' that gripped the French and Spanish monarchies and also much of Eastern and Northern Europe; or more generally that the ideas and passions that drove events originated in or resonated with ideas and passions driving conflict in Continental Europe.

We have already seen that foreign rulers itched to become involved in the war(s) in Britain and Ireland and that evident itch did have its effects on how the parties in Britain and Ireland behaved. But there were in fact no foreign banners or soldiers owing military allegiance to a foreign prince engaged in the archipelagic wars; and no troops owing allegiance to Charles or his enemies engaged in the continental theatres of the Thirty Years War and no British representatives at the treaties of Westphalia that ended that war. There is a European context for the British Wars as there is by definition a European context or dimension to everything that ever happens in British and Irish History. But it is no more necessary (or, of course, less necessary) to be aware of it for the 1640s than for any other decade.

Others, and notably Jonathan Scott, would look less at the interpenetration of events than ideas; and he would argue that the aspirations to new monarchy and its *alter ego*, the search for a puritan-republican commonwealth are both self-evidently rooted in the thought, writings and political cultures of contemporary Europe and that fear of Catholic monarchy and of the Catholic Church and Catholic religion were more powerful even than fears of their manifestations in Catholic Ireland in creating the militancy of Charles I's mortal enemies and in establishing the infant Commonwealth.[43] Exploring English Republican thought, or the articulation and forms (if not the psychological impulse) of English high millenarian thought, for example, one needs to cross the Channel and not the Irish Sea or the Pentland Hills. This is obviously true and important and is another area ripe for research and ignored by most of those who have written about the period.

Yet it can be suggested that the emergence of almost all the intellectual phenomena that require that approach followed and did not precede or make possible the collapse of the Stuart agglomerate. The rebellions of Scotland in 1638, England in 1640, Ireland in 1641 and all three in 1642–3 were not recognised by any of the principals as part of a European crisis. The Stuarts had not over-extended themselves militarily in the decades down to 1638 and the problems of managing their dynastic agglomerate – difficult though that had been proving – was not essentially a problem of sustaining a militarised state. Laud's programme, let alone its manner of introduction, can be understood within an insular intellectual and institutional environment; as can the passive and eventually the physical resistance of the godly.

The internal wars of the archipelagic kingdoms in the 1640s were not *caused* by a crisis whose lineaments resembled those of the continental rebellions of the 1640s.

The 'General Crisis' of the continental kingdoms was the result of the unprecedented attempts of government to increase levels of taxation and military supply; to develop institutions that could levy and deploy those massively-increased resources; and to impose central and centralising structures to supervise the new regional institutions. The result was a wave of revolts in the peripheries of the French, Spanish, Polish, Austrian and Russian dynastic agglomerates; and also revolts by elites who felt themselves disproportionately mulcted or inadequately consulted. None of this was true of Britain and Ireland. The crises in this agglomerate had very different *causes*; militarisation, bureaucratisation and centralisation were the *consequence* of the British crisis not the cause of it.

The parallels between the British and the Continental experience sometimes therefore flatter to deceive. They must never be ignored; but neither can they be used to replace or to be given higher priority than a study of the particular dynamics of a collapsing Stuart state system.

VIII

The problem with Russell's approach may be, then, that it is not radical enough: it looks *too* English. The more radical approach which I would suggest is worth investigating is that of John Pocock. Pocock's pioneering call in the mid 1970s for a new 'British History' has become ever more manifestly an attempt to locate an anglophone political culture with its own vital dialectic within the British Isles in the early modern period, around the Atlantic rim in the eighteenth century and around the globe in the nineteenth and twentieth century. It is no coincidence that the trail-blazing essay for this enterprise, and one of the most powerful reprises, was delivered in New Zealand, where Pocock grew up and to which he later returned as young teacher and scholar; or that his initial essay was published just when the United Kingdom made its first major move into the EEC and cut large parts of the anglophone diaspora adrift economically and culturally. Such concerns may have been instrumental in drawing Pocock's attention to the issues raised. And it seems to explain a central tension in his formulation of the problem. On the one hand he calls for an 'archipelagic' unit of study; on the other for the way the 'peoples of the British isles interacted so as to change the conditions of their own existence'. The latter means *both* the interaction of long-term anglophone settlers and recent anglophone colonists with the Celtic peoples; *and* the interaction of the peoples whose cultural identity had been modified as a result of *those* interactions with one another. I think there is very little doubt that Pocock's principal interest has not been in *state formation* but in *national identity* and what happens to national identity when a people encounters a physical and cultural environment different from its own.[44] Pocock is therefore drawn towards an Atlantic rim history as well as an Atlantic archipelagic history, and to the eighteenth century rather more than to the seventeenth century. But he has devoted time and thought to the mid-seventeenth century and especially to the difficulty of conceptualising the crisis within the archipelago at that period. This is how he construes the problem:

> Can we construct a holistic explanation of the War of the Three Kingdoms or must we concede that a multiple monarchy cannot have a single or holistic history? The issue turns on the extent to which the single dynasty ruling several realms had created a single polity or a complex of polities centred on itself, which had its own life and within which a series of things could go wrong: an entity which engendered or suffered its own crises, in short, and – above all – which had its own history.[45]

My answer to this conundrum has hitherto been that to some men in a position significantly to influence the outcome – Charles I himself, the Earl of Antrim, the Marquis of Hamilton, the Marquis of Ormond, almost all the leading Covenanters, many of the leading Confederates, it *was* one single conflict in several theatres. And for many humbler people who lived in the path of troops from a kingdom other than their own, it felt like one war. But for many leading Royalists in England, most leading Parliamentarians, and distinct minorities amongst the élites of Scotland and Ireland (and most humble folk in England and Scotland but not Ireland), the theatres other than their own were necessary short-term distractions or unwanted periodic intrusions into *their* war. It was both one untidy war and a series of interlocking wars in the minds of different leading actors; and it was therefore in reality both one war and three.[46]

Pocock's solution is rather different and more elegant. He argues that:

> In a history of the Three Kingdoms each kingdom has its own history, no matter how much it converges or interacts by refusing to converge and instead colliding, with the history of the others; particular histories do not cease to exist when it is seen that they cannot be written in isolation.[47]

I prefer 'each people' to 'each kingdom', but broadly speaking, this statement must be accepted. It follows from this that 'there was a War of the Three Kingdoms but it was several wars going on together.'[48] Pocock then ingeniously suggests that we draw down concepts developed by the Romans to understand the phenomenon of internal war within their Empire (and therefore known through Latin writings to the actors in the War(s) of the Three Kingdoms):

> It was a war among (and not between) the kingdoms comprising a multiple monarchy, and to find an appropriate label we should turn to the ancient Roman distinction between *bellum civile* and *bellum sociale* . . . A *bellum civile* was a war between *cives*, citizens of the same polity; a *bellum sociale* a war between *socii*, polities associated in a system comprising a multiplicity of states. The great *bellum sociale* of antiquity turned on the eligibility of Italian *socii* to be treated as *cives Romani*; it was a formal similarity with the Scottish endeavour to establish by military means that English and Scots should be members of a uniform ecclesiastical polity . . .[49]

The latter part of his essay considers more fully the implications of this distinction for an understanding of the various theatres of war within the archipelago in the 1640s. Elements of both kinds of war can be found in each kingdom. The King, the Scots – nobility and Kirkmen – the Protestant communities of Ireland and many of the leading figures in the Confederation of Kilkenny had as *a* principal objective a radical shift in the relationship of the kingdoms one to another as a result of the war, and fundamental changes in the rights of the peoples in relation to one another. They were fighting a *bellum sociale*. Most of them, most of the time, were also fighting a *bellum civile*, and other leaders in England and in Ireland, were fighting predominantly a *bellum civile*. But it may be that Pocock leaves out of account a third kind of internal war for which I do not know the Latin term: a war of independence (as exemplified by the Jewish Revolt of 67–70 CE). As far as I know, no one in Scotland was fighting for independence from the House of Stuart or for looser ties with England; on the contrary from 1640 to 1654 they were fighting for a con-federal union of the kingdoms and churches. All the Protestants of Ireland wanted a redefined relationship between the kingdoms; and most of the Catholics wanted to create an Irish kingdom independent of the English Parliament and courts but subject to the royal house of Stuart. However, it is becoming increasingly clear that there was – especially amongst the previously dispossessed Catholic septs of Ulster – a willingness, perhaps even a determination – to free Ireland from English and Stuart control, to recreate a Celtic realm initially under foreign Protectorship until such time as it might be possible to recreate the ancient Celtic high kingship.[50] And in 1649 the Rump of the English Parliament and its Council of State wished to secede from Scotland, to decouple the dynastic union of 1603 and to allow Scotland to float free as an independent monarchy to the North of an English and Irish Commonwealth.

Now, the point of this refining of Pocock's argument is to be clearer than he sometimes is about distinguishing two distinct processes: the structural stress engendered by the process of converting a dynastic agglomerate into a state system; and the fevers induced by the partly successful processes of acculturation of the Celtic peoples of the Atlantic archipelago into lowland English systems of law and inheritance, language, religion. The result was both the creation of new English, Irish, Scottish and Welsh identities very different from older English, Irish, Scottish and Welsh identities, and the creation within the peoples of the island of Britain, but not amongst most of the peoples of the island of Ireland, of an additional *British* identity. The Wars of the 1640s and the early 1650s were for many an attempt to command the first of those processes (and in that sense to be part of a holistic enterprise) and to withstand the second of them (and in that sense to seek to refuse to be part of that enterprise).

IX

So that is where things stand. The term 'The War(s) of the Three Kingdoms' for all its ungainliness on the page is the best available. It is a series of wars chronologically: 1639–40; 1641–6; 1648; 1649–50; 1650–5. All the wars saw battles in all three kingdoms. All those wars saw significant numbers of troops from at least two of the kingdoms engaged in the fighting in other kingdoms. Each war contained elements of *bellum civile* and *bellum sociale* and all the later ones saw elements of wars of independence. Of course, 'particular histories do not cease to exist when it is seen that they cannot be written in isolation', any more than different coloured wools do not cease to have their own identity when they tighten woven into a plaid, but it sometimes makes more sense to call such a tight weave a plaid rather than a weave of different coloured wools!

And yet, even then, new complexities appear. Ambiguity is indeed the essence of this problem. For the extent to which a 'plaid' approach to the War of the Three Kingdoms transforms our understanding of its/their dynamics varies with the kind of history we are attempting.

A *military* history gains immeasurably from a 'plaid' approach – it gives a shape to the campaigns, explains military decisions and military outcomes, for decisions about the deployment of armies, strategic prioritisation, under-resourcing, all deepen immensely if a holistic approach is taken.[51] It is self-evident in the case of the Marston Moor campaign in its narrow military sense – the Scots army was the largest single contingent on either side – and in the ill-will between Cromwell and senior Scottish commanders (not least over who should take prime responsibility for the victory) that resonated through the military campaigns and logistics for months afterwards. It might seem less obvious in the Naseby campaign, fought by two English armies, but as Norman Dore showed many years ago, the fact that the two armies met when, where and how they did, was contingent upon a number of decisions and complex movements of troops around the Midlands that might well have seen the decisive battle fought in the north west not in the south east midlands, and those complex movements were much concerned with the situations in Ireland and Scotland.[52]

A *political* history will benefit less regularly from such an approach. One could write at very great length about the Putney Debates and contextualise those debates in many ways without having to draw on an archipelagic perspective. But any account of the internal dynamics of the royalist or of the parliamentarian movements, of the factions amongst the Covenanters and Confederates, of any attempt to explain the failure of the peace process from 1641 to 1648 and beyond (in each and all of the kingdoms), any attempt to explain the strength of the army in the 1650s, when there were always between three and five times as many troops in Ireland and Scotland as in England, requires a recognition of the fact that the unresolved problem of constitutional incoherence and national identities provides a necessary dimension of any explanatory framework.

Any *religious* history will come up against the religious ambitions of groups in each kingdom for the whole archipelago; but it will also come up against a fact that this is a curdled mix in which the elements will not gel however stiffly beaten the historical whisk. And while the disruptive presence of the Scots in England needs more analysis even than it has yet received, the religious dimension of the War(s) more than any other needs both a European and an Atlantic rim dimension to make any real sense. New England experience and Counter-Reformation asceticism were central to the conflicts in England and Ireland in the 1640s after all.

Any *social* history will not only require a general sense of the dislocations caused by the kind of war we have already described, but a sense of English designs in the 1650s to destroy the social power of the

Scottish peerage and to develop a stout Scottish yeomanry grateful to the English for their liberation and dependent upon the English for their survival; and a sense of how English determination to expropriate more than a third of the land mass of Ireland to punish the Irish, and to give land to ex-soldiers, merchants and gentry as settlement of debts owed by the state, resulting in a revolution of land-holding proportionately greater and more traumatic than the Dissolution of the Monasteries in England a century before.

The Wars within, amongst and between the peoples of England and Wales, Scotland, and Ireland (note the care taken with sequence and punctuation) meant different things to different people at different times. And so the War(s) of the Three Kingdoms it needs to be: an unstable, unsatisfactory term for events that subverted everyone's sense of what was fixed and unalterable. For, uncomfortable though it is to admit it, the historian's task is sometimes to acknowledge the incoherence of the past and not to impose order upon it.

Notes to Chapter 3

1   J.S. Morrill 'Between War and Peace'; in eds. J.P. Kenyon and J. Ohlmeyer. *The Oxford Illustrated History of the British Civil Wars* (Oxford, 1998), 299–301 (these figures are themselves based on those of Henry Reece, 'The Military Presence in England 1649–1660', Univ of Oxford D Phil dissertation (1981), appendix 1).

2   J.S. Morrill, 'Three Kingdoms and One Commonwealth? The Enigma of mid-seventeenth century Britain and Ireland' in eds. A. Grant and K.J. Stringer, *Uniting the Kingdom? The Making of British History* (1995), 170–91.

3   Most obviously and effectively by Conrad Russell. See below, pp. 78–81.

4   See especially K.J. Lindley, 'The Impact of the 1641 Rebellion on England and Wales 1641–5', *Irish Historical Studies* 18 (1972), 143–76.

5   Joong-Lak Kim, *The Debate on the Uniformity of the Churches of England and Scotland in the British Revolutions, 1633–1647*, Univ. of Cambridge PhD thesis (1997).

6   A good recent survey is D. Stevenson, 'Cromwell, Scotland and Ireland' in ed. J. Morrill, *Oliver Cromwell and the English Revolution* (1990), 149–80.

7   There is and never has been a geopolitical term covering Britain and Ireland; and although from the Roman period and throughout the Renaissance period, European scholars and mapmakers had a clear notion of the *Insulae Britannicae* and Britons subsequently had no difficulty with the geographical term 'The British Isles', that term has been and is resisted and resented by the majority population of the island of

Ireland. The political unit was known as the United Kingdom of Britain and Ireland, and as United Kingdom for short, but only between 1801 and 1922 did it incorporate the whole of the islands of Britain and Ireland. The term the Atlantic Archipelago was coined by John Pocock in the 1970s (see below) pp. 81–3 and this is an artificial but real term, since the islands to the North and West of Scotland, together with the Isles of Man and Wight, the Scillies and the Channel Islands, have all been, for some parts of modern history, part of the polity. An archipelago it indubitably is.

8   See for example the discussion by John Pocock, 'The Atlantic Archipelago and the War of the Three Kingdoms' in eds. B. Bradshaw and J. Morrill, *The British Problem c.1534–1707: State Formation in the Atlantic Archipelago* (1996), 172–191 and J. Morrill, 'The Un-English Civil War' in ed. J.R. Young, *Celtic Dimensions of the British Civil Wars* (1997), 1–16.

9   ed. J. Ohlmeyer, *Ireland: from Independence to Occupation 1641–1660* (Cambridge, 1995), 89–112. See also the important thesis by T. O h'Annraichain, *The Mission of GianBattista Rinuccini to Ireland, 1645–1649*, PhD thesis, European University Institute, Florence (1995), esp. ch.1, in which he explores the views of the Pope and the Kings of Spain and France on the conflicts within the Stuart monarchies.

10   For John Kenyon's willingness to make these parallels with the European General Crisis, see his *The Civil Wars of England* (1988), 5–6.

11   Ohlmeyer coins the phrase in her important study of *Civil War and Restoration in Three Kingdoms: the Career of Randall Macdonell, Marquis of Antrim 1609–1683* (Cambridge, 1993), chapter 6 (entitled 'The War of the Five Kingdoms'); and she develops the idea in ed. Ohlmeyer, *Ireland: from Independence to Occupation,* 89–112.

12   The term was coined by J.C. Beckett, *The Making of Modern Ireland 1603–1923,* (London, 1966), ch. 4, as acknowledged also by John Pocock in his essay 'The Atlantic archipelago and the war of the three kingdoms' in eds. B. Bradshaw and J. Morrill, *The British Problem c.1534–1707: state formation in the Atlantic Archipelago* (Basingstoke, 1996), 172.

13   Edward Hyde, Earl of Clarendon, *The History of the Rebellion and civil wars in England.* (ed. W.D. Macray, 6 vols., Oxford, 1888).

14   If Clarendon was indeed the author (and it is not clear to me why his authorship has been so readily taken at face value) of the mis-titled *History of Rebellion and Civil Wars in Ireland* (in practice an elaborate defence of the Marquis of Ormond written from his papers to which Clarendon [d.1674] would not have had access) and published in 1719/20, then this silence in his *History of the Great Rebellion* would be even more eloquent. It was not that he was ignorant of Irish Affairs, but disinclined

to demonstrate the connection between Irish and British affairs. For bibliographical details, see G. Roebuck, *Clarendon and Cultural Continuity* (1981), 117–18, 127, 136. I am grateful to Glenn Burgess for drawing my attention to this.

15 and also the continental card, using foreign armies and mercenaries in an invasion of his own kingdoms.

16 What follows is based on a reading of my own copy (an edition of 1786)

17 Chapters LIII to LXII cover 1637–60 in some 160,000 words.

18 Covering the final paragraphs of chapter LVII and the early paragraphs of chapter LVIII.

19 S.R. Gardiner, *History of England from the Accession of James I to the outbreak of the civil war* (10 vols., 1883–4); *History of the Great Civil War, 1642–9* (4 vols., 1893); *History of the Commonwealth and Protectorate, 1649–56* (4 vols., 1903). After his death, the events of 1656–9 were written up by his close friend C.H. Firth in *The Last Years of the Protectorate* (2 volumes, 1911).

20 For which, see now S. Barber, 'Irish Undercurrents of the politics of 1653' *Historical Research* 65 (1992), 315–35.

21 In particular, the internal history of Scotland in 1642 and Ireland in 1647 are major casualties; and the internal history of Ireland in the winter of 1648–9 lacks a proper analysis on the destructive dynamics of political rivalry and military decay on the Catholic 'New Irish' side.

22 ed. L. Stone, *Social Change and Revolution in England, 1540–1640* (1965) in which the views of Professors Tawney, Stone, Trevor-Roper and many more are extracted and summarised. The whole book is a testament to how imposing historical castles built on sand can sometimes appear at the time.

23 For some fascinating preliminary thoughts on these groups, see E. O'Ciardha, 'Tories and Moss-troopers in Scotland and Ireland in the Interregnum: a political dimension' in ed. J.R. Young, *The Celtic Dimensions of the British Civil Wars* (Edinburgh, 1997): 164–84. For the same kind of reason, historians before the 1970s lavished interest and space on the Levellers and not on the much more numerous and widespread Clubmen (see the comments of David Underdown in eds. G. Eley and W. Hunt, *Reviving the English Revolution* (1988), 338–9).

24 For which, see below, pp. 75–8.

25 L. Stone, *The causes of the English Revolution 1529–1642* (London, 1972), 137–8.

26 An exception must be made for Godfrey Davies, *The Early Stuarts 1603–1660* (Oxford, 1959) in the Oxford History of England series. Designed both as school/university textbook and for the general reader. Davies was a dull and complacent historian, but he had been Sir Charles Firth's amanuensis in his later years, and he saw himself as the successor

and academic legatee of Gardiner and Firth: his book rather slavishly (but in terms of this essay effectively) reproduces their argument and balance with respect to the intersecting wars in three kingdoms as in so much else.

27   Thus Barry Coward, *The Stuart Age* (1980), 216, has the *Scots* hanging Hamilton (beheaded by the English after trial before the English High Court), as well as Huntly and Montrose; while J.P. Kenyon (*Stuart England [1978]*) 168, misrepresents both the Rump's Act of Settlement (for Ireland) and the nature of the annexation of Scotland. (The second edition of this book [1985, at pp. 181–2], which corrected many errors from the first edition, left these errors as they were).

28   Principally, I. Roots, *The Great Rebellion* (1966), witty and clear; J.P. Kenyon, *The Civil Wars in England* (1987), crisp and shrewd; M. Bennett, *The Civil Wars in Britain and Ireland* (Oxford, 1997), vivid and especially good on detailed local material. Each adopts an approach more in the tradition of 'let us concentrate on disaggregating the conflicts and look at each in turn' than that adopted by Wedgwood. Kenyon's undervalued book is in fact far more archipelagic than he was willing to admit; Bennett is, paradoxically, much more anglo-centric, with a deep sense of the particularism of the English regions. Yet a wonderful cartoon drawing of a Scottish officer in tartan pantaloons, his pointed nose and long face topped by a broad-brimmed 'puritan hat' (doodled on to the back of a tax receipt given by the officer in question – Major Andrew Leslie – to the Salvin family in Croxdale, County Durham) is magnificently evocative of how a three-kingdom (or, as Bennett rather contentiously prefers, four-nation) perspective can impinge on the work of the historian of the English locality.

29   As an example, as late as the mid 1980s when the current writer was an external examiner to the Modern History Department of a Scottish University, he was not invited to moderate the scripts for a special subject on The Personal Rule of Charles I in Scotland, the task instead being entrusted to the external examiner whose expertise lay in early medieval Scottish History.

30   G. Donaldson, *Scotland: James V to James II* (Edinburgh and London, 1965).

31   See my essays in ed. J. Morrill, *The Scottish National Covenant in its British Context* (Edinburgh, 1991), ch.1; and 'A British Patriarchy? Ecclesiastical Imperialism under the Early Stuarts' in eds. A. Fletcher and P. Roberts, *Religion, Culture and Society in Early Modern Britain* (Cambridge, 1994), 209–37. See also, Kim, *The Debate on the Uniformity of the Churches of England and Scotland,* chs.1–2.

32   W. Ferguson, *Scotland's Relations with England: a survey to 1707* (Edinburgh, 1977), 127, 128.

33   Eds T.W. Moody, F.X. Martin, F.J. Byrne, *A New History of Ireland*, Volume III, *1534–1691* (Oxford, 1976), esp. chs. IX-XIV.

34   See especially his essay 'The Genesis of the Ulster Rising of 1641' in ed.P.Roebuck, *Plantation to Partition: Essays in Honour of J.L. McCracken* (Belfast, 1981), 29–45.

35   A. Clarke, 'Ireland and the General Crisis', *Past and Present* 48 (1970), 79–99.

36   D. Stevenson, *Scottish Covenanters and Irish Confederates: Scottish-Irish Relations in the mid-Seventeenth Century* (Belfast, 1981).

37   D. Stevenson, *Alasdair MacColla and the Highland Problem in the Seventeenth Century* (Edinburgh, 1980). I think it fair to say that other figures working close to but not within the mid-seventeenth century field who had a major influence on the 'revisionist' scholarship of the wars of the 1640s include Jenny Wormald, for her essays on James VI and I and Anglo-Scottish Union and Steven Ellis, for his work on Irish History in a British context and on Ireland as just one of the Tudor borderlands.

38   J. Scally, 'The Political career of James, third Marquis and first Duke of Hamilton (1606–49) to 1643', Univ. of Cambridge PhD thesis (1992). For an example of his approach and findings, see his essay entitled 'Counsel in Crisis: James, Third Marquis of Hamilton and the Bishops' Wars, 1638–1640', in ed. J.R. Young, *Celtic Dimensions of the British Civil Wars* (Edinburgh, 1997), 18–34.

39   C. Russell, 'The British Problem and the English Civil War' *History*, 72 (1986), 395–415, reprinted in C. Russell, *Unrevolutionary England* (London, 1990), 230–59.

40   Russell, *Unrevolutionary England*, 233.

41   K. Brown, 'British History: a sceptical comment' in ed. R. Asch, *Three Nations – a common history?* (Bochum, 1993), 117–27, quotation from p. 127.

42   N. Canny, 'Irish Scottish and Welsh responses to centralisation c.1530–c.1640' in eds. A. Grant and K. Stringer, *Uniting the Kingdom? The Making of British History* (1995), 147–69, at p. 147–8. For further comment by Canny on these topics, see Canny, 'The attempted Anglicisation of Ireland in the Seventeenth Century: an exemplar of "British History"' in ed. Asch, *Three Nations*, pp. 49–81 and his review of Russell's *The fall of the British Monarchies*, in *Irish Economic and Social History* xix (1992), 112–15.

43   J.Scott, 'Britain's Troubles' in ed. M. Smuts, *The Stuart Court and Europe: Essays in Politics and Political Culture* (Cambridge, 1996).

44   Perhaps the most important of Pocock's most distinguished series of

articles are: (1) 'British History: a plea for a new subject', *JMH* iv (1975), 601–24; 'The Limits and Divisions of British History' *AHR* lxxxvii (1982), 311–36; 'History and Sovereignty: the historiographical response to Europeanisation in two British cultures' *JBS* xxxi (1992), 358–89; 'two kingdoms and three histories: political thought in British contexts', in ed. R.A. Mason, *Scots and Britons: Scottish political thought and the union of 1603* (1994); and (most directly relevant to this essay), 'The Atlantic archipelago and the war of the three kingdoms' in eds. B. Bradshaw and J. Morrill, *The British Problem c.1534–1707: state formation in the Atlantic Archipelago* (1996), 172–191.

45   Pocock, 'Atlantic Archipelago', 178.

46   J.S. Morrill, 'The Britishness of the English Revolution', in ed. Asch, *Three Nations*, 92–117.

47   Pocock, 'Atlantic Archipelago', 180.

48   Ibid., 182.

49   Ibid., 186.

50   I am trespassing as far as I think appropriate on an as yet unpublished paper by Jerrold Casway which looks at the way the O'Neills took inspiration from the Jewish Maccabees, a sect that sought to keep Israel pure from external corruption and to prepare the way for the Restoration of a prophetically-inspired monarchy. I am grateful to Jerrold Casway for permission to allude to this exciting essay.

51   For a demonstration see J.P. Kenyon and J. Ohlmeyer, *The Civil Wars in England, Scotland and Ireland: a military history* (Oxford, 1998).

52   R.N. Dore, 'Sir William Brereton's siege of Chester and the campaign of Naseby'. *T.Lancs & Chesh.Antiq.Soc.* 67 (1958 for 1957), 17–44.

CHAPTER 4

Restoration to Revolution: 1660–1690[+]

Clare Jackson

In 1685, Sir George Mackenzie of Rosehaugh observed that while 'these Kingdoms are unhappily divided, not in Nations, but in Opinions . . . the old Animosities among Scots, English, and Irish being forgot and buried', they had been replaced by 'modern Differences between the Episcopal and Fanatick, Cavalier and Republican, or as some term it, Whig and Tory'.[1] Mackenzie was one of the Stuart dynasty's most steadfast supporters who even acquired the unenviable sobriquet 'Bluidy Mackenzie' for his repressive actions as Lord Advocate of Scotland during the late-1670s and 1680s. The above observation was made within the context of a pamphlet controversy between himself and the Welsh bishop of St. Asaph, William Lloyd. Researching the antiquarian origins of the Welsh episcopate, Lloyd had concluded that the Scots could not have settled Scotland until the sixth century, thus fatally undermining Scottish claims to represent the most ancient monarchy in the world, founded originally in 330 B.C. by the mythical Fergus I.[2] In addition to his professional actions on behalf of the Stuart monarchs, Mackenzie also devoted considerable time to publishing demonstrations of the 'uninterrupted Obedience given by this Nation to an Hundred and ten Kings, in Two Thousand Years time, by exact Calculation'.[3] In 1683, his version of Scottish history had been granted official sanction when Charles II commissioned Jacob de Wet to paint the series of 111 portraits of those kings of Scotland which still hangs today in the Palace of Holyroodhouse in Edinburgh.

[+] I would like to thank Mark Goldie and John Morrill for their comments and suggestions on an earlier draft of this chapter.

Mackenzie's patriotic attachment to his Scottish national identity was inextricably linked with his personal loyalty to the Stuarts and his country's membership of the Stuart multiple monarchy. Like many of his contemporaries, however, Mackenzie frequently acknowledged a 'British' context to the events in which he participated and then recorded. Since Scotland, England, Ireland and Wales were ruled by the same monarch, the actions, intentions and welfare of that monarch and his government were evidently of common interest throughout his dominions. As Mackenzie later acknowledged, 'every honest man in Scotland rejoyces, when they hear of the Prosperity of the Royal Family in England . . . an Union in Principles, being stronger than that of Kingdoms'.[4] As this chapter will show, constitutional, political and religious parallels between events in one dominion and their implication for those of another were indeed frequently sought and found by all Restoration contemporaries. While not proposing that a single British perspective of events can either accommodate or rival single national histories of each kingdom, such a dimension often provides a crucial perspective on events throughout the multiple monarchy. The 'new British history' can thus provide parallels which enhance our understanding of the workings of multiple monarchy, but it cannot rewrite the national histories of England, Scotland, Wales and Ireland. The search for a wholly integrated history of the multiple monarchy between 1660 and 1690 may ultimately prove as distorting as traditional anglocentric historiography. For while contemporaries readily sought and applied British parallels to domestic situations, by no means was this appreciation of the practical workings of the multiple monarchy reflected in the simultaneous formation of a coherent British identity.

Historiographically, there has been less evidence of attempts to construct a 'British' history for the Restoration than for any other period in the seventeenth century.[5] Within the confines of space available, this chapter nevertheless explores some of the ways in which contemporaries themselves applied a British dimension to domestic situations. Considered first is the Restoration of the monarchy itself and the political and religious settlements that accompanied Charles II's return to power. From the outset, the catastrophic events of the mid-century civil wars dictated that Restoration actors ignored British history at their peril. As the earl of Clarendon notoriously recalled of England during the 1630s, 'when the whole nation was solicitous to know what passed weekly in Germany and Poland and all other parts of Europe, no man ever inquired what was doing in Scotland'.[6] Englishmen, at least, would be unwise to embrace such ignorance again.

Secondly, the chapter reviews the political implications of Charles II's administration for each nation within the multiple monarchy. For although Charles II and James VII and II were both obliged to seek different expedients for managing 'the British problem', they often proved as willing as their father to explore 'British solutions' to domestic predicaments. Thirdly, the chapter considers how the Stuart monarchs were also forced to devise policies which could accommodate the complex nature of religious affairs throughout the multiple monarchy. Since the confessional preferences of the majority of the population in each of the three kingdoms were different, religious affairs presented a unique challenge to the governments of Charles II and his brother. In this context, contemporaries were aware that if they faced opposition when practising their own religion in public, or even in private, they were as free as their monarchs to experiment with a 'British solution'. Hence they could make common cause with discontented subjects elsewhere in the Stuart dominions to undertake active and concerted action to seek freedom from persecution. Alternatively, they could also settle for peaceful internal exile. In 1689, Sir George Mackenzie himself ultimately sought refuge within the comfortably royalist walls of the University of Oxford when presbyterianism once again gained the ascendant and he found himself to be the focus of rumoured assassination plots circulating in Edinburgh.

Fourthly, the chapter investigates the different ways in which the constitutional relationships among the members of the multiple monarchy were conceptualised. The experiences of the civil wars had clearly demonstrated that early modern political arrangements were far from everlasting in nature or time. When intermittent continental hostilities and overseas colonial expansion contributed different and additional pressures, contemporaries also acknowledged the potential to renegotiate constitutional and economic arrangements within the British multiple monarchy. Fifthly, the chapter concludes by considering the particular impact of James VII and II's short rule on the constituent parts of the multiple monarchy as well as the British implications of the revolutions that followed.

I

In 1660 the Restoration of Charles II was greeted with near-universal enthusiasm throughout his dominions. While 'the world of England was perfectly mad . . . freed from the chaines of darkness which the presbyterians and phanaticks had brought',[7] once the news of the king's restoration arrived in Scotland, it was claimed that 'there was never [an] accident that altered the disposition of a people more than that did the Scottish nation'.[8] The Welsh cleric, William Phylip, privately rejoiced that 'God of Heaven by his power has brought the bones of Cadwaladr home', while across the Irish Sea, a Dublin crowd publicly enacted the funeral rites and effigy-burning of 'a certain monster they called the commonwealth, represented by an ugly mis-shapen body without an head, but with a huge insatiable belly and a prodigious rump'.[9] Apart from the personal return to power of Charles II, however, there was little domestic or British consensus about the precise nature of what was being restored. Underpinned by a desire to efface memories of the Cromwellian imperial experiment, the Restoration settlement was characteristically different in each of the Stuarts' dominions. In England and Wales, the monarchy was restored to its pre-1641 status, which preserved royal control of the militia as well as the king's right to appoint his own ministers, but sustained the illegality of Ship Money, the abolition of the Star Chamber and High Commission, the removal of the Crown's feudal rights and retained, temporarily, the Triennial Act. In order to secure as much support for the new régime as possible, the monarchy's first major legislative initiative was the Act of Indemnity and Oblivion in 1660 which pardoned all but a few individual regicides. Although honourable in intent, the Act was subsequently resented by former English and Welsh royalists who had endured considerable personal and financial hardship on the king's behalf. From their perspective, the Act only appeared to secure effective oblivion while indemnity was being offered to those of the king's former enemies who had also benefited materially under the intervening incumbencies.

The relative gains and losses incurred by English and Welsh royal-ists, however, paled by comparison with the enormous political and social revolution which had occurred in mid-seventeenth century Ireland. The official decision to make confiscated Irish land the cur-rency by which the war of the three kingdoms was principally to be subsidised had resulted in the Catholic share of Irish land-holding plummeting from around 59 per cent before the 1641 rebellion, to around 20 per cent by 1660, the majority of which land was in the less fertile counties of Clare and Connacht. Moreover, since the scheme remained incomplete in 1660, Charles II's administration was immediately overwhelmed with claims from former landowners seek-ing immediate restitution of their estates, together with the demands of numerous financial adventurers and unpaid soldiers who were still officially owed large tracts of land. In November 1660, the government responded by issuing a proclamation ordaining that former estates were to be restored to those Catholics innocent of rebellion since 1641, as well as to those who had served the crown in exile. As the proclamation also confirmed all those lands formerly granted to the soldiers, it was difficult to disagree with the duke of Ormonde's famous observation that if the proclamation were to be implemented as it stood, 'there must be discoveries made of a new Ireland, for the old will not satisfy these engagements'.[10] Although a court of claims was established by the Act of Settlement in 1662, its operations were suspended within a year, when over 85 per cent of its claims remained outstanding. Instead, the speedier alternative of an Act of Explanation (1665) was preferred, which required soldiers and adventurers to surrender one-third of their lands. Although the Acts of Settlement and Explanation modestly increased the Catholic land share, the conclusion of the Restoration land settlement was described by a subsequent lord lieutenant as 'flinging the reward upon the death of a deer among a pack of hounds, where every one pulls and tears for himself'.[11]

In Scotland, no immediate amnesties were granted until the Restoration political and ecclesiastical settlements had been concluded. As the presbyterian preacher, John Blackadder rued, while 'England and Ireland had the benefit of a general amnesty to obliterate their past misconduct', the Scots administration had 'contrived to put off the king's indemnity until their schemes of plunder were matured and iniquity established by law'.[12] Although most members of the Restoration political élite in Scotland had taken up arms against Charles I on at least one occasion since the late-1630s, the unlikely alliance between radical presbyterians and discontented nobles at the outset of the civil wars had subsequently proved unsustainable. The nature of the Restoration settlement in Scotland in 1660 thus reflected a prevailing élite anticlericalism. The belief that the wishes of the state should never again be subjugated to those of the church was demonstrated most vividly by the passage of the Act Recissory in 1661 which revoked all legislation passed in Scotland since 1633, thus formally invalidating the entire Covenanting revolution. Most significantly, the Act Recissory returned the government of 'the church by law established' from presbyterian to episcopalian, a decision commonly assumed to represent part of an official royal policy to secure religious conformity throughout Britain. Closer examination, however, suggests that the chief influence behind the Act Recissory was the earl of Middleton, a recent Anglican convert, in his capacity as commissioner to the Scottish Parliament. According to Charles II's Chancellor, the earl of Clarendon, the monarch himself was more concerned about domestic harmony in Scotland than about British congruity. From London, Clarendon relayed Charles II's view that albeit parliamentary assent for such a measure could easily be obtained, he did not consider that 'argument enough that it will be acceptable to the Kingdome'. Clarendon counselled caution, instructing that 'if the consequence of such rescinding, be the present suppressing of Presbitery, and erecting of Episcopacy ... it will not be safe'.[13] Notwithstanding, Middleton persevered and secured the passage of the Act Recissory, but the subsequently turbulent history of Restoration Scotland was to confirm the instinctive fears of Charles II and Clarendon.

II

Politically, Charles II's return to power was accompanied by the restoration of the ancient institutions of crown government throughout the multiple monarchy. In Scotland and Ireland, this ensured that royal policy would largely be directed by a high commissioner, acting in the king's name and on the advice of a separate privy council. In Scotland, the president of the Privy Council, the earl of Rothes, even ventured so far as to question the need to recall any parliament in Scotland, preferring a return 'to the good old form of government by his Maj[ties] privie councell'.[14] For, although the unicameral Scots Parliament remained the focus for constitutional politics, its potential for independent action was limited. Effective royal control from Whitehall was assured, since all legislative initiative was regulated by the Lords of the Articles, a committee of royal appointees, many of whom were also members of the Scottish privy council. Nor was parliament a regular constitutional entity; during the Restoration, Charles II summoned three parliaments, and his brother, only one, meaning that for half of the years between 1660 and 1689, no parliament was held in Scotland.

In Ireland, political influence was inextricably associated with the inequities of property distribution, since freehold ownership alone conferred the right of political representation. The entirely Protestant composition of the 1661 Irish Parliament clearly demonstrated the extent to which formal legal disenfranchisement of Catholics was unnecessary. Although restricted in its powers to initiate and amend legislation by the fifteenth-century enactment of Poyning's Law, the Irish Parliament provided the Irish political élite with a major forum for discussion, initiative and opposition in the years immediately following the Restoration. In 1666, however, the increasingly intractable nature of the Parliament led to its prorogation and it did not convene again until 1689. Parliaments in England were held more regularly, but the repeal of the Triennial Act in 1664 subsequently enabled Charles II to rule without a parliament for four years in the 1680s.

In Scotland and Ireland, the most inescapable political consequence of being part of a multiple monarchy was being ruled by an absentee monarch. In Ireland, the office of lord lieutenant had extended in scope from that of an administrator before the civil wars, to a position of considerable importance, not only for the government of Ireland, but also within the domestic administration. Originally conferred on the duke of Albemarle in 1660, the post passed to the duke of Ormonde in 1662 who held office until he was replaced in 1669 by Lord John Robartes. The following year, Robartes was succeeded by Lord John Berkeley, who was in turn followed by the earl of Essex in 1672. In 1677 the post once again reverted to the duke of Ormonde who remained lord lieutenant until Charles II's death in 1685. Throughout the Restoration, the committed support of the monarch was essential for each lord lieutenant to sustain his position, changes in the Irish administration generally reflecting changes of influence at Court. From Ireland, one such lord lieutenant, Essex, once confided to his brother that 'the nature of this people is very apt to trample on their superiors; and unless a man be thoroughly countenanced in England; there is no dealing with them'.[15]

In Scotland, effective political power was increasingly vested in the office of parliamentary High Commissioner. Under Charles II's administration, this post was held by the earl of Middleton from 1660 until 1663, by John Leslie, earl of Rothes until 1668 and then by John Maitland, earl of Lauderdale, until the duke of York was appointed in 1679. Particularly under Lauderdale, the post proved unpopular, as it was expensive to maintain, lacked specific powers outside parliament, and offered the potential to establish a quasi-perpetual dictatorship operating outside the normal framework of government and responsible only to the Crown. Charles II's unswerving loyalty to his Commissioner, however, vitiated all attempts to challenge Lauderdale's position, despite English parliamentary attempts at impeachment and complaints from Scotland that Lauderdale's 'very place & power is [i]n effect, so extraordinarie exorbitant we cannot bear it'.[16]

Despite its constitutional limitations, the very existence of an independent legislature in Scotland had important political implications for the Stuart multiple monarchy. As Sir George Mackenzie had long recognised, 'whilst the kingdoms stood divided, his Majesty had two Parliaments, whereof the one might always be exemplary to the other, and might, by loyal emulation, excite one another to an entire obedience'.[17] Throughout the Restoration, successful parliamentary management in Edinburgh was indeed frequently used by the royal administration to serve as a salutary example for political opponents elsewhere in Britain. Observing proceedings in the Scots Parliament as early as 1661, the earl of Clarendon informed its Commissioner, Middleton, 'that your excellent proceedings there with such harmony of affection, and the making so many good acts have given the King great advantage here which wee shall make good use of in our Parliament'.[18]

Similarly fulsome political support for the Stuarts was forthcoming from Scotland during the 'Exclusion Crisis' of the late-1670s and early-1680s, amid English parliamentary attempts to debar the duke of York from his lawful accession to the throne on account of his Roman Catholicism. To remove him from the volatile political atmosphere generated by such attempts at exclusion, Charles II twice sent his brother to Edinburgh in the capacity of High Commissioner for the Scots Parliament. Under York's presidency in 1681, the Scots Parliament proceeded fully to endorse York's right to the Scottish crown by passing a Succession Act which made explicit that 'no difference in Religion Nor no Law nor Act of Parliament made or to be made can alter or divert the Right of Succession and lineal descent of the Croun'.[19] Not only did this legislation serve to reinforce recognition that the crown of Scotland was independent and distinct from the crowns of England, Wales and Ireland, but the effective creation of a reversionary interest served an unambiguous warning to Exclusionist members of the English Parliament. As York's biographer subsequently recorded, '[t]he world was surprised at this testimony of the dutyfullness and Loyalty of the Kingdom of Scotland, which haveing been alwayes looked upon as the fountain of Presbiterie, should so strenuously assert the Prerogative of the Crown, when England it self flew so furiously in its face'.[20] Unsurprisingly, one of the most convincing arguments for an incorporative Anglo-Scottish Union in the early-eighteenth century was that the formation of a new British parliament would end former Stuart practice of 'playing one of the kingdoms against the other, making use of each (by turns) to oppress and enslave the other, whilst a body of formidable troops was always ready in Scotland to invade the liberties of England, and the riches of England [were] made use of to destroy both church and state in Scotland'.[21]

Members of the political opposition were, however, equally as vigilant as those of Charles's administration in following the British dimensions of Restoration Scottish politics. In 1667, for instance, an increasingly sizeable Scottish militia had been established for use in Charles II's service throughout the three kingdoms. Amid growing fears in England about the spread of popery and arbitrary government, such legislation could be construed as part of a grand political design to destroy Protestantism and rule by law. Campaigning in the English House of Commons against the maintenance of standing armies, William Sacheverell argued that 'the Scotch Act of Militia . . . puts the King in power plainly to alter any thing in Church or State, and so, by this army, Popery may be set up'. His fears were shared by his parliamentary colleague, Sir Thomas Littleton, who warned, '[i]t is in vain to act here, without converting our thoughts to Scotland'.[22] Domestic opposition in Scotland also swelled as further repressive legislation was enacted, such as the 'Clanking Act' of 1670 which made it a capital offence to preach at outdoor religious conventicles. To register their deep discontent, successive deputations of Scots nobles travelled to London where they were seen 'daily concerting a correspondence with Buckingham, Shaftesbury and others who were discontented there'.[23] Upon such information, the earl of Shaftesbury delivered a vehement speech to the English House of Lords in 1678, graphically depicting the manner in which the Scots were seeing 'their lives, liberties and estates sequestered to the will and pleasure of those that govern'. As he conceived, the Scots' predicament was of immediate domestic relevance, for 'until the pressure be fully taken off from Scotland', no reassurance could be gained that 'the principle is not changed at court, and that those men that are still in place and authority have their influence upon the mind of our excellent prince'.[24]

III

In an age of *cuius regio, eius religio*, when few early modern monarchs had ever successfully ruled over territories of different religious confessions, the greatest challenge faced by the Stuart monarchs throughout the Restoration was to offer sufficient liberty of conscience that would encourage political security throughout the multiple monarchy. In the Declaration of Breda of 1660, Charles II had declared 'a liberty to tender consciences', by which 'no man shall be disquieted or called in question for differences of opinion in matters of religion which do not disturb the peace of the civil magistrate'.[25] Theoretically this commitment encompassed not only spiritual freedom, but also the payments of tithes, the rights of lay proprietors, gentry pre-eminence and university monopolies over clergy training.

Despite the pledge made in the Declaration, the Restoration appeared to signal a return to the pre-civil war era throughout the multiple monarchy. Short of formal religious disestablish-mentarianism, contemporary logic denied the possibility for one monarch to possess a different religious conscience in each of his different dominions. In England, the Declaration had appeared to offer a sufficient guarantee for most presbyterians and former puritans in England to acquiesce in Charles' restoration. Nonetheless, a narrow form of Anglicanism was subsequently imposed, legislatively enshrined by the 'Clarendon Code' which included measures such as the Act of Uniformity (1662), enjoining consent to the Book of Common Prayer on pain of deprivation, the Conventicle Act (1664) proscribing attendance at nonconformist meetings and the Five Mile Act (1665) forbidding ejected ministers from residing within five miles of their former parishes. When episcopalian exclusivity was also restored in Scotland in 1662, an act was passed requiring all ministers ordained since 1649 to seek presentation from their patrons and col-lation from their bishops. A quarter of ministers refused and were thus subsequently deprived, the majority from parishes in the south-west of Scotland. Unlike the English and Scottish churches, the Church of Ireland had never formally been disestablished during the civil wars, but when the narrowly Anglican Act of Uniformity was enacted in 1666, it only reflected the religious sensibilities of around a third of Irish protestants and under one tenth of the country's whole population. Forced to compete with increasing numbers of English and Scots presbyterians, Independents and Quakers, the Church of Ireland's monopoly over Protestant worship had been ended forever by events during the civil wars.

Notwithstanding their attempts to impose religious conformity throughout the multiple monarchy, domestic peace was not secured immediately in an age when the defence of religion was perceived as one of the few legitimating pretexts for political resistance. In Scotland, as growing numbers of nonconformist clergy were ordained in England, Ireland and on the Continent, increasingly serious chal-lenges were mounted against the royal supremacy by theocratic presbyterians. In order to attract the loyalty of more moderate dis-senters, the government responded by drafting successive indulgences and schemes for accommodation in the late-1660s and 1670s.

Irreconcilable divisions between moderate presbyterians and more extreme elements emerged as a result of such initiatives. Particularly in the aftermath of the murder of Archbishop James Sharp of St. Andrews in May 1679, civil disobedience escalated and the subsequent effects of 'the Killing Times' soon reverberated outside Scotland. On his arrival in Dublin in 1683, the outlawed Scots Covenanter, James Renwick, proclaimed that 'the Lord has a special hand in my coming to this place . . . he has kindled a fire which I hope Satan shall not quench'.[26] Banished from Scotland in 1682, another Covenanter, James Fraser of Brea, similarly confirmed that he 'looked upon wicked folk, though Scotsmen, as the greatest aliens, foreigners, strangers to me; a godly man in England or Ireland is more my countryman than a wicked Scotsman'.[27] Among those presbyterians who elected to remain and suffer in Scotland, resentment was also directed towards those who had fled to 'Holland from Scotland, meerlie for their oun peace and quietnes, treacherouslie deserting the interest of the Lord and [l]eaveing their charges and the poor persecute flocks'.[28]

Apprehensions generated by the increased militancy of the Scots Covenanters were feared most acutely in northern Ireland. Particularly in Ulster, the government actively sought to achieve some form of accommodation with moderate presbyterians in order to deter them from combining with more extreme Scottish elements or with those English sectaries who remained unreconciled to the Restoration settlement. From 1672, therefore, presbyterian clergy in Ulster began to receive the *regium donum*, an official subvention derived from Irish customs revenue. That same year, the new lord lieutenant, the earl of Essex, was promised a list of proscribed persons in Scotland that would enable him to 'shut the doore upon them in Ireland, & soe prevent the Contagion they may bring of their doctrine into Ireland, from which they were banisht from their owne Countrey'. In this objective, Essex considered the Irish army as crucial to maintaining the security of all three kingdoms, given that 'the Kingdome of England is not in the most composd condition that could bee wisht, [and] that of Scotland very uneasy'.[29]

Elsewhere in Ireland, the religious situation was even more complex since economic realities alone dictated the need for *de facto* tolera-tion of Catholics who comprised around four-fifths of the total popula-tion. Although traditionally perceived as intrinsically disloyal and subversive on account of the 1641 Rebellion, various sections of the Catholic community resolved to demonstrate that political loyalty was not incompatible with religious nonconformity. With the outcome of the land settlement still pending in the early 1660s, for instance, a number of Irish Catholics formulated a remonstrance offering unqualified acceptance of Charles II as king and obedience to his authority in all temporal affairs. By firmly denying that political loyalty was compromised by recognition of the papacy's spiritual authority, their Gallican-style arguments sought to undermine the case for imposing civil disabilities upon the majority of the Irish population. Condemned outright by the Pope and other foreign observers, this initiative was, however, formally rejected by a national congregation in Dublin in 1666, after which an official anti-catholic reaction ensued across Ireland. To a large extent, the divisions that arose over the remonstrance reflected older civil war differences between those Old English factions who had remained loyal to the king and their more radical Gaelic co-religionists who had supported the endeavours of the papal nuncio, Cardinal Rinuccini.

Perhaps the greatest impediment to securing civil peace in Ireland was, however, the uncertain direction given by the court itself. As one Protestant magistrate complained of the Catholics in 1672, '[i]f the king would stand neuter, he doubted not but we were able to beat them into the sea'.[30] Suspicions about Charles II's own pro-Catholic leanings intensified during the 1670s and rumours circulated regarding the possible contents of a treaty which had been allegedly concluded between Charles II and Louis XIV at Dover in 1670. In Ireland, the removal of the staunchly Anglican duke of Ormonde as lord lieutenant was widely regarded as reflecting changing religious policies at court. As Thomas Carte later claimed, 'whoever notes the smiles and frowns which his grace of Ormond received at different seasons from the court, may form a good judgment of the church of England at those times'.[31] Two days before war was declared against the Dutch in March 1672, Charles issued a Declaration of Indulgence in England ordering that the execution of 'all manner of penal laws in matters ecclesiastical, against whatever sort of nonconformists or recusants, be immediately suspended'.[32] Not only was this declaration promulgated without parliamentary consent, but its timing coincided with extensive military preparations. When the English Parliament reconvened in February 1673, fears emerged that the Declaration was part of a design to establish absolutism and Catholicism by military means and French finance. Fuelled by such apprehensions, strong attacks were made upon Charles' use of the dispensing power and the Declaration was soon withdrawn.

Amid this atmosphere of mounting suspicion and distrust, few professions of political loyalty reassured English or Scottish Protestants of Ireland's fidelity. Exaggerated and fabricated rumours of Irish subversion thus became a structural feature of Restoration politics throughout the multiple monarchy. The most spectacular of these rumours concerned the putative revelations made by Titus Oates in 1678 of a 'Popish Plot' to murder Charles II and install his Catholic brother on the throne. The dramatic spectres generated by this alleged conspiracy ensured the random execution of eighteen priests and several Catholic laymen in England and the groundless execution for treason of Oliver Plunkett, archbishop of Armagh. In Scotland, graphic reports circulated of 'a plott of the papists and Irishes for cutting off the Inglish and Scotts, man, wife and child'.[33] Despite this widespread panic on the mainland, not a single execution of a Catholic priest or layman occurred in Ireland as a result of the plot. In the opinion of one Limerick gentleman in April 1680, '[a]s to the Irish plot . . . we believe more is spoken of it there [in England] than we hear of it here'.[34] Even after the Catholic James VII and II succeeded to the throne in 1685, entrenched perceptions of Irish disloyalty remained. Writing anonymously to James in 1685, one Irish priest condemned the manner in which 'the Irish that have not rebelld since 41 . . . must be still branded with the ignominious names of a rebellious barbarous & bloodthirsty nation but Munmouths & Argiles rebellions that struck so imediately at the very root of monarchy are already forgot as if they had bin a dream'.[35]

IV

In the absence of any imperial British vision emanating from the court of Charles II, it was initially unclear whether subsequent attempts would be made to redefine the relationships between the constituent parts of the multiple monarchy. Charles' hapless experiences at the hands of the Covenanters between 1650 and 1651 had engendered within him little desire to return to Scotland in person, or to seek a closer political relationship with his Scottish subjects after 1660. According to the earl of Clarendon, Charles was convinced he 'would not build according to Cromwell's models', apparently perceiving 'many reasons to continue Scotland within her own limits and bounds, and sole dependence upon himself'.[36] Such sentiments were evidently shared by his Scottish subjects who had been deeply disillusioned when the Cromwellian theory of incorporating union had translated into the unpleasant reality of military occupation. As the earl of Lothian reflected in May 1660, albeit 'we are in another world againe, and there are people newe moddelling this land . . . wee must be a free Independent nation, brethren and good friends, let us be under one soveraigne and head, but no parte of England'.[37]

Scotland's constitutional status may not have been openly challenged during the Restoration, but the same was not true for Ireland. Although it was not until 1698 that William Molyneux's *Case of Ireland being bound by acts of parliament in England, stated* provided the most extensive defence of Irish standing as an independent kingdom, the reality of such claims were often undermined during the Restoration. As a former Cromwellian soldier, Richard Lawrence, wrote in 1682, Ireland was 'governed by English laws, enacted by English parliaments, administered by English judges, [and] guarded by an English army'.[38]

The most significant constitutional shifts in Anglo-Irish relations arose, however, as a result of changing English economic policy. Before 1660, Irish and English trading interests had largely been treated as identical, with Irish merchants protected by the English Navigation Acts. After the Restoration, this policy was criticised, as the blame for falling English land values was increasingly placed on cheap Irish competition, particularly Irish cattle. Subsequent proposals to place a legislative embargo on the importation of Irish cattle into England encountered virulent domestic opposition in Ireland where cattle represented the chief export. In England, such motions were also recognised as undermining Charles II's assertion that '[h]e was equally King of all, and obliged to have a Care of all'.[39] Speaking in the House of Commons against a draft bill prohibiting the import of Irish cattle in 1665, the Solicitor General, Sir Heneage Finch, accepted that 'England is the older brother and noe doubt but all the priviledges and Advantages of primogeniture will bee preserved to you'. Nevertheless, Finch wondered 'can the King who is the Com[m]on father of his people, ruine the younger brother only to comply with the Impatient unmindedness of the older?'[40] Despite Finch's warnings, and the personal opposition of Charles II, in 1667 the importation of Irish cattle into English ports was entirely forbidden.

Ironically, the effects of the Act only served to assist the expansion of the Irish economy, in ways unforeseen by the English Parliament. Forced to develop a trade in barrelled beef, Irish merchants quickly exploited lucrative new Continental markets where they successfully undercut English commodities. In 1666, Finch had warned that 'Dutch Gazetts [will] bee very ready to boast if the King must have one of his kingdoms disabled to subsist', and indeed by 1672 it was universally known that Louis XIV's navy was being victualled by Irish provisions.[41] But apart from considerations of economic rivalry, the

Act also represented a change in English constitutional perspectives towards Ireland. As English acquisition of overseas territories expanded, increasingly colonial-style attitudes were also adopted towards Ireland. With reference to the Cattle Act, English ministers subsequently came to resent the fact that the Irish enjoyed growing economic prosperity while falling English rents conspicuously failed to recover. For this reason, Sir Edward Harley protested to the House of Commons, that since 'Ireland is but a colony of England . . . Can any story give any account that Colonies have been so indulged, as to prejudice the territory whence they came?'[42]

Changing economic priorities in England also carried implications for Scotland. Unlike their Irish counterparts, Scottish merchants had always been subjected to English protectionism as traders of an independent nation. But as members of the Stuart multiple monarchy, Scots frequently found themselves also excluded from Continental markets on account of Charles II's foreign policy. Complaining that '[t]he Scots are obliged to fight for maintaining the Trade of England', Sir George Mackenzie thus conceived it 'unjust, that we should be put to defend the Interest of such with our Lives and Fortunes who will not allow us any share in the Thing defended'.[43] Negatively contrasting their present situation with previous experience, Mackenzie pointed out that under the Franco-Scottish alliance which had subsisted before 1603, not only had the Scots enjoyed free trade with France and her colonies, but they had not incurred any reciprocal obligations to endorse French foreign policy. Fearful of any Scottish attempts to renew such alliances with English enemies, limited support for Anglo-Scottish free trade slowly emerged in England as traditional fears of cheaper Scots competition receded. In the House of Commons in 1667, for instance, the Cavalier MP, Sir Thomas Clifford, supported a relaxation of Anglo-Scottish trade restrictions, confident that '[w]hat we lose upon France, we gain upon Scotland . . . Manufactures they have few, because their people run most in clans, and the rest are slaves . . . Scotland is our Indies, as Colbert calls England the King of France's Indies'.[44] But when legislative proposals for an incorporative union based on free trade between England and Scotland were tabled in the late-1660s, mutual suspicions on both sides conspired to render such initiatives abortive. Writing to Sir Robert Moray from Edinburgh in November 1669, the earl of Lauderdale declared, '[y]ou cannot imagine what aversion is generally in the Kingdome to the Unione. The indeavour to have made us slaves by garrisons & the ruine of our trade by severe lawes in England frights all ranks of men from having to doe with England'.[45] As Sir

George Mackenzie later confirmed, it was unlikely that 'the proposal of an Union [could] have been less acceptable to the people at any time, than at this, in which the remembrance of their oppres[s]ion from the Usurper was yet fresh with them'.[46]

Similar proposals for an incorporative Anglo-Irish union remained confined to the private scheming of interested individuals. Albeit quixotic and impractical, the most comprehensive and detailed projects were devised by the political economist, William Petty, who admired the incorporating union between England and Wales in the early-sixteenth century as manifesting all 'the good effects of a union'. For Petty, one of the chief merits of an incorporating union would be that under a British parliament, 'the merit of the Rebellions of each of the 3 Kingdomes may be impartially scann'd and considered'.[47] By promoting Anglo-Irish intermarriage and the future resettlement of populations on both sides of the Irish Sea, Petty also trusted that incorporating union would permanently end 'all evils in Ireland, which by differences of birth, extractions, manners, languages, customs and religion that have continually wasted the blood and treasure of both nations for above 500 years, and have made Ireland for the most part, a diminution and a burthen, not an advantage to England'. Moreover, it could be argued that the 'union of all his majesties territories' would make England 'as strong and rich as the kingdom of France' and enable it to gain 'the real sovereignty of the seas and to undermine the Hollanders trade ... without war and bloodshed'.[48]

V

When James VII and II acceded to the throne in February 1685, there were those in Ireland who believed that Petty's projects for an incorporating British union could soon become reality. In 1686, one priest wrote anonymously to James, celebrating 'your Royal Ma[ties] line, in which al ye several rights and titles of the Irish Scotch Pictish Norman Saxon and British kings are so miraculously concentr'd that those 3 Kingdoms formerly so divided and distracted in themselves are now three in one'. According to the priest, the three kingdoms now required 'nothing to compleat the Union but Unity in religion that might joyn the heads hearts & hands of the 3 nations to make your Ma[tie] the most potent King upon Earth'.[49] In Edinburgh, the public proclamation of James as king was greeted with 'an Universal Acclamation from more than 30000 of all Ranks of people present

... and the Night concluded with all imaginable Demonstrations of Joy and Satisfaction'.[50] When the English House of Commons convened in May 1685, Whigs represented only around one-tenth of MPs and a rebellion raised in the west country by Charles II's illegitimate son, the duke of Monmouth, was quickly suppressed. The power and authority of the Stuart monarchy appeared invincible throughout their British dominions. Any threat to Protestantism posed by a reigning Catholic monarch was regarded as minimal, since the throne was to pass to James' Protestant daughter, Mary, upon her father's death.

Despite this theoretical reassurance, James' actions as king quickly provoked alarm throughout the multiple monarchy. In Ireland, control of the armed forces was immediately conferred upon a Catholic, Richard Talbot, later created earl of Tyrconnell. Following the disbandment of the largely Protestant militia in 1685, Tyrconnell radically restructured the Irish army; by the following summer Catholics comprised two-thirds of the rank and file and two-fifths of the officers. After Tyrconnell displaced the Protestant earl of Clarendon as lord lieutenant in February 1687, increasing numbers of Catholics continued to enter the army, as well as central and local government, the law courts and the bureaucracy. When the Restoration land settlement came under review in mid-1687, suggestions were mooted that Cromwellian and post-Cromwellian grantees should be required to surrender one-half of their estates to their former owners. Aware that any such alterations to the Restoration land settlement would require parliamentary consent, Tyrconnell also embarked upon a policy of packing city and burgh corporations with Catholic majorities. Among the Protestant community, the widespread panic generated by Tyrconnell's activities was reflected in a steep decline in trade and 'the retreat of several of the British into England'.[51] Nevertheless, despite a general act for liberty of conscience and exemption from paying tithes to the Church of Ireland, the Act of Uniformity remained on the statute book. No attempt was made to respond to calls for either the grant of established status for the Catholic church, or the formal repeal of all anti-Catholic legislation, or even a transfer of lands and ecclesiastical buildings from the Church of Ireland.

In Scotland, James VII and II continued to rely heavily on the political support he had forged during his time as commissioner in the early 1680s. Writing from London to congratulate the duke of Queensberry, as Commissioner, on his successful parliamentary management of the 1685 session, James expressed his hope that 'the parliament here will follow such good presedents as you have given them'.[52] But James's catholicising policies ultimately demonstrated that Scottish political obedience was not unconditional. Despite a royal tender of free trade between England and Scotland as an incentive, the Scots Parliament refused to be cajoled into enacting religious toleration by statute in 1686. Growing resentment was also engendered by the manner in which political power in Scotland was increasingly vested in the hands of a few Catholic converts, notably James Drummond, earl of Perth and his brother John, earl of Melfort. The rise of the Drummond brothers in Scotland reflected a wider power struggle throughout Britain in which Tyrconnell had gained the ascendant over Clarendon in Ireland, and Robert Spencer, earl of Sunderland increasingly supplanted Clarendon's brother, the earl of Rochester as James' chief political advisor in England.

In England, mounting opposition to James' rule culminated in the second Declaration of Indulgence in April 1688. When seven Anglican bishops were subsequently acquitted of seditious libel for having refused to read the declaration, a campaign of widespread civil disobedience ensued. An already volatile situation was exacerbated when James's wife, Mary of Modena, was reported to have given birth to a son in June. The Prince of Wales' appearance transformed the political scene by ushering in the prospect of a perennial Catholic succession. At the end of June 1688, a formal invitation was dispatched by a number of English politicians to James's son-in-law, William of Orange, which pledged full political support if William chose to mount an armed intervention from Holland. When William landed at Torbay on 5 December, James panicked and fled the country. In February 1689, a specially-convened Convention in London established William and Mary as joint monarchs and debarred all Catholics from future succession to the throne.

In Scotland, James' flight to the Continent presented a practical opportunity for the Parliament to vindicate its independent right to confer the Scottish crown on whomsoever it pleased, as had been widely proclaimed in 1681. As one anonymous memorial boasted in 1689, Scotland represented 'the ballance of Europe', for if Scotland declared for James VII rather than for his son-in-law, '[i]t is lyke that Scotland & Ireland with King James his pairtie in Ingland with the french assistance would have been too strong for King William and put a stope to his designes which might have broken the treasuries of all the princes in the league'.[53] In reality, however, the British dimension of revolutionary events heavily affected the Convention of Estates' decision to follow the English example and crown William and Mary as joint monarchs. As another anonymous pamphleteer conceded, 'it were a meer dream to imagine it possible to support and preserve K. James in his power here, without wronging the K. of England and his Interest'. For as most were aware, it was unlikely 'that K. James would value this Crown further then that he might thereby be enabled to recover that of England'.[54]

The Scots were, however, keen to derive some material advantage from their dutiful compliance with England in this juncture. In particular, James' departure presented an apparently propitious opportunity to seek incorporating union with England, since free trade was widely regarded as 'the only means to support an Impoverish'd and sinking Nation'. Construed within the context of a pan-British Protestantism, Anglo-Scottish union could also be depicted as the means by which 'the united strength of Great Britain may be intirely laid out for the Relief of our Neighbouring Protestants, yet groaning under the heavy yoke of their Antichristian Romish Tyrants'.[55] Nonetheless, it was eventually conceded that if the Scots postponed their decision to 'conferr the croun upon the king of Ingland before the Union be settled [t]hen the king and parlia[t] of Ingland will be so dissatisfied [t]hat certainly they will take occasione from this to make Scotland a province'. By that scenario, 'we most accept of what conditiones Ingland pleases to give us as Ireland hes done'.[56]

In Ireland, the Revolution provided an unprecedented opportunity to obliterate such precedents and instead secure independence by a successful military campaign to vindicate James' lawful right as monarch. Irish, Scots English, French, Dutch, German and Danish troops thus engaged in hostilities with one another on Irish soil between 1688 and 1691, before Williamite victories at the Boyne in July 1690 and at Aughrim in July 1691 prompted the eventual surrender of the Jacobite army in October 1691. During the military campaigns, however, it also became clear that while Irish reasons for supporting James were primarily domestic, James himself would settle for nothing less than the recovery of his British crowns. This conflict of interests appeared most clearly when the Irish Parliament reconvened in May 1689. The success of Tyrconnell's policy of remodelling political constituencies was clearly reflected in the fact that only six of its 320 MPs were non-Catholics. Once elected, those MPs pressed immediately for policies to bring domestic relief, such as a thorough recension of the Restoration land settlement and measures to reduce Ireland's political dependence on England. Upon James' arrival at the Parliament, however, such aspirations were soon frustrated by the prevention of attempts to repeal Poyning's Law and the Act of Settlement. As the French ambassador D'Avaux perceived of James, '[h]is heart is too English for him to agree to anything which could displease the English. He still counts on being re-established soon in the kingdom of England and . . . will do nothing to remove Ireland from its dependence on the English'.[57] Undeterred by James' additional refusal to establish a court of claims to hear applications regarding confiscated lands, the Irish Parliament independently produced an Act declaring that over 2,000 named Protestants had recently forfeited their life and property by rebellion, only to be infuriated by James' riposte, 'What, gentlemen, are you for another '41?'[58]

In the context of subsequent military defeat, James's caution ultimately proved accurate. The radical nature of the political aspirations articulated in the Jacobite Parliament not only exacerbated existing religious tensions in Irish society, but also served to polarise anti-Catholic opinion in England. Increasingly repressive penal legislation ensued and the foundations of the Anglo-Irish Protestant ascendancy were laid during the 1690s. By contrast, although often criticised for being 'the reluctant revolutionaries', it was the Scots who arguably experienced the most profound political and religious changes as a result of the events of 1688–89.[59] Having formally decreed that James VII had forfeited his right to the Scottish throne on account of his illegal actions as king, the Scottish Convention of Estates composed a Claim of Right establishing a number of fundamental constitutional principles upon which any future government of Scotland would be based. As a result of the abolition of the committee of the Lords of the Articles, Scottish parliaments became increasingly independent and intractable during the 1690s. Furthermore, presbyterianism was established as the state religion, episcopacy having been denounced in the Claim of Right as 'an intolerable grievance . . . hostile to this nation and contrary to the inclination of the generality of the people, ever since the Reformation'.[60] Henceforth, any attempts to create a unitary British state would thus need to accommodate formal religious pluralism. As far as the constitutional politics of the British multiple monarchy was concerned, the Revolution of 1688–90 provoked more questions than it resolved. While the fluctuating forces of convergence and divergence continued to dictate Anglo-Scottish relations into the eighteenth century, the prospect of Irish submergence remained.

Notes on Chapter 4

1   Sir G. Mackenzie, 'A Defence of the Antiquity of the Royal Line of Scotland', in *The Works of that Eminent and Learned Lawyer, Sir George Mackenzie of Rosehaugh*, T. Ruddiman ed., 2 vols., (Edinburgh, 1718–22), II, 357.

2   Cf. W. Lloyd, *An Historical Account of Church-Government*, (London, 1684).

3   Sir G. Mackenzie, 'A Discourse concerning the Three Unions between Scotland and England' in *Works*, II, 650.

4   Sir G. Mackenzie, *A Vindication of his Majesties Government & Judicatures in Scotland from some Aspersions thrown on them by Scandalous Pamphlets and Newsbooks*, (Edinburgh, 1683) p. 5.

5   The 'Further Reading' section provides a brief guide to relevant historiography.

6   E. Hyde, *The History of the Rebellion and Civil Wars in England*, W. D. Macray ed., 6 vols., (Oxford, 1888), I, 145–6.

7   A. Clark (ed.), *The Life and Times of Anthony à Wood, antiquary of Oxford, 1632–1695 described by Himself. Volume I: 1632–1663*, (Oxford, 1891), p. 317.

8   J. Kirkton, *A History of the Church of Scotland 1660–1679*, R. Stewart ed., (New York, 1992), p. 34.

9   Quoted by G. H. Jenkins, *The Foundations of Modern Wales 1642–1780*, (Oxford, 1987) at p. 173; Quoted by S. J. Connolly, *Religion, Law and Power. The Making of Protestant Ireland 1660–1760*, (Oxford, 1992) at p. 10.

10   Quoted by Connolly, *Religion, Law and Power* at p. 14.

11   *Ibid.*

12   A. Crichton (ed.), *Memoirs of the Rev. John Blackadder*, (Edinburgh, 1823), p. 75.

13   Bodleian Library, Oxford, Clarendon MSS. 74, ff. 290–3, 'Mine to my Lord Commissioner, March 26th 1660', f. 292r.

14   O. Airy ed., *The Lauderdale Papers*, 3 vols., (London, 1884–5), I, 172.

15   Quoted by J. C. Beckett, 'The Irish Viceroyalty in the Restoration Period' in *Confrontations. Studies in Irish History*, (London, 1972), pp. 67–86 at p. 82.

16   Scottish Record Office (hereafter 'SRO'), 'Ane short Accompt of affairs from Scotland, 1674', unfoliated.

17   Sir G. Mackenzie, *Memoirs of the Affairs of Scotland from the Restoration of King Charles II A.D.M.DC.LX.*, T. Thomson ed., (Edinburgh, 1822), p. 138.

18   Bodleian Library, Clarendon MSS. 74, ff. 290–3, 'Mine to my Lord Commissioner, March 26th 1660', f. 292r.

19   *Acts of the Parliament of Scotland*, T. Thomson and C. Innes eds., 20 vols., (Edinburgh, 1820), VIII, 239.

20   J. S. Clarke, *The Life of James the Second, King of England, &c. Collected out of Memoirs writ of his own Hand. Together with the King's Advice to His son, and his Majesty's Will*, 2 vols., (London, 1816), I, 697.

21   Quoted by C. Kidd, 'Protestantism, constitutionalism and British identity

under the later Stuarts', in B. Bradshaw and P. Roberts (eds), *British consciousness and identity: the making of Britain, 1533–1707*, (Cambridge, 1998) at p. 340.

22 A. Grey ed., *Debates of the House of Commons from the Year 1667 to the Year 1694*, 10 vols., (London, 1763), II, 238–42.

23 Mackenzie, *Memoirs*, p. 264.

24 A. A. Cooper, earl of Shaftesbury, 'Speech made in the House of Peers, by the Earl of Shaftesbury, November 1678, upon Consideration of the State and Condition of England, Scotland and Ireland' in *A Collection of Scarce and Valuable Tracts on the most interesting and entertaining Subjects, but chiefly such as relate to the History and Constitution of these Kingdoms*, W. Scott ed., 13 vols., (London, 1809–15), VIII, 49.

25 'The Declaration of Breda' in J. P. Kenyon ed., *The Stuart Constitution 1603–1688*, (Cambridge, 1966), p. 358.

26 Quoted by P. Kilroy, *Protestant Dissent and Controversy in Ireland 1660–1714*, (Cork, 1994) at p. 111.

27 J. Fraser, *Memoirs of the Rev. James Fraser of Brea*, A. Whyte ed., (Inverness, 1889), p. 290.

28 Anon., *The Protestatione of the Antipopish, Antiprelatick, Antieerastian, True Presbyterian But poor and Persecuted, church of Scotland. Against the Scottish Congregation at Rotterdam in Holland*, ([Glasgow], 1684), sig. A2v.

29 Quoted by R. L. Greaves, *Enemies under his Feet. Radicals and Nonconformists in Britain 1664–1667*, (Stanford, 1990) at pp. 108, 242.

30 Quoted by Connolly, *Religion, Law and Power*, at p. 31.

31 Quoted by J. I. McGuire, 'Why was Ormond dismissed in 1669?', *Irish Historical Studies*, 18 (1973), pp. 295–312 at p. 307.

32 'Declaration of Indulgence, 1672' in Kenyon ed., *Stuart Constitution*, p. 407.

33 R. Law, *Memorialls; or, the Memorable Things that fell out within this Island of Britain from 1638 to 1684*, C. K. Sharpe ed., (Edinburgh, 1818), p. 161.

34 Quoted by Connolly, *Religion, Law and Power*, at p. 31.

35 'A Series of Eight Anonymous and Confidential Letters to James II about the State of Ireland', *Notes & Queries*, 6th ser., V-VI (1882), VI, 22.

36 Quoted by G. Davies and P. Hardacre, 'The Restoration of the Scottish Episcopacy, 1660–1661', *Journal of British Studies*, 1 (1960) at p. 34.

37 Buckminster Estate Office, Tollemache MSS. 1041. Earl of Lothian to Earl of Lauderdale, 8 May 1660.

38 R. Lawrence, *The Interest of Ireland in its Trade and Wealth stated. In Two Parts*, (Dublin, 1682), II, 51.

39 Quoted by C. Edie, 'The Irish Cattle Bills: A Study in Restoration Politics', in *Transactions of the American Philosophical Society*, n.s., 60 (1970), pp. 1–66 at p. 25.

40 *Ibid.* at p. 18.

41 *Ibid.* at p. 20.

42 *Ibid.* at p. [4]7.

43 Mackenzie, 'Discourse concerning the Three Unions' in *Works*, II, 664–5.

44 Grey ed., *Debates of the House of Commons*, I, 39.

45 Airy ed., *Lauderdale Papers*, II, 154.

46 Mackenzie, *Memoirs*, p. 141.

47 W. Petty, 'An Expedient for the Union of England and Scotland and Ireland [1674]' in Marquis of Lansdowne ed., *The Petty Papers*, 2 vols., (London, 1927), I, 14.

48 Quoted by J. S. Kelly, 'The origins of the act of union: an examination of unionist opinion in Britain and Ireland, 1650–1800', *Irish Historical Studies*, 25 (1987), pp. 236–63 at p. 239.

49 'A Series of Eight Anonymous Letters', VI, 22.

50 *The Privy Council of Scotland's Letter to the King, together with the Arch-bishops and Bishops: As also several English Addresses to His Majesty*, (Edinburgh, 1685), p. 1.

51 *A Letter from a Gentleman to his Friend in Ireland*, (Dublin, 1688), p. 9. The pamphleteer explained that the term 'Irish' denoted 'the Native Irish Papist only'.

52 Historical Manuscripts Commission, Fifteenth Report, Appendix, Part VIII, *The Manuscripts of his Grace the Duke of Buccluch and Queensberry*, 2 vols., (London, 1897), I, 108.

53 SRO, GD 406/M9/200/10, 'A Memorial discussing past relations [1689]' – unfoliated.

54 Anon., *Allegiance and Prerogative Considered in a Letter from a Gentleman in this Country to his Friend Upon his being Chosen a Member of States for Scotland*, ([?Edinburgh], 1689), p. 5.

55 Anon., *Some Weighty Considerations, Humbly Presented to the Honourable Members of the Ensuing Assembly of the States of Scotland*, (Edinburgh, 1689), p. 8.

56 SRO, GD 406/M9/200/1, 'A resolution of tuo questiones [1689]' – unfoliated.

57 Quoted by J. Miller, *James II. A Study in Kingship*, (London, 1978), at p. 224.

58 Quoted by Connolly, *Religion, Law and Power* at p. 35.

59 The phrase was coined by I. Cowan in 'The reluctant revolutionaries: Scotland in 1688' in E. Cruickshanks ed., *By Force or by Default? The Revolution of 1688–89*, (Edinburgh, 1989), pp. 65–81.

60 'The Claim of Right', in Dickinson and Donaldson eds., *Source Book of Scottish History*, p. 205.

CHAPTER 5

'British' History in the Post-Revolutionary World 1690–1715

Tony Claydon

As other contributions to this volume make clear, there have been many reasons for the upsurge in interest in 'British' history in the early modern era. John Pocock's clarion call for a new subject has certainly played a part: as have contemporary political questioning of the legitimacy of the United Kingdom; cross fertilisation from the study of other periods; the pressure to invent new undergraduate courses; and the endless search by younger historians for new approaches with which to make their names. For the seventeenth century, however, one over-riding factor has been behind the fascination with Anglo-Celtic relations. This was the 'revisionism' which came to control early Stuart historiography towards the end of the 1970s. As revisionist scholars demolished old accounts of the origins of the English Civil War, they found themselves increasingly dependent upon 'British' scholarship, since without it they were unable to explain the most basic events of their period. Once they had rejected traditional interpretations of the slide to conflict (such as the rise of an assertive parliament, or a growing rejection of divine right), revisionists were at a loss to say how this terrible thing had happened, and were forced into 'British' history to make good their position.[1] Consequently 'the Atlantic archipelago' became the universal saviour of Civil War studies. By the late 1980s a whole industry had sprung up advancing 'three kingdoms' interpretations of the early Stuart era, and as a result, 'the British problem' became the central conundrum for all seventeenth-century specialists.[2]

This origin of 'British' history in early Stuart revisionism is interesting because it contains a considerable irony for scholars of the late Stuart world. Paradoxically, whilst something like revisionism has operated for the reigns of William III and Anne, the effect upon 'archipelagic' studies has been the opposite of that in the earlier era. Although scholars have been as busy demolishing traditional myths in the period 1690–1715 as they have for the early Stuart era, this has not noticeably bolstered 'British' history. Rather, the latest work seems to have confused and undermined an old sense of the importance of Anglo-Celtic interaction, and has, therefore, questioned the close link between 'revisionist' and 'three kingdoms' history which holds for other parts of the early modern era. In a strange reversal of the early Stuart situation, it was the older, established interpretations of the decades after 1688 which told clear and embracing 'British' stories. By contrast, whilst the latest accounts of William and Anne's reigns have stressed the entanglements of the three kingdoms, they seem to lack the encompassing sweep of the more ensconced versions of history, and no longer have a simple, archipelagic tale to tell.

I

To see the reversal clearly, it is necessary to consider the traditional accounts of post-revolutionary Britain. The most influential of these interpretations might be labelled the 'whig' vision. As embodied in the work of many historians, this account of the last two Stuart reigns saw the period in terms of the successful consolidation of the liberal achievement of the Glorious Revolution. It was a time when the Westminster parliament settled down as the central institution of the British state; when the monarchy finally came to accept limitations upon its power; and when a stable, free, representative, (and ultimately world-beating), political system was established in these islands.

At first glance, this whig vision may seem anglocentric in the extreme. Stressing the steady progress towards a parliamentary and liberal paradise, the account concentrated on the growing calm and openness of debate which characterised English politics under the last Stuarts, and played down the greater uncertainty, instability and potential violence of contemporary Scotland and Ireland. Thus much was made of the advent of peaceful and functional party politics at Westminster, whilst the fact that factional divisions were simultaneously bringing Scottish and Irish administration to the brink of collapse was treated as an inconvenient footnote. Similarly, the whig account concentrated upon moments of English parliamentary history, seeing these as staging posts to an emerging liberty and greatness, but gave much less coverage to events in other kingdoms which often seemed to point in the opposite direction. Much was therefore made of such statutes as the English Treason Trials Act (1696) which gave subjects greater guarantees of fair judicial process; of the English Act of Settlement (1701) which excluded absolutist-minded Stuarts from the throne and extended controls on the monarchy; and of the series of finance bills in the 1690s which set up a recognisably modern system of taxation and public credit. Rather less attention was given to the Irish penal laws which cut away at Catholics' basic civil rights; of the anarchy in parts of the Scottish Highlands; of the very real danger that the Scots parliament would not accept the principles of English succession after 1701; or of the continuing inability of either the Dublin or Edinburgh legislatures to arrange a sufficient flow of funds into the administration's coffers. Where such events were covered, they were treated as Macaulay treated the Glencoe Massacre of 1692 (an incident in which troops supported by William III's ministers in Edinburgh killed members of a formerly Jacobite clan, despite the clansmen's capitulation to the new government, and their extension of hospitality to its soldiers).[3] These were lawless, shameful actions, well outside the proper standards of English liberalism, and if they were to be analysed at all, they were so chiefly to be condemned. For whiggishly-inclined historians, it was late Stuart England which most clearly moved towards the free and great Britain of later decades. These writers, therefore, pushed England into the spotlight.[4]

However, whilst England was undeniably at the centre of the traditional whig interpretation, this never meant that that account lacked a 'British' dimension. Events in the north and west might receive relatively short shrift, but that did not mean the old interpretation had no sense of a wider archipelagic story. In fact, 'whiggism' had a clear vision of English interactions with the Celtic kingdoms, which could occasionally lead historians writing in the tradition to quite extensive coverage of the three kingdoms. This vision of interaction centred upon the gradual extension of English achievements out into the north-western hinterland, and the encouraging convergence of Scotland and Ireland with the enlightened English model. Progress in this area might be slow, and Scotland and Ireland might be neglected in periods when they were not making rapid advances towards the south-eastern utopia, but among whig historians, belief in the progress was real. Where Celtic convergence with English politeness and liberalism could be demonstrated, whig scholars celebrated it; and their idea of steady harmonisation with England provided a strong framework for interpreting the development of Britain and Ireland as a whole.

Two areas of the whig historiography of 1690–1715 demonstrated its 'British' sense particularly clearly. The first was the treatment of the Act of Union of 1707. Almost uniquely amongst events outside England, the decision by the Scots parliament under Queen Anne to merge itself with its Westminster counterpart was seen by whig scholars as a thing of great moment. In fact, it was canonised as a crucial stage of national history. In whig works it became one of the key foundations of the British constitution: a step towards a liberal Britain very nearly as significant as the Magna Carta, the Protestant Reformation, the 1688 revolution or the 1832 Reform Act. The reason for this apotheosis of 1707 was that it could be fitted into the strong whig vision of archipelagic development. Whilst much that had happened in Scotland and Ireland was disappointing for historians who believed in liberal convergence, the Union stood as a shining beacon. In the whig interpretation, 1707 could be presented putting a seal on nearly two centuries of development towards a free, English-style polity. Effectively, the Scots had guaranteed the future of their representative institutions, their limited monarchy, and their protestantism, by joining them to the more robust models for these achievements south of the border. Similarly, the Union could be shown to have aided further convergence towards liberal England once it had been effected. 1707 could be shown leading to economic boom and intellectual enlightenment in eighteenth-century Scotland, and so to have underpinned the free political system with a propertied and educated society. Taken overall, therefore, the Union could be moulded into a powerful symbol of the whole whig version of British history, whose prominence demonstrated the strong archipelagic awareness of this historical school.[5]

The second feature of whig historiography to reveal its 'British' sense was its vigour amongst historians of Scotland and Ireland. Whilst the whig history written by English scholars was strongly anglocentric, the importance of whiggism's British dimension meant that it could be used by Irish and Scots scholars to interpret their own national pasts. From the eighteenth to the twentieth centuries, historians of the north-western kingdoms wrote national stories in terms of a steady progress towards a liberal apotheosis, and celebrated the closer ties or parallels with England which this had brought about. Thus, as Colin Kidd has recently shown, many Scots were happy to share the English whigs' view of 1707.[6] For them, incorporation within Britain set the seal upon centuries of Scottish advance. It demonstrated that Scotland had abandoned a backward and barbaric past and had embraced a prosperous, polite and prestigious future in her partnership with another great nation. Similarly, scholars such as W.E.H. Lecky, who have been identified as Ireland's 'whigs', were relieved that that nation remained within the English sphere under William and Anne.[7] William's victory over James II's forces in 1689–91 might have allowed a vicious anti-popery and a high-handed English administration of Ireland which whigs could not condone – but it at least prevented a backsliding into the ignorant tyranny of Jacobitism, and provided a space in which Irish protestants could begin to develop and demand a parliamentary system on the English model. Indeed, for writers such as Lecky, the 1690s were – in some ways – a time of great liberal progress. Saved from James II's absolutism by the new English ruler, and perhaps inspired by the new importance of the Commons at Westminster, Irish legislators secured regular parliamentary sessions, greater control over revenue and the initiation of statutes, and closer scrutiny of the functions and finances of the administration.

If whig historians had a strong 'British' interpretation of history in the late Stuart period, the same was true of other traditional accounts of the post-revolutionary period. These were the nationalist historiographies of Ireland and Scotland, which insisted on the separateness of those countries, and which centred on the creation, survival and resurgence of national feeling within them. Among nationalists, an archipelagic interpretation of 1691–1715 was virtually inevitable. Whilst these historians insisted on the differences between the English and their neighbours, the conditions in which these differences had to be asserted, and the challenges which they met, were always considered in a British framework. For nationalists, after all, the past only made sense as a record of Anglo-Celtic interaction. In their view, the English had devoted centuries to illegitimate expansion into the north and west; whilst the peoples of Scotland and Ireland had resisted and had heroically pursued their national destiny through their struggle with the London-based state.

Within such a broad interpretation, it was easy for nationalists to find late Stuart examples to fit their historical understanding, and so to interpret post-revolutionary events in a three kingdoms framework. For example, for Scots, the years 1703–05 assumed a special importance. Then, the Edinburgh parliament had stood out against English imperialism, insisting on new limitations on the crown to protect its independence, and threatening to break the dynastic link with England if it did not get them. Such defiance was a potent reminder of the autonomy of Scotland before the Union, and could be an inspiration to those who wished to regain that freedom. Similarly, the English response to 1703–05 was held up as an illustration of the southern attitudes. Commercial retaliation, the threat of force, and the browbeating of the Scots parliament to vote itself out of existence in 1707, demonstrated the ruthless expansionism of England and so emphasised that London's 'British' ambition was the chief dynamic of Scots history.[8]

Irish nationalist historians also utilised the late Stuart period to show the importance of archipelagic interactions. For example, all agreed that the Irish Woollen Act (1698), passed at Westminster, was a central event of the period. By preventing the export of Irish wool, and therefore legislating for Ireland without its consent, the English had again demonstrated that colonial desire to control both islands which had been evident from the first the medieval invasions, and which would culminate in the absorption of the Irish parliament in 1800. Irish resistance to English expansion within the archepelago was similarly crucial to nationalist interpretations of the period. In this case, however, divisions within the tradition meant there was some dispute about what to highlight. Some nationalists could celebrate the independent-mindedness of the Irish parliament in this period, thus joining in a curious alliance with liberal historians such as Lecky. Legislative scrutiny of a largely English executive was a nationalist as well as liberal virtue, and contemporary claims about the constitutional autonomy of the Irish parliament – most notably Molyneux's *Case of Ireland stated* (1698) – could be celebrated as cogent denunciations of English ambitions. In fact so close could certain nationalist interpretations come to liberal accounts, that some scholars have seen a third strand of Irish historiography, explicitly termed 'whig-nationalist', which has borrowed assumptions from both visions.[9] However, whilst this strand of interpretation has been important (perhaps too dominant for some scholars), it was not the only brand of nationalism available. For some historians, the protestant nature of the Irish parliament (Catholics had been excluded under an English statute), and its role in passing the anti-Romanist penal laws, meant it could not be an appropriate representative of an essentially catholic Ireland. At best it could be the mouthpiece of a colonial Ireland – a body representing privileged and alien settlers who cooperated with their metropolis in the oppression of a brutally conquered people. For the 'anti-whig' nationalists who thought in this way, the archipelagic struggle against England was still crucial: but it took the form of heroic survival in the face of persecution.[10]

Thus for nationalists, as for whigs, a British approach to the late Stuart period was important. Although these historiographic traditions had pedigrees some centuries older than the 'new British history', they were aware of Anglo-Celtic interactions and placed them near the centre of their analyses. Given this, the impact of the recent scholarship of the period 1689–1715 has been the reverse of what one might expect. New generations of scholars have challenged old accounts: but, far from making readers more aware of an archipelagic story, the challenge has confused the 'British' interpretations which the established traditions contained. In the latest scholarship, much attention is still given to the ways the peoples of Britain and Ireland have affected each other. However, the patterns of relationships have been shown to be far more complex and ambiguous than older visions asserted. More interestingly, and perhaps more importantly, evidence deployed in the latest scholarship has even suggested that 'Britain' might not be the most appropriate level on which to understand the events of the period.

II

To illustrate these trends this essay will examine two areas which are crucial to understanding Stuart Britain and Ireland, and in which scholars have recently been active. The first of these is the developing relationship between the three separate legislatures in Westminster, Edinburgh and Dublin. In broad outline, this development can be briefly summarised. In the aftermath of 1689, all three parliaments experienced a renaissance. They began to meet far more frequently, took a closer role in scrutinising their local executive, and handled a greater quantity of legislative business than any of them had before. Unfortunately, this common parliamentary resurgence created problems in the coordination of policy. Whilst the monarchs in London could still exercise some control of the legislatures through their right to choose ministers in all three realms, and whilst the Irish body remained legally subordinate to the English Privy Council, growing opposition within – and competition between – the three parliaments meant that it became even more difficult for the court to construct a coherent strategy for ruling all its kingdoms. In the 1690s, the Irish parliament disputed the right of the English parliament to legislate for it in areas such as foreign trade and the allocation of confiscated land. At the same time an Irish 'country' movement criticised the conduct of William's government (especially over its generous treatment of catholic Jacobites after the 1689–91 war) and demanded greater control over the initiation of Irish money bills. In Scotland, a similar spirit of autonomy existed, and was made more threatening both by the northern kingdom's legal independence from London, and by the fact that bitter factional rivalries among Scots politicians guaranteed overwhelming opposition to whoever had been appointed ministers by the king. Under William, Scots dissatisfaction with England came to a head over the vandalisation of the Darien scheme. This scheme – an attempt to establish a Scots commercial settlement in central America – had failed after hostile interests in the English parliament had persuaded the English ministers to hamper it, and had blocked English investment in the proposed trading company. Resentment at such conduct fed a vigorous opposition to whatever ministry the king tried to construct in Scotland, and made stable administration virtually impossible. Later, under Anne, Scots protested at the way the English had settled the succession of the crown on the house of Hanover, without consulting the Edinburgh parliament. In the famous Act of Security (1703), the northern legislature insisted on tight limitations on the prerogatives of any new monarch, and asserted that the Scots had the right to choose a different ruler from that chosen by the English.

Given such instability and challenge, it was vital for the crown and ministers in London to find a way of coordinating the different legislatures. In Ireland this was achieved through English ministers coming to terms with leading Irish politicians known as 'undertakers'. In return for granting such men as Henry Boyle influence over policy and patronage, these local legislators 'undertook' to manage the king's business in parliament, carefully building alliances which would vote the necessary business through. In Scotland, a more dramatic solution to parliamentary separatism was found. From 1703, English ministries pursued a vigorous policy of persuading the northern parliament to accept a union with its counterpart in the south. In 1707, this policy succeeded, when the Scots legislature voted itself out of existence. Henceforth, statutes and financial supply throughout Britain would be granted by a united body in Westminster – with the proviso that Scots law, education and established religion would remain distinct from their English equivalents, and would be dealt with separately by the new assembly.[11]

As we have seen, there was much in the above story which could fit into the whig and nationalist traditions with their strongly 'British' interpretations of the period. For example, English difficulties in Dublin, and the eventual compromise which ended them, could be celebrated as the birth pangs of a liberal nation which would support or challenge London's rule (according to whether one took a whig-unionist, or a whig-nationalist, view). Alternatively, the Dublin parliament, and the undertaker system which made it work, could be vilified as another example of English ability to reduce Irish populations to colonial lackeys. Similarly the 1707 Union could be celebrated as the creation of a liberal polity to embrace the whole of Britain, or could be denounced as the final stage in England's ruthless annexation of Scotland. What all these interpretation have in common is their virtual demolition by the latest 'revisionist' scholarship. Recent accounts of parliamentary development have contradicted whig and nationalist assumptions, and have consequently obscured the archipelagic vision they contained.

With 1707, for example, work since the 1960s has undermined any notion that the union resulted from the gradual convergence of Scotland with England, or from any widespread desire to create a strengthened parliamentary polity. William Ferguson and P.W.J. Riley, examining the process by which the Edinburgh legislature came to abolish itself, have concluded that it was simply a political 'job'. The ministry in London bribed unprincipled Scots magnates to throw their weight behind the idea, and a semi-feudal, and highly factionalised, political class lacked the independence to take a different line from their masters.[12] In the new view, Scots public opinion was both deeply hostile to the idea of union, and utterly irrelevant to the course of events. As Mark Goldie has argued in a recent article, Scottish and English political cultures were probably diverging rather than coming together in the late Stuart period (Scots were showing greater attachment to their distinctive society, political assumptions, religion and legal code); and as David Hayton has suggested, Union could probably have been achieved at any point after 1689 since determined English efforts to manage magnate opinion would have been successful as soon as it was tried.[13]

Clearly such an interpretation sinks the whig vision of late Stuart Britain. It might, of course, support a nationalist view by suggesting that English ministers cynically extinguished Scots autonomy – but in fact, this alternative analysis has also been weakened by trends in recent scholarship. First, the very investigation which revealed the jobbing nature of 1707, has called attention to the behaviour of Scots magnates. Quite apart from the obvious moral question of whether it was more cynical of the English to offer bribes than for the Scots to accept them, close investigation of the events of 1703–07 shows that Scots leaders were not simply capitulating in the face of superior

English influence, but were actively calculating their own political advantage and exploiting the political situation as it evolved. Scotsmen voted for Union because they thought it would increase or preserve their access to local power and court patronage.[14] Some of them, as Hayton has shown, gained influence as they became the equivalent of Irish 'undertakers'. They came to manage the Scots representation in the new united parliament.[15] In this perspective, the Union may seem less an English takeover of Scotland, than merely one stage in the endless battle among the leaders of Scottish factions to displace each other from positions of power.

A second trend to weaken any nationalist interpretation of 1707 has been a new interest in its ideological background. Perhaps in reaction to simple 'jobbing' interpretations of the union, some historians have looked at the intellectual arguments surrounding the event, and have found a surprisingly rich vein of political argument.[16] Unfortunately for the whig tradition, the pamphlet debates of Queen Anne's reign provide little evidence for liberal convergence between England and Scotland. Between 1703 and 1707 Scots were debating many alternative political futures, of which Union was only one; and the arguments for joining with the southern kingdom were generally economic rather than constitutional. Despite this, however, public discussions in Scotland contained a more reasoned, solid and widely-accepted case for union than any nationalist vision of English bribery would imply. The economic arguments for union were not simply those of particular merchants who wished to gain access to the English commercial system, or were frightened of English customs being used against Scots goods if the two countries went separate ways. Rather, as work by John Robertson and David Armitage has shown, union was advocated as part of a sophisticated theory of competing European imperialisms.[17] This stated that Scotland would need global commercial expansion if it were not to be dominated by foreign powers busy tying up the world in their own commercial empires. It also suggested that Scotland could not build an empire on her own (the too bitter experience of Darien demonstrated this); and then offered amalgamation with England as a solution. In such a view the Scots would not be annexed by the English, but would join with them to fulfil their own destiny as an imperial nation. Such arguments were very cogent in the late Stuart era. Even those who rejected Union, such as Andrew Fletcher of Saltoun, wrestled with the problem of Scotland's position among global empires, and were prepared to see changes in Scotland's constitutional and national status as a way out. Fletcher's analysis led him to suggest that Scotland (and all other

European polities) should be broken up into a series of smaller city states in order to save the world from universal domination by one power. For our purposes, the central point about all such 'imperial' thinking was that it was neither whig nor nationalist in character, and consequently was perhaps not particularly 'British' in focus. It concentrated, not on Edinburgh's relationship with London, but on Scotland's position in a much wider world.

Trends in the history of the Irish parliament have similarly undermined the old interpretations. 'Whig' and 'whig nationalist' celebrations of the vigour and independence of the Irish parliament in the 1690s have been undermined both by new emphasis on Irish unionism, and by new thoughts on the strength of contemporary parliamentarianism. Work by James Kelly has disinterred the strength and depth of the desire for parliamentary union with Westminster among the Irish political classes under William and Anne. Union was formally requested by the Dublin parliament on several occasions in the late Stuart era, and even men such as Molyneux – most closely associated with the Irish patriot cause – argued for greater independence as a second-best, since union was 'a happiness not to be hoped for'.[18] Given this, the survival of the Irish parliament until 1800 can hardly be ascribed to its proud spirit of autonomy. Rather, as David Hayton has shown, it stemmed from the fact the Ireland had fewer great magnates than Scotland (so a system of 'undertaking' could work without political rivals of the undertakers having an automatic majority in parliament), and from the insecurity of Ireland's protestant rulers which meant they could not threaten the sort of separation whose prospect had converted Westminster to union with Edinburgh.[19] In the same article, Hayton further detracted from the gloriousness of Irish parliamentary achievement by putting it into the context of a general renaissance of representative bodies in all three kingdoms in the 1690s. With William's desperate search for the finance with which to fight France, all sorts of such institutions revived. William, and his successor Anne, tried to use parliaments as places where they could meet, placate and negotiate with the political classes which would have to approve wartime taxes. We have seen the strength of the Dublin, Edinburgh and Westminster legislatures in the period: Hayton reminds us of the revival of the Anglican church's convocations, of the General Assembly of the Church of Scotland, and the Convocation of the Stannaries in Cornwall. In such a context, the vigour of the Irish body looks much less remarkable. Furthermore, the monarch's use of parliaments in order to gain revenue suggests that the body able to deliver most money would become most influential. Since this was the English parliament, and since this assembly had ambitions to legislate for Ireland, the situation actually limited Dublin's autonomy. Monarchs could not afford to block demands made by Westminster – as the history of the woollen and land forfeitures acts demonstrate. Irish parliamentary spirit was real in the 1690s, but it was founded on conditions which ultimately led to its humiliation.[20]

Of course, the relative helplessness of the Irish parliament might support the vision of a subservient, colonial Ireland which lies at the heart of non-whiggish nationalism. Yet here again, recent interpretations have questioned the basic assumptions of the model. Whilst the late Stuart era may have been no golden age for the Irish parliament, it is becoming increasingly doubtful that Ireland can be regarded simply as exploited by the English. As work by several scholars has shown, Irish protestants, at least, found ways round the institutional subordination of their parliament, and gained considerable freedom to run their own affairs. Although English ministries could over-rule Irish opinion at times of crisis, they realised that in day-to-day management they would have to work with the local inhabitants, and would have to grant degrees of influence and independence to them. Thus Irish 'undertakers' came to have considerable influence of policy making and government appointments; Irish suggestions for legislation were usually taken up and approved by the English Privy Council; the English representative in Dublin – the Lord Lieutenant – trod sensitively in his dealings with parliamentary leaders; and the English administration proved flexible when its actions proved unpopular in the other island (a fact proved dramatically soon after the end of this survey, when the Wood's Halfpence crisis resulted in a complete reversal of policy in the face of Irish protests).[21] Moreover, any English high-handedness towards their subordinate kingdom usually took the form of indifference and ignorance rather than interference. English ministries had no grand plan for the future of England's relations with Ireland, and seem to have been happiest when they could ignore what was happening on the other side of the Irish Sea. This attitude created a situation where the London government preferred to leave Ireland to run itself when this did not create problems elsewhere. In the work of Sean Connolly such findings are taken further to question whether any notion of Ireland as an English colony is appropriate. Connolly accepts that the English in North America (colonists by any definition) enjoyed a freedom from central interference comparable with that of the Irish: but he points out that American colonial autonomy stemmed more from distance than from the unwillingness to interfere which governed English relations with Ireland, and also points out that the Irish were in a different position from the Americans because of their reciprocal influence over English affairs. Geographical proximity, and the lack of cultural barriers to Irish activities on the British mainland, meant that Irishmen had a considerable impact in the metropolis. They sat in the Westminster parliament; married into leading English families; corresponded with important English politicians; wrote books, sermons and plays for London audiences; and owned economic enterprises operating on both islands. Given this, Connolly doubts that those represented in the Dublin parliament can be seen as a colonial class and thus casts further doubt on any nationalist interpretation of relations between the two polities.[22]

Overall, then, work on the three parliaments under William and Anne has blurred the old historiographies, and caused problems for their clear interpretations of archipelagic development. More profoundly, however, they have also questioned whether 'Britain' is the correct level of analysis for the phenomena they have discovered. Whilst the latest scholarship provides many interesting examples of interaction between peoples in the islands, often a more local or a more global focus seems appropriate. For example, understanding the 1707 Union has become a matter of working out what advantages Scot politicians saw *in Scotland*, and what factional games they were playing with other Scots groups. Again, if Irish politicians were largely left to themselves in this period, then local, Irish ambitions and conditions would have been the greatest influence on action in the Dublin parliament. At another level, recent work suggests that contexts wider than the British Isles need to be taken seriously in any interpretation of the period. For instance, we have seen that those Scots constructing intellectual cases for and against the Union were most worried about the competing world empires of European powers. Parochial relations between London and Edinburgh were only a subsidiary part of their thinking. Again, if the crucial problem in the late Stuart period was the simultaneous renaissance of three competing legislatures, then attention should be focused on the continental factors which caused this. After all, the parliaments of Westminster, Edinburgh and Dublin could seize their opportunities only when a Dutch king, determined to lead a European alliance against France, called upon his subjects to become involved in this overseas enterprise. The various legislatures exploited both the royal need for wartime finance, and a royal willingness to allow indigenous politicians to run their kingdoms so that the monarch would be free to devote most of his attention to his international conflict. They may also have benefitted from a foreign-born king's more relaxed attitude to legislatures. William's political experience in the Netherlands had taught him to expect to have to deal with representative assemblies. In the light of all this, it seems local and extra-Britannic contexts are central to understanding parliamentary history in the late Stuart era.[23] They will become evident again in consideration of national identities in the period – the second area of recent scholarly activity to which this essay will now turn.

Traditional accounts of the development of national identities in the late Stuart era have had a strongly archipelagic focus. Either they posited a new transnational identity which embraced all the peoples of the islands, or they stressed the survival and strengthening of individual nationalities in the face of imperialistic expansion throughout the region by the English. On the island of Britain, for instance, whiggish historians, celebrating the creation of the novel liberal polity through the 1707 Union, were keen to stress that this had been accompanied by a pride in the new country. From the eighteenth century, Scots writers in particular had tried to present people both north and south of the border embracing the new nationality, and had rewritten the past to demonstrate a long-standing and developing identification with it.[24] Much more recently, this 'British' reading of late Stuart national feeling has become popular with a new generation of historians who have seen it as one foundation of later imperial expansion. Whilst scholars such as Linda Colley and John Brewer have not recognised a liberal paradise in the state created in 1707, they have been at one with the whigs in seeing Britain as a country marked out for greatness by its peculiarly inclusive political system, and in seeing a new 'Britishness' as a sentiment which could harness popular energies to this destiny.[25] In contrast to this, nationalist historians of Scotland denied the authenticity of any all-embracing identity in the late Stuart age. If there was any new feeling for the island group as whole, it was confined to those few Scots who had been duped by the English into aiding their absorption of the other kingdom. However, whilst nationalists attacked 'Britishness', their own accounts of identity in the period still had a 'British' focus, since they argued that London's expansion into its Celtic hinterland had triggered reactions among the Scots population. They suggested that English aggression strengthened and defined Scottishness and gave that identity clear content, enemies and voices. Thus for some historians, late Stuart spokesmen against England (especially

Fletcher of Saltoun) came to be heroes who provided a developing nationalism with greater intellectual rigour. Again, some nationalist writers saw a sort of purification of Scotland in 1707, as certain Scots ruled themselves out of their nation by cooperation with England. True patriotism came to mean unsullied opposition to the Union. If this was joined by an attachment to the indigenous, but displaced, Stuart dynasty (of the sort which produced heroically unsuccessful Jacobite risings in Scotland in 1708 and 1715), so much the better.[26]

In Ireland, issues of national identity between 1688 and 1715 were somewhat different and more complicated. Partly this was because there was no late Stuart union of parliaments, but mainly it stemmed from a series of parliamentary acts attacking Catholicism which deepened old difficulties in defining a real Irish nation in the face of religious divisions. From 1695, the protestant parliament in Dublin passed a series of statutes, soon to be known as the penal laws, which mounted a sustained attack on the faith of the bulk of the population. Over two decades, statutes were enacted to hinder the operation of the Roman church (bishops and regular clergy were to be expelled); to remove non-protestants' political and civil rights (catholics were banned from public office and eventually from voting); and to erode the economic position of followers of the Roman faith by denying them entry to certain professions and disqualifying from inheriting land. Given the depth of the confessional divide which these acts revealed, it has been impossible for historians to treat Ireland's population as a single, united community, and this shaped both national and liberal approaches to Irish identity. For whigs (either unionist or nationalist), the penal laws had to be condemned. They broke basic tenets of representative government, and, perhaps worse, they bred faction and bigotry in a community whose identity should centre on an enlightened liberal consensus. Lecky's trenchant denunciation of the acts was therefore widely borrowed, both by those who thought a united and liberal Ireland must develop into a sovereign state, and by unionists (like Lecky himself) who believed that it should not.[27] Non-whiggish nationalists were less embarrassed by the penal laws, but their hostile interpretation of them had the cost of casting the protestants who had promoted them out of the national community. A group which had tried to degrade the bulk of the Irish people were enemies of that people, and the penal laws confirmed that only the oppressed catholics were the true Irish nation.

Clearly these interpretations of the penal laws and of Irish identity were divergent. Once again, however, the different visions were united by their strong archipelagic focus. For non-whiggish nationalists, the penal laws were only what was to be expected given English imperialism within the British Isles. English expansion had garrisoned conquered territories with alien and intolerant settlers who had imposed a sort of apartheid which was yet another instrument of colonial power. Whiggish condemnations of the penal laws were similarly dictated by 'British' considerations. 'Whig nationalists' saw these act as dividing a community whose claims to proper representative government would eventually counter English expansion. In this view, protestant spokesmen such as Molyneux, or Jonathan Swift, saw some of the injustices of English rule – but failed to realise that the best way to end it would be to include catholics in the political nation; establish a common, liberal identity with them; and then lead the united community in resistance to the occupying power. Unionist whigs on the other hand, worried that the penal laws revealed an Ireland incapable of sharing in a wider 'Britishness'. Such religious discrimination threatened the shared enlightenment which was bringing the different populations of the islands together, and so ran against the most important trend in the late Stuart archipelago.[28]

Yet as with the history of parliaments, so with that of national identity. Recent scholarship has questioned old whig or nationalist accounts, and led to far more complex, and perhaps less obviously 'British' centred interpretations. In the latest work, ambiguity, confusion, and multiple levels of identity abound; and it has become harder to tell any clear story of archipelagic development. These trends are clearest in writing on the identity of the ascendant Anglicans of Ireland. In traditional interpretations, this group was either discovering its essential 'Irishness' in the period (coming to lead challenges to English hegemony); or was revealing itself as a agent of English domination; or as a third possibility, was coming to share more deeply in a wider 'British' culture. In recent work, however, none of these developments is readily apparent. Instead of clarifying their identity in one of the ways suggested, Irish protestants appear increasingly caught between different ways of thinking about themselves, so that Jim Smyth (quoting a contemporary source) has likened them to 'amphibious animals'.[29] On one hand, ascendancy protestants were unlikely to think of themselves as Irish. 'Irish' had been the term they had always used to describe the native catholic population, and was therefore tied up in their minds with images of superstition, ignorance, barbarity, poverty, hostility and treason. On the other hand, 'British' was also an unavailable label. This was partly because the adjective 'British' had never been in common use, and partly because it suggested identity with Scots presbyterian settlers in Ulster – a group to which ascendancy Anglicans were as hostile as catholics. By tradition, the protestant ascendancy had called itself 'English', or the 'English in Ireland'. Unfortunately, tensions with the Westminster government from the 1690s onwards made this an unworkable description as well, since it was hard to talk of people as English, when it was English policy to which they objected. Irish Anglicans could, of course, describe themselves as protestants. However, this tag identified the group with an international community of faith which spread far beyond Ireland or Britain, and was therefore little use in locating their precise position in the world.[30] In the face of these difficulties, Irish protestants seem to have adopted the practice of changing their identity according to momentary calculations. For example, they could insist on their own Englishness when facing English contempt; claim to be the true Irish nation when defending the kingdom's constitutional rights; and make a play of their protestantism when travelling in Europe and seeking hospitality from reformed Christians. Similarly, and according to specific audience, they could justify their privileged position in Ireland by saying they had participated in an English conquest of the country; or by claiming to be a superior sort of Irishmen whose rational and unsuperstitious religion gave them the right to rule unenlightened papists. In such rapid shifts and equivocations, there are none of the neat patterns of identity developing within a 'British' context which were evident in the older historiographies.[31]

As one might expect, interpretations of the penal laws have matched the greater complication of other studies of Irish identity. In the light of recent work, it has become more difficult to use the discriminatory code as a measure of how far the Irish had advanced towards any true 'Irishness'. Scholarship has tended to downplay and deconstruct the late Stuart penalties against catholics, so that it has become harder for nationalists to portray them as instruments of foreign colonialism, or for whigs to be sure they represented a betrayal of Ireland's liberal destiny. For example, studies on the passage of the laws has revealed no systematic plan behind them. The acts were passed haphazardly over several parliamentary sessions; they did not form a coherent system when they were in place; they sprang from a great variety of individuals and pressure groups; and they appeared to lack an underlying philosophy. Thus the terms of different acts contradicted each other as to whether the catholic church should be allowed to function at a simple, parish, level; and from the legislation as a whole, it was unclear whether the intention was to force mass conversions to protestantism, or merely to exclude catholics from positions of any power.[32] If the penal code was, in reality, no code at all, it becomes more difficult to draw any overall conclusions about it, and it therefore become harder to say what the discrimination said about Irish identity, or Ireland's relationship with the rest of Britain. Similarly, recent suggestions about the effects of the laws have implied that they did not perform any of the roles previously ascribed to them. Sean Connolly, in particular, has argued that the penal legislation of the late Stuart period had a rather limited impact. He has suggested that powerlessness in eighteenth century Ireland stemmed primarily from not owning land – and then points out both that this was true in all *ancien regime* societies, and that the penal laws were not the main reason for catholic landlessness, since catholics had been dispossessed well before 1689.[33] What Connolly leaves us with is not an Ireland defined by – or defined against – the penal legislation, but a fairly typical European community of its day. In all countries real estate carried political and social influence, and everywhere religious allegiance affected the chances of holding land. Such a conclusion not only questions the urgency of finding archipelagic interpretations of the penal legislation, it also asks if such a level of analysis would be appropriate. If Ireland was just a typical European community, then it should not be treated as if relations with England or Britain affected its every feature.

Work on other national identities within Britain and Ireland in the late Stuart era is less advanced than that on the Irish protestant ascendancy and its penal legislation. However, future efforts in these areas appear likely to reveal similar levels of confusion and ambiguity. For example, Irish catholics may not have come to see themselves as the real Irish nation in the way that some nationalist accounts have insisted that they did in the penal era. The history of Irish catholic Jacobitism in this period, for instance, is less the history of a nationalist *risorgimento*, than of Irishmen fighting for a far broader cause. They joined French armies, and saw action across the continent as they attempted to restore the Stuarts to the English and Scottish, as well as the Irish, thrones.[34] Similarly, if Sean Connolly is right about social relations in rural Ireland, then the catholic population viewed protestants not as an alien force of occupation, but primarily as landlords. Attitudes to the ascendancy were those of tenant or peasant groups elsewhere, and protestants were seen as economic, not national, enemies (if they were seen as enemies at all).[35] Scots national feeling too, is coming to seem a complex and ambiguous thing. As has been shown, debates on the union were not simply between

'British' or 'Scots' visions of Scotland's future, but between sophisticated intellectual positions which viewed Scotland as a European community, as well as a separate nation or as a part of a United Kingdom. Again, work on the Scots Highlands at the time of the Glencoe Massacre has confirmed how little highlanders had in common with other Scots, and how much more important old ties to kinsmen and locality were than any feeling of wider nationality.[36]

Obviously, by itself, such questioning of older interpretations of national identity does not mean that a 'British' level of analysis is inappropriate. More recent accounts may lack the simple archipelagic vision of whiggery and nationalism, but they often retain the importance of interactions between peoples in the British Isles. In the case of the Irish ascendancy, for example, national identity appears to have been ambiguous, precisely because these people were caught up in webs of relationships with Scots presbyterians, Irish catholics and English administrations which rendered any way of describing themselves difficult. In many ways the latest scholarship calls, not for an abandonment of the 'British' approach, but for a more complete and less simplistic understanding of the 'British' context. Yet, at other levels, there is again a sense in which doubt has been case on the new British history. As with parliamentary history, surveying recent scholarship suggests that more local, and more universal, layers of analysis must at least run alongside any Britannic focus. In the late Stuart period, it has become clear that people had many different identities from which to choose. Alongside 'British' and 'national' feelings, these included both subnational identities (such as Highland clan loyalty, or the sense of being tenants of a particular Irish landlord) and supranational identities (such as protestantism, Stuart legitimism, or a sense of participation in a general European culture). Moreover, it is not obvious that the choice of which identity to adopt would always be taken using a 'British' perspective. Often very personal, particular and momentary circumstances must have dictated the decision. People would have taken on and changed personae to gain advantage within small scale family disputes, conflicts within their immediate neighbourhood or political battles *within* each constituent nation of the British Isles. They may also have presented different faces to match extra-British audiences – from foreign governments, to international churches, to hosts encountered during European tours. In all this, the sort of interactions between different British nations which has dominated the new British history may not have been central. The archipelago certainly influenced identity, and provided one of the spheres in which it would be enacted or altered. 'The three kingdoms', however, were not the only important context.

To conclude this essay it is worth reflecting on what wider lessons can be learned from this survey of relations between parliaments and national identities in the late Stuart British Isles. The first of these, undeniably, is the extraordinary richness and complexity of interactions between inhabitants of England, Scotland and Ireland after the Glorious Revolution. Despite the scepticism about the 'new British history' which has been expressed, the stories told above throw up many examples of different peoples 'modifying the conditions of one another's existence' in Pocock's much quoted phrase. Yet the scepticism is also important. The latest scholarship demonstrates the importance of examining the 'British' background to late Stuart events – but it also suggests that archipelagic studies produce as much confusion and ambiguity as deeper understanding, and also reminds us (more clearly than traditional accounts of the three kingdoms did) that the archipelago cannot explain everything. Indeed, recent work on the period 1690–1715 may sound a warning about the 'new British history' more generally. Calls for a 'three kingdoms' approach have become so loud that they risk imposing a methodological monopoly on early modern history, a monopoly which may be as distorting as the anglocentrism and Celtic isolationism it was supposed to replace. The work reviewed here suggest that insistence on the British context may sometimes be as dangerous as ignorance of it.

Notes on Chapter 5

1   Conrad Russell's publishing history is instructive – compare his retrospective collection of essays, *Unrevolutionary England* (London, 1990) with his more recent *Fall of the British monarchies* (Oxford, 1991).

2   The work of many of the historians active in this explosion is contained in Brenden Bradshaw and John Morrill (eds), *The British problem, c.1534–1707* (Basingstoke, 1996) and Steven Ellis and Sarah Barber (eds), *Conquest and union: fashioning a British state, 1485–1725* (London, 1995).

3   For Macaulay's denunciation of Glencoe, see Thomas Babington Macaulay, *The history of England to the death of William III* (London, 1848–1861), ch. 18.

4   The tendency is most marked in the books which concentrated on English history, with subsidiary, short (and often despairing) chapters on Scotland and Ireland. For one such – otherwise excellent – work, see David Ogg, *England in the reigns of James II and William III* (Oxford, 1955).

5   Note, for example, the works listed in footnote 1 of Mark Goldie, 'Divergence and union: Scotland and England 1660–1707' in Bradshaw and Morrill (eds), *British problem*, p. 220. Also note the ability of the great 'whig' historian G.M. Trevelyan to write full 'British' history when dealing with the Union in the second volume of his *England under Queen Anne*, (3 vols, London, 1930–4).

6   Colin Kidd, *Subverting Scotland's past: Scottish whig historians and the creation of an Anglo-British identity, 1689–c.1830* (Cambridge, 1993).

7   Lecky's great work was *A history of Ireland in the eighteenth century* which can be consulted in the Longman edition (5 vols, London, 1913).

8   The historical importance of the period 1703–7 for Scots nationalists is charted in Paul H. Scott, *Fletcher of Saltoun and the treaty of union* (Edinburgh, 1992), chs. 1, 18. The classic nationalist *exposés* of English campaign for Union have been William Ferguson, 'The making of the Treaty of Union', *Scottish Historical Review* 43 (1964), 89–110, and Ferguson *Scotland's relations with England: a survey to 1707* (Edinburgh, 1977).

9   For debates on the existence and influence of an Irish 'whig-nationalist' historiography, see the exchanges between Steven Ellis and Brendan Bradshaw in *Irish Historical Studies*, 15 (1986), 1–18; 16 (1989), 329–51; 17 (1991), 289–308. Echoes of 'whig-nationalist' assumptions can be found, for example, in J.C. Beckett, *The making of modern Ireland, 1603–1923* (London, 1966), p. 155–7 where the struggles of the Irish parliament for independence in the 1690s are suggested as precursors of later battles for Irish nationality.

10   The most influential work in this tradition was Daniel Corkery, *The hidden Ireland* (Dublin, 1924).

11   The best summary of these processes is David Hayton, 'Constitutional experiments and political expediency', in Ellis and Barber (eds), *Conquest and union*, pp. 276–305.

12   See, Feguson, 'The making of the Treaty'; Ferguson, *Scotland's relations*; P.W.J. Riley, 'The union of 1707 as a episode in English politics', *English Historical Review*, 84 (1989), 498–527; P.W.J. Riley, *The union of England and Scotland* (Manchester, 1978).

13   Goldie, 'Divergence and union'; Hayton, 'Constitutional experiments', p. 277.

14   See works in note 12 above. For background on Scots political attitudes as interpreted by this school, see P.W.J. Riley, *King William and the Scottish politicians* (Edinburgh, 1979).

15   Hayton, 'Constitutional experiments', pp. 303–5.

16   See in particular, John Robertson (ed), *A union for empire: political thought and the British union of 1707* (Cambridge, 1995).

17 John Robertson, 'An elusive sovereignty: the course of the union debate in Scotland, 1698–1707' in Robertson (ed), *Union for empire*, pp. 198–227; David Armitage, 'Making the empire British: Scotland and the Atlantic world, 1542–1717', *Past and Present*, 155 (1997), 34–63.

18 James Kelly, 'The origins of the act of union: an examination of unionist opinion in Britain and Ireland, 1650–1800', *Irish Historical Studies*, 25 (1987), 236–63.

19 Hayton, 'Constitutional experiments'.

20 Ibid.

21 Other work arguing for a fair level autonomy for Ireland includes Francis Godwin James, *Ireland in the empire, 1688–1770* (Cambridge, Mass., 1973), pp. 43–4; David Hayton, 'The beginnings of the undertaker system', in Thomas Bartlett and David Hayton (eds), *Penal era and golden age* (Belfast, 1979), pp. 32–54; Daniel Szechi and David Hayton, 'John Bull's other kingdoms: the English government of Scotland and Ireland', in Clyve Jones (ed), *Britain in the first age of party* (London, 1987).

22 Sean Connolly, *Religion, law and power: the making of protestant Ireland, 1660–1760* (Oxford, 1992), pp. 103–144. The analysis based in Ireland's proximity is supported by Jack P. Greene, *Peripheries and centre: constitutional development in the extended polities of the British empire and United States, 1607–1788* (Athens, GA, 1986).

23 For this see Hayton, 'Constitutional experiment', and the conclusion to David Hayton, 'The Williamite revolution in Ireland', in Jonathan Israel (ed), *The Anglo-Dutch moment* (Cambridge, 1991), pp. 185–214.

24 Kidd, *Subverting Scotland's past*.

25 Linda Colley, *Britons: forging the nation, 1707–1837* (New Haven, Conn., 1992), ch. 3; John Brewer, *The sinews of power* (London, 1989), especially pp. 13–14.

26 For Fletcher as the intellectual backbone of Scots nationalism, see Scott, *Fletcher of Saltoun* ch. 18, which also points out that the major biographical studies of Fletcher – G.W.T. Ormond, *Fletcher of Saltoun* (1935); W.C. Mackenzie, *Andrew Fletcher of Saltoun* (1935); and, Scott might have pointed out, his own work – all appeared at times of agitation for Scots' home rule. For close association between Scots nationality and Jacobitism after 1707 see Bruce Lenman, *The Jacobite risings in Britain, 1689–1746* (London, 1980), p. 87 and after.

27 For Lecky's denunciation, see Lecky, *History of Ireland*, vol 1 – especially pp. 136–171.

28 Such fears lay behind Lecky's attacks on the penal laws. For comment on Irish attitudes to protestant 'patriots' such as Molyneux and Swift, see Ian McBride, "The common name of Irishman": protestantism and patriotism in eighteenth-century Ireland', in Tony Claydon and Ian

McBride (eds), *Protestantism and national identity in Britain and Ireland, c1650–c1850* (Cambridge, 1998). Echoes of the attitudes described in the last two paragraphs can still be heard in the recent leading works on the penal laws, such as Maurine Wall, *The penal laws, 1691–1760* (London, 1961); Edith Mary Johnston, *Ireland in the eighteenth century* (Dublin, 1974); Patrick J. Corish, *The Irish catholic experience* (Dublin, 1974); P.J. Corish, *The catholic community in the seventeenth and eighteenth centuries* (Dublin, 1981).

29 Jim Smyth ' "Like amphibious animals": Irish patriots, ancient Britons, 1691–1707', *Historical Journal*, 36 (1993), 785–797.

30 For this ambiguity about how to describe Irish protestants, see Smyth, 'Like amphibious animals'; David Hayton, 'Anglo-Irish attitudes: changing perceptions of national identity among the protestant ascendancy in Ireland, c.1670–1750', *Studies in Eighteenth-century Culture*, 17 (1987), 145–157.

31 Something of the flexibility of Irish protestant identities in this period will be explored in Toby Barnard, 'Protestantism, ethnicity and Irish identities, 1660–1760' in Claydon and McBride, *Protestantism and National Identity*.

32 For the lack of system behind the penal laws, see Sean Connolly, 'Religion and history', *Irish Economic and Social History*, 10 (1983), 66–80; Thomas Bartlett, *The rise and fall of the Irish nation: the catholic question, 1690–1830* (Dublin, 1992), pp. 18–20. Both scholars leant heavily on J.G. Simms 'The making of a penal law, 1703–5', *Irish Historical Studies*, 12 (1960), 105–18; and J.G.Simms, 'The bishop's banishment act of 1698', *Irish Historical Studies*, 10 (1970), 185–99.

33 Connolly, *Religion, law and power*, ch. 7.

34 For this Jacobite internationalism, see Frank McLynn, *The Jacobites* (London, 1985), ch. 2; Daniel Szechi, *The Jacobites: Britain and Europe, 1688–1788* (Manchester, 1994).

35 Connolly, *Religion, law and power*, chs. 4 and 7.

36 For a flavour of Highland society at the time, see Paul Hopkins, *Glencoe and the end of the Highland war* (Edinburgh, 1986); McLynn, *Jacobites*, ch. 3

CHAPTER 6

Patterns of British Identity: 'Britain' and its Rivals in the Sixteenth and Seventeenth Centuries[*]

Arthur Williamson

'. . . a new history of Britain should be written with the utmost regard to accuracy.'

– Sir Thomas Craig, *De unione regnorum Britanniæ tractatus*, 1605[1]

THE CONSTRUCTION OF PATRIOTISM

Andrew Melville memorialized Queen Elizabeth's death in 1603 with verses describing her as 'the divine mother of the Britons.'[2] Strange-sounding indeed, for whatever Elizabeth's varied titles, 'her Britannic majesty' was not one of them. Moreover, the queen had utterly rejected Melville's Presbyterian church polity, discounted much of his theology, and eventually destroyed his English colleagues and counterparts. Yet, despite such drastic faults, Melville applauded Elizabeth's 'great love of religion': she had been the terror of the Iberians, the protector of Scotland, France, and the Netherlands – and, implicitly, of the reformations within each of them. Through these commitments her long reign had restored the golden age. However severe her shortcomings, she had undertaken what Melville regarded as the British project.

What made Elizabeth 'mother of the Britons' involved still more

[*]This essay was made possible through the support of the Committee for Research and Scholarly Activity at California State University, Sacramento. I am also most grateful to my friend and colleague, Paul McGinnis, who kindly translated the poems of Andrew Melville and of David Hume of Godscroft, as well as part of Godscroft's *De unione insulæ Britanniæ. Tractatus I.* In addition, Professor McGinnis discussed a number of the themes in this essay with me, conversations that did much to clarify my thinking.

than her British policies. Most immediately, she was the progenitrix of King James VI and I, whom Melville proclaimed as 'rex Britanniarum.' Far beyond being merely the 'rex Britannorum,' James was literally king of the 'Britannias' – that is, of Scotland and England, and, more generally, the British Isles. Melville's enthusiasm for Britain fully equalled that of the king whom he celebrated, even if their British visions turned out to differ significantly.

Melville the Briton was also Melville the Scot. British effusiveness in no way qualified his Scottish patriotism. Melville was one of the very few early modern poets to undertake a Scottish national epic. Known today as 'The Gathelus,' the poem draws on the full range of Scottish patriotic mythologies, materials through which at least since the high Middle Ages Scots had averred their realm's autonomy and dignity. Yet in Melville's hands, Scotland's epic experience would culminate in an apocalyptic British crusade, led by its 'Scoto-Britannic' champions. Scottish destiny achieved fulfilment in the latter-day British struggle against the gigantic Iberian Empire – a contest Melville imagined as taking place between Isaac and Ishmael, between the spirit of justice and the spirit of conquest, between religious freedom and religious tyranny.[3]

Melville was by no means alone. His younger associate, David Hume of Godscroft, seems to have had no interest in an anti-Spanish crusade, very limited interest in imperial expansion, and, so far as we can tell, precious little interest in the apocalypse as any kind of organizing category. He was also one of the most committed and articulate promoters of Scotland's autonomy and parity during this period. In fact, he is one of the very earliest to introduce the neologism 'patriot' into the vernacular. His attitude towards Middle Scots, the Scottish variant of the southern language, was equally determined. Although Hume noted in his history of the house of Douglas that Archibald Douglas, the 6th earl of Angus (c.1489–1557), had learned 'the English tongue and tone which he did thereafter delight much to use,' this was in no way admirable. For Hume learning the southern forms was simply 'affectation.' It was a mean occupation to study what was no more than a dialect of one's own speech – and just possibly an inferior one at that. Hume spoke 'Scottish' – 'and why not, to Scottish-men?' – a language which *he* thoroughly enjoyed using.

During the first decade of the seventeenth century Hume entered into a pamphlet campaign against James' newly intruded bishops, vigorously defending Scottish institutional integrity against English 'tyranny.' His appeal could prove arrestingly direct. 'I may say as a

Scotishman,' he expostulated to James Law, the bishop of Orkney, 'to you as a Scotishman and, I trust, not without some regarde unto your native countrie.' By the end of his life he had become obsessed to publish his great history of the Douglases, a history exemplary of the aristocratic patriotism he saw as in decline.[4]

Perhaps surprisingly, none of this was in any way incompatible with the new Britain, nor deflected him from what were genuinely British commitments. Hume described himself as a 'Scoto-Britannus,' and with manifest ardor wrote tracts and poems advocating union. The union he sought would be neither federal nor confederal, but a fusion and synthesis of the two realms, a Britain that in some ways supplanted both Scotland and England. Mere federalism could only be 'inferior,' the result of larger failure.

Nor did any of these aspirations simply arise from the highly charged years surrounding 1603. Quite the reverse. Here were ideas long in the maturation. One of Hume's early poems was addressed to the young James VI – 'De Iacobo Sexto Scotorum Rege adhuc puero, Expectatio' (Anticipation concerning James VI, king of the Scots though still a child) – and it cannot have been written much later than 1580 when James was 14 and Hume between 20 and 24. James would bring Scotland – otherwise 'buried in shameful darkness' (a play on the traditional derivation of 'Scot' from the Greek σκοτος, meaning 'darkness' or 'obscurity') – 'into the light of day,/ Now more brightly shining than all other shores.' And how would James achieve this much-sought return of the golden age? It would be accomplished by nothing less than the creation of *British* public space.

At nunc perpetuam spondent tibi sydera pacem,
  Et locant regno medium Britanno.[5]
  [And now the stars promise you lasting peace,
  Finding the public good in the British kingdom.]

Scotland's emergence issued in a British order, and thus Scottish identity generated British consciousness.

If Melville and Hume strike us today as very odd patriots, they did not seem at all that way to their age. When Hume began speaking of 'the good patriot' in the mid 1580s, he was probably not alone and he would soon be joined by growing numbers of others from many places within 'Britain.' The armada crisis stimulated reflection about notions of nation (and loyalty to it) in England no less than in Scotland. Those who were most determined to resist the Hapsburgs, who saw the struggle through broad, often apocalyptic lenses, and who therefore saw themselves as the most loyal to the nation, were naturally the most committed Protestants. As in Scotland, 'patriots' inclined to seek further reform, whether in religion or in political institutions. As in Scotland, the word 'patriot' entered England's speech as a term monopolized by opponents of the crown.[6] Within both realms 'patriots' would most likely see themselves as actors within larger, extra-national frameworks. Even if English political culture – uniquely articulate, uniquely integrated, uniquely coherent[7] – increasingly refracted, constricted, and reshaped the southern outlook, patriotism in the early modern period typically carried reformist, dissentient, and internationalist implications largely alien to nineteenth and twentieth century traditionalisms and utterly alien to nineteenth and twentieth century nationalisms.

To be sure, the dense and, to us, strange textures of early modern patriotism, even in their Scottish forms, did not necessarily lead to British conclusions. During the 1550s, that peculiarly French moment in British history, George Buchanan imagined a powerful Valois dynasty, embracing both Scotland and England, that dedicated itself to the defeat of the Hapsburgs' universal empire. Buchanan's 'Epithalamium' on the marriage of Mary Stewart to Francis of Valois contained a patriotic passage that stirred Scottish hearts long after the French cause had evaporated. Patriotism did not inherently mean corporate autonomy, as it reflexively does today, while its potential forms ranged widely. Patriotism might often assume a British turn, it could briefly adopt a French accent or even an Hispanic inflection, it might become articulate in still other voices. But, whatever the voice and whatever the register, there was certainly no necessary reason at all for it to become *either* an extension of English political culture *or* the fulfilment of some pre-existent identity.

Melville, Hume, and even Buchanan need to be approached – and probably can only be approached cogently – through the recently-developed categories of the new British history. During the past twenty years an idea of British history has emerged that visualizes the experience of the Atlantic archipelago as an interactive process. So conceived, societies within this region continually reformulated one another in ever shifting kaleidoscopic patterns, as kin and administration, feudal law and blood traditions interpenetrated one another, and as a remarkable range of literatures, genres, and languages were employed to make all these ongoing developments intelligible. From the new British perspective anglocentric triumphalism becomes a distorting teleology and thus untenable. In exactly the same way, nationalist histories – really no more than the other side of the same teleological coin – become similarly untenable. If the whiggish

England-as-Britain falls before the new historiography, so too do its equally nineteenth century ethnic competitors.

Because of the powerful nationalist revival that has swept the West (and perhaps the world) since the mid-1970s, the latter enjoys greatly more credibility today than does discredited anglocentricism.[8] But English whiggery, however distorting, at least has the virtue of recognizing an empirical dynamic: the expansion of the government based at London (if also to a lesser extent at Edinburgh, Dublin, and Inveraray) was the signal factor in the history of the region. Romantic nationalism, however, has no virtue at all. No community, no group, no kindred, no 'gens' within this pre-Kantian world could ever have comprehended the notion of a collective 'soul' or the unfolding common 'spirit' that underwrites modern nationalist historiography. No one in that age could ever have imagined Edmund Burke's 'genius of the nation philosophically considered.' No one then would ever have proposed (much less accepted) his social group as being a unique and autonomous 'spiritual communion.'

The peoples of that time frequently did have a sense of prophetic destiny – as did Andrew Melville – but that destiny was always universalist human redemption. Depending on political context and institutional development, they could speak of national covenants or of national election. But we will look in vain for the modern preoccupation with essentialist authenticity. There are no 'sons of destiny' in early modern Europe. We will find martyrs aplenty in that era – overwhelmingly Protestant[9] – but these martyrdoms bore witness to larger, non-ethnic causes. We will find often conflicting languages of peoplehood. But we will never lose a European horizon, and we will never find a priori transcendence. Reformers and counter-reformers conducted spiritual and political crusades against each other. But they were no less concerned to conduct crusades against 'barbarism' and to transform their communicants. Both sides were summoned for mission, but not for self-actualization.

Before there were 'patriots,' and long before there was anything as abstract as 'patriotism,' there was 'pietas': the classical world's spiritual commitment to kin and country, to the citizen and the public good. Here arose the most profound avowal of this world and involvement in it, for only through such involvement could one's humanity be fulfilled and any further salvation be achieved. The notion entered Renaissance Europe through civic humanism, and the term 'pietas' long coexisted with today's familiar neologism, patriot. As we would expect, the antique concept suffuses the writing of George Buchanan, but even so establishment a figure as the lawyer Sir Thomas Craig would use it in the fully humanist sense. His *De unione* . . . (1605) celebrated James VI and I as a wise and excellent prince, 'inspired by wisdom and patriotism' (cum sapientia conjuncta pietas). James's unionist policies similarly derived from the highest wisdom, patriotism, and regard for the well being of his united (British) people ('ex summo Iudicio, sic ex pietate, et summa in populum benevolentia conjunctum').[10] Protestant spirituality absorbed with unique success this profoundly civic commitment, along with so much else in the humanist enterprise.[11] If, as conservative historians have recently insisted, the Reformation produced no revolutionary ideology or 'theory of resistance,' its radicalism nevertheless remains in its uncompromising commitment to public space and in its remarkably politicizing soteriology. The classical citizen and the Protestant saint tended to merge and, with thinkers like Buchanan, could become all but coterminous.[12] Calvin and Cato turned out to be surprisingly complementary. Protestant 'pietas' lay at the heart of early modern patriotic and civic identity. With these intellectual foundations we are recognizably on the road to the Enlightenment and to the democratic revolutions – but a vast way indeed from the romantic sensibility.

SCOTLAND: BRITISH STATE, BRITISH NATION

'Pardon me, mother Scotland. I call upon you as witness on my behalf – myself as the examiner of my innermost feelings. You are not dearer to anyone than to me, nor is your name sweeter to anyone. But what is my purpose? Public utility draws all to itself, and you yourself are not unwilling to say so. The common mother [Britannia] requires it as well – in whose way it is not right that you stand. I think that the debate [about union] has become irksome to you, and [the prospect] that thereby the common body would be torn asunder.'

– David Hume of Godscroft, 1605[13]

Just as late twentieth century nationalist ideologies distort beyond recognition the world of earlier peoples, so too does late twentieth century cynicism. The Renaissance and then the Reformation deeply penetrated the tissues of Scottish political culture, propagating in the process an extraordinary range of powerful minds. A surprising number of these, though far from all, found themselves attracted to the idea of creating a British polity, and in most cases they did so for reasons we could only describe as idealistic. From the late medieval scholastic John Mair, to Hector Boece, John Bellenden, John Knox, Robert Pont, Patrick Adamson, Andrew Melville, Thomas Craig, David

Hume of Godscroft, and many lesser figures, all looked to Britain as the engine of reform – even though the reform these individuals sought, political, social, religious, varied greatly and conflicted frequently. Mair's *History of Greater Britain* (1521), with its unionist agenda of anti-magnate political reform, is well-known today, and its readership and impact in the sixteenth century is doubtless greater than now recognized. But it was altogether superseded for contemporaries by Hector Boece's hugely influential *The History and Chronicles of Scotland* (1527). Deriving from humanist models, more visibly civic, resolutely aristocratic, offering a different vision of reform and, above all, manifestly patriotic both in its posture and mythologies, Boece's history is in all these respects a riposte to Mair's. Regarded as a Scottish Livy, Boece became a touchstone for sixteenth century Scots, whatever their politics or religious commitments. His would be the only Scottish history to see print in translation during that century, eventually in both Scots and English. It initiated a new genre of Scottish historiography. Perhaps surprisingly it became a kind of court ideology during the 1530s, and not even Buchanan's *History of Scotland* (1582), authoritative for nearly two centuries, would fully eclipse it.

But if Boece appealed powerfully to Scottish patriotic sensibilities, that circumstance still did not preclude union with England. John Bellenden's translation was prefaced with a poem that spoke of the Scots as 'Ay [= always] fechtand for thair liberteis and richtis,/ With Romanis, Danis, Inglismen, and Pichtis.' Despite such stirring sentiments, the creation of a new state remained manifestly desirable.

> Heirfore I dar boldlie affirme, gif the Albianis had sic grace that they micht leif with concord amang thaimself, or gif thair realmes, be ony honest way, micht cum under the empire and senyourie of ane king; thay micht nocht allanerlie haif all necessaries within thaimself, uncoft; bot, with small difficultie, micht daunt all nichtbouris and cuntreis liand tham about . . .[14]

Boece's patriotism caused him to prefer 'Alba' to 'Britain,' 'Albanians' to 'Britons' (against classical historians and geographers): Anglo-Welsh mythologies associated Britain with the south and, potentially, with English suzerainty. Writing at a moment of exceptional cultural self-confidence, when the court of the young James V appeared filled with promise, 'Alba' (or 'Albion') seemed plausible. After 1550 it seemed 'poetic,' as deepening classicism, domestic repression, and a double foreign invasion refocused Scottish thinking. 'Britain' became 'indifferent' – as England's Lord Protector, Edward Seymour, Duke of Somerset, had claimed it to be in 1548 – largely because it eliminated the question of precedence implied by saying 'England and Scotland.' Further, by late century, both Scottish and English mythologies, if not the claims they supported, increasingly failed to carry conviction among the learned elites.

It was only natural for Somerset to appeal to both Mair and Boece when he urged the union of the realms through the marriage of the Princess Mary to the young Edward VI. His famous 'An Epistle or exhortacion, to unitie and peace . . . to . . . the Realme of Scotlande' (1548) was issued in the midst of invasion and an exceptionally brutal war, but it spoke of Scottish freedom from foreign servitude and, replacing servitude, of the liberty, amity, equality between the two realms. Here was something 'whiche your writers hath alwayes wisshed mighte once [i.e., at one time] come to pass.'[15] Whatever the Protector's true intentions, both his Scottish and English advisors – most notably the Edinburgh merchant James Henrisoun who surely played a central role in drafting the document – looked to a new era of reform and justice, under the auspices of a latter-day Constantinian empire that fulfilled the promises of both sacred and secular prophecy.

When people began speaking of union in terms of the providential and the prophetic, a distinctly new dimension entered British politics. Britain might now appear as integral to the sacred drama, inherent within the final stages of the historical redemption before the end of time. The language of the apocalypse had always been available, but it assumed new significance with the Reformation. When John Ireland (c.1440–1495) or William Dunbar (c. 1460–1514) spoke of Antichrist, in medieval fashion they meant an individual not an institution; the term bore no political implications; there was nothing even remotely imminent about it.[16] By 1550 all that had changed: the apocalypse organized the European experience into a coherent, linear process that made contemporary events intelligible. Its meaning became immediate and urgent. We encounter one indication of the new apocalyptic, conceived institutionally rather than personally, when the earl of Glencairn in 1539 denounced the Catholic clergy as 'Monsters with the Beast's marke.' In 1550 John Knox fully outlined the apocalyptic programmatic underlying human experience in what would be his most remembered sermon.[17] During the intervening years Somerset's publicists had promoted such a providential vision of the British union with striking effectiveness. While there was nothing particularly British about the apocalypse (it could and did shape the aspirations of such anti-British structures as the Iberian empires), and while it certainly was possible to seek radical reform without recourse to its organizing principles, the apocalypse by mid-century would become a driving force behind the creation of Britain.

Somerset, like Henry VIII and so many English rulers before him, continued to insist on the superiority of the southern crown. And yet, despite this, the 'Epistle' emerges as one of the decisive documents in the forming of the British state. A remarkable writing by any standard, the letter subsequently acquired an international status when it appeared in Latin as part of Johannes Sleidanus's widely-read *De statu religionis et reipublicæ, Carlo Quinti, commentarii* (1557). No less than Knox's famous unionist tract, the *First Blast of the Trumpet against the Monstrous Regiment of Women* (1558), at junctures develops strikingly similar arguments to those found in the 'Epistle' and it is hard not to think that Knox found inspiration from it. Subsequently the letter would feature prominently in the writings on union of such major Scottish intellects as Robert Pont, Thomas Craig, and David Hume of Godscroft.[18] There was a great deal of Scottish thought about a British union during the later sixteenth century, and, unarguably, Somerset's evocative tract was important to much of it.

The prospect and then the event of James VI's uncontested accession to the southern crown resolved British thinking into concentrated focus. Andrew Melville's British crusade found itself complemented by (and in competition with) a more court-oriented, hierarchical British vision. Based on the memory of the Roman emperor Constantine the Great, who was seen as a British figure, the court version similarly interwove a dense fabric of mythology and prophecy. Like Melville, it looked to Prince Henry – though in deference to the king it frequently tended to be rather anti-Turkish than anti-papal. Yet it was no less apocalyptic than its Melvillian rival: as the 'British' Constantine had established the faith and banished Satan's public kingdom, so latter-day Britain might restore the faith and overthrow its enemies at the end of time. Both sprang from similar aspirations and shared hopes. Both need to be seen as expressions of a common culture. Variations of the establishment version found their poets and promoters in successful, powerful courtiers like Sir William Alexander, as well as in failed, if learned academics like James Maxwell. For Alexander, imperial Britain grew from a crusade led by Prince Henry into colonial enterprise in the New World – empire in the full range of its meanings.[19]

To be sure, Scottish enthusiasts for Britain at the regnal union always resolutely insisted on parity with England. Thus the Edinburgh lawyer John Russell urged union evoking full-blown Constantinian imagery, and yet also asked James to treat England as auxiliary to his prime responsibilities in Scotland. The one arose immediately in default of the other, and it is not even odd to find both postures in a single tract.[20] In the event English resistance to Britain, as well as the south's often ugly xenophobia, caused Scots to recoil into a defense of the realm against anglicization – a transition neatly illustrated in the career of Hume of Godscroft. During those charged years on either side of the regnal union, even Hume briefly adopted the perspective of Melvillian imperialism. His dauntingly complex poem 'Daphn-Amaryllis' (London, 1605) urged James's succession and union (Amaryllis-Elizabeth-England/Daphnis-James-Scotland). James's succession to the marble chair (now in London) would lead to great things:

> . . . haud Roma Britannos
> Maxima iam metuet frustra: aut terrebit inultos
> Tarpeius torquens fremebunda tonitrua flamen,

[Not at all in vain will Rome fear the British. Nor will the Tarpeian flamen (i.e., the pope) twisting his lightning bolts, be unavenged]

Subsequently, Hume added, '. . . et ad quæuis maxima aggredienda, propagandis quam longissime extra insulam imperii finibus' (with the boundaries of the empire to be extended far beyond the island).[21] Let the pope beware, the British are coming. But things changed quickly. In little more than a year after the poem came off the London press, Hume became embattled in a long term struggle on behalf of the Scottish church and thereby Scottish identity. Hume never lost sight of Britain at least as an ideal, even if the new politics forced him to shift his priorities. The power of the idea of a British crusade and a British mission is difficult to exaggerate. It had captured the imagination of the Scottish public, enjoying a widespread currency in the north long after such expectations had ceased to be fashionable at Whitehall.[22]

There consequently exists an enormous irony in the 1638 Scottish revolution against Charles I and the provincialization of the realm brought about by his rule. Charles's authoritarian, repressive kingship – 'British' only in the sense that it stood above the constitution of any of the realms he governed – provoked Scotland to what eventually became a British response. Even if an alliance with English reformers and subsequently with the English parliament became necessary to preserve Scottish autonomy, it remains hard to deny that an unmistakable idealism informed Scotland's involvement in England. The Westminster Assembly, the Committee of Both Kingdoms, the *conservatores pacis*, all at once addressed visionary preoccupations no less than hard-headed practical security concerns. Here were the first serious efforts to create genuinely British institutions.[23]

But the Britain they envisioned differed considerably from attitudes at the time of the regnal union, for England and Scotland would now be federated or confederated rather than fused. From the later years of the sixteenth century Scots had continuously developed and refined exceedingly rich vocabularies for imagining sacralized confederation, vocabularies that long had become commonplace within Scottish political culture. Confederal Britain more convincingly spoke to the universal reform that had exercised Scottish thinking since the days of Melville and Alexander. Confederal Britain seemed plausible to Scottish court moderates who sought to preserve the monarchy. Confederal Britain spoke with singular cogency to the House of Argyll. Britain had been integral both to Campbell identity and to Campbell territorial expansion at least from the 1560s, and it can hardly surprise us that the eighth earl doggedly promoted British confederation in the mid-1640s or that he all but single-handedly forced through Scotland's treaty with Charles II that made him king of 'Great Britain.' For the elites generally at mid-century, Britain underwrote Scottish social stability, protecting heritable jurisdictions and aristocratic power against the claims of clerical radicalism – and, still more, against the revolutionary commonwealth that eventually succeeded the covenanting regime. Scottish elites were unwilling to see their realm either as an independent quasi-republic or as integrated within a larger English polity.

The English republic initially undertook the conquest of Scotland only with the greatest reluctance. But it did so in the name of social liberation, a voice unmistakably anticipating that of the democratic revolutions in the next century, and indeed all the political revolutions that have subsequently grown out of them. Fired by apocalyptic visions of universal freedom, the radical commonwealth – the first Britain – attacked and altogether overthrew the Scottish elites. Despite dreadful devastation and the horror of conquest and occupation, the republic attracted some Scottish communities and some remarkable individuals from the elites, outstandingly James Hope of Hopetoun.[24] If the republican tradition eventually failed everywhere within the British Isles, the seventeenth century experiment nevertheless led directly to modern politics.

Scotland's British experience could therefore be both radical and conservative, reforming and preserving. Britain might promise a new world as it did for Scots like James Henrisoun in the 1540s and like

James Hope in the 1650s. But instead it might simply protect local power. Moreover, as James VI found in the first decade of the seventeenth century, Britain would enable him to undo earlier radicalism. Buchanan's civic *respublica* might seem plausible in the unstable world of the 1560s and 1570s, but it could hardly carry conviction within the larger British order. Scotland's Presbyterian church government triumphed in 1592, but turned out to be vulnerable in the context of the regnal union.

It was one thing to create a British state, quite another to create a British nation. Categories of genuine British identity emerge only slowly and indirectly on the margins and interstices of traditional politics. Britain as a cultural entity probably first emerged in the later sixteenth century with the earls of Argyll and the growth of Gaelic Protestantism. The Campbell challenge to the MacDonalds and other clans in the west Highlands inevitably confronted memory of the Lordship of the Isles, the powerful Gaelic principality that till 1493 had straddled the northern channel between what eventually became Scotland and Ireland. Possibly in part because their origins in Strathclyde were too well known, the Campbells could not lay claim to the defunct Lordship, but instead portrayed themselves in Arthurian and in specifically British terms. The Campbells thereby challenged and reimagined the traditional Highland world they inhabited, the adoption of an anglicizing 'p' to the spelling of their name being perhaps emblematic of their outlook.[25]

What is arresting about them is not so much their proverbial expansiveness and 'aggression,' but their hybridization. It is not simply their increased use of written records, or their vigorous manipulation of feudal legal procedures that were always a dimension of the Scottish Highlands, or their relatively successful efforts to improve agricultural practice, or even their sponsoring of lowland settlers as 'spiritual kindred' in newly acquired territories. It is the integration of quite disparate cultural elements and the resulting reformulation of tradition that must strike us today. Their activities parallel the contemporaneous thinking of the Highlander Buchanan and of the Borderer Godscroft, thinking that sought to interweave Calvinist humanism and civic identities into the militarized kin structures of traditional Scotland. It is perhaps no accident or at least curiously appropriate that Hector Boece had links with the bardic traditions of ClanCampbell. The Campbells' language indicates how fully conscious they were of the integrative character of their endeavors: they were among the earliest in using the terms 'North British' for

Scotland and 'British' for the settlers in Ulster.[26] Naturally enough ClanCampbell adopted the language of the court and portrayed its mission as 'civilizing' – though today with greater distance and more developed social thought, we might rather characterize it as 'revitalizing.'

The eighth earl and first marquis of Argyll contrasts revealingly with his MacDonald counterpart and bitter antagonist, the second earl and first marquis of Antrim. Central figures in the great upheaval of the mid-seventeenth century, the two marquises inhabited both a Gaelic world and the world of the Stewart court. Each was bilingual in the non-verbal symbol systems he negotiated no less than in his speech.[27] But Argyll pursued visions that went well beyond both the court and the expansion of his lands at the expense of his rival. Antrim recalled the Lordship, Argyll sought a new order. Antrim was bifurcated, Argyll was British.

These developments on Scotland's western seaboard potentially held great significance. The earls of Argyll were powerful well beyond other aristocratic families within Britain. Indeed they were emerging as almost a third force, behind London and Edinburgh. Immediately in the wake of the 1560 Reformation, the fifth earl proposed an unprecedented rapprochement with England that might well have changed the trajectory of Irish and thus British history. Even so, the Campbells, as integral to James VI's policies of expansion, colonizing, and 'civilizing,' were also integral to developing both British imperialism and a common British identity.[28] Campbell power reached its apex during the early 1640s when the Covenanting Movement extended Campbell influence into all three kingdoms. At the heart of these events lies the irony that the Protestant Gael emerged as the first modern Briton.

British identities developed in still other subtle and tentative ways. Scotland shared with its neighbors common attitudes toward the customs of the realm, and appeals to the authority of such 'ancient' custom had been a commonplace in most of Europe for an exceedingly long time. Scots often spoke of 'loveable custom,' the English spoke typically of 'laudable custom,' the French of 'louable coutume.' Like their neighbors Scots would resist royal policy in the name of custom, as they all had done since the emergence of feudal monarchy during the middle ages.

But during the course of the sixteenth century England's customary law had acquired cogency in English political thought unparalleled elsewhere. Custom appeared as a single, coherent, and immemorial fabric of profound wisdom, animated through the enactments of a sovereign crown in parliament. By the end of the century this entire structure could be described as 'fundamental law,' and was seen as secure as the property relations on which it was founded.

Parliament had proved to be a highly important institution in sixteenth century Scotland, but neither parliament nor Scots law occupied a comparable place within the Scottish political imagination. Other assemblies, both lay and ecclesiastical, enjoyed a status unlike anything in the south, while parliament itself might be variously constituted. Scots appealed to their laws when they resisted French domination at mid-century, but custom obviously held a different significance for John Aylmer than it did for John Knox and, doubtless, most Scots. Scottish statute did not enjoy an authority comparable to its southern counterpart. The eminent Scottish jurist and minister Robert Pont could reject the 'Black Acts' of 1584 in part by noticing that in practice parliamentary statutes frequently never went into effect. Patriot dynasties rather than highly developed institutions underwrote the upheavals of 1559–60 and 1567–73. But the language of immemorial custom and fundamental law moved more to the center of Scottish consciousness at the very end of the century as the prospect of Anglo-Scottish union loomed. Scots not only confronted the English legal attitudes and claims, but were constrained simply by the Stewart accession itself to think increasingly in terms of formalized governing structures.[29]

In 1606 Andrew Melville, his nephew James Melville, and six other Scottish Presbyterian ministers found themselves detained indefinitely in London by order of the crown, and their response to this act of government terrorism is illuminating. At an important juncture they were questioned individually by the Scottish council. James Melville responded in terms of legal right claiming that

> he wes a frie subject of the kingdome of Scotland, quhilk had lawis and priveledges of its awin, as any in the world, to quhilk he would stand. He thoucht thair had bein no lawfull summonds lawfully execut againes him: The Nobilmen thair sitting, nor yit he, wes not at home in thair awin native countrey: The chairge *super inquirendis* wes long syne put away and abolischit, as iniquouse and injust: He wes of no law or reasoun bound to accuse himselff, be furniseing dittay againes himselff. He desyrit the Nobillmen quho were thair present to remember quhat they wer, and to deal with him (howbeit ane poor man, yit a frie-born gentil Scotis-man) as they would be content to be usit thaimselffis, that is, by the lawis of Scotland.

Personal liberties, rights against self-incrimination, the privileges and protections of the law do not feature prominently in the politics of late sixteenth century Scotland. Liberty did not normally or primarily derive from writ, but from civic engagement, from public life, from the exercise of virtue. Andrew Melville subsequently spoke in a far more familiar way when he told the assembled aristocrats 'flattly that they . . . wer degenerate from the antiant nobilitie of Scotland, quho wer wont to give thair landis and liffes for the fridom of the kingdome and the Gospel.'[30]

Englishmen would have found James Melville's statement immediately recognizable; many would have applauded it. Andrew's would have sounded far more foreign and, we might expect, darkly troubling. The new politics enjoined new language, but it would be wrong to see James Melville as simply 'anglicizing.' Melville was speaking about Scots law and Scottish autonomy. 'Free-born' Englishmen and 'free-born' Scots might turn out to be strikingly similar figures. Despite significantly divergent political cultures, common languages of liberty would emerge in the face of authoritarian government. Thus, that deeply un-English instrument, the National Covenant, nevertheless based part of its appeal on the largely un-Scottish notion of 'fundamental law' and privileges secured in property.

ENGLAND: THE LAW FUNDAMENTAL

During the 1530s Thomas Cromwell, Thomas Cranmer, and Henry VIII successfully tapped into cultural energies that would not dissipate fully until the twentieth century. The legislation of that decade proclaimed English sovereignty in terms unduplicated elsewhere in Europe at the time because it derived neither from dynastic claims nor ethnic mythologies, but from an unparalleled assertion of institutional coherence and continuity. English institutional integration under a common law, imagined as customary, may well have been unique; in its institutional self-consciousness England was indeed unique. The foundations of such attitudes reached far back into the English past, and Lord Chief Justice Fortescue's well-known statement in his *De laudibus legum Anglie* of the late fifteenth century is illustrative of it.

> The kingdom of England was first inhabited by Britons, then ruled by Romans, again by Britons, then possessed by Saxons, who changed its name from Britain to England. Then for a short time the kingdom was conquered

by Danes, and again by Saxons, but finally by Normans, whose posterity hold the realm at the present time. And throughout the period of these nations and their kings, the realm has been continuously ruled by the same customs as it is now, customs which, if they had not been the best, some of those kings would have changed for the sake of justice or by the impulse of caprice, and totally abolished them, especially the Romans who judged almost the rest of the world by their laws. Similarly, others of these aforesaid kings, who possessed the kingdom of England only by the sword, could, by that power, have destroyed its laws. Indeed, neither the civil laws of the Romans . . . nor the laws of the Venetians . . . nor the laws of any Christian kingdom, are so rooted in antiquity. Hence there is no gainsaying nor legitimate doubt but that the customs of the English are not only good but the best.[31]

It will come as no surprise that Fortescue's text first saw print in about 1537 or that Robert Mulcaster's translation appeared in no less than three editions during Elizabeth's reign. This frequent republication comprises an important element within the 'great hardening and consolidation' of common law thought that John Pocock describes as taking place between 1550 and 1600. Increasingly detached from continental sources and from universal concepts of law, English legal and political thinking became focused on the laws of the realm as a single, self-generated fabric. By 1604 members of the House of Commons could claim that all their privileges were integral within England's immemorial legal structure and thus of a piece with all right and all heritages, indeed of a piece with property itself. Thus, to think of England then was to think of its longevity, its continuity, it cohesion, its autonomy, and, in so saying, its inviolable institutional integrity.

If the *De laudibus* was, in Sir Walter Raleigh's words, 'that noble bulwark of our laws,' it had become the bulwark of much else as well. The 1530s initiated political no less than institutional consolidation and rationalization, in what was a curiously well integrated and yet still far from centralized state. Not only did parliament and statute acquire new authority, not only did public administration become more articulate, political integration also extended still further – to the borders, to the new Irish 'kingdom,' to Calais, to Scotland, and, outstandingly, to Wales. No doubt, a British strategy and vision came only haltingly. It probably only emerged under Edward VI, to be reformulated importantly, if briefly, by William Cecil at Elizabeth's accession. Thereafter something recognizably like Melville's British project was promoted by 'advanced Protestants' with leaders who included Leicester and Philip Sidney. As with Melville, Leicester and

Sidney sought a monarchy at once limited and yet also oddly imperial: reform at home, leadership for Protestant Europe, hegemony in the region, and, sotto voce, empire across the ocean.

Again analogously to Melville, increasing numbers of English men and women imagined their realm as performing a central role within scripture's great sacred drama that was now seen as entering upon its final acts. Yet precisely here arose insurmountable differences. English apocalyptic expectations had become interwoven into the dense fabric of English institutions. Like its law, England's spiritual destiny was self-generated, immanent, autonomous. The larger British project might prove a manifestation of English mission – or it might not – but, either way, it was marginal if not irrelevant to English identity. Scoto-Britanni abounded at the regnal union, but the Anglo-Britannus was a bird rare almost to the vanishing point.

Englishmen like Andrew Willet, Thomas Brightman, and Miles Mosse, who actually did welcome a new British state, saw it as an agency of reform and imagined it within a recast and deepened apocalyptic vision. Much more Judaic and biblicist, their reformulated apocalypse pointed away from English institutions rather than reinforcing them: Scotland and England, in Willet's words, would as 'louing sisters and fellow tribes . . . go up to Jerusalem together.' With such writers as these emerged the beginnings of English philo-Semitism and of a radicalism that had a long history before it.[32] But their voices would not be heard in the House of Commons at the union of crowns. Nor did their themes then exercise the English elites. Even if publicists associated with the Protector Somerset had developed a powerful British vision, 'Britain' had come to sound distinctly un-English half a century later.

If Britain were to be in any way imagined as a supranational state, then English institutional integrity (and the sovereignty of king-in-parliament) would become inherently qualified and was thus radically unacceptable. The only union that could make sense within this mental world would be the incorporation of Scotland through the expansion of English law – following the Welsh model. As the English MP Laurence Hyde argued in 1607,

> I am persuaded that the commons and all the Scottish nation except some few great persons that have liberties unfitt for subjects, as power to pardon treasons, felony, murder, manslaughter, and other like, would gladly yield to the subject of our laws.[33]

It is in response to this situation that Thomas Craig's discussion of English law in the *Jus feudale* (1603, first printed 1655) and the *De unione* (1605, first printed 1909) needs to be read. Craig untiringly insisted that the Norman conquest marked a profound rupture in English society. 'So great was [William's] hatred of the English, that the Conqueror spoiled them of their arms and distributed their nobles' estates as booty among his Normans.' 'There is no manner of doubt that the law of real property which today obtains in England is not that which held in the days preceding the Norman Conquest.' 'It was . . . feudal law which the Conqueror imposed on England.' The purpose of all this was not so much to assert Scottish dignity and its unconquered antiquity against English aspersions. Nor was it simply to show the Norman dynasty (and its successors) to be illegitimate, while the Scottish line (and James VI) emerged the true heir to Edward the Confessor. Rather, Craig's central purpose was to subvert the English claim to a sui generis constitution and to recontextualize institutions of the southern realm: 'Our English neighbors are therefore far out in their reckoning in their belief that their legal system is indigenous and unlike those of other countries.'[34] Common feudal principles (organized about Roman law categories), common cultural assumptions, made a truly British partnership possible.

The English laws, seen as 'ancient' and yet only defined and made authoritative through the acts of a sovereign crown in parliament, undoubtedly promoted insularity and, at moments, a notoriously nasty xenophobia. But, however unpleasant English anti-Scottish senti-ment could be, it is crucial to recognize that its motivation was institutional and not ethnic, prompted by a concern for political integrity and not by racism. As Laurence Hyde indicated, the Scots (and presumably anyone) could become English simply by adopting English laws and liberties – an experience imagined as liberating rather than involving subjection. Attitudes that begin to sound like modern racism enter English discourse only occasionally at the margins and from the most resolute opponents of Anglo-Scottish union and of any British state: the English Catholics. Catholic writers like Richard Verstegan, as Christopher Highley has recently shown, went to great lengths in stressing the Saxon roots of Englishmen, thereby distinguishing them ethnically from altogether alien Scots and Britons. This unbridgeable ethnic chasm precluded a modern Britain, while simultaneously linking the people of England to the peoples of the continent.[35] Scotophobia at court or in the House of Commons thus differed qualitatively from the Scotophobia that motivated Guy Fawkes and his associates. The former derived from the Cromwellian Reformation, the latter derived from its rejection. The former arose from institutional preoccupations, the latter from racial preoccupations. Miles Mosse was undoubtedly right when he saw opposition to James's succession (and certainly to the union) as coming in large part from 'our mutinous and seditious Papists' who 'slandered his native realm of Scotland.'[36]

By the 1590s there had emerged a new English apocalyptic: reformist, British-oriented, philo-Semitic, and focused on the future rather than the institutional past. At about the same time there also emerged a Catholic counter-historiography: oriented toward the continent, emphatically ethnic and racial, resolutely anti-British and anti-apocalyptic, and eventually anti-Semitic. During the earlier seventeenth century the more apocalyptic an Englishman's outlook, the more likely he would find a British perspective to be congenial, the more likely he would have favorable attitudes toward the Scots, and the more likely he would find himself interested in contemporary Jewry, possibly to the point of seeking their readmission. Conversely, anti-apocalypticism and anglocatholicism encouraged a negative conflation of both Jews and Scots, and there may well turn out to be an conservative anti-Semitic tradition in England extending from this period to the era of T.S. Eliot and Evelyn Waugh.[37]

But most English people, and certainly the elites, found themselves drawn at this juncture neither to revolution nor race, neither to an imminent new world nor to ethnic self-discovery. The late twentieth century obsession with race no more provides insight into the intellectual life of early modern Englishmen than does contemporary nationalism or contemporary cynicism.

THE PRIMITIVE AND THE CIVILIZED

'. . . it is but even the other day since England grew civil.'

– Edmund Spenser (?)[38]

'We have met the enemy, and he is us.'

– Pogo[39]

If race was not the preoccupation of the early modern peoples of the Atlantic archipelago that it has since become, we will nevertheless find it variously visible on the margins of British and Irish political life. Thus the Celtic veneration of genealogy led to mythologies that proclaimed the ethnic superiority of the *Gael* over the lowland and foreign *Gall*. Precisely this identity with blood informed and heightened highland opposition to the Campbells and their policies of cultural assimilation with the racially inferior Lowlander.[40]

More portentous for the future was the racism philosophically constructed by the scholastic John Mair. A virulent anti-Semite, Mair defended the 1290 expulsion of the Jews from England and urged all contemporary princes to take similar action. Although Mair enjoys a extraordinary reputation today as an innovative and critical rationalist who either debunked or ignored popular myth, his *History* duly recounted tales of the medieval blood libel. This reputation for enlightenment is all the more remarkable, for he in fact served on the infamous commission at the University of Paris that in 1514 condemned Johannes Reuchlin and Jewish studies for Christians.[41] Mair undoubtedly applauded the contemporary expulsion of the Jews from the Iberian peninsula (1492–98), and, given these attitudes, he may well have endorsed the sixteenth century laws that increasingly restricted the New Christian converts because of their 'impure' and 'unclean' blood.

Mair supported still other Spanish projects, most notably its newly conquered empire in the Americas. The Americans, Mair insisted, were the natural slaves described in Aristotle's *Politics*, and thus their conquest and dispossession was both in accordance with nature and ultimately in their own interest. Inevitably defenders of the Spanish monarchy and its policies, like the royal confessor Juan Ginés de Sepúlveda, found aid in the renowned Scottish theologian. But Mair did not stop there. He went on to identify the Americans with the Highlanders. For Mair, the latter inhabited a semi-nomadic, tribal, and militarized society whose pastoralism only at times could be used by royal authority to contain its banditry. Mair's *History* inescapably pointed to a policy of dispossession similar to that adopted by the Spanish monarchy in the New World.[42]

We visibly encounter racism or proto-racism during this period in England, Scotland, and the Celtic world. Yet both traditional racism and philosophical racism held considerably more limited significance for British identities and the politics of this period than people with today's sensibility might expect. Mair seems to have exerted vastly less influence in Britain than in Iberia, and policies of 'extirpatioun' were never consistently pursued. More important, neither our own obsession with race nor even the sixteenth century Iberian obsession with blood finds anything approaching a full analogue within the British Isles.

The central matrix was not race but civility, learning, and political life – not the imposition of civilization on the racially inferior, but the creation of civilization itself within the putatively unpropitious northern latitude that all these peoples inhabited. Here was a concern well worthy of obsession: for to think of the north often enough was to move into the dark margins of the western imagination. Traditionally, from both biblical and classical sources, the north was pictured as quintessentially the place of the primitive, the bestial, the satanic. Imagining a civilization or the creation of a civilization, at once cultured, independent, and yet relevant to Europe exercised many of the best minds in Scotland, England, and Ireland from the late middle ages into the Enlightenment – at which point the edge of civilization shifted from the long-standing latitudinal north-south horizon to a longitudinal east-west frontier.[43]

Figures like George Buchanan, Thomas Craig, David Hume of Godscroft, John Milton, Edmund Spenser, and to some extent even Mair himself, found themselves reflecting on the problem of civilization with great seriousness and at moments with great urgency, if also great perplexity. At issue was no anticipation of the patronizing 'white man's burden,' nor cultural denigration cynically manipulated to legitimate conquest, but a universal transformation involving the home regions no less than the outlying ones – a transformation seen as liberating and empowering, and, at times, also as redeeming.[44] The Hapsburgs had no doubt what to do in Bohemia, never wavered in their commitment to global empire, and had precious little doubt about their undertaking in the Americas. In different circumstances they would have made quick work of Ireland – whose Celtic societies the Counter-Reformation in no way idealized. Much greater ambivalence existed in Britain both about empire and also about Ireland. That is why Catholicism survived there, while the rich Protestant cultures of central Europe were all but entirely extirpated.

True to its humanist roots, Calvinist 'discipline' entailed a transformation of self that its propagators imagined as enabling and even politicizing rather than as simply subjecting and coercive. It might not be too anachronistic to see the reforming agenda as seeking to turn peasants into Scotsmen – or perhaps simply the citizen. The sometime Edinburgh court minister Robert Bruce provides a 'conservative' example of this phenomenon. His famous sermons of the 1590s sought to supplant kin-ties, the traditions of Scottish 'kindness,' and the appeal of blood, with the more articulate ties founded on formal law. As Christ rejected the claims of blood amongst his disciples, so we too need to reject such ties within the Christian community. As we are not joined to Christ through His blood in the mass but through His spiritual presence, so we are not joined to one another through blood. Instead, we join each other in Christian fellowship through what Bruce notably called a 'spiritual glue.' The new community, more self-conscious and more self-created, possessed a civic and juridical character unimaginable within traditional Scotland. Bruce's words spoke every bit as compellingly to the court and the city of Edinburgh as they did to the Highlands and Borders.[45]

At the other end of the Calvinist spectrum stood George Buchanan. The most consistent theme throughout his long life and extensive writings was the creation of the classical citizen and civic life – realized through severely moralist values he saw as the antithesis of clerical power. Initially he had looked to royal authority as the instrument for restraining clerical pretensions and protecting public space. James V, Henry VIII, João III, Henry II, and at one brief point possibly even Charles V, all seemed potential candidates to implement such politico-moral reform. Buchanan never imagined these rulers as 'absolute' but as protectors who would leave the 'reins' loose: law at least ideally would be self-imposed. During the 1550s his view became increasingly anti-imperial: he bitterly criticized the new global empires established by the Iberian kingdoms and strenuously supported the Valois cause against Hapsburg pretensions to universal monarchy. He portrayed empire in almost all its senses as utterly incompatible with the civic ideal and thus with human purposes. Buchanan returned to Scotland following the 1559–60 revolution where his 'constitutional' ideal shifted from an increasingly civic conciliarism to something much more closely resembling the morally autonomous polis of antiquity. This new quasi-republicanism assumed its fullest articulation with Buchanan's 'Genethliacon,' a poem celebrating the birth of James VI in 1566, and then with his famous *De jure regni apud Scotos: dialogus* written on behalf of the Scottish revolution of the following year.[46]

Unlike Bruce, for Buchanan traditional Scottish society underwrote – or potentially underwrote – civic capacity. Scotland would be imagined as Livy's virtuous republic, ruled by abstemious aristocrats who, rising above private interests, were utterly committed to the pursuit of the public good – aristocrats precisely like those who led the Scottish revolutions. The point then was not to replace kin-ties but to revalue them. Traditional social structures would become politicized, as the ancient military virtue acquired (or rediscovered) its civic meaning, as Latin supplanted Gaelic, as patriotism supplanted barbarism.[47]

Bruce's objective was more narrowly juridical, Buchanan's more broadly political. But both sought civility and, each in his way, salvation, while neither man had his eye exclusively or perhaps even mainly on the remote 'rude partes' of the realm.

Calvinist conversion lay at the heart of Bruce's civilizing dynamic; something broadly like it featured in Buchanan's revaluation of 'ancient' Scottish tradition. Yet the result was in both instances social rather than theological, politicizing rather than spiritual. Nevertheless, Scots possessed still other, more secular matrices for imagining the sources of civility. Even the deeply anti-clerical Buchanan seems downright religious – and certainly more the moralist – when compared with a contemporary civilizing process that competed both with his vision and with Bruce's: trade and industry. Commerce, not conversion, exercised the government of Buchanan's sometime pupil, King James VI. The king was deeply hostile to the peoples of the Highlands and the Outer Isles and their 'barbarous and deteastable form of living.' At particularly angry moments they seemed nothing less than 'cannibals' – the ultimate mark of the barbaric. But he was emphatic that the problem of civility also concerned the Lowlands in ways that were at least broadly similar. In response the king at moments appealed to the authority law against kinship and friendship; at other moments he appealed to the civic ideal; at still different moments he entertained 'extirpatioun and plantatioun' in ways that would likely have met with Mair's approval (and that of the Hapsburgs as well). But in the end the royal government concluded decisively that the route to civilization lay through 'lawfull traffique and handling.' For the Outer Isles that mean fishing and, perhaps significantly, competition with that most commercial of societies, the Dutch republic. What it did not mean, or what became at most an afterthought, was religious conversion.[48]

The view developing at Edinburgh in the 1590s surfaced contemporaneously with altogether similar, if more articulated views emerging at London and Dublin – the latter growing out of an extraordinarily sophisticated proto-sociology. When seen outside the self-serving lenses of late twentieth century nationalism and today's taste for tales of delicious victimhood, the later Tudor and early Stewart Irish tracts emerge as amazingly insightful and unexpectedly humane.[49] The best known of these writings is *A View of the Present State of Ireland* (1596), normally attributed to the poet Edmund Spenser. The *View* evinces genuine sympathy for the native Irish, people portrayed as long exploited by the Anglo-Irish settlers who denied them access to English liberties. But the simple importation of the Common Law could not solve the problem. The author faced the far larger problem of the general barbarism of all the northern peoples, English as well as Irish. The recent memory of medieval

England made clear that civilization had been a long and complex process, and in some matters the adoption of Anglo-Saxon procedures rather than post-Conquest laws might intially make more sense and offer better hope. Even so, 'it is to be thought that the use of all England was, in the reign of Henry the Second when Ireland was first planted with English, very rude and barbarous.'[50]

Here was a problem that had exercised virtually every sixteenth century Scottish intellectual, and it is hardly surprising that the author made extensive use of the history written by that 'Irish Scot or Pict by nation,' George Buchanan.[51] Buchanan had claimed that a number of peoples had variously converged on the British Isles from what was or became Gaul – the Scots first coming to Ireland from northern Spain and thereafter populating northern Britain. The *View* adopted Buchanan's ethnography (though not his linguistic analysis) at least insofar as to suggest that part of the Irish population had Spanish origins. But the inhabitants of Ireland appeared to comprise an amalgam of a great many other northern peoples as well: Scyths from a generalized and primitive north, Britons from across the Irish Sea, and then 'rude' Englishmen as well. Even the Spaniards themselves were no other than a thorough mixture:

> ... though afterward they [the Moors and other Africans] were beaten out by Ferdinand of Aragon and ... his wife, yet they were not so cleansed, but that through the marriages which they made, and mixture with the people of the land during their long continuance there, they left no pure drop of Spanish blood; no, nor of Roman or Scythian; so that of all the nations under heaven I suppose the Spaniard is the most mingled, most uncertain and most bastardly.[52]

These remarks in no way seek to denigrate a mongrelized Irish population, and thereby, presumably, legitimate English conquest. Utterly the reverse. The author clearly is *attacking* racism, and specifically the Iberian obsession with 'pure' and 'clean' blood (pureza de sangre, limpiezas de sangre). His analysis subverts the governing ideology of the monarchy with which England was locked in the most dangerous post-medieval war prior to our own century. It was the singular providence of God, the author insisted, 'to mingle nations so remote, so miraculously, to make as it were one kindred and blood of all people, and each to have knowledge of him.'[53] We are a long, long way indeed from John Mair and the Spanish conquistadors.

Civilization in Ireland required strengthening the peasant against the power of the magnate by creating secure tenures and eliminating traditional exactions like coign and livery. This reformation of

Ireland's economic base would undermine tribal authority while at the same time creating modern agriculture. From the improved agriculture and its new surpluses would emerge exchange, the growth of trades, respect for labor, new towns, expanding commerce. Urban life was the key, the ultimate aim, and the *View* looked to the 'example' of 'those free boroughs in the low Countries, which are now all the strength thereof.'[54] Spenser, if he is its author, and then Sir John Davies proposed for Gaelic Ireland precisely what Mair had thought culturally and racially impossible for Gaelic Scotland.

The reformation of Ireland's political economy would not involve a reformation of religion, or at least not right away. The author of the *View* clearly believed the papacy to be the prophesied Antichrist, but he twice specifically states that he has little to say of religion.[55] Building bridges seems to be more immediately important than preaching the Gospel. If he scolded the reformed ministers for lacking the zeal of their opponents, he nevertheless accepted that 'instruction in religion needeth quiet times, and ere we seek to settle a sound religion in the clergy, we must purchase peace unto the laity.' Besides, Ireland was a dangerous place right now (it is hard to think what a Franciscan or Jesuit in the New World would have made of this). When religion eventually did come to Ireland it would come through parliament.[56] The author *apparently* felt that free men would choose a religion of freedom. Commerce was crucial, conversion little more than a side effect.

Boece, Bellenden, and Buchanan had all undertaken to transform aristocratic martial virtue into civic virtue – not altogether unlike what happened with the rise of the antique polis itself, from which such ideas first originated. All of these writers, and outstandingly Buchanan, held nothing but contempt for commerce, again in common with the classical world. King James rejected his tutor's views in a great many ways: not least his notion of what it meant to be virtuous and 'manly.' In the process the king's governments were also rejecting the Iberian world, both its proselytizing religion and its fervent racism. Sir William Alexander eventually redirected his objectives away from the Melvillian-style crusade associated with Prince Henry and from its militarism ('that violent kind of vanity') toward peaceable commercial empire. Further, this perspective on a future at once commercialized and civilized was genuinely British. It would underwrite the anglophone empire. And it also ensured the survival of Catholicism.

DUTCH REPUBLIC, IRISH 'KINGDOM': POLITICAL AUTONOMY AND THE CHRISTIAN BODY

'. . . What ish my nation?'

– Captain Macmorris[57]

In 1558 John Knox insisted that the Lord 'hath not created the earth to satisfy the ambition of two or three tyrants, but for the universal seed of Adam; and hath appointed and defined the bounds of their habitation to diverse nations, assigning diverse countries.'[58] These brave words nevertheless appeared in a tract intended to promote Anglo-Scottish union and thus the creation of an empire in at least its traditional meaning of a composite monarchy. But Knox hoped for still more, a British state that would inspire reformation and sincere religion. In that way Britain might provide leadership and thereby 'headship' for all Europe.

In fact political independence in a full and final sense proved surprisingly difficult for northern Europeans to imagine during the sixteenth and early seventeenth centuries. Despite courageous proclamations of imperial and historical autonomy, despite 'closed' imperial crowns on heads and on steeples, despite the shattering effects of confessional conflict, the idea of 'the common corps of Christendom' proved surprisingly resilient.[59] Universal empire long would have its eccentric apologists: Italy's Tommaso Campanella, England's John Dee, France's Guillaume de Postel and Isaac La Peyrere, Sweden's Johannes Bureus, Scotland's James Maxwell. But their eccentricities deflect us from core attitudes that were remarkably widespread. Universal empire offered considerable plausibility in the mid-sixteenth century and long attracted far more mainstream figures. Even those who stoutly resisted both the idea and its Hapsburg manifestation still wanted to think in terms of the Christian body. The views on the subject of James VI and I and of Francis Bacon, as well as of the Valois and Bourbon kings, are well known.[60]

In a world that instinctively looked to 'headship' and hierarchy on the one hand and to kin and dynastic ties on the other, the morally and politically independent republic posed a particularly acute mental challenge. In 1575 the Dutch revolutionaries offered sovereignty in the lowlands to Queen Elizabeth, an idea that possessed continuing appeal nearly a century later. Up till the last moment Catalonia's Pau Claris continued negotiations with Madrid, hoping (apparently sincerely) that Olivares might yet see the error of his ways, while simultaneously working out an arrangement with Richelieu. The

Catalan republic itself lasted a grand total of one week, with a primary purpose of administrative transfer.[61]

Yet the Renaissance and then the Reformation had powerfully encouraged Ciceronian civic values, even if they were far more difficult to translate into the politics of the northern monarchies than they had been in the city states of classical antiquity or the quattrocento. Such values had deeply entered Scottish discourse with the writings of Boece, Bellenden, and Buchanan. They became much more immediately plausible with the Scottish revolutions of the 1560s. Margaret Sanderson recently noted of the Lords of the Congregation: 'the wonder is that they acted together at all.' Similarly the decision of some 2500 Ayrshiremen in 1559 not simply to protect their local churches, but to march off and join the Congregation – and together challenge a professional French army for which they were patently no match – is enormously telling of their sense of common purpose and public good. The distance to the national capital elsewhere in Europe was often much further than from Ayrshire, but mentally it proved far further still.[62] Precisely this national horizon and shared undertaking promoted (and was promoted by) Buchanan's vision of the Scottish *respublica*. In this polity of self-ruled citizens, where law was its own authority and external coercion unnecessary, the king needed only to be an exemplar, the archetypal citizen.

> The descendants of Romulus saw Numa offering sacrifice,
>> fostering peace and tranquility,
> The palms of the Euphrates saw mighty Solomon.
> Neither the deadly sword nor the snorting warhorse
> strengthened their kingdoms,
> Nor did the doubled-edged axe, nor the legions in densely packed columns,
> But the love of piety and virtue injurious to no one,
> And majesty supported by the power of unarmed law.

The virtuous Scottish republic fulfilled human purpose and provided the direct antitype to the grotesque, distended Iberian empires – just as the classical republic had been to imperial Rome.

> But the conqueror who made his way to the riches of India,
>> The Macedonian general [i.e., Alexander], and those kings
> Whose arrogant imperium prevailed in Ausonia [i.e., Caesar, Augustus, etc.],
>> They died by the sword, they died by poison, and
> their blood paid for the blood they had shed.

* * * *

And if he could truly be king of himself and king of his own people,
He would think his kingdom more extensive by far than it would be
If it stretched from the Indies to the shores of Hesperia [i.e., Iberia].[63]

If Buchanan's republicanism became attenuated through the politics of the later sixteenth century and the less qualified royalism of his successors Melville and Hume, Calvinist *civisme* remained a powerful current within Scottish political life.

From this perspective the contrast between covenanted Scotland in the years after 1638 and the various Irelands during the period of the Confederation in the years after 1641 is striking and profound. The Covenant formulated the purposes of a single, coherent Scottish realm. The Confederation occurred between different nations or perhaps different tribes. Similarly, the Solemn League and Covenant between Scotland and England of 1643 was intended as a species of sacralized confederation. The Irish Confederation suffered from utterly divided leadership for perfectly good reasons, reasons that distinguish it decisively from Scotland or even Catalonia. There was not a fractured elite, but fractured peoples, not conflicting policies but conflicting nations. Some time after the demise of the Confederacy an exasperated contemporary noted the seemingly irreconcilable gulf that had existed between the Old English Catholics and the Gaelic Catholics: 'Are not five hundred years powerful enough to make one people of the English and the Irish?'[64] The fissures reach in many directions. In what sense can we call the earl of Antrim 'Irish,' whose central purpose was the restoration of a vast north channel principality?

It is certainly true that the Confederates imitated features of emergent Scottish and English political organization. It is also certainly true that early modern elites often faced broadly similar challenges and parallel difficulties. But in the end functional comparisons of composite monarchies and their problems will prove only somewhat more useful than nationalist *Leidensgeschichte*. Protestantism and Catholicism provided their constituencies with quite different tools by which to make their options and aspirations articulate. More than merely political differences separate Confederation from Covenant. The former, however dramatically sworn, has none of the *spiritual* significance of the latter. Reformation biblicism and humanism provided a richer range of vocabulary for autonomy than did Counter-Reformed neo-scholasticism with its preoccupation with integration and classification.

It is therefore grossly misleading to portray the Confederation as a power, even a third rank power, within a European state system.[65]

Neither the Confederates nor their various backers thought in terms of autonomy. Overwhelmingly, they all were deeply uncomfortable with any such an idea. The mental world of the Confederates was heavily keyed to suzerainty and hierarchy; that world made independence particularly difficult to imagine. A rising in itself does not make a republic, and the Confederates look rather more like a British Vendée than proto-Eire.

Unlike the Scottish Highlands, feudal law was altogether alien to the more tribal world of Celtic Ireland. Resistance to the incursion of central government in Ireland came to assume a religious character, quite unlike the political and dynastic preoccupation it adopted in the Highlands.[66] Yet it was precisely Henry VIII's creation of the Irish 'kingdom' that tended to stimulate pan-island identity[67] – as opposed to *Gaedhil* ethnic solidarity or channel states. Of course the new 'constitution' led back to the Stewarts and to Whitehall, and it becomes hard to avoid the conclusion that Ireland was an English invention, unimaginable outside of a British context. Nevertheless, in the end, despite the 'Irish crown,' there would remain multiple Irelands within a highly conflicted frontier region. Here was a situation that contrasted radically with circumstances across the Irish Sea. Precisely for this reason, Scottish and Welsh nationalism have proven anemic in the modern period and even today, while English and British nationalism have been virtually non-existent. Precisely for this reason, Irish politics eventually came to follow the pattern of continental nationalism.[68]

From the waning of French influence in the 1550s to the collapse of the Stewart monarchy nearly a century later, it became almost impossible to visualize Scotland, England, and Ireland (or any of their regions) outside of a British context. Dynastic loyalties, the protection of local privileges, the upholding of tradition, all increasingly ran to a London-based, multiple British monarchy. Religious and political reform also looked to Britain, if one differently and also variously conceived. Civilization itself seemed to require Britain. Along the margins we can detect something more, elements of a genuinely – that is, interactive – British culture: a Protestant Gaeldom, a shared apocalyptic spirituality, a burgeoning commercial empire whose assumptions were truly British in origin, parallel notions of liberty visualized as English-style freedoms. Even patriotism itself not only could coexist with a British vision, but actually reinforce it.

The most coherent and highly wrought dissent came from the left rather than the right, not from Catholic resistance to a Protestant dynasty, nor Irish resistance to a centralizing regime. The present day quest for nascent Irish nationality during this period is as desperate as it is futile. Altogether against our expectations, it is with George Buchanan rather than the Irish magnates and their publicists that we hear the true voice of autonomy. Buchanan emerges as a genuine little Scotlander, as well as a quasi-republican well ahead of the Dutch, and all this despite being in no sense a nationalist. Still, even he seems to have imagined some sort of Achaean league with England.[69] As events turned out, the upheavals of 1559–60 and 1567–73 required much heavier English intervention in Scottish affairs than Buchanan's vision could have comfortably allowed. But things went much further. Scottish politics and dynastic aspirations generated a crusade for Britain (and, in addition, for some, a British crusade) and created considerable pressure for 'conformity with England' – if also, though more hesitantly, 'conformity with Scotland.'

In the end the 'matter of Britain' became an imperative that neither the most imaginative radicalism nor the most blinkered conservatism ultimately could defeat.

CONCLUSION

A contemporary writer has recently observed that the account of the civilizing process in the Tudor-Stewart Irish tracts differs in utterly unexpected ways from that proposed such twentieth century theorists as Max Weber, Mikhail Bakhtin, and Michel Foucault. For today's most fashionable thinking on 'modernization' turns out to be at once more cynical and more nostalgic.[70] That observation about the Irish tracts can be extended to nearly all early modern British reflection about civilization and its meanings. Not only do racism, authoritarianism, and even militarism far more characterize the marginalized than the marginalizers. Not only did the prevailing forces experience grave self-doubt, develop intellectual structures that most modern people regard as attractive (often out of archaic vocabularies like the apocalypse), and ultimately lay the foundations of social science. The very categories of marginal-dominant themselves eventually tend to breakdown. We find far less cynical denigration than concern for effective comprehension, less focus on some putative 'other' than preoccupation with problems regarded as universal.

The world of Rudyard Kipling, Éamon De Valéra, and Eion O'Duffy does not find direct roots in the early modern period. Only in a context of nationalist revival and authoritarian religious revanche might it seem otherwise.

Notes to Chapter 6

1   C.S. Terry (ed. and trans.), *De unione . . .* (Edinburgh, 1909), p 468; '. . . et nova totius Britanniæ Historia servata veritate publicetur' (p 200).

2   'Britannorum inclyta mater': all references in this paragraph and the next are to the two poems, 'Ad Elizabetham Angliæ Reginam ægrotantuem 1603.8.calend. Aprilis' and 'Anno 1603 calend. April. Votum pro Iacobo Sexto Britanniarum Rege,' in *Viri clarisimi A. Melvini musæ et P. Admosoni vita et palinodia . . .* (np, 1620), p 12. Melville emphasized Elizabeth's British character by describing her as 'queen of the waves' (undaram regina), a phrase visibly anticipating the eighteenth century anthem.

3   See P.J. McGinnis and A.H. Williamson (eds.), *George Buchanan The Political Poetry* (Edinburgh, 1997), 'Introduction: Poetry and Politics,' and Appendix C (forthcoming).

4   David Hume, *History of the Douglases,* (Edinburgh, 1643), p 278 (second part); 'To the Reader'; A.H. Williamson, 'A Patriot Nobility? Calvinism, Kin-Ties, and Civic Humanism,' in *Scottish Historical Review* 72 (1993), pp 1–21; A.H. Williamson, *Scottish National Consciousness in the Age of James VI* (Edinburgh, 1979), chapter IV; David Calderwood, *Historie of the Kirk of Scotland,* ed. by Thomas Thomson (Edinburgh, 1842–49), vol VI, p 730. In the immediate wake of the 1603 union Hume did adopt what seems to be, for him, an uncharacteristically imperialist view. See note 19.

5   David Hume of Godscroft, *Poemata omnia . . .,* ed. by James Hume of Godscroft (Paris, 1639), 'Lusus poetici,' pp 58–59 (separately paginated). Regarding the alleged etymology of 'Scot,' see A.H. Williamson, 'The Jewish Dimension of the Scottish Apocalypse: Climate, Covenant, and World Renewal,' in Y. Kaplan et al. (eds.), *Menasseh Ben Israel and his World* (Leiden, 1989), p 30, n59, and *passim.*

6   C. Russell, *The Crisis of Parliaments: English History 1509–1660* (New York, 1972), p 209.

7   And thus uniquely modern. See for example David Cressy, 'The Protestant Calendar and the Vocabulary of Celebration in Early Modern England,' in *The Journal of British Studies* 29 (1990), pp 31–52, and Cressy, *Bonfires and Bells: National Memory and the Protestant Calendar in Elizabethan and Stuart England* (London, 1989). Sacred time became English time during the Elizabethan period in ways unparalleled elsewhere till the age of the democratic revolutions.

8   See A.H. Williamson, *Images of Blood: Ethnic Identity and the Destruction of the Left in Europe and America, 1972–1992* (Sacramento, 1995).

9   See J.S. Morrill, 'The British Problem, c.1534–1707,' in Brendan Bradshaw and John Morrill (eds.), *The British Problem, c. 1534–1707: State Formation in the Atlantic Archipelago* (London, 1996), p 36.

10   Craig, *De unione* . . ., pp 25 (240), 41 (262). Anthony Pagden has considered the idea within a somewhat different context in his *Lords of All the World: Ideologies of Empire in Spain, Britain and France, c. 1500–c. 1800* (New Haven, 1995), pp 29–31.

11   Richard Tuck, *Natural Rights Theories: Their Origin and Development* (Cambridge, 1979). p 32ff.

12   See McGinnis and Williamson, *George Buchanan The Political Poetry*, 'Introduction.'

13   *De unione insulæ Britanniæ. Tractatus I* (London, 1605), p 17. 'Da mater veniam Scotia, te testor; & intimorum sensuum scrutatorum illum: non tu cuiquam charior; aut dulcius hoc nomen. Sed quid agam? rapit ad se utlitas publica, te puto non invitâ; rapit comunis maater, cui nec te obniti fas est. et puto cladium te jam tædet, & sic disrumpi communia viscera.'

14   Hector Boece, *The History and Chronicles of Scotland*, trans. by John Bellenden (reprint; Edinburgh, 1821), p xxiv.

15   J.A.H. Murray (ed.), *The Complaynt of Scotlande* . . . (London, 1872), p 239.

16   John Ireland, *The Meroure of Wyssdome, composed for the use of James IV, King of Scots, AD 1490*, ed. C. Macpherson (Edinburgh and London, 1926), vol I, pp 72–74; William Dunbar, 'Lucina schynnyng in silence like the night,' in James Kinsley (ed.), *Wiliam Dunbar Poems*, (Oxford, 1958), p 49 (line 29). Cf. Richard K. Emmerson, *Antichrist in the Middle Ages* (Seattle, 1981), esp. pp 3–20, 206–221.

17   Calderwood, *Historie*, vol I, p 136; Williamson, *Scottish National Consciousness*, chapter I. Probably the earliest Scots to speak of Antichrist in the institutional rather than the medieval sense were the Lollards of Kyle during the early 1490s. See John Knox, *History of the Reformation in Scotland*, ed. W.C. Dickinson (Edinburgh, 1949), vol. I, p 9.

18   A detailed discussion of the history of Somerset's 'Epistle' appears in Williamson, *Scottish National Consciousness*, pp 151–52, n44. For the British-orientation of the Knox's *First Blast*, see *Scottish National Consciousness*, pp 9–13; Williamson, 'Union with England Traditional, Union with England Radical: Sir James Hope and the Mid Seventeenth-Century British State,' in *English Historical Review* 110 (1995) p 305; R.A. Mason, 'Usable Pasts: History and Identity in Reformation Scotland,' in *Scottish Historical Review* 76 (1997), pp 63, 67–68.

19   See A.H. Williamson, 'Scotland, Antichrist, and the Invention of Great Britain,' in J. Dwyer et al. (eds.), *New Perspectives on the Politics and Culture of Early Modern Scotland* (Edinburgh, 1982), pp 34–58; Williamson, 'Jewish Dimension of the Scottish Apocalypse.'

20   John Russell, 'A treatise of the happie and blissed Unioun,' in B.R. Galloway and B.P. Levack (eds.), *The Jacobean Union: Six Tracts of 1604* (Edinburgh, 1985), pp 79–80.

21 'Daphn-Amaryllis,' pp 10, 11, 15; cf. Melville's poem to Prince Henry,'Principis Scoti-Britannorum natalia' (Edinburgh, 1594). Yet in contrast to Melville's poetry, these comments appear a momentary flicker, the product of excitement surrounding 1603, and nothing like it surfaces in Hume's other work, not even in his discussion of the 'pseudo-episcopacy' of the hierarchical church. Godscroft is treated in Williamson, 'A Patriot Nobility?.'

22 Note for example the views expressed by the people of Dumfries to James on his visit in 1617, in J. Adamson (ed.), Τά τῶν μοσῶν ἔξοδια, *The Muses Welcome* (Edinburgh, 1618), 288.

23 See J.S. Morrill's essays listed in the bibliographical essay below.

24 Williamson, 'Union with England Traditional, Union with England Radical.'

25 See A. Grant, 'Scotland's "Celtic Fringe" in the Late Middle Ages: The Macdonald Lords of the Isles and the Kingdom of Scotland,' in R.R. Davies (ed.), *The British Isles, 1100–1500* (Edinburgh, 1988), pp 118–41; Grant, *Independence and Nationhood: Scotland 1306–1469* (London, 1984), pp 200–15.

26 A.I. Macinnes, *Clanship, Commerce, and the House of Stewart, 1603–1788* (East Linton, 1996), pp 60, 69–70, 74–75; John Bannerman, 'Literacy in the Highlands,' in I.B. Cowan and Duncan Shaw (eds.), *The Renaissance and Reformation in Scotland* (Edinburgh, 1983), pp 229–30; A.H. Williamson, 'From the Invention of Great Britain to the Creation of British History: A New Historiography,' in *Journal of British Studies* 29 (1990), pp 267–76.

27 J.H. Ohlmeyer, *Civil War and Restoration in the Three Stuart Kingdoms: The Career of Randal MacDonnell, Marquis of Antrim, 1609–1683* (Cambridge, 1993); E.J. Cowan, *Montrose for Covenant and King* (London, 1977).

28 See the essays of Jane Dawson cited in the bibliography below and David Armitage, 'Colonial Theory in a Provincial Society: Scotland before 1707,' (forthcoming). My thanks to Professor Armitage for sharing the essay with me in advance of publication.

29 Williamson, *Scottish National Consciousness*, pp 80–82.

30 R. Pitcairn (ed.), *Autobiography and Diary of Mr James Melville* (Edinburgh, 1842), pp 665, 666.

31 Sir John Fortescue, *De laudibus legum Anglie* (In Praise of the Laws of England), ed. and trans. by S.B. Chrimes (Cambridge, 1949), pp 38–41.

32 Willet, *Ecclesia Triumphans* (Cambridge, 1603), sig. 7ᵛ, cited and discussed in B.P. Levack, *The Formation of the British State: England, Scotland, and the Union, 1603–1707* (Oxford, 1987), p 107; cf. Willet, *De universali et novissima Iudaeorum vocatione . . .* (Cambridge, 1590).

33 Cited by C. Russell, 'Composite Monarchies in Early Modern Europe:

The British and Irish Example,' in A. Grant and K.J. Stringer (eds.), *Uniting the Kingdom? The Making of British History* (London, 1995), p 145.

34 Craig, *De unione*, pp 223–24, 242, 309, 311, and *passim*.

35 Highley, 'Antiquarians, Catholics, and Anglo-Scottish Union.' My thanks to Professor Highley for sharing his paper with me prior to publication.

36 Mosse, *Scotland's Welcome* (London, 1603), pp 78–79; cf. Levack, *The Formation of the British State*, p 107.

37 See A.H. Williamson, '"A Pil for Pork-Eaters": Ethnic Identity, Apocalyptic Promise, and the Strange Creation of the Judeo-Scots,' in R.B. Waddington and A.H. Williamson (eds.), *The Expulsion of the Jews: 1492 and After* (New York, 1994), pp 237–58; Williamson, 'Latter-day Judah, Latter-Israel: the Millennium, the Jews, and the British Future,' in *Chiliasmus in Deutschland und England im 17. Jahrhundert* (Göttingen, 1988), pp 149–65.

38 *A View of the Present State of Ireland*, ed. W.L. Renwick (Oxford, 1970), p 67; J.R. Brink and C.G. Canino question whether Spenser is in fact the author of this extraordinary tract. See Brink 'Constructing the *View of the Present State of Ireland*,' in *Spenser Studies: A Renaissance Poetry Annual* 11 (1994), pp 203–27; Canino, 'Reconstructing Lord Grey's Reputation: A New View of the *View*,' in *The Sixteenth Century Journal* 29 (1998), pp 1–18.

39 Walt Kelly, *Pogo: 'We have met the enemy, and he is us.'* (New York, 1972), p 11.

40 Macinnes, *Clanship*, pp 3, 99.

41 Williamson, 'George Buchanan, Civic Virtue, and Commerce: European Imperialism and its 16th-Century Critics,' in *Scottish Historical Review* 75 (1996), pp 19–36; B.P. Copenhaver and C.B. Schmitt, *Renaissance Philosophy* (Oxford, 1992), p 97.

42 Williamson, 'Scots, Indians, and Empire.'

43 Williamson, 'Scots, Indians, and Empire'; Larry Wolff, *Inventing Eastern Europe: The Map of Civilization in the Mind of the Enlightenment* (Stanford, 1994), esp. pp 4–5, 91, 141, 157, 190–91, 204, 318; cf. D. Shuger, 'Irishmen, Aristocrats, and other White Barbarians,' in *Renaissance Quarterly* 50 (1997), pp 494–525.

44 Cf. D. Hirst, 'The English Republic and the Meaning of Britain,' in *Journal of Modern History* 66 (1994), p 462. Concerning 'denigration' and 'conquest,' a vast, largely Irish historiography has arisen since the 1970s with the new nationalism. Particularly characteristic of it are: John Gillingham, 'Images of Ireland, 1170–1600: The Origins of English Imperialism,' *History Today*, 37 (1987), pp 16–22; N.P. Canny, *Kingdom or Colony: A Pattern Established, 1565–76* (New York, 1976), esp. ch. 6. For the intellectual context from which this literature derives, see Williamson, 'Images of Blood.'

45 Williamson, *Scottish National Consciousness*, pp 69–72.

46 See McGinnis and Williamson, *George Buchanan The Political Poetry*, Introduction. Also Williamson, 'Unnatural Empire: George Buchanan, Anti-Imperialism, and the Sixteenth-Century Syphilis Pandemic,' in J.E. Force and D.S. Katz (eds.), *Everything Connects: In Conference with Richard Popkin* (forthcoming).

47 Williamson, 'Scots, Indians, and Empire'; Williamson, *Scottish National Consciousness*, chs. 5 and 6.

48 Williamson, 'George Buchanan, Civic Virtue, and Commerce,' esp. pp 32–37; Williamson, 'Scots, Indians, and Empire,' esp. pp. 61–66.

49 For more serious and less lachrymose discussions of the Irish tracts, see the following. On John Davies' *A Discoverie of the True Causes why Ireland was never entirely Subdued* (1612), see J.G.A. Pocock, *The Ancient Constitution and the Feudal Law* (Cambridge, 1957), pp 59–64. Pocock observes that *A Discoverie* is 'perhaps the most outstanding piece of historical writing achieved by an Englishman in James I's reign' and a book that 'may still be read with profit.' On Richard Beacon, *Solon His Follie: Or a Politique Discourse, Touching the Reformation of commonweales conquered, declined or corrupted* (1594) see Markku Peltonen, *Classical Humanism and Republicanism in English Political Thought, 1570–1640* (Cambridge, 1995), pp 73–102; a comprehensive discussion of these along with *A View of the Present State of Ireland* (1596), Fynes Moryson's 'Itinerary' (1617), and William Herbert's *Croftus sive de Hibernia liber* (*c.* 1591) appears in D. Shuger, 'White Barbarians.'

50 *A View of the Present State of Ireland*, ed. W.L. Renwick (Oxford, 1970), pp 67, 143–44, also 5, 10, 13, 24, 36, 81, 147, 149, 151. This theme is examined in greater detail by Shuger, 'White Barbarians,' pp 504–7.

51 *View*, p 40, cf. pp 38, 45, 54, 57, 59. The author intimates, without quite saying, that Buchanan was a native Gaelic speaker. Of all historians Buchanan received 'most credit,' although the author clearly missed the significance of his analysis of language.

52 *View*, p 44. British writers frequently twitted Spaniards for their preoccupation with blood and race. See Buchanan's 'Ad Henricum II Franciæ Regem . . .' and Melville's 'Gathelus,' in McGinnis and Williamson, *George Buchanan The Political Poetry*, 15/2 and Appendix C4; Knox's *First Blast of the Trumpet against the Monstrous Regiment of Women*, reprinted in R.A. Mason (ed.), *Knox on Rebellion* (Cambridge, 1994), p 40.

53 *View*, pp 44–45; see A.H. Williamson, 'The Cultural Foundations of Racial Religion and Anti-Semitism,' in A. Maidenbaum et al. (eds.), *Lingering Shadows: Jungians, Freudians, and Anti-Semitism* (Boston, 1991), esp. pp 137–39.

54 *View*, pp 81–83, 128, 132, 139, 142, 145, 167. Cf. Shuger, 'White Barbarians,' esp. pp 508–10, 514.

55 *View*, pp 85, 84, 161.

56 *View*, pp 164, 162, 86, 143.

57 William Shakespeare, *The Life of King Henry V*, III.ii.121.

58 *The First Blast of the Trumpet*, in Mason, *Knox on Rebellion*, p 41.

59 See Dale Hoak, 'The Iconography of the Crown Imperial,' in Dale Hoak (ed.), *Tudor Political Culture* (Cambridge, 1995), pp 54–103; R.A. Mason, '*Regnum et Imperium*: Humanism and the Political Culture of Early Renaissance Scotland,' in Mason, *Kingship and the Commonweal: Political Thought in Renaissance and Reformation Scotland* (East Linton, 1998), pp 104–38.

60 F.L. Baumer, 'England, the Turk, and the Common Corps of Christendom,' in *American Historical Review* 50 (1944–45), pp 26–48; James VI, *The Lepanto* (Edinburgh, 1591); reprinted in J. Craigie (ed.), *Poems of James VI* (Edinburgh, 1955), vol. I, pp 198–269.

61 G. Parker, *The Dutch Revolt* (Ithaca, 1977), p 146; J.H. Elliott, *The Revolt of the Catalans* (Cambridge, 1963), esp. pp 470–73, 505–6, 521–22.

62 *Ayrshire and the Reformation: People and Change, 1490–1600* (East Linton, 1997), pp 143, 99.

63 Buchanan, 'Genethliacon,' in McGinnis and Williamson, *George Buchanan The Political Poetry*.

64 Cited by Jane Ohlmeyer, 'Introduction: A Failed Revolution?,' in Jane Ohlmeyer (ed.), *Ireland from Independence to Occupation, 1641–1660* (Cambridge, 1995), pp 14, 20. This essay dissents utterly from Ohlmeyer's nationalist thesis.

65 Cf. Jane Ohlmeyer, 'Ireland Independent: Confederate Foreign Policy and International Relations during the Mid-Seventeenth Century,' in Ohlmeyer (ed.), *Ireland from Independence to Occupation*, pp 89–111, esp. 93.

66 Macinnes, *Clanship*, pp 6–7, 58–59.

67 Cf. Brendan Bradshaw, *The Irish Revolution of the Sixteenth Century* (Cambridge, 1979).

68 It is significant that Ireland is the only English-speaking society in the 1930s where fascism attracted a large-scale following, the only such society to aid materially the Nationalists against the Spanish republic.

69 See, for example, the closing lines of his 'D. Gualtero Haddono Magistro libellorum supplicum Serenissimæ Angliæ Reginæ,' in McGinnis and Williamson, *George Buchanan The Political Poetry*.

70 Shugar, 'White Barbarians,' p 510.

CHAPTER 7

Is a British Socio-Economic History Possible?

Ian Whyte

Most of the recent outburst of writing on British history has been political in focus. Much less attention has been given to social and economic issues within a British context.[1] Early-modern English economic and social history can – and often has – been written with only a handful of references to Wales, Scotland and Ireland,[2] a legacy perhaps of the Whig interpretation of English history.[3] The biases of anglocentric history linger on in deceptively 'neutral' themes such as demographic change, industrialization, urbanization and the transformation of social structures[4] with approaches which emphasise English uniqueness and 'individualism'.[5] Even 'British' economic histories of the eighteenth century and after are often heavily anglocentric.[6]

In relation to English history, for instance, it has been commented that the Scots only appear as nuisances, villains or curiosities;[7] as Border raiders in the sixteenth century, fanatical Covenanters in the seventeenth and rebel Jacobites in the eighteenth. Much the same could be said for the Irish and even, to a degree, the Welsh. Reviewing English perspectives on the social and economic history of early-modern Scotland, Wrightson has written 'If these "kindred adjoining kingdoms" have experienced a complex social, political and cultural interrelationship throughout most of their recorded histories – an involvement which became closer in the course of the early-modern period – it is one which has attracted surprisingly little disciplined historical analysis outside the political and diplomatic spheres'[8] This applies with as much justification to Ireland and Wales. In terms of economic history Wales tends to disappear after the early sixteenth century union until it reemerges as a source of coal and iron during the Industrial

Revolution. Ireland and Scotland are seen mainly as sources of raw materials, livestock and poor migrants.

Yet the view from outside England is a rather different one. Cullen has pointed out that the dominant theme in Irish history is Anglo-Irish relations.[9] The same can be said for seventeenth century Scotland. It is important in this context to appreciate that the author's standpoint is that of an historical geographer who has worked mainly on aspects of the society and economy of early-modern Scotland. Hence the focus of this chapter is on Scotland with comparisons drawn from Ireland and Wales. Although Scottish historical studies have sometimes in the past been as parochial as those of England,[10] seeking to distance themselves from their southern neighbour by emphasising features which were distinctive and unique rather than drawing meaningful parallels and contrasts, no historian writing today could seriously consider discussing the economic history of Ireland, Scotland or Wales in the seventeenth century without taking into account the influence of England.[11] Nevertheless, wide-ranging, comparative studies of economic development within the British Isles before the later eighteenth century have been rare, although there have been important developments in the study of Irish and Scottish economic history.[12] Progress in adopting broader perspectives on the social history of this period has been even more limited.

The political context forms an important framework for British economic and social development in the seventeenth century. It was during this period especially that the various regional and national economies within the British Isles began to converge and integrate. The differing nature of the political relationships between England, on one hand, and Wales, Ireland and Scotland, as well as linkages within the 'Celtic fringe', influenced the ways in which economies and societies within the four nations developed. Equally, economic issues and social differences precipitated political changes, notably in the case of the Anglo-Scottish union of 1707.[13] The later Middle Ages was a period of divergence within the British Isles in social and economic as well as political terms.[14] The early-modern period emphasised increasing convergence although the process was not an inevitable one. The story was not just one of the coming together of the economies and societies of the four kingdoms into a single unit, dominated by the interests of lowland England.[15] It also involved divergence and deepening regional variation.[16] For example, contrasts between Highland and Lowland society in Scotland were probably at their sharpest during the seventeenth century.[17] At this period the Highland line was one of the most impenetrable barriers to population movement within Britain and in economic terms the Highlands did not supply the Lowlands with much more than harvest labour and lean cattle.[18] Thus it is important to emphasise the scale of economic and social differences within Scotland (Highland/ Lowland), Ireland (north/south) and Wales (north/south). The story of growing economic integration within Britain during the seventeenth century is partly one of increasing interaction between regions within each of the four nations.

In considering a case for the need to adopt a British dimension to the study of seventeenth-century socio-economic history it is useful to review the nature of the economic links between the four nations, focusing especially on those with England, so as to highlight the broad similarities as well as identifying reasons for differences in detail. Themes in social and cultural development will then be examined.

ECONOMIC TRENDS

The economic history of Britain in the seventeenth century can be considered within various spatial frameworks. At its simplest, one can consider Britain in terms of a core-periphery model driven by an arable-oriented, more industrialised, wealthier southern and eastern England, centred on the rapidly-growing metropolis of London with its concentration of trade, its role as a major food market, and its attraction for migrants.[19] From late medieval times outlying areas of England, as well as Wales, Scotland and Ireland, became increasingly linked to this core region as suppliers of livestock, pastoral products, raw materials and low-grade manufactures like coarse woollen and linen cloth.[20] Such areas were characterised by more difficult environments with poorer soils, more rugged terrain and harsher climates. They were less suited to arable farming, and had an emphasis on pastoralism. They had lower population densities, less commercialised farming systems and limited urbanization. A more refined version of this approach is Wallerstein's modern world-system with its division into core states, semi-peripheral and peripheral areas.[21] In this context South Wales, central Scotland and south east Ireland could be classed as semi-peripheral. In another sense there were four expanding core areas in late-medieval Britain: southern England, Lowland Scotland, the Englishries of Wales, and south eastern Ireland.[22] In the early seventeenth century expansion by each was incomplete, as was the spread of control over the rest by lowland England.

The use of a core-periphery model based on environmental characteristics focuses attention on divisions other than national boundaries. Was, for example, the Highland line a more significant socio-economic divide than the Anglo-Scottish Border? But national boundaries were nevertheless significant in economic terms. Sometimes this simply reflected political differences: thus tariff barriers were applied on the Anglo-Scottish Border until 1707. In other cases variations in the rate of evolution of regional economies and deeper-seated contrasts in institutional structures were involved. For example the famine of 1623 highlighted a basic environmental contrast between upland and lowland zones within Britain as both Scotland and northern England were severely affected.[23] By the 1690s, however, the geography of famine had taken on national dimensions. Scotland was badly hit but not northern England. Reasons for this included better regional economic integration south of the Border and the development, from the early seventeenth century, of important contrasts in the effectiveness of the systems of parish poor relief operating in England and Lowland Scotland.[24]

The terms 'core' and 'periphery' imply relationships based on superiority and dependency. In economic terms this was sometimes true. Dependence of the periphery on the core for luxury items, and even at times basic foodstuffs, went back to late medieval times at least. Ireland and Wales were seen as being economically dependent on England as early as the twelfth century. Wales was unable to feed its population without grain imports from England.[25] By 1500 the markets of London and other large English towns were attracting raw materials from Ireland, Scotland and,Wales. Wool was imported from Ireland and Wales, cattle from Scotland and Wales, coal from Wales and Scotland.[26]

The seventeenth century was characterised by the spread of commercialization into the periphery as part of the wider process of transformation from feudalism to capitalism. Common elements in this process included the spread of a rash of new market centres,[27] a significant increase in levels of urbanization,[28] and the spread of rural industry.[29] Agricultural change also occurred. A good deal of this involved sectoral shifts within existing agrarian systems.[30] Some changes, however, represented real improvements in productivity. The focus of attention on the more rapid pace of change in English agriculture from the sixteenth century has led to a view that agrarian systems within the periphery were archaic, inefficient and unchanging.[31] More recently the real significance of the technical changes in English agriculture during the sixteenth and seventeenth centuries, claimed by Kerridge as an 'agricultural revolution', has been questioned,[32] and the role of agricultural change elsewhere reassessed. There is growing evidence, for example, that Scottish agriculture was not unresponsive to change. For the West Highlands Dodgshon has shown that some features of agriculture in the seventeenth and eighteenth centuries, such as the use of intensive spade cultivation rather than ploughs, were not archaic features, but recent responses to population pressure in an environment where scope for expanding the arable area was limited.[33] In Lowland Scotland infield-outfield farming was capable, under the stimulus of demand from urban markets, and possibly the injection of urban capital, of adopting innovations like liming and the use of legumes to evolve into relatively sophisticated four- and five-course rotations.[34] While the onset of the main phase of agricultural improvement in Lowland Scotland is still considered to lie in the later eighteenth century, recent research has highlighted the importance of earlier structural changes such as reductions in tenant numbers, holding amalgamation and the granting of longer written leases in laying a foundation on which later more rapid and spectacular transformation was based.[35] There is more tentative evidence for a phase of agricultural development in the western Lowlands during the early seventeenth century.[36] Growing commercialization encouraged more efficient livestock farming in areas like the Borders from the 1660s.[37]

At a local scale population growth within the periphery generated increased demand for commodities like grain. In broader terms, during the seventeenth century the economies of peripheral areas became increasingly geared to the production of commodities which complemented rather than competed with those generated within the core.[38] In doing so Ireland, Scotland and Wales came into competition with each other, something which helps to explain the small scale of trade between them in many commodities.[39] The nature of political relations with England could aid or undermine the success of such commercial developments though. The qualtity of Irish woollen cloth exported to England led to a ban in 1699.[40] This helps to explain the emphasis by both Ireland and Scotland on the development of linen manufacture.[41] England supported this shift by imposing tariffs on imported French linen in 1693 and 1696 and by removing duties on Irish linen in 1696.[42] English producers might lobby Parliament to impose restrictions on the import of goods from other parts of the British Isles.[43] In the case of the cattle trade the Welsh had a head start due to more immediate overland access to English markets, and the earlier dovetailing of the Welsh and English economies. During the seventeenth century the Irish so successfully overcame the disadvantages of greater distance from English markets, and a sea crossing, that by the mid-1660s over 50,000 cattle and 100,000 sheep were being sent from Ireland to England each year.[44] English producers were moved to object, leading to a ban on the import of Irish cattle in 1667, encouraging English and Welsh cattle rearers.[45]

The Welsh economy was integrated with that of England at an earlier date than those of Ireland and Scotland. Union with England from 1536–43 had major economic and social impacts on Wales, which gained significantly from easier access to a wider market for the products of her industries as well as her agriculture.[46] The impact of the English food market in the sixteenth century changed Wales as much as the Reformation or the political and judicial aspects of Union.[47] The trade in livestock and livestock products to England, already established in late medieval times, expanded substantially although the scale of the growth cannot be quantified. The manufacture of woollen cloth, the mining of coal and the production of grain were also stimulated.[48] Increasingly commercial attitudes to agriculture led to the engrossing of holdings, the intake and improvement of much common land, and sharper polarisation within rural society, trends similar to those which were being experienced in many parts of England.[49] The Union, by introducing English law and English administrative systems, stimulated a convergence between the two societies, starting with the Welsh landed elite. This was reflected in the development in the new Welsh shires of 'county communities' similar to those of England.[50]

Parliamentary representation in Westminster, and various offices within the new Welsh judicial and administrative structure, provided opportunities for a rising and dynamic class of Welsh gentry who were also benefiting from closer economic links with England. Contemporary Welshmen wrote of the 'joyful metamorphosis' in the economic and social life of Wales as a result of the Union.[51] Yet at the same time, despite the spread of the English language and English protestantism,[52] the Welsh gentry retained their traditional language, remaining conscious of the origins of their families and the history of their nation. While Wales lost her legal systems and did not have any institutions of higher education, the adoption of English laws and the necessity of seeking educational opportunities outside Wales did not lead to a rapid decline in Welsh culture and language because there remained a firm, widely-diffused sense of cultural identity. In particular the gentry class were able successfully to fuse the desirable features of English society, manners and attitudes with their own traditions.[53]

If the Tudor settlement preserved Welsh national heritage to a remarkable degree, the Welsh eagerly seized the wider opportunities offered by the Union. The movement of Welsh into administrative, legal and ecclesiastical posts in Tudor England was striking. At this level opportunistic Welshmen made a mark out of all proportion to their numbers. Some 2,000 Welshmen were students at Oxford and Cambridge between 1570 and 1642 while at least 700 entered the Inns of Court.[54] Some of the latter were the sons of gentry families who returned home to use their skills in local administration. Others carved out careers on a larger stage as equal citizens in a new British realm. This process was paralleled by the migration to England of many Welsh of lower social status. They moved to towns like Bristol, Shrewsbury and Chester but also to London.[55] The distribution of Welsh immigrants in London in 1638 – scattered throughout the city and its suburbs with no marked evidence of clustering in specific areas – shows how easily they were assimilated into the general population.[56] The Welsh in England may have remained distinctive on account of their accent and mannerisms of speech as well as their predilection for pedigrees but the stage image of the stereotype Welshman was much more sympathetic than that of Sawney or Teague, the caricature Scotsman and Irishman.[57]

Union with Wales successfully integrated the Welsh elite into that of Western England, making Wales the least rebellious region in Britain. Success in the assimilation of Wales led to the belief that peace and civility could be imposed elsewhere using the same administrative structures, transposed from lowland England, that had worked in Wales.[58] This led to problems in Ireland. Although the act of 1541 provided a mechanism for incorporating Ireland into the Tudor state along similar lines to Wales,[59] seventeenth-century Ireland was treated, effectively, as an English colony. The Irish economy reflected the colonial nature of the political relationship with England.[60] As well as being subservient politically and economically Ireland received civil and ecclesiastical administrators from England, as well as large numbers of more humble immigrants.[61] Irish producers were liable to arbitrary interference by the English Parliament while Irish merchants were excluded from direct participation in trade with England's colonies, though there was considerable evasion in practice.[62] Even so, the Irish did remarkably well. Ireland's seventeenth-century commercialization, with both indigenous and immigrant landowners eager to seize commercial opportunities, was impressive.[63] Irish exports grew in value by 2% per annum in the later seventeenth century.[64]

Opinions have differed regarding the relative strength of the Irish and Scottish economies in the late seventeenth and early eighteenth centuries. To Cullen and Smout, it was the Irish rather than the Scottish economy which seemed poised for further growth in the early eighteenth century[65] They suggested that by 1700 Irish exports may have totalled 6 shillings per person per annum against only 4 shillings for Scotland, and that even in the mid-eighteenth century per capita exports from the two countries were about level.[66] It was not until the later eighteenth century that the Scottish economy showed signs of pulling ahead. This positive view of the Irish economy has been challenged more recently by suggestions that the steadier overall pace of economic change in Scotland, generated internally rather than imposed from outside, demonstrated greater long-term potential.[67] Despite the much greater size of Dublin compared with Edinburgh in the later seventeenth century, at a lower level Ireland did not have the dense network of small burghs which existed in Lowland Scotland.[68] The English connexion made for growth in seventeenth-century Ireland but there was a price to pay in the longer term.[69] The seventeenth-century land settlement in Ireland created a gulf between landlord and tenant which did not exist in Scotland, fostering class war in the countryside.[70] This helps to explain the very different pace of agricultural improvement in the two countries during the eighteenth century.[71] Agricultural change in Scotland was already significant in the early eighteenth century; there was no sign of similar improvement among Scots settlers in Ulster.[72] The limited ability of Irish farmers to accumulate reserves, and the basic poverty of Irish rural society compared to that of Lowland Scotland, is shown by the fact that the last major famine to affect the Lowlands was in the 1690s while Ireland continued to suffer throughout the eighteenth century, notably in 1728–9 and 1740–1.[73]

The most significant feature of the Scottish economy during the seventeenth century was the fact that Scotland remained a separate state. She was forced, by the different nature of her political relationship with England, to be more self sufficient in basic commodities like grain than Wales or Ireland, though the degree to which the Scottish economy operated in isolation from England diminished significantly during the seventeenth century. The significance of English markets to Scottish exporters increased markedly between the late sixteenth and late seventeenth centuries, but France, the Netherlands and Scandinavia remained major trading partners.[74]

It is easy to exaggerate the extent to which Scottish society was moving closer to that of England in the later sixteenth century. Admittedly there were some signs of convergence: the rise of the legal profession in Scotland, the reduction of feuds, the growth of a new nobility based on service, the growing social and political influence of the gentry, a developing bureaucracy, higher taxation, and imitation of English legislation.[75] But the pace of convergence was slow. The Union of 1603 linked two countries which differed more sharply than in the late thirteenth century and were too deeply divided to allow any real integration in the short term.[76] There was a long-standing legacy of mistrust and even hatred between England and Scotland where the disasters of Flodden, Solway Moss and the Rough Wooing were still vividly recalled.

As a result, the union of 1603 did not mark a major watershed in economic relations between England and Scotland. Despite the wishes of James VI and I neither country was keen on the idea of a closer economic union.[77] English opposition was based on national prejudice as much as rational economics. Efforts by Charles I to bring the two countries closer together in areas such as a common fisheries policy were viewed with suspicion by the Scots.[78] The Union allowed the Scots to trade with England on slightly more favourable terms. Nevertheless, customs duties continued to be applied on Scottish goods entering England, including coal, salt, linen and cattle. Much of the boom in Scottish trade during the first quarter of the seventeenth century was generated by trade with Europe, not England though Scotland's inability after the Union of 1603 to formulate an independent foreign policy led to the disruption of overseas trade as a result of unwanted wars with the French and later the Dutch.[79] Scottish horizons in the seventeenth century were still firmly fixed on Europe, as mercenaries and traders, or on Ireland as emigrant farmers and tradesmen. There may have been around 30,000 Scottish pedlars in Poland in the first half of the seventeenth century but the numbers of Scottish chapmen in England are not likely to have been more than a small fraction of this figure.[80] It took time to break the 300-year-old perception of England as the 'auld enemy'. Samuel Johnson's 'high road to England' for ambitious Scotsmen was very much an eighteenth century construction.

The Scottish economy was too shattered by war and heavy taxation in the 1650s to reap any benefit from the short-lived Cromwellian union. After 1660 the Scots were debarred from direct access to England's American colonies by the English Navigation Act, though this did not stop some Glasgow merchants from trading illegally with America. Nevertheless, the volume of trade with England increased. By the later seventeenth century England was probably Scotland's most important trading partner, taking perhaps 50% of Scottish exports.[81] The pull of the English market affected even the more remote parts of Scotland. The Highlands especially benefited from the cattle trade. By the end of the seventeenth century animals from areas as distant as Skye were being driven to East Anglia where they were fattened for the London market.[82] Profits from the droving trade helped ease the increasing burden of debts which Highland chiefs were accumulating through their growing preference for more expensive Lowland lifestyles. Indirectly, the cattle trade helped the assimilation of Highland landowners into the rest of British landed society. Some of the profits also went to the clan gentry, allowing them to gain an entry into the land market by lending money to their chiefs on wadset. These sources of profit gave both chiefs and tacksmen a vested interest in peace and encouraged a decline in interclan violence.[83]

After the export boom of the later 1670s, when Scottish exports to the Continent seemed to be thriving, the Scottish economy came under increasing pressure as countries across Europe imposed more protectionist policies and raised tariff barriers to protect their own industries. Scotland's limited range of exports rendered her vulnerable to shifts in overseas markets. Attempts to stimulate domestic industry to improve Scotland's balance of trade were unsuccessful, hampered by lack of skills, limited capital and the small size of the home market. The Revolution of 1688 marked the start of a period of increasing difficulty. Scotland was dragged into wars with France which lasted from 1689 to 1697 and from 1701 to 1713. To the loss of French markets was added the depredations of French privateers on Scottish shipping inadequately protected by the Royal Navy.[84] The later 1690s brought widespread harvest failure, severe famine and also the ill-fated Darien Scheme. By 1700 perhaps a quarter of Scotland's liquid capital had been lost in the venture, a severe blow for a small, poor country. While the scheme had misconceived from the start, part of the disaster was directly attributable to English opposition.[85] There was a growing feeling that the Union of 1603 was proving unworkable and that Scotland's current economic position was untenable. The failure of the Darien venture may have helped to create an atmosphere in which the possibility of closer union with England began to be taken more seriously by the Scots.

In 1702 negotiations towards a parliamentary union were started but neither the English commissioners or Parliament were fully committed to the project. This encouraged the Scottish Parliament of 1703 to adopt a tough, independent line which forced England in turn to take the question of Union more seriously. In 1703 and 1704 the Scottish Parliament passed several pieces of legislation which alarmed English politicians. The Act of Security and Succession imposed major conditions on Scotland accepting the Hanoverian succession. The Act Anent Peace and War required the consent of the Scottish Parliament before war could be declared or treaties negotiated. This, and other legislation, does not seem to have been aimed at forcing an immediate split between the two countries but English politicians believed that this was the Scots' ultimate aim. They revised their views on the desirability of union with Scotland. To achieve this it would be necessary to grant significant concessions to the Scots. The prospect of how the Scottish economy would fare in the event of a total break with England helped concentrate Scottish minds, as did the English Parliament's response to the Scottish acts of 1703–04. In 1705 an Alien Act was passed which stated that unless the Scots agreed by Christmas to start talks on an incorporating union, or had accepted the Hanoverian succession within the framework of the Union of 1603, all Scots resident in England would be treated as aliens, and their lands would be liable to seizure. The import of Scottish coal, cattle and linen to England would be banned and a blockade imposed to prevent Scottish trade with France. This crude but effective blackmail was directed particularly at the Scottish nobility, a number of whom had acquired English estates through marriage with many more being active in the cattle trade. After the initial fury which the act aroused, more careful consideration of the various options followed. There was general agreement about the depth of Scotland's economic crisis, and that this was the result of an unfavourable balance of trade. The pro-union faction saw open access to English markets for Scottish cattle, linen, coal, wool, grain and salt as the only way of reversing decline. Anti-unionists believed that the Scots needed to improve their competitiveness so that they could regain European markets and make themselves independent of England. There is little doubt that the economic understanding of the pro-unionists was sounder and more practical.[86]

The Anglo-Scottish union of 1707 remains a controversial topic. It ended Scotland's independence and has also been viewed as an economic and social watershed. Much of Scotland's economic history in the seventeenth century has been seen, with hindsight, as leading inexorably towards union. For the eighteenth century, the union is often considered as an inevitable and necessary foundation for the economic and social progress which ultimately led to the Industrial Revolution.[87] In recent years research has emphasised the extent to which eighteenth century changes in Scotland's economy and society – in agriculture for instance or business practices – were based on seventeenth century foundations.[88] Nevertheless, the significance of the Union in providing a suitable milieu for these developments cannot be gainsaid, despite the fact that economic growth in Scotland was limited for three decades after 1707.

The Union was entered into by England principally for political reasons, and by Scotland mainly for economic motives. The importance of economic issues within Scotland in the Union debate has been played down by some historians who have stressed the role of political management, patronage and bribery of the Scottish commissioners. Behind such short-term manoeuvrings, however, loomed broader economic issues. 15 of the 25 articles of Union were directly economic in character.[89] The commissioners, and many Scottish parliamentarians involved in the union debate, were landowners with a range of economic interests; cattle and corn, coal and salt, linen and woollens, herring and salmon. Some economic bribery was offered to particular Members of Parliament who received private concessions exempting them from the general conditions of the treaty. On a larger scale there was the promise of £2,000 sterling a year for encouraging Scottish industry. A bigger bribe still, aimed mainly at the nobility, was the repayment of money lost by Darien investors, with interest, in return for liquidating the company.

Taken together the treaty included a package of economic concessions which, considered impartially, was fair to the Scots, even generous in places.[90] In return, the Scots only conceded a marginal reduction in real power.[91] This was due to the fact that England's concerns about Scotland were essentially political. Scotland was not seen as a major economic threat; her coal and salt industries were geared largely to domestic markets, the linen industry did not compete with English production while the Scottish fine woollens industry, which did, was already on its last legs before 1707.[92] Opposition to the Union from the parliamentary representatives of the Scottish royal burghs, and the relative poverty of the merchant class, did not suggest that major competition with England's colonial trade was likely, especially once the Darien Company had been wound up.

The above discussion, especially the fluctuating state of Anglo-Scottish relations, demonstrates the extent to which seventeenth century political and economic change were closely inter linked, necessitating a truly British perspective in economic history. A similar macro scale approach is equally valuable in studying evolving social, cultural and institutional structures.

SOCIAL AND CULTURAL DEVELOPMENT

The history of English denigration of the languages, cultures, customs, morals and living conditions of the inhabitants of the other nations within the British Isles and Ireland is a long one. Of particular significance were the topographical, antiquarian and historical writers who pioneered the 'rediscovery of England' in Tudor times.[93] They were succeeded in the seventeenth and eighteenth centuries by a series of smug, superior travellers whose views, biased and preconceived, have often been echoed in modern scholarship.[94] It has been widely assumed by anglocentric historians that because southern and eastern England emerged as a wealthy and powerful area from late medieval times there was automatically something superior in English institutions, cultural values and social structures. Institutional and social structures elsewhere in Britain, particularly in those areas where Celtic cultures survived, have often been dismissed as primitive and inefficient. The transfer of southern English norms to secondary core areas such as Lowland Scotland and south east Ireland further encouraged the attack on Celtic society. In Scotland, the Lowlanders' view of the Highlanders from the sixteenth to the eighteenth century was one of contempt tinged with fear, perhaps reinforced by the subconscious realisation that typically 'Celtic' institutions such as the bloodfeud, and strong kinship structures had only recently vanished from the Lowlands.[95] The subconscious survival of such attitudes, compounded by a lack of acquaintance with the Celtic languages or an understanding of Celtic culture, have continued to influence modern historians.

Again, some Scottish examples will illustrate the point. Late medieval Scotland has, in the past, been dismissed as a wasteland of warring factions with, at the top, a continuing power struggle between a weak crown and over-powerful magnates. However, new interpretations suggest that the relationship between the Stewarts and their magnates was, in general, based on cooperation rather than conflict, on a consensus view that a balance between royal and noble power had to be maintained for the good of all. Crown and nobility worked to retain a responsible partnership and a generally peaceful and positive relationship. The traditional picture of over-mighty magnates and struggling kings has been shown to have been based largely on sixteenth-century chroniclers whose works are riddled with bias and invention. Despite the fact that James I and James III were murdered and Mary Stewart deposed, there was no serious challenge to the dynasty; a very different situation from fifteenth century England.[96]

A similar reappraisal has extended to Scottish administrative and legal structures. Compared with England these have, in the past, been seen as simple and ineffective. By English standards the Scottish crown was impoverished. Lack of money prevented the development of a sophisticated central administration, but at the same time a lack of complex institutions reduced the need of Scottish kings for money to run them. Compared with England, Scotland's population was taxed infrequently and lightly so that a complex and expensive money-gathering apparatus was not needed. It has been customary to write off Scotland's system of heritable sheriffdoms, regalities and baronies as inefficient and weak compared with the sophisticated centralised system of justice which developed in England. Under the Scottish system local disputes and problems were dealt with by local people under a system of amateur justice. This contrasted with the early professionalisation of English justice. But while the English legal system became increasingly cumbersome and even unworkable, the Scottish one retained a more flexible, commonsense approach which may have worked at least as well in its way.[97]

Scottish society, down to the seventeenth century, has often been portrayed as excessively and inherently violent. However, Brown and Wormald's research on the nature of bloodfeud has shown this institution in a more positive light, often less violent than had sometimes appeared, a traditional form of kin-based justice which integrated well with the decentralised Scottish legal system offering a realistic way of maintaining stability in the localities.[98] If bloodfeud survived as a characteristic feature of Lowland society to the end of the sixteenth century, other kinds of violence and protest, relatively frequent in England, such as popular rebellions, were rare or unknown in Scotland. Scotsmen who travelled in England during the seventeenth century were surprised at the amount of aggression displayed by the lower levels of English society. The close personal structure of Scottish society may have helped to diminish tensions of this sort.[99]

This revision of ideas relating to Scottish society and its institutions has wider implications as it throws English society into sharper perspective. In particular, it challenges the assumptions that the structures which were characteristic of lowland England were necessarily more advanced and more effective than those of the 'backward' periphery. The Scots faced many broadly similar problems to the English but often tackled them in different ways. For instance, population pressure in Scotland from the sixteenth century to the eighteenth was accommodated in part by a major shift in diet from meat and livestock products to one based overwhelmingly on cereals, first in the Lowlands then in the Highlands.[100] The new diet was no less nutritious than the old one but enabled a larger population to be maintained than would have otherwise have been possible[101] Similarly, in a less urbanised society, emigration provided a major demographic safety net in seventeenth-century Scotland, taking the place of migration to London which served as an important regulator of population in England[102]

While much of the social history of seventeenth-century Britain can be viewed in terms of a gradual convergence towards English patterns the persistent differences are often as striking as the growing similarities. This can be seen in relation to population. England, Wales and Scotland (though not always Ireland) had many demographic features in common; there were similar long-term chronologies of change with rising population in the sixteenth and early seventeenth centuries, producing population pressure, inflation, rising poverty and other social problems; slower growth or even decline in the later seventeenth century then renewed growth in the eighteenth. Features such as the central importance of the nuclear family, mean household size, high levels of population mobility, and a high mean age of first marriage were also comparable. The demographic regimes of the four nations were clearly all set within the same overall framework but there were also interesting variations. Such differences within this broad framework are often imperfectly known and poorly understood. Demographic history within Britain has tended to be undertaken within national frameworks, partly due to differences in the nature, survival and quality of source materials. However, more comparative approaches are now being undertaken.[103]

Patterns of nuptiality in late seventeenth and early eighteenth century Scotland were broadly similar to those of contemporary England but seem to have been less varied over time. The mean age of first marriage for Scottish women, and levels of celibacy, remained high while they fell in England.[104] Levels of illegitimacy were also less changeable.[105] In Ireland, whose demography has been described as being, in 1600, over 100 years behind the rest of Europe,[106] women seem to have married comparatively early though still within the bounds of the North West European marriage pattern, while celibacy was also relatively low.[107] One possible reason for this was the ready availability of land in an underpopulated country with abundant waste and a willingness by proprietors to allow subdivision of holdings, especially compared with Lowland Scotland where, in the seventeenth century, unauthorised squatting and excessive holding fragmentation was resisted by landowners.[108] Marital fertility was comparatively low in England but was consistently higher in Ireland with shorter birth intervals and larger completed family sizes. These factors combined with immigration to encourage faster population growth in Ireland than in England or Scotland. Marital fertility may also have been higher in Scotland, balancing, to some degree, higher levels of mortality. Expectation of life at birth was lower in Scotland than in England due to higher levels of infant, child and adult mortality. Scottish levels of illegitimacy were higher than in England during the later seventeenth and early eighteenth centuries, but less changable and with marked, persistent regional variations. However, pre-marital pregancy was much less common in Scotland than England.[109] There is much scope for further research to establish more clearly such national and regional variations within early-modern Britain and to attempt to explain them in terms of underlying social differences.

The impact of such social variations can also be seen where institutions which worked successfully in Lowland England were exported to other parts of the British Isles. The introduction of the English system of shire and local government into Wales succeeded largely because it met the needs and aspirations of the upwardly-mobile Welsh gentry class.[110] By contrast, efforts to introduce features of English local government to Scotland met with little success. In the late sixteenth and early seventeenth century James VI encouraged legislation relating to the provision of poor relief, the control of vagrancy and the establishment of Justices of the Peace, all clearly modelled on Tudor legislation[111] The attempt to introduce justices to Scotland was a failure. There was no room among the decentralised franchises for a new tier of local administration; the holders of baronies and regalities were not prepared to give up any of their power to a new set of officials. It was only after 1667, when the powers of Justices were increased at a time when some of the activities of the franchise courts were declining, that they began to develop a useful role.[112] Because of the different distribution of power at a local level, efforts to introduce a system of poor relief into Scotland comparable with the English model were also unsuccessful. Because of the lack of any secular officials at parish level and opposition to their establishment, poor relief was delegated to the church through its kirk sessions. Instead of adopting a system of levying poor rates, as developed in England, poor relief in Scotland during the seventeenth century remained based on voluntary contributions and was much less generous than south of the Border. In England, poor relief provided a basic level of subsistence; in Scotland, payments were seen only as a supplement to aid provided by family, friends and neighbours.[113] Lacking a uniform system of poor relief, Scotland did not need settlement laws like England. Ireland followed the Scottish model of provision of poor relief, only more slowly and even less successfully due to the fact that the established Church of Ireland was a minority religion over much of the country.[114] The impact of such differences on demography, population mobility, vagrancy and other aspects of society have yet to be fully addressed, far less evaluated.

If variations in society between England and Scotland necessitated different approaches to similar problems the same was true within Scotland in terms of the contrast between the Lowlands and the Highlands. The Highlands provide the best example of a major regional divergence in society within any of the nations making up the British Isles during the seventeenth century. Social differences from the rest of Scotland were underlain by demographic ones. Although the evidence so far is limited, and mainly relates to the eighteenth century, there are indications that average age of first marriage for women in the Highlands was earlier than in the Lowlands or England, more directly comparable with Ireland.[115] In the seventeenth and early eighteenth centuries population in the Highlands may have been growing faster, over a longer period of time, than in the Lowlands.

However, to isolate Highland society as an archaic, freakish survival by over-emphasising its peculiarities merely perpetuates the prejudices of seventeenth-century Lowlanders and English visitors. More recently, Scottish historians have tended to view contrasts in society between the Highlands and the Lowlands as ones of emphasis and chronology rather than of kind. Smout's suggestion that Highland society was based on kinship modified by feudalism, Lowland society on feudalism modified by kinship, emphasises this.[116] It is also misleading to consider Highland society as geographically uniform; the balance between Celtic and feudal tradition varied within the Highlands on a gradation from the more feudalised east towards the north and west.[117]

Despite all that has been written about Highland clans we still know remarkably little about how they evolved and functioned. A reassessment which focuses less on their antiquated, outlandish features and more on their effectiveness as social systems is long overdue. Highland clans have for too long been viewed through an over-romanticised swirl of tartans and bagpipes. It is only in recent years that serious scholarship has been able to demonstrate the important continuities which underlay Highland society; for example in terms of spatial patterns of economic and social contacts.[118] Dodgshon's application of anthropological models to the structure of clans and the evolutionary cycles which they underwent provides a much needed framework for understanding how they operated and what they meant to the ordinary inhabitants of the Highlands.[119] Equally clear is the increasing evidence that, far from remaining feudalised and archaic until the eve of Culloden, Highland society changed steadily from the sixteenth century onwards as the region became more integrated first with the rest of Scotland and then, politically, with Britain as a whole.[120] This was seen first in terms of the Highland aristocracy. The more conservative response of the ordinary clansmen to social and economic influences from outside produced tensions in seventeenth-century Highland society which were articulated by gaelic bards who condemned the adoption by chiefs of new expensive lifestyles and their neglect of traditional obligations and values. Their comments mirrored those of bards in gaelic Ireland at a slightly earlier date and also echoed the bards of sixteenth-century Wales.[121] This in turn highlights the need for more comparative research on the Celtic societies of late medieval and early-modern Britain, and the ways in which they responded to the impact of external and internal forces for change.

CONCLUSION

In the limited space available it has only been possible to touch on a few themes. These should, nevertheless, highlight the need to consider economic and social history at a British as well as a purely English, or Scottish, Irish or Welsh level. The political relations between the 'four nations', which has been the mainstay of recent work on British history, had profound effects on economic and social patterns and their variation through time, but economic development and differing rates of social change likewise affected political relationships. During the seventeenth century growing convergence led to increasing levels of contact and integration between core and periphery within Britain, especially with the commercial penetration of the periphery, yet at the same time deep-seated, long-established differences remained prominent. There is considerable scope for further research drawing parallels, exploring differences and explaining contrasts within the British Isles. If British history aims to examine 'the totality of the relationships between the peoples of the British Isles'[122] and to show how the component parts of the British Isles 'interacted so as to modify the conditions of each others existence,[123] this can hardly be done without a concern for its economic and social dimensions.

Notes on Chapter 7

1   Kearney, Hugh F. *The British Isles. A History of Four Nations.* (Cambridge, 1989) p. 4.

2   eg. Clay, C.G.A. *Economic Expansion and Social Change: England 1500–1700.* 2 vols. (Cambridge, 1984).

3   Wrightson, Keith E. 'Kindred and adjoining kingdoms'; an English perspective on the social and economic history of early-modern Scotland. In R.A. Houston & I.D. Whyte (eds.) *Scottish Society 1500–1800.* (Cambridge, 1989) pp. 247–8.

4   Ibid. p. 248.

5   Macfarlane, Alan. *The Origins of English Individualism.* (Oxford, 1978).

6   eg. Floud, Roderick (ed.) *The Economic History of Britain Since 1700.* 2nd ed. (Cambridge, 1994).

7   Houston, Robert A & Whyte, Ian D. 'Introduction'. In R.A. Houston & I.D. Whyte: *Scottish Society* p. 2.

8   Wrightson: 'Kindred and adjoining kingdoms' p 248.

9   Cullen, L.M. *The Emergence of Modern Ireland.* (London, 1981) p. 11.

10   Wrightson: 'Kindred and adjoining kingdoms' p. 245.

11   Mitchison, Rosalind.' Ireland and Scotland: the seventeenth-century legacies compared'. In T.M. Devine & D. Dickson (eds.) *Ireland and Scotland, 1600–1850.* (Edinburgh,1983) p. 2. Devine, Thomas M, 'The English connection and Irish and Scottish development in the eighteenth century'. In Devine and Dickson: *Ireland and Scotland.* p. 12.

12   Cullen, L.M., & Smout, T. Christopher, (eds.) *Comparative Aspects of Irish and Scottish Economic and Social History 1600–1900.* (Edinburgh, 1977), Devine & Dickson, *Ireland and Scotland,* Mitchison, Rosalind &. Roebuck, Peter (eds.) *Economy and Society in Scotland and Ireland 1500–1939.* (Edinburgh, 1988). Connolly, S.J., Houston, Robert A. & Morris, Robert J, *Conflict, Identity and Economic Development. Ireland and Scotland 1600–1939.* (Preston, 1995).

13   Whatley, Christopher A. *'Bought and Sold for English Gold'? Explaining the Union of 1707.* (Edinburgh, 1994).

14   Kearney: *The British Isles,* p. 104.

15   Ibid. p. 91.

16   Grant, Alexander J & Stringer, Keith A. 'The enigma of British history'. In A. Grant & K.J. Stringer (eds.) *Uniting the Kingdom ? The Making of British History.* (London, 1995), p. 5.

17   Wormald, Jenny. *Court, Kirk and Community. Scotland 1470–1625.* (London, 1981) p. 63.

18   Mitchison 'Ireland and Scotland', p. 20.

19   Fisher, F.J. 'The development of the London food market 1540–1640. *Economic History Review* 5 (1935) pp. 46–64 Kitch, M.J. 'Capital and

kingdom: migration to later Stuart London'. In A.L. Beier & R. Finlay (eds.) *The Making of the Metropolis: London 1500–1700*. (London, 1986) pp. 224–51. Wareing, J. 'Changes in the geographical distribution of the recruitment of apprentices to the London Companies 1486–1750'. *Journal of Historical Geography* 6 (1980) pp. 241–9.

20 Mitchison, 'Ireland and Scotland' p. 20.

21 Wallerstein, Immanuel. *The Modern World System*. Vol I (London, 1974).

22 Ellis, Steven.G. 'The concept of British history'. In S.G. Ellis & S. Barber *Conquest and Union. Fashioning a British State 1485–1725*. (London, 1995) p. 22.

23 Appleby, Andrew B. *Famine in Tudor and Stuart England*. (Liverpool, 1978). Flinn, Michael (ed.) *Scottish Population History*. (Cambridge, 1977).

24 Mitchison, Rosalind. 'The making of the old Scottish poor law'. *Past and Present* 63 (1974) pp. 58–93.

25 Gillingham, J. 'Foundations of a disunited kingdom'. In Grant & Stringer: *Conquest and Union* p. 61.

26 Kearney: *The British Isles* p. 108.

27 Cullen: *Modern Ireland* p. 59. Everitt, Alan. 'The marketing of agricultural produce. In J. Thirsk (ed.) *The Agrarian History of England and Wales* IV (Cambridge, 1967) pp. 467–80. Kearney, *The British Isles*, p. 108. O'Flanagan, P. 'Markets and fairs in Ireland, 1600–1800: index of economic development and regional growth'. *Journal of Historical Geography* 11 (1985) pp. 364–78. Whyte, Ian D. 'The growth of periodic market centres in Scotland 1600–1707'. *Scottish Geographical Magazine* 95 (1979) pp. 13–26.

28 Whyte, Ian D. 'Urbanization in early-modern Scotland: a preliminary analysis'. *Scottish Economic and Social History* 9 (1989) pp. 21–37. Whyte, Ian D. 'Scottish and Irish urbanisation in the seventeenth and eighteenth centuries: a comparative perspective'. In Connolly, Houston & Morris: *Conflict, Identity and Economic Development*. pp. 14–28.

29 Whyte, Ian D. 'Proto-industrialization in Scotland'. In P. Hudson (ed.) *Regions and Industries*. (Cambridge, 1989) pp. 228–51.

30 Dodgshon, Robert A, *Land and Society in Early Scotland*. (Oxford, 1981) pp. 253–63.

31 Wrightson: 'Kindred and adjoining kingdoms' p. 251.

32 Kerridge, Eric, *The Agricultural Revolution*. (London, 1967). Overton, Mark. *Agricultural Revolution in England*. (Cambridge, 1996).

33 Dodgshon, Robert A. 'Strategies of farming in the Western Highlands and Islands prior to crofting and the Clearances'. *Economic History Review*. 46 (1993) pp. 679–701.

34 Whyte, Ian D. 'Infield-outfield farming on a seventeenth-century Scottish estate'. *Journal of Historical Geography* 5 (1979) pp. 391–407.

35 Devine, Thomas M, *The Transformation of Rural Scotland. Social Change and the Agrarian Economy 1660–1815*. (Edinburgh, 1994) pp. 19–32.

36 Whyte, Ian D.' Poverty or prosperity? Rural society in Lowland Scotland in the late sixteenth and early seventeenth centuries'. *Scottish Economic and Social History*. Forthcoming.

37 Dodgshon, Robert A. 'Agricultural change and its social consequences in the Southern Uplands of Scotland 1660–1780'. In Devine & Dickson: *Ireland and Scotland* pp. 49–59.

38 Cullen, L.M. 'Economic trends 1660–91'. In T.W.Moody, F.X. Martin & F.J. Byrne (eds.) *A New History of Ireland III 1534–1691*. (Oxford, 1976) p. 392.

39 Mitchison: 'Ireland and Scotland' p. 6. Cochran, L.E. *Scottish Trade with Ireland in the Eighteenth Century*. (Edinburgh, 1985).

40 Mitchison: 'Ireland and Scotland' p. 8.

41 Ibid. p. 9.

42 Devine: 'The English connection' p. 15.

43 Mitchison: 'Ireland and Scotland' p. 2.

44 Woodward, Donald. 'A comparative study of the Irish and Scottish livestock trades in the seventeenth century'. In Cullen & Smout: *Comparative Aspects* pp. 147–64.

45 Ibid. pp. 151–2, Mitchison, 'Ireland and Scotland' p. 4.

46 Ellis: 'The concept of British history' p. 18.

47 Kearney, *The British Isles*. p. 119.

48 Ibid. p. 97.

49 Williams, G. *Recovery, Reorientation and Reformation. Wales c1415–1642*. (Oxford, 1987) p. 386.

50 Ellis: 'The concept of British history' p. 18.

51 Jones, J.Gwynfor. *Early Modern Wales c1525–1640*. (London, 1994) p. 1.

52 S.G. Ellis (1995) op.cit. p. 18.

53 Jones: *Early Modern Wales*. p. 45.

54 Ibid. p. 27.

55 Williams: *Recovery, Reorientation and Reformation*. pp. 458–62.

56 Jones, Emrys. 'The Welsh in London in the seventeenth and eighteenth centuries'. *Welsh Historical Review* 10 (1980–1) pp. 461–79.

57 Williams: *Recovery, Reorientation and Reformation*. p. 463.

58 Ellis, Steven.G. 'Tudor state formation and the shaping of the British Isles'. In Ellis & Barber: *Conquest and Union* p. 55.

59 Ellis: 'The concept of British History' p. 17.

60 Devine: 'The English connection' p. 14. Mitchison & Roebuck. Introduction. p. 2 Mitchison, 'Ireland and Scotland' p. 9. Wormald, Jenny. 'The creation of Britain: multiple kingdoms or core and colonies?' *Transactions of the. Royal Historical. Society*. 6th ser. 2 (1992) pp. 175–94.

61 Cullen: *Modern Ireland* p. 35.

62 Cullen: 'Economic trends' p. 399. Cullen & Smout: Comparative Aspects p. 5. Devine: 'The English connection' p. 16.

63 Cullen: *Modern Ireland* p. 15.

64 Ibid. p. 39.

65 Ibid. p. 61.

66 Cullen & Smout: *Comparative Aspects* p. 4.

67 Cullen, L.M. 'Scotland and Ireland 1600–1800; their role in the evolution of British society'. In Houston & Whyte: *Scottish Society* 228–29. Devine: 'The English connection' pp. 18–19 Mitchison & Roebuck: 'Introduction' p. 4.

68 Cullen: *Modern Ireland* p. 26.

69 Mitchison: 'Ireland and Scotland' p. 9.

70 Cullen: *Modern Ireland* p. 18.

71 Cullen & Smout: *Comparative Aspects*. p. 9.

72 Roebuck, Peter. 'The economic situation and functions of substantial landowners 1600–1815. Ulster and Lowland Scotland compared'. In. Mitchison & Roebuck: *Economy and Society* pp. 85–86.

73 Cullen & Smout: *Comparative Aspects* p. 9.

74 Lythe, Sydney G.E. *The Economy of Scotland in its European Setting, 1550–1625.* (Edinburgh, 1963).

75 Brown, Keith M. *Kingdom or Province? Scotland and the Regal Union, 1603–1715.* (London, 1992). pp. 33–59.

76 Dawson, J.A. 'Anglo-Scottish Protestant culture and integration in sixteenth-century Britain'. In Ellis & Barber: *Conquest and Union* pp. 87–114.

77 Galloway, Bruce. *The Union of Scotland and England 1603–1608.* (Edinburgh, 1986).

78 Macinnes, Alan. *Charles I and the Making Of the Covenanting Movement.* (Edinburgh, 1991).

79 Brown, James, J. *The social, political and economic influences of the Edinburgh merchant elite 1600–38.* Unpublished PhD. thesis, University of Edinburgh, 1985.

80 Smout, T. Christopher, Landsman,N.C, & Devine, Thomas M. 'Scottish emigration in the seventeenth and eighteenth centuries'. In Canny, Nicholas (ed.) *Europeans on the Move: Studies in European Migration 1500–1800.* (Oxford, 1994) pp. 77–87.

81 Smout, T.Christopher. *Scottish Trade on the Eve of Union, 1660–1707.* (Edinburgh, 1963) pp 237–38.

82 Woodward: 'Irish and Scottish livestock trades'.

83 Macinnes, Alan. 'Gaelic culture in the seventeenth century: polarization and assimilation'. In Ellis & Barber: *Conquest and Union* pp. 181–93.

84   Smout: *Scottish Trade* p. 245.

85   Ibid. pp. 250–3.

86   Ibid pp. 261–70.

87   Riley, P.W.J. *The Union of Scotland and England.* (Manchester, 1978). Ferguson, W. *Scotland's relations with England: a Survey to 1707.* (Edinburgh, 1977).

88   Devine: Rural Scotland. Devine, Thomas M. 'The Scottish merchant community 1680–1740'. In Campbell, Roy, H & Skinner, A.S. (eds.) *The Origins and Nature of the Scottish Enlightenment.* (Edinburgh, 1982) pp. 26–41.

89   Whatley: *Bought and Sold* p. 33.

90   Ibid. p. 47.

91   Devine: 'The English connection' p. 12. Ellis: 'Concept of British history'. p. 23.

92   Campbell, Roy H. *The Rise and Fall of Scottish Industry 1707–1939.* (Edinburgh, 1980) pp. 6–7.

93   Hoskins, William G. 'The rediscovery of England'. In W.G. Hoskins. *Provincial England.* (London, 1965) pp. 209–30.

94   Hume Brown, Peter. *Early Travellers in Scotland.* (Edinburgh, 1891).

95   Whyte, Ian D. *Scotland's Society and Economy in Transition c1500–c1760.* (London, 1997) pp. 94–96.

96   Grant, Alexander. *Independence and Nationhood. Scotland 1306–1469.* (London, 1984) pp 171–99. Wormald: *Court, Kirk and Community.* pp 3–26.

97   Wrightson: 'Kindred and adjoining kingdoms' pp. 246–47. Davies, S.J. 'The courts and the Scottish legal system 1600–1747: the case of Stirlingshire'. In Gatrell, V.A.C. Lenman, Bruce & Parker, Geoffrey (eds.) *Crime and the Law.* (London, 1980) pp. 54–79.

98   Brown, Keith M. *Bloodfeud in Scotland 1573–1625.* (Edinburgh, 1986) Wormald, Jenny. 'Bloodfeud, kindred and government in early-modern Scotland'. *Past & Present* 87 (1980) pp. 54–97.

99   Brown: *Kingdom or Province?* pp. 22–23.

100 Gibson, Alexander & Smout, T. Christopher. 'Scottish food and Scottish history, 1500–1800'. In Houston & Whyte: *Scottish Society* pp. 59–84.

101 Ibid.

102 Wrigley, E Anthony. 'A simple model of London's importance in changing English society and economy 1650–1750' *Past & Present.* 37 (1967) pp. 44–70.

103 Tyson, Robert E. 'Contrasting regimes: population growth in Ireland and Scotland during the eighteenth century'. In Connolly, Houston & Morris: *Conflict, Identity and Economic Development.* pp. 64–76. Houston, Robert A. *The Population of Britain and Ireland 1500–1750.* (London, 1992).

Mitchison, Rosalind & Leneman, Leah. *Sexuality and Social Control. Scotland 1660–1780.* (Oxford, 1989).

104 Houston: *Population of Britain and Ireland* p. 37.

105 Ibid. p. 46.

106 Cullen: *Modern Ireland* p. 83.

107 Devine: 'The English connection' p. 20. Houston: *Population of Britain and Ireland* p. 39.

108 Devine: 'The English connection' p. 20.

109 Mitchison & Leneman: *Sexuality and Social Control.*

110 Jones: *Early Modern Wales.* pp. 2–18.

111 Mitchison, Rosalind. 'North and South: the development of the gulf in Poor Law practice'. In Houston & Whyte: *Scottish Society* p. 202.

112 Ibid. p. 215.

113 Mitchison, Rosalind. 'Who were the poor in Scotland, 1690–1830?' In Mitchison & Roebuck: *Economy and Society* pp. 140–48.

114 Dickson, David. 'In search of the Old Irish Poor Law'. In Mitchison & Roebuck: *Economy and Society* pp. 149–59.

115 Tyson: 'Contrasting regimes' pp. 70–71.

116 Smout, T. Christopher. *A History of the Scottish People 1560–1830.* (London, 1972) pp 313–314.

117 Dawson, J.E.A. 'The origins of the "Road to the Isles". Trade, communication and Campbell power in early-modern Scotland'. In R.A. Mason & N. MacDougall (eds.) *People and Power in Scotland.* (Edinburgh, 1992), pp. 74–103.

118 MacPherson, A.G. 'Migration fields in a traditional Highland community' *Journal of Historical Geography* 10 (1984) pp. 1–14.

119 Dodgshon, Robert A. 'Pretense of blude and plaice of thair dwelling': the nature of Highland clans 1500–1750'. In Houston & Whyte: *Scottish Society* pp. 169–98.

120 Stevenson, David. *Alastair McColla and the Highland Problem in the Seventeenth Century.* (Edinburgh. 1980). MacGregor, M.D.W. *A political history of the MacGregors before 1571.* Unpublished PhD. thesis, University of Edinburgh, 1989.

121 Jones: *Early Modern Wales* p. 37. Dodgshon: 'Pretense of blude'.

122 Ellis: 'The concept of British History' p. 5.

123 Ibid. p. 9.

PART TWO:
ASSESSMENTS

CHAPTER 8

British History and Irish History

T.C. Barnard

In 1688 two tourists visited the Jesuit college in Rome. Among the sights was an image of Ireland. The personification, although decked out with sceptre and harp, was crowned only with a ducal coronet. When the observant sightseers enquired why Ireland was not honoured as a kingdom, their guide agreed that the island had indeed been recognized as such by the pope. However, when Henry VIII assumed the kingly title in 1541, it had not been endorsed by the papacy. As a result, several Jesuits within the community 'did not think fit to call the country a kingdom'. Furthermore, while priests eulogized the Catholic James II, it was as 'king of England or Great Britain without mentioning Ireland.'[1]

This incident introduces an important theme. It reminds that in the seventeenth century, as in the sixteenth and eighteenth, Ireland's precise status was puzzling. But what often confused contemporaries may look clearer to confident modern investigators. The essence of Ireland's constitutional position within the *imperium* of the English monarch as a distinct kingdom annexed to the crown of England was agreed throughout this period. Less clear was how the relationship should work.[2] Malfunctioning regularly caused trouble, and trouble, whether in paper controversies or on the battlefield, attracts historians. The latter have boldly deduced the history of Ireland from the numerous disquisitions on the idea of Ireland. Conceptual frameworks have been added. Thus, the notions of colony,[3] empire,[4] province,[5] frontier marches,[6] composite monarchy,[7] multiple kingdoms,[8] *anciens régimes*[9] and confessional states[10] have all been enlisted. In addition, distinct strands of thinking in and about Tudor, Stuart and Hanoverian Ireland have been isolated: an embryonic unionism,[11] conservative constitutionalism,[12] provincial particularism[13] and incipient nationalism.[14] These bold characterizations have enabled those outside the Irish historical community to fit Ireland into their larger constructs.[15] Specialists on Ireland itself have often been less happy with these arresting models. Just as novelists or film-makers who convey too well the ordinariness of daily life are in danger of boring their audiences, so too those scholars who report the confusions, inconsistencies and complexities of Ireland may quickly lose their readers. At the risk of doing so, it is nevertheless worth illustrating the range of opinions among the inhabitants of seventeenth- and eighteenth-century Ireland about the nature of their country and themselves, as well as how they were regarded by outsiders. Then it will be easier to understand how British approaches have elucidated these attitudes, and to consider what such perspectives distort or conceal.

I

In 1682 a recent English settler in Ireland declared happily that 'Ireland was become West England'.[16] What is striking here is that Ireland is associated fruitfully with *England* not *Britain*. This thinking embodied a tradition which had persisted since settlers from England had first planted Ireland in the twelfth century. Their successors, designated as 'the English of Ireland', 'Old English' or 'the English Irish', together with the New English who had arrived since the sixteenth century, by insisting on their Englishness requested rights as free-born Englishmen equal to those of the English who had remained in England and Wales.[17] Furthermore, the stress on Englishness as a defining attribute revealed a reluctance about identifying too closely with their domicile or its aboriginals. Otherwise the settlers would more quickly have thought of themselves as Irish, and have been content to be so described by others. Only in the mid-eighteenth century, it would seem, did a stronger feeling of Irishness develop within the planter settlements.[18] In part it was a response to the insensitive treatment meted out by England. It also coincided with, and may have been fostered by, a more relaxed view of the Catholic Irish among whom they dwelt and of the scary landscape which they inhabited.[19] Even so, the willingness to think of themselves as Irish lagged behind the propensity of the English (and Britons) to call all within Ireland Irish. This idea of Irishness, now applied so promiscuously and without respect to ethnicity or confession, dealt still in the stereotypes of the Irish current since the twelfth century. What hitherto had differentiated the English and Scots in Ireland from one another and from the indigenes was blurred.[20] The primitivism, backwardness and barbarism thought to mark Gaelic society were transferred from natives to newcomers. Novel notions of politeness, civility and moderation separated the English in Ireland from their originals still in England. Unsympathetic observers at best mocked the Irish Protestants as uncouth provincials; at worst, as degenerates who had gone native.[21]

An alternative to the stark polarities of English or Irish was to be British. Yet, as Colin Kidd has demonstrated, throughout the seventeenth century, Britishness appealed to few in Ireland.[22] The pamphleteer in the Dublin of 1682 had not proposed West *Britishness* but West *Englishness* as the quality which now defined the more populous and prosperous Protestant community. New images and imaginings of Britain could include Ireland. John Morrill has noticed how, as early as the sixteenth century, atlas makers lumped together Ireland and Britain under the title *Magna Britanniae*.[23] In a similar spirit, an Irish antiquary in the 1680s wrote of 'the empire of the British Isles (among which we rank Ireland).'[24] Maps were especially important in determining how their owners conceived the places where they lived. However, by that reasoning, the availability by the later seventeenth and eighteenth centuries of detailed maps, first of Ireland alone, then of the particularities of its topography and ultimately of individual counties, towns and estates, encouraged a localism which centred on the neighbourhood, province and Ireland itself rather than on Britain.[25]

Thoughts of Britain and Britishness occurred intermittently in Ireland. As early as 1673 a writer celebrated Ireland as 'one of the chiefest members of the British empire', and predicted that soon the island would be transformed into 'an orderly commonwealth, civil in itself and in time like to prove profitable to the prince, and at all times a good additional strength to the British Empire'.[26] This anonymous analyst disclosed a number of traits which would recur. Once a British Empire expanded beyond Europe, it offered a framework other than the Tudors' and Stuarts' *imperium* of England, Scotland and Ireland in which to set the last. Increasingly Ireland was looked upon and treated as the original and nearest component in that empire. By the later eighteenth century, the aggrieved Irish compared their lot not with that of the Scots and Welsh (as they had earlier), but with other colonists, particularly in North America.[27] The invocation of Englishness dwindled as the preferred means of

Protestants (and Catholics) in Ireland to protest against English mistreatment. This tendency for the inhabitants of Ireland to think of themselves as members of the British Empire was further strengthened by their increasingly easy access to it.[28] Britishness was born of the benefits some in Ireland derived from the Empire. Yet, when Ireland was belatedly brought within the Union in 1801 it was not as a component of Great Britain but of a United Kingdom.[29]

Another noteworthy feature of the 1673 account of *The Present State of Ireland* common to many more contemporary surveys was the inconsistency with which the terminology of British and English was used. The writer described how those of English descent had conquered and colonized Ireland. Simultaneously he contended that Ireland had first been settled from Britain and praised the industry of recent 'Protestant British planters'. He was also keen to advise how 'the Protestant British interest' could be fortified.[30] As he switched, apparently at random between 'British' and 'English', he aimed more at stylistic liveliness than ethnographical exactness. However, others who favoured 'British' rather than 'English' to qualify the settlers, may have had stronger motives. It has been noted, for example, that the inclusive term 'British' was employed at moments of crisis. During the 1640s and after 1688, Protestant solidarity had to be promoted. 'British Protestant' served better than the discrete designations of 'English' and 'Scots', since the latter too accurately mirrored the ethnic, political and confessional disunity.[31] In the eighteenth century, 'British' continued to be preferred by those, like Samuel Madden and William Henry, who either lived among or were descended from families which had originated in Scotland.[32] Again its use told of a wish to end the fierce divisions between Ulster Scots, their distinctiveness preserved by confessional difference, legal discriminations and continuing links with Scotland, and the generally conformist Protestants of English stock.

Britain as something other than an aery notion or antiquarian's invention took on greater solidity after 1707. But the statutory incorporation of Britain added to the anomaly of Ireland.[33] Whereas in Scotland the Presbyterian kirk was now ensconced as the state church, concurrently its offshoots in Ireland were harassed.[34] By asserting their Britishness, Ireland's inhabitants, although themselves denied the legal benefits of Union, might add to their claims to be treated like their sovereign's other free-born subjects. Except among a minority, mainly in the British province of Ulster, until the later eighteenth century disgruntled Irish Protestants requested appropriate rights still as the English of Ireland, not as Britons.

As the pamphleteer of 1673 showed both individual identities and perceptions of Ireland were contingent, multiple and inconsistent. Concocted for topical purposes, as these purposes altered, so too did the characterizations. In consequence, while reflections on Ireland and Irishness abound from the sixteenth to the eighteenth centuries, they offer treacherous evidential foundations for grand theoretical structures.[35] In general, those historians who favour the British approach are not responding with acute sensitivity to the cadences they catch in the voices from the Irish past. It is irrelevant to the merits of this British perspective that few in Ireland thought of themselves as British. Whatever they thought they might nevertheless be British. Imposed retrospectively, Britishness may make sense of much that otherwise is incomprehensible or overlooked.

Champions of British history can remind sceptics how, for better or worse, since 1169 parts of Ireland have been ruled by and from England. Between 1541 and 1719 Ireland was universally regarded as 'united and knit to the imperial crown of England'.[36] After 1603 a single monarch wore 'the imperial crowns of England, Scotland and Ireland'.[37] Only the practical consequences of this theory bred disputes. One interpretation saw Ireland as 'a distinct kingdom', and therefore to be ruled 'according to the ancient customs, laws and statutes thereof'.[38] An alternative, which was embodied in the British statute of 1719, was to emphasize how the kingdom of Ireland was 'subordinate unto and dependent on the imperial crown of Great Britain, as being inseparably united and annexed thereunto'.[39] Despite the action of the British parliament in subjecting Ireland more thoroughly, throughout the eighteenth century Ireland enjoyed its own institutions faithfully copied from English prototypes, by which it could govern itself. Through council, parliament, law courts, municipal corporations, the shrievalty, commissions of the peace and county militias, a functional autonomy prevailed.[40] By manning these posts, the Protestants of Ireland may have identified more with the interests of Ireland. Also, insensitive interference by the British government retarded the growth of British loyalties and incubated Irishness. In some accounts, this is characterized as 'colonial nationalism'.[41] But the situation was further complicated as insidious forces, especially of economy and culture, promoted an involuntary integration into and assimilation to British ways.[42]

Identities were rarely exclusive. Indeed they could be donned and discarded as occasions required. It was possible to hold the responsibilities as head of a house, dynasty or affinity with an attachment to barony, county, province, kingdom and empire.[43] Moreover, the same person could belong simultaneously to tangible and intangible communities arranged around religious denomination, voluntary associations, regiments, guilds and recreational circles. Sometimes these contracted into the immediate neighbourhood; others expanded across the seas. How the rival claims of these affiliations were balanced and how individuals experimented with a sequence of identities, including Anglo-Irish and Hiberno-Scots as well as Irish, English and British, have not long detained British historians. For the most part, the latter have interested themselves in supplementing or enriching earlier histories by stressing what hitherto has been neglected: the British context of Irish lives. Almost inevitably this requires a concentration on public lives which can be reconstructed from accessible evidence. Thus, politics and political ideas bulk large in the new British history. At a time when much of the most innovative writing on Ireland's past concentrates on topics other than high politics, and on the private as much as the public sphere, the impact of British historians might be thought retrograde.[44] However, before looking more closely at that and other objections to the British movement, it is necessary to sketch its origins and impact.

II

1972 and the publication then of the memorable rodomontade by J.G.A. Pocock are conventionally taken as inaugurating the latest manifestation of British history.[45] Pocock's exhortation can be located in a time of doubt and dissatisfaction. His programme offered a means to assuage guilt among the thoughtful for the mess Britain had made of Ireland. Not only did violence engulf a part of the United Kingdom which many had forgotten belonged to it, the Union itself might shortly be dismembered. This possibility, coupled with the power of irredentist surges within other states, reminded how artificial and unstable were many long-established countries.

Those who have obeyed Pocock's injunctions quickly appreciated that Ireland (and Scotland), traditionally at the bottom of the English government's priorities (and therefore of English historians'), might unexpectedly climb to the top. Restiveness, sometimes indeed outright rebellion, regularly forced Ireland on England's attention. John Morrill, one of the most energetic and prolific practitioners of British history, has identified four periods in which Scotland and Ireland – either in unison or alone – decided the priorities of the English government: 1534–47; 1559–72; 1592–1609; 1637–60.[46]

Others might be included, notably the years between 1688 and 1691[47] and several episodes in the eighteenth century. There existed, too, occasions when the interconnectedness of Irish and English events expressed itself in something other than rebellion. From time to time Ireland was valued as a laboratory in which to test policies for later use in England. Richard II, the first sovereign since John to visit Ireland, realised this.[48] Then Wentworth in the 1630s, Henry Cromwell between 1655 and 1659 and Tyrconnell after 1686 turned Ireland into a model for what might be essayed elsewhere.[49]

Well-known moments when the usually parallel histories of Ireland and England converged, often with destructive results for one if not both kingdoms, bewitch the exponents of British history. Their renewed enquiries, while they throw fresh light on Ireland, document best the flawed nature of the English state. As a result, the new British history has been seen by some in Scotland and Ireland as incorrigibly anglocentric.[50] It rests, too, on premises and evidence which disregard many important aspects of Ireland simply because they do not impinge sensationally on England or Britain.

Notoriously, the apparatus of the English or – after 1707 – British state in Ireland never permeated all areas of Irish life. Numerous relationships survived or revived which owed little or nothing to the English link. Some were introspective and parochial; others, more expansive, revealed cultural and confessional communities which encompassed a transnational Gaeldom, Protestantism or Catholicism. Kinship, language and trade united some within Ireland with others in the ports, cities and regiments of continental Europe and North America.[51] Ideas, fashions and goods could enter Ireland without first being mediated through England. Nevertheless, the English connection, evident in the governance or the simple physical propinquity, was something Ireland could not escape.[52] Also, being so copiously documented, it is readily retrieved.

Long before 1972, indeed well before 1922, three staples dominated Irish historical writing: politics, land and religion. An English or British slant was unavoidable, thanks to the way in which the topics were conceived and because of the surviving evidence. It is a truism that the winners write history. Although, after 1922, the independent Irish emerged as final victors, they had to reconstruct their chronicle from the materials generated and preserved by their adversaries, for long ascendant. The British state spawned the principal archive. Moreover, the bullish government in Tudor and Stuart Ireland, like its counterparts elsewhere in Europe, worsted its opponents – in part – through bureaucracy, written laws and standardized and printed documents. Similarly the beneficiaries of this order utilized the law, formal leases, accounts, maps and surveys. Ruling through paper and print the English state in Ireland, together with its accessories, left many traces. Historians have long been collecting, calendaring and deciphering them.

Two archival accidents have tilted treatments of Ireland's past further towards the English or British side. Because of losses within Ireland (notably the burning of the Public Records in 1922), it is to the records of the state and its servants now preserved mainly outside Ireland to which historians have to turn. Letters, memoranda and petitions which passed between Dublin Castle and Whitehall abound. They are supplemented by what politicians associated with Ireland collected and then abstracted when they left office. The muniments of the Cecils, Carews, Hydes, Boyles and Butlers fuse, and so confuse, the public and private activities of their owners. These notables, like others whose estate and family papers have been preserved, seldom concerned themselves only with Ireland. Usually their archives have survived because the families retained or acquired interests in Britain. Thither they, or their descendants, removed, along with their papers. Historians, aware of the British or Anglo-Irish contexts in which these grandees of Ireland functioned, have been willing enough to proclaim what these collections demonstrate: Irish lives which necessarily linked with, and sometimes were ended in, England.

Historians of Ireland do sometimes chafe at the restrictions imposed by such evidence, and the British bias which it perpetuates. Jealous of the virgin territory annexed by historians elsewhere, the ambitious have explored how to evoke and resuscitate the mentalities and behaviour of the modest or humble, the vanquished and marginal. Largely destroyed are the parish registers, wills, inventories and series of routine judicial and administrative records utilized by historians of other societies. Even so, familiar materials when approached from novel angles can yield unexpected insights. Recently such topics as popular belief and recorded crime, long felt to be beyond the ken of Irish historians, have been wonderfully illumined, thanks to the discovery of unsuspected materials or the imaginative use of the familiar.[53] Fragments of Irish verse and prose have been pieced together, and their codes cracked, in order to understand more of indigenous responses to the newcomers in Ireland. Yet this evidence has been used principally to elucidate the perennial obsession of the Irish with English conquest and rule. Sadly, the erudite interpreters have failed to agree on the messages they hear in these reflections.[54]

Independent of any quest for the lost worlds of the obscure, even before 1922 reliance on tainted British sources could be reduced by mining continental deposits, Such researches catalogued exhaustively the disabilities loaded onto Irish Catholicism and enlarged its martyrology.[55] If these enquiries traced relationships – with the papacy and Catholic states outside the British ambit – the findings were presented often as a triumph over English repression. Once more, those who most stridently denounced the centuries of English authority could not but accept it as the framework in which most activities within Ireland had occurred.

A wish to inventory past misdeeds, correct present evils and shape the future through the writing of history was pronounced before 1922. Many nineteenth-century scholars, such as Prendergast, Froude, Lecky, Gilbert and Hickson, were partisans either of unionism or nationalism.[56] Partial independence in 1922 may have weakened the imperative to write in order to redress injustices. Since then, even those historians active in politics, have been more reticent about obtruding their current preoccupations. Discretion was also enjoined by academic training. In obedience to the precepts of an objective, even 'scientific' history, the past was to be approached dispassionately.[57] Such coyness disappointed traditionalists who accorded the historian a public duty akin to that of the *seanchaidhe* as seer in Gaelic society.[58] Less overtly, Pocock's call that the historian attend more closely to what present circumstances revealed about the fabrication and failures of Britain revived the notion of a civic function.[59] As fresh troubles spread between Ireland and Britain in the later 1960s, history was seen as a prime culprit and as a possible palliative. Penitence and prophecy were now expected from historians.

The apocalyptic forebodings of the early 1970s engendered the demands for an integrated history of Britain and Ireland. That atmosphere of expectancy as the Union apparently edged towards dissolution is now as hard to recreate as the similar mood which greeted the execution of Charles I in 1649 or the assembling of the Nominated Parliament in 1653. Yet, even if something of that intense anxiety has abated, what it created – the need to write truly British history – thrives. Nevertheless, since 1972 the injunction has been obeyed more readily by historians of England, for whom it had the allure of novelty, than by historians of Ireland, who had long practised what was being preached.

Like it or not, even those historians of Ireland who wished to escape from the constraints of the British connection, seldom succeeded completely. Britain, so close and intrusive, loomed as a continual presence. Much of the best work undertaken between 1922 and 1972 accepted England's or Britain's intermittent interventions as a neutral fact. A pioneer, a British historian *avant la lettre*, is D.B. Quinn. Often counted as one of the triumvirs, along with T.W. Moody and R.D. Edwards, who introduced a new professionalism into Irish history during the 1930s, Quinn's career, unlike that of the other two exemplars, lay mostly outside Ireland. In consequence his historical interests diverged from theirs. Starting with two of the familiars of study – the apparatus of the English state in Ireland and land ownership – Quinn placed them more firmly in their times.[60] Thus, Ireland added detail and new understanding to the processes through which the Tudors had expanded their authority and their subjects had pushed westwards. Others who related Tudor and Stuart Ireland to what was happening in Britain and Europe included another trio, Hugh Kearney, Terence Ranger and Aidan Clarke. Attracted by the theories utilized by European, American and British historians in the 1950s and 1960s they applied them to the Irish evidence.[61] The coincidence of several 'contemporaneous' rebellions across Europe during the 1640s had long prompted scholars to speculate about common causes.[62] The hypothesis of 'a general crisis' was advanced. The crisis was variously characterized. It might have resulted from rapid economic transformations and consequent social dislocations. More centralized monarchies with willing bureaucracies antagonized privileged groups. These animosities between rulers and ruled then expressed themselves in refusals to contribute enough men and monies to win wars. At the same time global chilling ruined harvests.[63] Kearney, Ranger and Clarke revealed that Ireland, on the edge of Europe, could not escape from its maladies.

For historians of Britain these reminders of Irish experiences were especially timely. The former had long pondered over the causes of the English civil wars. These were routinely allowed to have been 'a War of Three Kingdoms'.[64] However, such an admission did not resolve the ferocious skirmishing over the wars' causes, and whether long- or short-term.[65] The infusion of Irish (and Scottish) evidence refreshed controversies which were losing momentum. Yet the fresh acknowledgement of the roles of Ireland and Scotland supported, according to inclination, either those who believed in the contingent and personal or those who argued for a structural and ideological content. By the 1970s, the historians of early-seventeenth-century Ireland, like their counterparts in England,[66] retreated from the grand theories of causation into the particular and local. By examining minutely the chronology of developing crises, the accidents and personalities were thrown into sharper relief.[67] Also, the local contexts out of which conflict arose were exhaustively recreated, especially in the provinces of Ulster and Munster where natives had been displaced by new British settlers.[68] To those engaged on researches of this sort the admonitions of Pocock and his acolytes, when not an irrelevance, merely justified what already was in hand.

Unpredictable conjunctures which issued in the uprising of 1641 were now more sharply delineated. But behind these episodes was sensed the bigger problem, often discerned by historians of Ireland. The state in Ireland might faithfully replicate the English original. However it did not function like the prototype. In understanding why this should be so historians of Ireland were helped by work on other early modern kingdoms. The notion of the general crisis was being refined so that the nature of the crisis between sovereigns and subjects was better understood. First H.G. Koenigsberger with his analyses of 'composite states',[69] and then J.H. Elliott with an incisive discussion of 'multiple monarchies',[70] offered models with which the Tudor and Stuart polity could be compared. Immediately, Ireland looked less exceptional. The predicaments of the United Provinces, the Spanish Netherlands, Portugal, Catalonia, Milan, the two Sicilies, Bohemia, Hungary, Poland and Lithuania may not exactly match Ireland's.[71] Nevertheless, the parallels, convergences and divergences are suggestive.

Enthusiasm to learn from historians of Europe is connected with a wish, long entertained by some students of the Irish past, to insist on the European dimension of Irish history. The wars of the 1640s or 1680s and 1690s respond well to such treatment.[72] Ireland, itself convulsed by its own wars over religion, was drawn into the strategies of continental powers.[73] Frequently England's anxiety about Ireland centred on the threat that it posed for security. As a result Ireland might be viewed in London primarily as an issue of foreign policy.[74] However, illuminating as this European perspective is, it can hardly supplant but only supplement the English and British approaches. Meanwhile, a different force had been at work, distinct from those so far considered, which was to complicate the task of the historian of Ireland in the wake of Pocock's proposals.

III

Pocock's article in 1972 included a critique of the naivete and negligence of some who had been writing England's story. Judged by these standards, historians of Ireland were generally less culpable. However, they were soon attacked for *trahison des clercs* in other quarters.[75] Much of the historical work on Ireland between 1922 and the 1970s, sketched impressionistically above, used British, American and European contexts and comparisons. If these helped to make sense of otherwise baffling incidents, they also questioned whether Ireland was unique in its history. Many of the most dramatic events – conquest, famine, dispossession and colonization – had numerous close if not exact parallels in and beyond Europe. Renewed enthusiasm after 1972 for an explicitly British approach only strengthened the search for apt comparisons. Of course, it was possible, and it has often happened, that Ireland when integrated into or juxtaposed with the histories of Britain resists incorporation because so idiosyncratic. Yet if the unique qualities of Ireland have emerged more strongly from these sustained exercises in British history, this was not always the aim. Rather the invention (or reinvention) of a British history which includes Ireland could be regarded as a further phase in the enterprise of normalizing (and by implication devaluing) what Ireland had suffered. As such, it was a sinister manifestation of a hydra-headed 'revisionism'.[76]

'Revisionism' is largely the creation of scholars eager to extract from diffuse and empirical historical researches into Ireland's past a shared core of theory. When not a figment in the fertile minds of those obsessed with ideological and theological systems, it is a movement the impact of which has been greatest in the history of Ireland after 1800. However, it does not always ignore earlier centuries.[77] The relationship between 'revisionism' and the new British history is at best ambivalent and at worst antagonistic. The British approach was born of an unease about the divergent directions taken by historians of England, Wales, Scotland and Ireland. The revisionists, as characterized by their critics, had utilized the methods and insights of British, European and American colleagues, and had tended to treat Ireland as a hybrid or variant of the states to be found throughout Europe or the emergent colonies rather than as an exception. Whatever their adversaries might contend, the so-called revisionists adhered to no single intellectual school. However, many were, either consciously or unwittingly, precocious exponents of British history. Seldom were they content to detach Irish experience from larger contexts. Ironically, those dissatisfied with the achievements of the revisionists are themselves disciples of other movements in continental and American historiography. In so far as they wish to recreate what life may have been like for the unseen and unheard majorities who lived beyond the reach of the English state in Ireland, they reject a history written solely by and about the male members of the ascendancy.

Practical difficulties, notably in the sources, impede the evocation of the everyday or the evaluation of the irrational and imagined. Any continuous and comprehensive account of popular beliefs, culture and politics or of gender relations, age, authority and material life, eludes even the most adept. Nevertheless, by studying such themes the historian of Ireland might be freed from the thrall of the British state. Recent studies of popular religion after the Reformation, recorded crime in the eighteenth century and, more tentatively, of popular cultures, show what the ingenious and industrious can accomplish.[78] More often than not these pioneers have been inspired by English or British innovators. Inhabitants of an overwhelmingly anglophone world, historians of Ireland also look eagerly to America for directions, less frequently to Europe.[79]

The main thrust of the new British history has forwarded that old familiar, political history. Recent work concentrates still on those episodes when Ireland either showed up the flaws in the British state or intervened sensationally in English affairs. These moments when Ireland impinged on England (or Britain), as well as being the best documented, have traditionally attracted the closest scholarly scrutiny, long before 1972. They edge out the duller scenes of provincial or colonial life and obscure the lives of women and the unimportant. They also encourage the opinion that convergence, even violent collision, rather than parallel courses normally characterized the relationship between Ireland and England.

A notable example of the vitality of this orthodox political history is the continuing division of sixteenth-century Ireland into the reigns of the viceroys. Shorter than regnal years, viceregal tours of duty compartmentalize and personalize the past. In the early modern world, such an approach may be helpful. Individual lords lieutenant imprinted policy with their own distinctive stamp. From the rise and fall in 1534 of the Kildares,[80] through the sequence of St. Leger, Sussex, Crofts, Sidney and Perrot,[81] to the rigour of Wentworth and Henry Cromwell[82] or the relaxed dexterity of Ormonde,[83] through the alarms raised by the Catholic Tyrconnell to the final supersession of the Irish-born in 1713,[84] the identity of the viceroy has been seen as a key to initiatives. Indeed, a recent impressive analysis of the mid-Tudor epoch, posits 'the age of the viceroy'.[85] The best of these studies untangle the mesh which linked incumbents in Dublin Castle with courtiers and councillors in England or grandees and clients in the Irish provinces. Conceptual tools handled with good effect in the contemporary histories of France and England, such as bastard feudalism, faction and *clientèles*, have opened up some of the secrets of Irish government.[86] *Par excellence*, the politics of the viceroyalty is the stuff of British history. The approach may attribute too much to individuals, with the implication that each was empowered to set fresh objectives. As a result, policy is represented as starkly polarized: between coercion and conciliation or sword and word.[87] Essential similarities in the problems and solutions may accordingly be overlooked.

This habit of seeing the viceroyalty chiefly through its occupants uncovers a failing which besets other parts of Irish history. Only in David Hayton's largely unpublished discussion of the structure and workings of politics in the reign of Queen Anne is the viceroyalty as an institution anatomized.[88] Changes in the status and powers of the lords lieutenant have still to be inferred from the discrete studies of individuals.[89] This makes it difficult at present to assess how much the institution assisted or retarded the synchronization of Ireland's government with that of England, let alone Britain. Any history of the Irish viceroyalty as political and administrative institution would certainly fortify the prevailing anglocentric, if not the British, interpretation of early modern Ireland. More usefully it might stimulate explicit treatment of a theme which should be, but so far has not been, central to the questioning of British historians: the process of anglicization and the creation – both at political and cultural levels – of a vibrant Britishness. Remembering the limited patronage, attenuated court, increasingly brief stays and – from 1713 – the English birth of the viceroys, the tentative conclusion must be that the office failed fully to integrate the political elites of Protestant Ireland into a British system.[90] Other agencies which reproduced and upheld English government, such as the privy council, law courts, county and borough magistracies, grand juries, municipal corporations and local militias, have received equally patchy coverage.[91] The absence of systematic studies of these aspects of government, understandable owing to the destruction of many essential records, hampers any satisfactory evaluation of success or failure of the Irish government in imposing itself on the localities. As a result, extended comparison between what was or was not achieved in Ireland with the successes of the state in remoter parts of England and Wales looks not only premature, but foolhardy.

Historians of Britain, England and Ireland, suddenly keen to trace the jerky process of state formation, need to compare and combine what was happening in the discrete parts of the Tudors', Stuarts' and Hanoverians' realms. Here they face a hazard too little appreciated.

If government and administration in England and Wales evolved constantly in response to opportunities and problems, so too did the state in Ireland. It is, perhaps, too easy to assume that what administrators in Dublin and the Irish provinces contended was true: namely that Ireland's government and society more nearly resembled England's as the decades passed. Most acute Irish observers, even when impressed by the pace of change, acknowledged that Ireland still lagged behind England. By the eighteenth century some boasted that the gap had been narrowed: from one hundred to perhaps eighty or fifty years.[92] The ideal to which the apologists of the English order in Ireland aspired – an Ireland which reproduced the social organization, economy and government of England – was not itself a fixed one. It needs hardly to be stressed how quickly and fundamentally England was changing. If, as some analysts assert, Ireland underwent unusually rapid and profound social, economic and cultural transformations between the sixteenth and late eighteenth centuries, these were not always conforming it more closely to the English norm. Behind the superficial assimilation of Ireland to English practices of dress, tenure, language and behaviour, other accelerating forces in the Irish economy and society may have widened its divergence from English standards.[93]

The gaps in the thematic treatment of institutions extend to Irish society in the early modern period. Again this weakens the case of those who have resorted to explanatory modes, such as a rapid shift from a lineage to a civil society in seventeenth-century Ireland or the characterization of Hanoverian Ireland as an *ançien regime*.[94] Too much is unclear about the structures, members and values of the social hierarchies to allow confident comparison between the Irish and British or European manifestations.

At first glance, the elites of Tudor and Stuart Ireland appear the best documented element in that society. The process through which the established were supplanted by interlopers has been exhaustively considered. Furthermore, the ingenuity and opportunism with which the defeated lessened their losses have been explored. In some places as proprietors, in many more as occupiers, older owners hung on.[95] Certainly the new order can be apprehended in outline. But little detail – about total numbers county by county, the relationship between landed income, status and office-holding, ethnic and geographical origins, exogamy or endogamy – has, as yet, been added.[96] By the eighteenth century, members of this order performed the same functions as their counterparts in England and Wales. They sat in parliament, administered their counties, ruled their parishes and manors. This Protestant Ascendancy is customarily thought to have been composed of landowners.[97] Such a misjudgment is easy to explain. For Irish nationalists, loss of land encapsulated Irish subjection to England. As a grievance, its extent could be quantified, the losers identified and the beneficiaries pilloried. More recently, the misapprehension persists because the other, more numerous groups in Protestant Ireland lurk unseen and unconsidered.

The majority of Protestants in later seventeenth- and eighteenth-century Ireland did not own land. They may not even have lived on the land, but in the many middling and small towns.[98] For the minority which did possess land, it rarely supplied the sole or an adequate income. Revenues had to be supplemented from office, trade and professions. But the latter activities, and those who followed them, have attracted scant attention. Studies of such groups outside Ireland show what might be attempted.[99] In another sense as well, such enquiries represent a missed chance to practise a useful British history. How the clergy of the established Church of Ireland (and of the dissenting congregations and Catholic Church), barristers, attorneys, doctors, surveyors, bankers and merchants were constituted might reveal the fluctuating interplay of integrative and separatist pressures. Lawyers, for example, before they could practise in Ireland had to qualify themselves through residence at a London Inn of Court.[100] Similarly, if less formally, the requirements of the established Church, especially after the 1666 Act of Uniformity passed, obliged its personnel to adopt English norms of doctrine and ritual. In 1708 the English academic set over the Church of Ireland as primate could state confidently that 'the Church of England and Ireland are one and the same Church'.[101] British historians, keen to trace a development from congruity through uniformity to fusion, may find vindication for their approach.[102] Again, though, outward integration can mask a continuing or increased separatism.[103] Other groups whose training and business spanned the Irish Sea and often involved them in continental Europe and colonial America need to be investigated. In the interlinked worlds of banking, trade and politics, after 1689 the shift in the centre of gravity towards Ulster, strengthened bonds both with London and Scotland.[104] These, together with the prevalence in Ulster of Scottish and English settlers which sanctified the usage 'British', may have fostered an Ulster Protestant feeling of Britishness. Such forces did not combine in the other provinces where different tendencies prevailed.

Social and occupational hierarchies have lately interested historians of England and Wales. The latter may not have agreed any single

classificatory system, but the problems of nomenclature and evaluation have been clarified.[105] The implications of this work for historians
of Ireland, whether or not they consciously follow the British agenda,
have yet to be felt. This is the more surprising as social organization
was one of the ways in which England intended to subordinate Ireland.
English or Scottish models of urban and manorial settlement were to
be substituted for the apparent haphazardness of Gaelic society. By
proscribing and uprooting the indigenes and by importing newcomers from Wales, Scotland and England, this goal was pursued. The
results are all too clear. By the end of the seventeenth century, those
recorded as owners of land, holders of office and members of parliament, showed that a new elite had been installed. Not only had the
membership of the elites been transformed, but also their values and
behaviour.

Contemporary observers routinely lampooned the quirks of Gaelic
life; few lamented the passage of old habits., Such observations,
frequently accepted as objective reports, fed off one another.[106] How
often the pundits confronted the awkward realities of Irish society,
especially in its remoter and demotic manifestations, may be doubted.
Throughout the island, as newcomers encountered natives, sports
appeared. Yet, in order to describe these local hybrids, reporters
usually resorted to explanatory schemes and vocabulary filched from
England. Often, this was apposite. Did not Ireland have peers, knights,
esquires, gentlemen, yeomen and husbandmen? Occasionally special
nouns were improvised, such as scurloges, middlemen, gneevers and
squarsons.[107] Such terms, although hazy, at least attested to the
peculiarities in the Irish social scene not covered by the existing
English idioms.

The invented terminology alerts us to a larger problem which the
British approach has hardly helped. Elites could be expected to assist
political, cultural and perhaps confessional integration. Those in
Wales and Scotland, ambivalent towards England and Britain, varied
in the speed and enthusiasm with which they adapted to English
practices. Some hardly did so. Despite the penetrating studies for
Scotland, notably by Keith Brown, and for Wales by Philip Jenkins
and J.G. Jones, the question of how far the elites in Ireland, whether
long or lately established, were assimilated to British values has been
little pondered.[108] This is the more regrettable as the uppermost strata
of Irish society, notably the aristocracy and gentry, look amenable to
such enquiries.

Part of the reluctance to tackle this problem may arise from the
fact that England's plans for Ireland included a peerage. As a result,

the caste may be dismissed as another alien import. Nevertheless, in the sixteenth century, local chiefs readily exchanged older styles for titles granted by the English monarch. The peerage included families of different vintages, and was not simply a further ruse for replacing the indigenous with interlopers. Even so, the Irish peers of the seventeenth and eighteenth centuries, when they embraced English manners, were thought to betray their weak footing in local society. If only the peers permanently absent in England are considered, such contempt may be justified.[109] However, the fact that a minority was loosely attached to Ireland does not merit the neglect of the entire order. The one recent study, focussed on the eighteenth century, begins to correct the prevalent myopia.[110] Otherwise only individual aristocrats have been considered. The subjects – the first and second earls of Cork,[111] the first marquess of Antrim,[112] the first and second dukes of Ormonde[113] and the first earl of Orrery[114] – have been noticed because they acted outside as well as within Ireland. Therefore they are well documented. Only two of them, Antrim and Orrery, knew all three kingdoms intimately. Even then they could work successfully only in two rather than in all three at the same time. The remainder, like their counterparts in Scotland such as Hamilton and Lauderdale, followed careers at home and in England. Aristocrats, preeminent in wealth and standing, welcome at their sovereign's court, enjoyed the best opportunities to participate in something larger than their locality or a single kingdom. A transnational artistocracy, its tastes and outlook increasingly cosmopolitan, could have helped in incorporating Ireland into a powerful Britain. As yet, sadly, the particular studies, when not riddled with anachronisms, do little to illumine the issues of honour, nobility and civility. Historians of Ireland have been slow to learn from the excellent studies of Welsh, Scottish, English and European aristocracies.[115] In consequence we lack either an integrative or comparative treatment of the Irish peerage. A suspicion lingers, despite the absence of solid discussion, that by the eighteenth century Irish peers thought of themselves as English or Irish, or sometimes as both depending where they were, not British.[116] The same may well have been true of other groupings like the gentry and urban patriciates in Ascendancy Ireland.

The list of the social and occupational groups or institutions within Ireland which want detailed analysis could be lengthened to include virtually all. Notwithstanding the interest in Ireland evinced by British historians, cross-pollination remains rare. Perhaps because the interest of outsiders is suspected as a new example of cultural imperialism, historians of Ireland have not slavishly copied the crazes current in

England. Often there has been a greater readiness to learn from historians of Scotland, western Europe or North America: fellow victims of English arrogance. But these preferences have still locked Irish history into familiar chambers. The fad of British history alone cannot be blamed for the neglect of themes and topics such as institutional and cultural integration or the roles of aristocracy, gentry, merchants, town-dwellers, women or peasants. Recent suggestions for a more imaginative use of the British framework, to understand peoples, the mythic and imagined as well as the material, promise to enliven the study of Ireland.[117] But until such injunctions are obeyed, grave problems obtrude. As historians of England or Britain turn to Ireland in the hope that it might either be merged into their histories or furnish evidence for their interpretations, inadvertently they compare like with unlike. Too often ideas about how Ireland was governed or how its social structures might be remodelled are mistaken for the actuality. When institutions such as parliament, council, magistracy, militia or manor are discovered in Ireland, or groups composed of peers, esquires, gentlemen, yeomen or husbandmen, it is reasonable to conclude that each resembled its English original. Tentative findings indicate that this is not always so.

Students of Irish history, too trusting of the numerous though frequently derivative accounts of social and economic transformations, tend to emphasize convergence with, rather than divergences from, British norms. Even in the eighteenth century it was conceded that some districts, such as the Beara or Iveragh peninsulas in the south-west or Iar Connacht and parts of Donegal, still evaded British authority.[118] But these occasional exceptions have not weakened a stress on the growing homogeneity both within Ireland and between Britain and Ireland. Just as the continuing existence of strong regional variegation may need to be included in treatments of Britain, seventeenth- and eighteenth-century Ireland becomes incomprehensible without it. A difficulty in deciding how to balance integrationist and modernizing forces in Ireland with those that tended towards custom, stasis and centripetalism lies – once again – in the nature and quality of the evidence. Contemporary descriptions of Ireland from the sixteenth to the eighteenth centuries accepted English assumptions. Change was noticed and praised. What was seen was immediately equated with English phenomena. Herein began the approach which successive analysts have been unable to escape.

Would-be ethnographers in the early modern era accepted that peoples progressed at varying speeds. There existed simultaneously societies at different stages of development. If some looked to America for contemporary examples of savagery and barbarism, others were to be found closer to hand: in the peripheries of Europe, including Wales, Scotland and Ireland. Because it was also agreed that civilizations underwent cycles of improvement, apogee, decline and decay, it was possible to view Ireland either cheerfully or gloomily. Some stressed the traces of a once prosperous and cultivated people or the likelihood that under benign British rule the potential of Ireland would be realised. Others were chastened by the slow pace of change and by indigenes impervious to confessional, economic and cultural pressures.[119] The neophytes of British history, keen to adduce Irish evidence to resolve English historiographical puzzles, generally consider the concurrent events in the two (or three) kingdoms. Again this impedes any satisfying investigation of the nature of Irish government and society. Those struck by the inappropriateness of comparing Ireland with lowland England have turned to areas which may have lagged behind metropolitan developments. As a result, the marcher areas of Britain, outposts set up in France or the colonies planted in North America have been favoured.[120] Each has been fruitful, but none exactly matches the case of Ireland. Indeed, a problem may be to regard Ireland as an entity instead of as a congeries of distinctive territories. Ireland, in the hands of its most accomplished historians, splinters into bewildering fragments. As such, it is not much use to historians of Britain, who, in the main, have preferred the most coherent but simplistic evocations of Ireland.

Thus, the notion of Ireland lagging behind much of Britain, common throughout the early modern era, has not been much employed by recent writers. Much about anglicized Ireland as it emerged through the sixteenth, seventeenth and eighteenth centuries recalled medieval England. Parallels with the marches or the settlements in Lancastrian France have been traced. England itself was a land which had been settled by a succession of invaders and conquerors. The processes through which the locally powerful sorted themselves into a social and economic pecking order had similarities in the two kingdoms of England and Ireland, but, separated by several centuries, these have not been analysed.[121] Instead, when the values and attributes of the notables of Ascendancy Ireland are mocked as antiquated and anomalous, the reasons why they deliberately espoused behaviour throught to have prevailed in later medieval and Tudor England are not discussed.[122]

The English past offers some clues as to how and why English Ireland evolved as it did. Ireland's own past furnishes others. Defeat and conquest in the sixteenth and seventeenth centuries inevitably ruptured much. Discontinuities are legion. Yet some unexpected continuities have also been rediscovered. A minority willingly accommodated itself to the new order; larger numbers retained something of their customary power and prestige. What is being appreciated more slowly is the degree to which those intruded into the commanding positions as landowners, magistrates, lawyers and clergy entrenched themselves through strategies borrowed from their displaced predecessors. The importance of heredity and affinity in upholding the new political bosses, like the Boyles, Conollys, Gores and Ponsonbys, successful professionals in the law, church, armed services and government office, or as local magnificoes, suggests that the interlopers realised that authority depended still on customary ways. Yet most forms and dynamics in this new state hide in the shadows. In part this is because a captivating British history has diverted scholarly energies elsewhere.

This neglect of so many topics vital to an understanding of Ireland cannot be blamed wholly on the zest for British history. Numerous historians of Ireland have happily collaborated in the latter enterprise. They have good reasons to be grateful since they benefit from an enlarged readership and lusher fields of patronage. Like Laudianism in the 1630s, Britishness in the 1990s offers the key to academic preferment. These material gains seem to outweigh the intellectual ones. Much that historians of Ireland had laboured at long before 1972 has now been endorsed as useful. But investigators of Ireland, already fertile in their use of concepts and contexts, have received no noteworthy innovations in method or subject from the infusion of Britishness. Historians of England and Ireland sometimes congratulate themselves that they have brought Ireland at last into the mainstream of their own historical endeavours and explanations. The best of them, alert to the connotations of mainstream, echoing those of 'mainland', guard against the accusation of a fresh campaign of English cultural aggression. Through cant circumlocutions like 'these islands' or 'the Atlantic archipelago', the scrupulous search for concepts into which Ireland can be fitted quietly without exciting fears of a new conquest. Behind these commendable niceties lies a sharper sense among outsiders of guilt over Ireland's repeated mistreatment. Guilt, however, is not always the most illuminating emotion with which to recover the past.

Bent on their programme, the Britishers cry up the writing on Irish history which will forward their cause. Only a tithe of what now is published annually is likely to be read outside Ireland, such is the proliferation of small and local publications. Increasingly, even within Ireland, it is impossible to keep track of what may be useful.[123] Some of the most exciting investigations of Ireland's past ignore the new British history, obsessed still with old-fashioned politics. Yet, few other than specialists wish to luxuriate in the formlessness, ordinariness and sheer intractability of Ireland, unless they can be communicated with literary and mental brio. Instead, there is a worrying reliance on offerings of stolid Irish fare, tricked out with eye-catching English or British trimmings to render them palatable to dainty foreign stomachs. Historians of Ireland, knowing too well the problems of evidence, often find themselves at variance with British historians about what is jejeune, unsubtle or simply inaccurate.[124] These disagreements may stem from differing levels of knowledge; they can also speak of a territoriality as the locals resist a new annexation by Britain. Even so, and whatever the misgivings, the histories of Ireland and England so regularly intertwine that to separate them is to falsify much of the past. English and British approaches will continue, as they always have. Who knows? In time, they may popularize in Ireland the themes so far strikingly neglected: institutions,[125] social stratification, urbanization,[126] professionalization, immiseration, gender and sexualities.[127] In its turn, Ireland may suggest that sometimes historians of Britain have been too quick to bury regionalism, violence, crises of subsistence and the individual in societies whose small scale allowed encounters face to face. So long as no single prescription instructs the historians of Ireland and Britain what they are to do, the older, permissive historiographical regimen will yield its treasures.

Notes to Chapter 8

1   The accounts of the two travellers are: 'Journal of Samuel Waring', Public Record Office of Northern Ireland, Belfast, D 695/228; M. Misson, *A new voyage to Italy*, 4th edn. (London, 1714), ii, part i, p 177.

2   A. Clarke, 'The history of Poynings' Law: 1614–41', *Irish Historical Studies* xviii (1972), pp 207–22; Clarke, 'Colonial constitutional attitudes in Ireland, 1640–1660', *Proceedings of the Royal Irish Academy* sect C, 90 (1990), pp 357–75; R.D. Edwards and T.W. Moody, 'The history of Poynings' Law, 1494–1615', *Irish Historical Studies* ii (1941), pp 415–24; Pawlisch, *Sir John Davies and the conquest of Ireland: a study in legal imperialism* (Cambridge, 1985); D.B. Quinn, 'The early interpretation of Poynings' Law, 1494–1534', *Irish Historical Studies*, ii (1940–41), pp 241–54.

3   The most succinct summary of the merits and weaknesses of this concept

is K.S. Bottigheimer, 'Kingdom and colony: Ireland in the westward enterprise 1536–1660', in K.R. Andrews, N.P. Canny and P.E.H. Hair (eds), *The Westward Enterprise: English activities in Ireland, the Atlantic and America* (Liverpool, 1978), pp 45–65. Other treatments include: N.P. Canny, *Kingdom and Colony: Ireland in the Atlantic World 1560–1800* (Baltimore 1988); A. Clarke, 'Colonial identity in early seventeenth-century Ireland' in T.W. Moody (ed.), *Nationality and the pursuit of national independence: Historical Studies XI* (Belfast, 1978), pp 57–71.

4   F.G. James, *Ireland in the empire, 1688–1770* (Cambridge, Mass., 1973).

5   T.C. Barnard, 'Crises of identity among Irish Protestants, 1641–1685', *Past & Present* 127 (1990), p 42; J.G.A. Pocock, 'The limits and divisions of British history: in search of an unknown subject', *American Historical Review* 87 (1982), p 327.

6   S.G. Ellis, *The Pale and the Far North: government and society in early Tudor borderlands* (Dublin, 1988); Ellis, *Tudor Frontiers and Power: the making of the British state* (Oxford, 1995).

7   M. Perceval-Maxwell, 'Ireland and the monarchy in the early Stuart multiple kingdom', *Historical Journal* 34 (1991), pp 279–95; C. Russell, 'The British problem and the English civil war', *History* 72 (1987), pp 395–415.

8   T.C. Barnard, 'Scotland and Ireland in the later Stewart monarchy', in S.G. Ellis and S. Barber (eds) *Conquest and Union: Fashioning a British State 1485–1725* (London, 1995), pp 250–75.

9   S.J. Connolly, *Religion, Law and Power: the making of Protestant Ireland 1660–1760* (Oxford, 1992); J.R. Hill, 'Corporate values in Hanoverian Edinburgh and Dublin', in S.J. Connolly, R.A. Houston and R.J. Morris (eds), *Conflict, Identity and Economic Development: Ireland and Scotland, 1600–1939* (Preston, 1995), pp 114–24.

10 C.D.A. Leighton, *Catholicism in a Protestant kingdom: a study of the Irish 'Ancien Regime'* (London, 1994).

11 J. Kelly, 'The origins of the act of Union: an examination of unionist opinion in Britain and Ireland, 1650–1800', *Irish Historical Studies* xxv (1987), pp 236–63.

12 T.C. Barnard, 'The Protestant Interest, 1641–1660', in J. Ohlmeyer (ed), *Ireland: From Independence to Occupation 1641–1660* (Cambridge, 1995), pp 238–40; Clarke, 'Colonial constitutional attitudes'; J.R. Hill, 'Ireland without Union: Molyneux and his legacy', in J. Robertson (ed), *A Union for Empire: Political thought and the British Union of 1707* (Cambridge, 1995), pp 271–92.

13 T.C. Barnard, 'Conclusion: Settling and Unsettling Ireland: the Cromwellian and Williamite Revolutions', in Ohlmeyer (ed), *Independence to Occupation*, pp 288–89; J.T. Leersen, 'Anglo-Irish patriotism and its

European context: notes towards a reassessment', *Eighteenth-Century Ireland* iii (1988), pp 7–24.

14   B. Bradshaw, 'The beginnings of modern Ireland', in B. Farrell (ed), *The Irish parliamentary tradition* (Dublin, 1973), pp 68–87; Bradshaw, 'Geoffrey Keating: apologist of Irish Ireland', in B. Bradshaw, A. Hadfield and W. Maley (eds), *Representing Ireland: literature and the origins of conflict, 1534–1660* (Cambridge, 1993), pp 166–90.

15   C. Russell, The British background to the Irish rebellion of 1641', *Historical Research* 61 (1988), pp 166–81; Russell, 'The British problem and the English civil war'; Russell, *The causes of the English civil war* (Oxford, 1990); Russell, *The fall of the British monarchies, 1647–42* (Oxford, 1991); J.S. Morrill, 'The Britishness of the English Revolution, 1640–1660', in R.G. Asch (ed), *Three Nations – A Common History? England, Scotland, Ireland and British History c. 1600–1920* (Bochum, 1993), pp 83–116; Morrill, 'Historical introduction and overview: the un-English Civil War', in J.R. Young (ed), *Celtic dimensions of the British civil wars* (Edinburgh, 1997), pp 1–14.

16   R. Lawrence, *The Interest of Ireland in its trade and wealth stated* (Dublin, 1682), part ii, p 51.

17   R. Frame, '"Les Engleys Nées en Irlande": the English political identity in medieval Ireland', *Transactions of the Royal Historical Society*, 6th ser. iii (1993), pp 83–104; Hill, 'Ireland without Union'; L. O'Malley, 'Patrick Darcy, Galway lawyer and politician', in D.G. O'Cearbhaill (ed), *Galway: town and gown* (Galway, 1984), pp 90–109; J.G. Simms, *William Molyneux of Dublin* (Dublin, 1982).

18   D.W. Hayton, 'Anglo-Irish attitudes: changing perceptions of national identity among the Protestant ascendancy in Ireland, *ca* 1690–1750', in *Studies in Eighteenth Century Culture* xvii (1987), pp 145–57; Hayton, 'From Barbarian to Burlesque: English images of the Irish, c. 1660–1750', *Irish Economic and Social History*, xv (1988), pp 5–31; P.W[alsh]. *The Irish Colours Folded* (London, 1662), p 11.

19   T.C. Barnard, 'Art. architecture, artefacts and Ascendancy', *Bullan* 1/2, (1994), pp 25–26.

20   T.C. Barnard, 'Protestantism, ethnicity and Irish identities, 1660–1760', in A. Claydon and I. McBride (eds), *Chosen Peoples: Protestantism and National Identity in Britain and Ireland* (Cambridge, 1998); Hayton, 'From Barbarian to Burlesque'.

21   T.C. Barnard, 'Integration or Separation? Hospitality and display in Protestant Ireland, 1660–1800', in L. Brockliss and D. Eastwood (eds), *A Union of Multiple Identities: the British Isles, c. 1750–1850: essays in memory of A.D. Macintyre (1935–1994)* (Manchester, 1997), pp 127–46.

22   C. Kidd, 'Protestantism, Constitutionalism and British Identity under the

later Stuarts' in B. Bradshaw and P. Roberts (eds), *British Consciousness and British Identity: The making of Britain, 1533–1707* (Cambridge, 1998), pp 321–42.

23   'The British problem, c. 1534–1707', in B. Bradshaw and J. Morrill (eds), *The British Problem, c. 1534–1707; state formation in the Atlantic archipelago* (Basingstoke and London, 1996), pp 4–5. This revises the contrary statement in J. Morrill, 'The fashioning of Britain', in Ellis and Barber (eds), *Conquest and Union*, p 17.

24   R. O'Flaherty, *Ogyia* (London, 1685), translated by J. Hely (Dublin, 1793), i, p xvi.

25   J.H. Andrews, 'Maps and mapmakers', in W. Nolan (ed), *The shaping of Ireland: the geographical perspective* (Cork and Dublin, 1981), pp 99–110; T.C. Barnard, 'Learning, the learned and literacy in Ireland, c. 1660–1760' in T.C. Barnard, D. O Croínín and K. Simms (eds), '*A Miracle of Learning*' (Aldershot, 1998), p 222; T.W. Moody and W.E. Vaughan (eds), *A New History of Ireland, IV Eighteenth-Century Ireland, 1691–1800* (Oxford, 1986), pp 751–52.

26   *The Present State of Ireland* (London, 1673), sig. A2ᵛ–A3, pp 78–79. I am grateful to Dr. David Dickson for discussing with me the possible author of this tract. Even so, neither of us has been able to penetrate the anonymity of the writer.

27   T.C. Barnard, 'Robert French of Monivae 1716–1779: the worlds of a Galway squire', in G. Moran and R. Gillespie (eds), *Galway: History and Society* (Dublin, 1996), pp 271–96.

28   L.M. Cullen, 'The Irish diaspora in the seventeenth and eighteenth centuries', in N.P. Canny (ed), *Europeans on the move* (Oxford, 1994), pp 134–35, 141–48; R.B. McDowell, *Ireland in the age of imperialism and revolution, 1760–1801* (Oxford, 1979), pp 59–63.

29   The essentials of the act are printed in E. Curtis and R.B. McDowell (eds), *Irish historical documents 1172–1922* (London, 1943), pp 208–13.

30   *Present State*, pp 2, 6, 9, 12, 14, 22, 65, 71–72, 144–45, 152, 185, 248.

31   Barnard, 'The Protestant Interest', pp 239–40; Barnard, 'Settling and Unsettling Ireland', pp 281–91; Barnard, 'Protestantism, ethnicity and Irish identities'; Barnard, 'The government and Irish dissent, 1704–1780', in K. Herlihy (ed), *The politics of Irish dissent* (Dublin, 1997), pp 9–27.

32   W. Henry, 'Some hints towards a natural and typographical [sic] history of the counties of Sligo, Donegal, Fermanagh and Lough Erne', National Archives, Dublin, M 2533, pp 344, 408; [W. Henry], *An Appeal to the people of Ireland* (Dublin, 1747), pp 9–10; Henry, *A Philippic Oration against the Pretender's Son* (Dublin, 1745), pp 13, 23; S. Madden, *Memoirs of the Twentieth Century* (London, 1733), i, pp 15–16; Madden, *Reflections and*

Resolutions proper to the gentlemen of Ireland (Dublin, 1738, reprinted 1816), pp 82–83, 94–96; Madden, *Themistocles, the lover of his country* (Dublin, 1729), prologue and epilogue; Barnard, 'Protestantism, ethnicity and Irish identities'.

33 D.W. Hayton, 'Constitutional experiments and political expediency, 1689–1725' in Ellis and Barber (eds), *Conquest and Union*, pp 276–305.

34 J. Agnew, *Belfast merchant families in the seventeenth century* (Dublin, 1996), pp 91–104; D.W. Hayton, 'Exclusion and Conformity: the impact of the Sacramental Test on Irish dissenting politics', in Herlihy (ed), *Politics of Irish dissent*, pp 52–73; I. McBride, 'Presbyterians in the penal era', *Bullan*, 1/2 (1994), pp 2–23.

35 N. Canny, 'Identity formation in Ireland: the emergence of the Anglo-Irish' in N.P. Canny and A. Pagden (eds), *Colonial identity in the Atlantic world, 1500–1800* (Princeton, 1987), pp 159–212.

36 Curtis and McDowell, *Irish historical documents*, pp 77–78.

37 [John Wilson], *A Discourse of Monarchy, more particularly of the Imperial Crown of England, Scotland and Ireland* (London, 1684).

38 Curtis and McDowell, *Irish historical documents*, p 169.

39 Curtis and McDowell, *Irish historical documents*, p 168.

40 Connolly, *Religion, law and power*; D.W. Hayton, 'Walpole and Ireland', in J. Black (ed), *Britain in the age of Walpole* (London, 1984), pp 95–119; Hayton, 'The beginnings of the "Undertaker System"', in T. Bartlett and D.W. Hayton (eds), *Penal era and golden age: essays in Irish history, 1690–1800* (Belfast, 1979), pp 32–54; E.M. Johnston, *Great Britain and Ireland, 1760–1800* (Edinburgh and London, 1963); R.B. McDowell, *Ireland in the age of imperialism*.

41 J.G. Simms, *Colonial nationalism 1698–1776* (Cork, 1976).

42 L.M. Cullen, *Anglo-Irish trade, 1660–1800* (Manchester, 1968); T.C. Barnard, 'The world of goods and County Offaly in the early eighteenth century', in T. O'Neill (ed), *Offaly: History and Society* (Dublin, forthcoming).

43 Barnard, 'French of Monivae'; Barnard, 'Crises of identity'; Barnard, 'Protestantism, ethnicity and Irish identities'.

44 For example, S.J. Connolly, *Priests and people in pre-famine Ireland, 1780–1845* (Dublin, 1982); L.M. Cullen, *The emergence of modern Ireland 1600–1900* (London, 1981); D. Fitzpatrick, *Oceans of consolation: personal accounts of Irish migration to Australia* (Cork, 1995).

45 J.G.A. Pocock, 'British history: a plea for a new subject', *Journal of Modern History*, 47 (1975), pp 601–28; Pocock, 'Limits and divisions of British history'.

46 Morrill, 'The British problem', p 19.

47 Barnard, 'Settling and Unsettling Ireland'; K. Bottigheimer, 'The

Glorious Revolution and Ireland', in L.G. Schwoerer (ed), *The Revolution of 1688–89* (Cambridge, 1992), pp 234–41; D.W. Hayton, 'The Williamite Revolution in Ireland, 1688–91', in J.I. Israel (ed), *The Anglo-Dutch moment: essays on the Glorious Revolution and its world impact* (Cambridge, 1991), pp 185–212; P.H. Kelly, 'Ireland and the Glorious Revolution: from kingdom to colony', in R.A. Beddard (ed), *The Revolutions of 1688* (Oxford, 1991), pp 163–90.

48   N. Saul, *Richard II* (New Haven and London, 1997), pp 270–92.

49   T.C. Barnard, 'Planters and policies in Cromwellian Ireland', *Past and Present*, 61 (1973), pp 31–69; Barnard, 'Scotland and Ireland in the later Stewart Monarchy'; H. Kearney, *Strafford in Ireland, 1633–41: a study in absolutism* (Manchester, 1959); J. Miller, 'The earl of Tyrconnell and James II's Irish policy', *Historical Journal* xx (1977), pp 802–23; T.O. Ranger, 'Strafford in Ireland: a revaluation', in T. Aston (ed), *Crisis in Europe, 1560–1660* (London, 1965), pp 271–93.

50   K. Brown, 'British history: a sceptical comment', in Asch (ed), *Three Nations*, pp 117–27; N. Canny. 'The attempted anglicization of Ireland in the seventeenth century: an exemplar of "British history", ibid. pp 49–82.

51   N. Genet Rouffiac, 'Jacobites in Paris and St Germain-en-Laye', in E. Cruickshanks and E. Corp (eds), *The Stuart court in exile and the Jacobites* (London and Rio Grande, 1994), pp 15–38; G. Henry, *The Irish military community in Spanish Flanders, 1586–1621* (Dublin, 1992); R.A. Stradling, *The Spanish monarchy and Irish mercenaries: the wild geese in Spain, 1618–68* (Dublin, 1994); M.K. Walsh, '"Destruction by peace": Hugh O'Neill after Kinsale* (Armagh, 1986).

52   J. Fenlon, 'French influence in late seventeenth century portraits', *Irish Arts Review Yearbook 1989–90* (Dublin, 1989), pp 158–68; N. Figgis, 'Irish artists and society in eighteenth century Rome', *Irish Arts Review*, 3, no. 3 (1985), pp 28–36; S. Foster, 'Going shopping in Georgian Dublin: luxury goods and the negotiation of national identity', unpublished M.A. dissertation (Royal College of Art/Victoria and Albert Museum, 1995), pp 40–43.

53   N. Garnham, *The courts, crime and the criminal law in Ireland, 1692–1760* (Dublin, 1996); R. Gillespie, *Devoted People: belief and religion in early modern Ireland* (Manchester, 1997).

54   N. Canny, 'The formation of the Irish mind: religion, politics and Gaelic Irish literature, 1580–1750', *Past and Present* 95 (1982), pp 91–116; T. Dunne, 'The Gaelic response to conquest and colonization: the evidence of the poetry', *Studia Hibernica* xx (1980), pp 7–30; B. O Buachalla, 'James our true king: the ideology of Irish royalism in the seventeenth century' in D.G. Boyce, R. Eccleshall and V. Geoghegan (eds), *Political thought in Ireland since the seventeenth century* (London and New York, 1993), pp 7–35; M.

O'Riordan, *The Gaelic mind and the collapse of the Gaelic world* (Cork, 1990) (see also the reviews by B. Bradshaw in *Bullan* 1/1 [1994], pp 119–22, and B. O Buachalla in *Eighteenth-Century Ireland* 7 [1992], pp 139–75).

55   Much of the archival material is calendared or reported on in *Archivium Hibernicum* and *Collectanea Hibernica*. For particular uses of some of it: P.J. Corish, *The Catholic community in the seventeenth and eighteenth centuries* (Dublin, 1981); H. Fenning, *The undoing of the friars of Ireland* (Louvain, 1972); Fenning, *The Irish Dominican province, 1698–1797* (Dublin, 1990); B. Millett, *The Irish Franciscans 1651–1665* (Rome, 1964).

56   T.C. Barnard, 'Irish images of Cromwell' in R.C. Richardson (ed), *Images of Oliver Cromwell: essays by and for Roger Howell* (Manchester, 1993) pp 192–200; Barnard, '1641: a bibliographical essay' in B. MacCuarta (ed), *Ulster 1641: aspects of the rising* (Belfast, 1993), pp 173–86; R.F. Foster, 'History and the Irish question', *Transactions of the Royal Historical Society*, 5th Series, 33 (1983), pp 169–92; D.A. McCartney, *W.E.H. Lecky: historian and politician (1838–1903)* (Dublin, 1994).

57   C. Brady (ed), *Interpreting Irish history: the debate on historical revisionism* (Dublin, 1994).

58   B. Bradshaw, 'Nationalism and historical scholarship in Modern Ireland', *Irish Historical Studies* xxvi (1988–89), pp 329–51, reprinted in Brady (ed), *Interpreting Irish history,* pp 191–216.

59   Pocock, 'British history: a plea'.

60   'Anglo-Irish local government, 1485–1534', *Irish Historical Studies* i (1939), pp 354–81; 'Ireland and sixteenth-century European expansion' in T.D. Williams (ed), *Historical Studies,* I (London, 1958), pp 20–32; 'Henry VIII and Ireland', *Irish Historical Studies*, xii (1960–61), pp 318–44; 'The Munster plantation: problems and opportunities', *Journal of the Cork Historical and Archaeological Society* lxxi (1966), pp 19–40.

61   H. Kearney, 'Ecclesiastical politics and the counter-reformation in Ireland, 1618–48', *Journal of Ecclesiastical History* xi 1960), pp 202–12; H.F. Kearney, *Strafford in Ireland*; T.O. Ranger, 'The career of Richard Boyle, first earl of Cork, in Ireland 1588–1643', unpublished D.Phil. dissertation (Oxford, 1959); Ranger, 'Richard Boyle and the making of an Irish fortune', *Irish Historical Studies* x (1957), pp 257–97; Ranger, 'Strafford in Ireland: a revaluation': A. Clarke, *The Old English in Ireland, 1625–42* (London, 1966); Clarke, *The graces, 1625–41* (Dundalk, 1968); Clarke, 'Ireland and the general crisis', *Past & Present* 48 (1970), pp 79–99.

62   H.B. Meriman, *Six contemporaneous revolutions* (Oxford, 1938).

63   T. Aston (ed). *Crisis in Europe*; H.R. Trevor-Roper, 'The general crisis of the seventeenth century' in Trevor-Roper, *Religion, the Reformation and social change* (London, 1967), pp 46–89; G. Parker and L.M. Smith (eds), *The general crisis of the seventeenth century* (London, 1978).

64 The concept is implicit throughout S.R. Gardiner, *History of the Great Civil War* 3 vols (London, 1886–91), and explicit in J.C. Beckett, *The making of modern Ireland 1603–1923* (London, 1966), chapter iv

65 C. Hill, *The English Revolution, 1640* (London, 1940); L. Stone, *The causes of the English revolution 1539–1642* (London, 1972); B.S. Manning, 'The aristocracy and the downfall of Charles I', in Manning (ed), *Politics, religion and the English civil war* (London, 1973), pp 36–80.

66 J. Morrill, *The revolt of the provinces* (London, 1976); A.J. Fletcher, *The outbreak of the English civil war* (London, 1981).

67 K.J. Lindley, 'The impact of the 1641 rebellion upon England and Wales, 1641–5', *Irish Historical Studies* xviii (1972), pp 143–69; M. Perceval-Maxwell, 'Strafford, the Ulster Scots and the Covenanters', *Irish Historical Studies* xviii (1973), pp 524–51; Perceval-Maxwell, 'The Ulster rising of 1641 and the depositions', *Irish Historical Studies* xxi (1978), pp 144–67; A. Clarke, 'The genesis of the Ulster rising of 1641' in P. Roebuck (ed), *Plantation to Partition: essays in Ulster history in honour of J.L. McCracken* (Belfast, 1981), pp 29–45; R. Gillespie, 'The end of an era: Ulster and the outbreak of the 1641 rising' in C. Brady and R. Gillespie (eds), *Natives and Newcomers: essays on the making of Irish colonial society 1534–1641* (Dublin, 1986), pp 191–213; J.H. Ohlmeyer, *Civil war and restoration in three Stuart kingdoms: the career of Randal MacDonnell, marquess of Antrim, 1609–1683* (Cambridge, 1993).

68 R. Gillespie, *Colonial Ulster*, (Cork, 1985); Gillespie, 'The murder of Arthur Champion and the 1641 rising in Fermanagh', *Clogher Record* xiv (1993), pp 52–62; M. MacCarthy-Morrogh, *The Munster plantation: English migration to southern Ireland 1583–1641* (Oxford, 1986); B. MacCuarta (ed), *Ulster 1641*; M. Perceval-Maxwell, *The Scottish migration to Ulster in the reign of James I* (London, 1973); P. Robinson, *The plantation of Ulster: British settlement in an Irish landscape 1600–1670* (Dublin, 1984).

69 H.G. Koenigsberger, '*Dominum regale* or *Dominum politicum et regale*' in Koenigsberger, *Politicians and Virtuosi: essays in early modern history* (London, 1986), pp 1–25.

70 J.H. Elliott, 'A Europe of composite monarchies', *Past and Present* 137 (1992), pp 48–69.

71 J.H. Elliott, *The revolt of the Catalans* (Cambridge, 1963); Elliott, 'The Spanish monarchy and the kingdom of Portugal, 1580–1640', in M. Greengrass (ed), *Conquest and coalescence: the shaping of the state in early modern Europe* (London, 1991), pp 48–67; R.J.W. Evans, *The making of Habsburg monarchy 1550–1700* (Oxford, 1979); H.G. Koeningsberger, *The government of Sicily under Philip II of Spain* (London, 1951).

72 G.C. Gibbs, 'The European origins of the Glorious Revolution' in Maguire (ed), *Kings in conflict*, pp 9–28; Israel (ed), *The Anglo-Dutch*

moment; J. Ohlmeyer, 'Ireland independent: confederate foreign policy and international relations during the mid-seventeenth century' in Ohlmeyer, (ed), *Ireland from independence to occupation,* pp 89–111; J.G. Simms, *Jacobite Ireland 1685–91* (London, 1969); W. Troost, *William III and the Treaty of Limerick (1691–1697)* (1983); B. Whelan (ed), *The last of the Great Wars: essays on the war of the three kingdoms in Ireland, 1688–91* (Limerick, 1995), especially chapters 1–4.

73 T.ó hAnnracháin, 'The mission of Gian Battista Rinuccini in Ireland 1645–9', unpublished Ph.D. dissertation, (European University Institute, 1995).

74 W. Palmer, *The problem of Ireland in Tudor foreign policy 1485–1603* (Woodbridge, 1994).

75 Bradshaw, 'Nationalist historiography'.

76 The collaboration of Brendan Bradshaw, the fiercest scourge of 'revisionists', and John Morrill, enthusiast for British history, as editors of *The British Problem* has a particular piquancy, conveyed at pp 8, 275, n.31.

77 Brady (ed) *Interpreting Irish history;* D.G. Boyce and A. O'Day (eds), *The making of modern Irish history: revisionism and the revisionist controversy* (London, 1996).

78 Garnham, *The courts, crime and the criminal law;* Gillespie, *Devoted People;* K. Whelan, *The tree of liberty* (Cork, 1996); S.J. Connolly, 'Approaches to the history of Irish popular culture', *Bullan* 2/2 (1996), pp 83–100; Connolly, 'Popular culture: patterns of change and adaptation' in Connolly, Houston and Morris (eds), *Conflict, identity and economic development,* pp 103–13.

79 D. Cressy, *Literacy and the social order* (Cambridge, 1980); Cressy, *Birth, marriage and death: ritual, religion and the life cycle in Tudor and Stuart England* (Oxford, 1997); R.A. Houlbrooke, *The English family 1450–1750* (London, 1984); M. Prior (ed), *Women in English society 1500–1800* (London, 1985); B. Reay (ed), *Popular culture in seventeenth century England* (London, 1985); J. Sharpe, *Crime in early modern England 1550–1750* (London, 1984); Sharpe, *Early modern England: a social history 1550–1760* (London, 1987); P. Slack, *Poverty and policy in Tudor and Stuart England* (London, 1989); K.V. Thomas, *Religion and the decline of magic* (London, 1971); K. Wrightson, *English society 1580–1680* (London, 1985).

80 B. Bradshaw, 'Cromwellian reform and the origins of the Kildare rebellion, 1533–34', *Transactions of the Royal Historical Society,* 5th series, xxvii (1977), pp 69–93; S.G. Ellis, 'Tudor policy and the Kildare ascendancy in the lordship of Ireland', *Irish Historical Studies,* xx (1976–77), pp 235–71; Ellis, 'The Kildare rebellion and the early Henrician reformation', *Historical Journal* xix (1976), pp 807–30; Ellis, *Reform and revival: English government in Ireland, 1470–1534* (Woodbridge and New York, 1986).

81 B. Bradshaw, *The Irish constitutional revolution of the sixteenth century* (Cambridge, 1979); C. Brady, *The chief governors: the rise and fall of reform government in Tudor Ireland 1536–1588* (Cambridge, 1994): N.P. Canny, *The Elizabethan conquest of Ireland: a pattern established 1565–76* (Hassocks, 1976); J.G. Crawford, *Anglicizing the government of Ireland: the Irish privy council and the expansion of Tudor rule 1556–1578* (Dublin, 1993); S.G. Ellis, *Tudor Ireland: crown, community and the conflict of cultures 1470–1603* (London, 1985); H. Morgan, *Tyrone's rebellion: the outbreak of the Nine Years War in Tudor Ireland* (Woodbridge and New York, 1993).

82 Barnard, 'Planters and policies'; Barnard, *Cromwellian Ireland* (Oxford, 1975); Kearney, *Strafford in Ireland*; Ranger, 'Strafford in Ireland'.

83 Barnard, 'Scotland and Ireland in the later Stewart monarchy'; Barnard (ed), *From Kilkenny to Avignon: the dukes of Ormonde (1610–1745)*, forthcoming; J.C. Beckett, *The cavalier duke: a life of James Butler, first duke of Ormond* (Belfast, 1990).

84 D.W. Hayton, 'The crisis in Ireland and the disintegration of Queen Anne's last ministry', *Irish Historical Studies* xxii (1981), pp 193–215; Miller, 'Tyrconnell and James II's Irish policy'.

85 Brady, *The chief governors*, p xi.

86 Brady, 'Faction and the origins of the Desmond rebellion of 1579', *Irish Historical Studies* xxii (1980), pp 289–312; Brady, 'Court, castle and country: the framework of government in Tudor Ireland' in Brady and Gillespie (eds), *Natives and newcomers*, pp 22–49; Brady, *The chief governors*; J.I. McGuire, 'Why was Ormond dismissed in 1669?', *Irish Historical Studies*, xviii (1973), pp 295–312; M. Perceval-Maxwell, 'Protestant faction, the impeachment of Strafford and the origins of the Irish civil war', *Canadian Journal of History*, xvii (1982), pp 235–55; Perceval-Maxwell, *The outbreak of the Irish rebellion of 1641* (Dublin, 1994).

87 B. Bradshaw, 'Sword, word and strategy in the reformation in Ireland', *Historical Journal* xxi (1978), pp 475–502; Bradshaw, 'Robe and sword in the conquest of Ireland' in C. Cross, D. Loades and J.J. Scarisbrick (eds), *Law and government under the Tudors* (Cambridge, 1988), pp 139–42; A. Ford, *The Protestant reformation in Ireland 1590–1641*, 2nd edition (Dublin, 1997), pp 7–12.

88 D.W. Hayton, 'Ireland and the English ministers, 1707–1716', unpublished Oxford dissertation (Oxford, 1975).

89 T. Bartlett, 'The Townshend viceroyalty' in Bartlett and Hayton (eds), *Penal era and golden age*, pp 88–112; Hayton, 'The beginnings of the "undertaker system"'; Hayton, 'The crisis in Ireland'; Hayton, 'Walpole and Ireland'.

90 T.C. Barnard, 'The viceregal court in Ireland under the later Stuarts' in E. Cruickshanks (ed), *The Stuart Court* (Stroud, forthcoming).

91   Help is offered by: Crawford, *Anglicizing the government of Ireland*; Ellis, *Reform and revival*, pp 181–205; Ellis, *Tudor Ireland*; P. McNally, *Parties, Patriots and Undertakers: parliamentary politics in early Hanoverian Ireland* (Dublin, 1997).

92   W. Henry, *Love of our Country* (Dublin, 1756), pp 17–21; T. Leland, *Sermons on various subjects*, 3 vols (Dublin, 1778), iii, p 18; S. Shepherd, *Sermons on various subjects* (Dublin, 1790), i, pp 192–93.

93   L.M. Cullen, 'Incomes, social classes and economic growth in Ireland and Scotland, 1600–1900' in T.M. Devine and D. Dickson (eds), *Ireland and Scotland 1600–1850: Parallels and contrasts in economic and social development* (Edinburgh, 1983), pp 248–59.

94   Connolly, *Religion, law and power;* R. Gillespie, 'Lords and commons in seventeenth-century Mayo' in R. Gillespie and G. Moran (eds), *'A Various Country': essays in Mayo history 1500–1900* (Westport, 1987), pp 44–66; Gillespie, 'The transformation of the borderlands, 1600–1700' in R. Gillespie and H. O'Sullivan (eds), *The Borderlands: essays in the history of the Ulster-Leinster border* (Belfast, 1989), pp 75–92.

95   L.J. Arnold, *The restoration land settlement in County Dublin, 1660–1688* (Dublin, 1993); K.S. Bottigheimer, *English money and Irish land: the 'Adventurers' in the Cromwellian settlement of Ireland* (Oxford, 1971); M. Brennan, 'The changing composition of Kilkenny's landowners, 1641–1700', in W. Nolan and K. Whelan (eds), *Kilkenny: history and society* (Dublin, 1990), pp 161–96; L.M. Cullen, 'Catholic social classes under the Penal Laws' in T.P. Power and K. Whelan (eds), *Endurance and Emergence: Catholics in Ireland in the eighteenth century* (Dublin, 1990), pp 57–84; K.J. Harvey, 'The family experience: the Bellews of Mount Bellew' in Power and Whelan (eds), *Endurance and emergence*, pp 171–97; J.G. Simms, *The Williamite confiscation in Ireland 1690–1703* (London, 1956); K. Whelan, 'An underground gentry? Catholic middlemen in eighteenth century Ireland', *Eighteenth-Century Ireland* 10 (1995), pp 9–66, reprinted in Whelan, *The tree of liberty*, pp 3–56.

96   Helpful local studies include: D. Dickson, 'An economic history of the Cork region in the eighteenth century', unpublished Ph.D. dissertation (Trinity College, Dublin, 1977); H.F. Morris, 'The "Principal Inhabitants" of County Waterford in 1746' in T.P. Power and W. Nolan (eds), *Waterford: history and society* (Dublin, 1992), pp 309–30; T.P. Power, *Land, politics and society in eighteenth-century Tipperary* (Oxford, 1993); L.J. Proudfoot, 'Landownership and improvement, c. 1700–1845' in L.J. Proudfoot (ed) *Down: history and society* (Dublin, 1997), pp 203–38.

97   J. Smyth, '"Like amphibious animals": Irish Protestants; ancient Britons', *Historical Journal*, xxxvi (1993), p 786. Cf. B. Fitzpatrick, *Seventeenth-Century Ireland* (Dublin, 1989), p 4.

98   Totals of Protestants in each county are in: *An abstract of the number of Protestants and Popish families in the several counties and provinces of Ireland* (Dublin, 1736). A useful corrective is offered by J.R. Hill, *From patriots to unionists: civic politics and ideology in Protestant Dublin, 1660–1840* (Oxford, 1997).

99   P. Corfield, *Power and the professions in Britain 1700–1850* (London, 1995); G. Holmes, *Augustan England: professions, state and society 1680–1730* (London, 1982); W. Prest (ed), *The professions in early modern England* (London, 1987).

100 T.C. Barnard, 'Lawyers and the law in later seventeenth century Ireland' *Irish Historical Studies* xxviii (1993), pp 256–82; D.F. Cregan, 'Irish Catholic admissions to the English Inns of Court, 1558–1625', *Irish Jurist* v (1970), pp 95–114; Cregan, 'Irish recusant lawyers in politics in the reign of James I', *Irish Jurist* v (1970), pp 306–20; C. Kenny 'The exclusion of Catholics from the legal profession in Ireland, 1537–1829', *Irish Historical Studies* xxv (1987), pp 337–57.

101 Bodleian Library, Oxford, Ms. Smith 52, p 151.

102 A. Ford, 'Dependent or Independent? The Church of Ireland and its colonial context, 1536–1649', *The Seventeenth Century* x (1995), pp 163–81; J. MacCafferty, '"God bless your free Church of Ireland": Wentworth, Laud, Bramhall and the Irish Convocation of 1634' in J. Merrett (ed), *The political world of Thomas Wentworth, earl of Strafford*, (Cambridge, 1995), pp 187–207; J. Morrill, 'A British Patriarchy? Ecclesiastical imperialism under the early Stuarts' in A. Fletcher and P. Roberts (eds), *Religion, culture and society in early modern Britain* (Cambridge, 1994), pp 209–37.

103 Tentative explorations include: T.C. Barnard, 'Improving clergymen, 1660–1760'; in A. Ford, J. McGuire and K. Milne (eds), *As by law established: The Church of Ireland since the Reformation* (Dublin, 1995), pp 136–51.

104 National Archives, Dublin, M 2533, p 418; T.C. Barnard, 'The Irish government and dissent, 1704–1780' in Herlihy (ed), *The politics of Irish dissent,*

105 P.J. Corfield, 'Class by name and number in eighteenth century Britain' in P.J. Corfield (ed), *Language, history and class* (Oxford, 1991), pp 101–30; Corfield, 'The rivals: landed and other gentlemen' in N. Harte and R. Quinault (eds), *Land and society in Britain 1700–1914* (Manchester and New York, 1996), pp 1–23; D. Cressy, 'Describing the social order of Elizabethan and Stuart England', *Literature and History* 3 (1976), pp 29–41; G.S. Holmes, 'Gregory King and the social structure in pre-industrial England', *Transactions of the Royal Historical Society*, 5th series 27 (1977), pp 41–68; K. Wrightson, '"Sorts of people" in Tudor

and Stuart England' in J. Barry and C. Brooks (eds), *The middling sort of people* (Basingstoke, 1994), pp 28–51.

106 J. Loveday, *Diary of a tour in 1732* (Edinburgh, 1890); E. MacLysaght, *Irish life in the seventeenth century*, 3rd edition (Shannon, 1969); C. Maxwell, *Country and town in Ireland under the Georges* (Dundalk, 1949); *Richard Pococke's Irish tours*, ed. J. McVeagh (Dublin, 1995); D.B. Quinn, *The Elizabethans and the Irish* (Ithaca, 1966).

107 T.C. Barnard, 'The gentrification of eighteenth-century Ireland', *Eighteenth-Century Ireland*, 12 (1997), pp. 137–55.

108 K. Brown, 'Aristocracy, anglicization and the court, 1603–37', *Historical Journal* xxxvi (1993), pp 543–76; Brown, 'Courtiers and cavaliers: service, anglicization and loyalty among the royalist nobility' in J. Morrill (ed), *The Scottish National Covenant in its British context 1638–51* (Edinburgh, 1990), pp 155–92; Brown, 'The origins of a British aristocracy: integration and its limitations before the treaty of union', in Ellis and Barber, *Conquest and Union*, pp 57–77; P. Jenkins, *The making of a ruling class: the Glamorgan gentry, 1640–1790* (Cambridge, 1983); J.G. Jones, *Concepts of order and gentility in Wales 1540–1640* (Llandysul, 1992).

109 T.C. Barnard, 'Introduction' in Barnard (ed), *The Dukes of Ormonde*.

110 F.G. James, *Lords of the Ascendancy: the Irish House of Lords and its members 1600–1800* (Dublin, 1995); and the remarks on it in *Parliamentary History* xv (1996), pp 420–22.

111 T.C. Barnard, 'Land and the limits of loyalty: the second earl of Cork and first earl of Burlington (1612–98)' in T. Barnard and J. Clark (eds), *Lord Burlington: architecture, art and life* (London and Rio Grande, 1995), pp 167–200; N. Canny *The upstart earl: a study of the social and mental world of Richard Boyle, first earl of Cork, 1566–1643* (Cambridge, 1982); P. Little, 'Family and faction: the Irish nobility and the English court, 1632–42' unpublished M.Litt. dissertation (Trinity College, Dublin, 1992); Little, 'The earl of Cork and the fall of the earl of Strafford, 1638–41', *Historical Journal* xxxix (1996), pp 619–35; Ranger, 'The career of Richard Boyle'; Ranger, 'Richard Boyle and the making of an Irish fortune'.

112 Ohlmeyer, *Antrim*.

113 J.C. Beckett, *Cavalier duke*; W. Kelly, 'The early career of James Butler, twelfth earl and first duke of Ormond, 1610–43', unpublished Ph.D. dissertation (Cambridge, 1996); Kelly, 'James Butler, twelfth earl of Ormond, the Irish government and the Bishops' wars, 1638–40', in Young, *Celtic dimensions of the British civil wars*, pp 35–52; essays by D. Edwards and P. Little in Barnard (ed), *The Dukes of Ormonde*.

114 T.C. Barnard, 'Planters and policies'; Barnard, 'The Protestant interest'; Barnard, 'Settling and unsettling Ireland'; Barnard, 'The political, material and mental culture of the Cork settlers, c.1650–1700' in P.

O'Flanagan and C.G. Buttimer (eds), *Cork: history and society* (Dublin, 1993), pp 309–65; K.M. Lynch, *Roger Boyle, first earl of Orrery* (Knoxville, 1965).

115 J.S.A. Adamson, 'The baronial context of the English civil war', *Transactions of the Royal Historical Society*, 5th series 40 (1990), pp 93–120; L. Bourquin, *Noblesse seconde et pouvoir en Champagne aux XVIe et XVIIe siècles* (Paris, 1994); K.B. Neuschel, *Word of honor: interpreting noble culture in sixteenth-century France* (Ithaca, 1989); E. Schalk, *From valor to pedigree: ideas of nobility in France in the sixteenth and seventeenth centuries* (Princeton, 1986); H.M. Scott and C. Storrs, 'Introduction: the consolidation of noble power in Europe, 1600–1800' in H.M. Scott (ed), *The European nobilities in the seventeenth and eighteenth centuries*, 2 vols (London, 1995), i, pp 13–51.

116 Barnard, 'Land and the limits of loyalty'; Barnard, *The Dukes of Ormonde*.

117 R.R. Davies, four presidential addresses on 'The peoples of Britain and Ireland, 1100–1400' in *Transactions of the Royal Historical Society* 6th series iv-vii (1994–97).

118 British Library, Additional Ms. 47001B, f.64; S. Burdy, *The life of Philip Skelton* (ed) N. Moore (Oxford, 1914), pp 110–12, 141; S.J. Connolly, 'The Houghers: agrarian protest in early eighteenth century Connacht' in C.H.E. Philpin (ed), *Nationalism and popular protest in Ireland* (Cambridge, 1987), pp 139–62; M.F. Cusack, *A history of the kingdom of Kerry* (London, 1871), pp 282–87. *The letters of Lord Chief Baron Edward Willes to the earl of Warwick, 1757–62* (ed) J. Kelly (Aberystwyth, 1990), p 90.

119 T.C. Barnard, 'The Hartlib circle and the cult and culture of improvement in Ireland' in M. Greengrass, M. Leslie and T. Raylor (eds), *Samuel Hartlib and universal reformation* (Cambridge, 1984), pp 281–97; Barnard, 'Gardening, diet and "improvement" in later seventeenth century Ireland', *Journal of Garden History* 10 (1990), pp 71–85; J.R. Hill, 'Popery and protestantism, civil and religious liberty: the disputed lessons of Irish history, 1690–1812', *Past and Present* 118 (1988), pp 96–129; C. O'Halloran, '"The island of saints and scholars": views of the early church and sectarian politics in late eighteenth century Ireland', *Eighteenth-Century Ireland* v (1990), pp 7–20; O'Halloran, 'Ownership of the past: antiquarian debate and ethnic identity in Scotland and Ireland' in Connolly, Houston and Morris (eds), *Conflict, identity and economic development*, pp 135–47.

120 See, for example, C.T. Allmand, *Lancastrian Normandy 1415–50: the history of a medieval occupation* (Oxford, 1983); T. Barry, R. Frame and K. Simms (eds), *Colony and frontier an medieval Ireland: essays presented to J.F. Lydon* (London, 1995); essays by R. Bartlett, R.R. Davies and R. Frame in R. Bartlett and A. Mackay (eds), *Medieval frontier societies* (Oxford, 1989);

THE NEW BRITISH HISTORY, 1603-1715

Ellis, *The Pale and the far north*; Ellis, *Tudor frontiers and noble power*; R.A. Griffiths, 'The English realm and dominion of the king's subjects in the later middle ages' in J.G. Rowe (ed), *Aspects of late medieval government and society* (Toronto, 1986), pp 83–105; R. Massey, 'The land settlement in Lancastrian Normandy' in A.J. Pollard (ed), *Property and politics: essays in later medieval English history* (Gloucester and New York, 1984), pp 76–90.

121 P.R. Coss, 'The formation of the English gentry' *Past and Present* 147 (1995), pp 38–64; M.E. Jones (ed), *Gentry and lesser nobility in later medieval Europe* (Gloucester, 1986); S. Payling, *Political society in Lancastrian England: the greater gentry of Nottinghamshire* (Oxford, 1991); N. Saul, *The Gloucestershire gentry in the fourteenth century* (Oxford, 1981).

122 W. Harris and C. Smith, *The antient and present state of the county of Down* (Dublin, 1744), pp 3–4; T.C. Barnard, 'Hospitality and display'; Barnard, 'The gentrification of eighteenth-century Ireland'.

123 The bibliographies in *New History of Ireland* ii–1v and the survey, J.J. Lee (ed), *Irish historiography 1970–79* (Cork, 1981) can be supplemented by the annual lists published in *Irish Economic and Social History* and by A. Clarke, R. Gillespie and J. McGuire (eds), *A New History of Ireland. Bibliographical supplement 1534–1691* (Oxford, 1991).

124 As with the divergent judgments on Canny, *Kingdom and Colony* in Morrill, 'The British problem', p 276, n 45, and by V. Treadwell in *English Historical Review* cvii (1992), p 200.

125 There is little sign as yet of applying to Ireland the insights in M.J. Braddick, 'State formation and social change in early modern England: a problem stated and approaches suggested', *Social History* 16 (1991), pp 1–17; Braddick, *The nerves of the state: taxation and the financing of the English state, 1558–1714* (Manchester, 1996); J. Brewer, *The sinews of power: war, money and the English state, 1668–1783* (London, 1989); P. Langford, *Public life and the propertied Englishman 1689–1798)* (Oxford, 1991).

126 Individual Irish towns are well served by: Agnew, *Belfast merchants;* H.B. Clarke (ed), *Irish cities* (Cork, 1995); D. Dickson, '"Centres of motion": Irish cities and the origins of popular politics' in Bergeron and Cullen (eds), *Culture et pratiques politiques,* pp 101–22; Dickson (ed), *The gorgeous mask: Dublin 1700–1850* (Dublin, 1987); R. Gillespie, 'The origins and development of an Ulster urban network', *Irish Historical Studies,* xxiv (1984), pp 15–29; Gillespie, 'Small towns in early modern Ireland' in P. Clark (ed), *Small towns in early modern Europe* (Cambridge, 1995), pp 148–65; D.W. Harkness and M. O. Dowd (eds), *The town in Ireland: Historical Studies XIII* (Belfast, 1981); Hill, *From Patriots to Unionists;* Royal Irish Academy, *Irish historic towns atlas* i (Dublin, 1996); A. Simms and J.H. Andrews (eds), *Irish country towns* (Cork, 1994); Simms and Andrews (eds), *More Irish country towns* (Cork, 1995).

127 If a synthesis such as T. Hitchcock, *English sexualities 1700–1800* (London, 1997) is not yet possible, guidance is given by: A. Cosgrove (ed), *Marriage in Ireland* (Dublin, 1985); M. MacCurtain and M. O'Dowd (eds) *Women in early modern Ireland* (Edinburgh, 1991); M. O'Dowd and S. Wichert (eds), *Chattel, servant or citizen: women's status in church, state and society: Historical Studies XIX* (Belfast, 1995); K. Simms and C. Meek (eds) *"The fragility of her sex": medieval Irishwomen in the European context* (Dublin, 1996).

CHAPTER 9

Seducing the Scottish Clio: Has Scottish History Anything to Fear From the New British History?

Keith M. Brown

The reasons for the current interest in British History are now well known. Since the debate was started by John Pocock in 1974 changes in Britain's world role, the devolution debate, the disappearance of a common enemy, the advent of multi-culturalism and post-modernism have all made the old Anglocentric imperial and constitutional history more problematic. The self-doubt that has crept into British History practitioners has brought Scottish and Irish History to centre stage.[1] Chronologically, a History of Britain can be divided into a number of major epochs not all of which lend themselves equally to a British reinterpretation.[2] Historians discuss Roman Britain without any difficulty, although the Roman presence in the land mass that is now Scotland was never total and always semi detached. Thereafter British History is more uncertain as the tribal invaders carved out their own kingdoms. From the eleventh to the end of the thirteenth centuries a British History is particularly relevant with Henry II establishing lordship over most of the archipelago and Edward I standing on the threshold of peacefully creating a united Britain in the 1290s.[3] By contrast, from c.1300 to the mid-sixteenth century is much less convincing, and Scottish historians of this period are least likely to be persuaded of the need to subsume their subject in it.[4] Ironically, while the Victorians looked with satisfaction on an Empire as the fulfilment of Britain's destiny, Scottish historians of the nineteenth and twentieth centuries are vulnerable to being categorised as regional while British History is at its least self-conscious.[5] Clearly British History is a more useful vehicle for some periods than for others, and with Scotland altering its relationship with Westminster more than at any time since 1707 who knows how appropriate it will be for the twenty first century? But in whatever form or shape it is introduced, British History is essential to an understanding of early modern England, Ireland, Scotland and Wales. The spinal cord of this history is political, the constitutional relationships established between the constituent parts from the union of England and Wales in 1536 to the creation of the United Kingdom in 1800. Here in this early modern period lies the often exciting and controversial opportunity to explain how and why Britain came about, and it is unsurprising that the most intense debate about British History has taken place among historians of this era.

An English historian told me recently that there was no such subject as British History and no such creature as a British historian. There are historians of England, as he is, and historians of Scotland, as I am, but British historians are a sort of bastard breed with an expertise in one kingdom who exploit the work of others for those parts of Britain about which they know very little. There is some truth in this, just as most European historians turn out, on closer inspection, to be French, Italian or Swedish experts who synthesise the work of their colleagues in other countries. Lurking here, I suspect, is also an English national-ism that rather likes the idea of Charles I as an English king, presid-ing over an English court, refusing to summon an English parliament on the road to an English civil war.[6] Of course, there is nothing new in such English insularity, and in the seventeenth century John Milton was just as unwilling to see England's story swallowed up by Britain.[7] English uniqueness and the apparent self-sufficiency of its history make it resistant to the idea of British History. After all, what could be usefully learned from the 'Celtic' societies that 'inevitably followed a logic of historical development first worked out in England'. That self-confidence may be waning just a little, but even those prepared to give some room to British History cannot give up their English myths so that 'English distinctiveness is best understood through her impact on her neighbours'.[8]

But English historians are not alone in wanting to deny a place for British History. Irish historians have problems in writing a nationalist history that does not keep the English at bay. Nicholas Canny has been most forthright in attacking the abandonment of the compara-tive history of Britain and Ireland for an integrationist British History.[9] Canny, however, wants to have it both ways, impressing the significance of Ireland on the world, but trying to distance Ireland from England when it was the latter that brought the Irish to the rest of the world's attention. For nationalist historians, British History represents a snare that denies Irish identity and is a betrayal of the nationalist cause. As one historian of Ireland described the problem: 'in nationalist Ireland, 'British' is the antithesis of 'Irish', is frequently synonymous with 'English', and it refers to the modern British state'.[10] S.J. Connolly has also recognised this in writing about eighteenth-century Irish patriotism, suggesting it was 'more British than it looked at first sight', an unpopular view with those who prefer their Irish History to be green and nationalist.[11] Here Irish historians face a particularly difficult task in reconciling popular perceptions of Ireland's past with a British History that sits uncomfortably alongside the nation's cherished myths.[12] In fact Irish History is a part of British History and cannot be fully understood either in isolation from Britain, or only in comparative terms, just as British History makes no sense without bringing Ireland into the story.[13]

Scottish historians face a similar dilemma, and in an earlier foray into this territory I expressed some scepticism about the attractiveness of British History.[14] The writing of Scottish History, as opposed to the memorising of a distinctly Scottish tradition that had its origins in the seventh century, began in the 1290s in response to English aggression.[15] Since that date there always has been an important strand to the writing of Scotland's past that is intimately tied up with the preservation of a national identity in which English 'otherness' is an important ingredient.[16] Even eighteenth-century historians, that most unionist of generations, retained some ambivalence towards England and its contribution to their own nation.[17] What historians must do is ensure that such ambivalence is never allowed to become a vehicle for anti-English sentiments, and here ignorance is as much a danger as bad history. The union of 1707 was not brought about by English invasion as thirty-seven per cent of Scottish school children appear to believe.[18] When a historian can publicly argue that the 'Anglo-Scottish ruling class' have for centuries been engaged in 'falsifying actual Scottish History since 1707' it is unsurprising to find politicians hijacking the subject.[19] What must be avoided, therefore, is a debased and populist Little Scotlander history in which 'we' figures largely in the telling of folk tales.[20] Unfortunately, there is in Scotland, as in Ireland, a massive popular interest in a 'Braveheart' past sustaining myths that may or may not be culturally and politically useful, but that are a long way from good history. On the other hand, Scotland is experiencing a deep cultural awakening that is linked to political developments, and this popular interest and enthusiasm should be brought into contact with professional academic history.[21] Scottish History is now more energetic, innovative and stimulating than ever, being sustained by a powerful presence in all Scotland's older universities, by journals like the *Scottish Historical Review*, associations like the Scottish History Society, and a whole professional network designed to promote the subject. There is no doubt that over the last four decades the subject has exploded into life, and there are a great many interesting questions still to be answered which do not need the conceptual framework of British History.[22]

But British History will not go away, even if the United Kingdom does disappear. The problem facing those of us who are Scottish historians is that if we refuse to participate in the debate, and insist on pursuing Scottish History in isolation, British History will simply be another rewrite of English History.[23] The days when Hugh Trevor-Roper could offend Scots in the knowledge that few voices would be raised in protest are long over, and the inferiorism that many Scottish academics, or academics working in Scotland, colluded in propagating is no longer an issue.[24] Nevertheless, most attempts at British History fail because it is conceived as English History with Scottish or Irish add-ons that seek to demonstrate how Westminster came to govern the entire archipelago while highlighting the 'peculiarities' of what are often mistakenly described as the 'Celtic' nations.[25] Jeremy Black's recent foray into this territory is exasperating for precisely this tendency to practise tokenism with regard to Scotland, and Mark Kishlansky's history of the seventeenth-century Stuart monarchy is equally disappointing.[26] Sustaining many of these efforts, both consciously and subconsciously, is Michael Hechter's core and periphery model which did British History no favours, and as its title suggests was concerned to explain how England, the core, triumphed over peripheral regions.[27] Scotland as periphery is offensive. There were at least two cores with difficult peripheries to administer, one located in the south of England, the other in central Scotland, with perhaps a third at Dublin, and each of these overlapped, sliding in and out of one another's vision depending on circumstances.[28] This cut and paste British History, in which Scotland is slotted into an English narrative, makes Scottish History conceptually dependent on an anglocentric context: thus twelfth-century Scotland was some sort of Anglo-Norman colony; the fourteenth-century struggle for independence was just one of a number of fronts on which the English crown waged territorial wars; the Scottish Reformation was merely the tidying up of religious change in mainland Britain; eighteenth-century Scotland was little more than a provincial subculture of Great Britain; and Scottish identity in the twentieth century cannot be national and must only be understood as regional. This anglocentric contextualisation has had the greatest impact on the seventeenth century which becomes, in David Stevenson's phrase, 'twilight before night or darkness before dawn'. Fortunately, recent research has done a great deal to dispel both of these unhelpful myths.[29]

Unfortunately, British History presently leads down one road to the examination of the origins of the British state, and risks taking us back to a more sophisticated version of old-fashioned anglocentric constitutional history.[30] Thus Brian Levack has made a strong case for the emergence of Britain solely from developments in the state apparatus rather than elite integration or the appeal of ideology.[31] Meanwhile, John Morrill has explicitly located state formation in Britain within British History, arguing that without this context it is not possible to make sense of the nature of the state system that came to govern these islands in the early modern era. He has also avoided alienating Scottish and Irish historians by delicately arguing that the story of that state formation is one of growing English dominance while at the same time denying that this history need be anglocentric and triumphalist.[32] The underlying question appears to be why did the Anglo-Norman medieval monarchy and its Protestant-Whig successor end up dominating the geographic space we call Great Britain and Ireland?

That is both a legitimate and an important question, and it is one that Scottish and Irish historians cannot avoid asking however much they might resent the fact that in any British History the major player is always going to be England. That is a simple fact: England is bigger, it has always been more populous, wealthy and powerful, and the advantage has been moving in England's direction at an exponential rate for centuries. Population alone guarantees that England has a deeper cultural heritage, because it has more towns, more shires and more famous people than Scotland. British History cannot help being heavily weighted towards England because at least from the reign of Alfred economic and political power in Britain has been centred in the south of England, even if medieval Scotland successfully resisted that power.[33] It was the 1650s that marked the crucial watershed in establishing English political and military superiority within Britain, even if the English themselves were ambivalent about empire and some Scots were prepared to imagine union.[34] It might stick in the gullet to say it, but from the perspective of those English lords and gentry at Westminster, or of the city of London, the union of 1707 was little more than 'a straightforward enlargement of England's empire'.[35] As Lord Belhaven, an anti-unionist, said in the last Scottish parliament at the height of the union debate in 1706–07, the Scots 'are an obscure, poor people..[living in]..a remote corner of the world'.[36]

This does not mean that Scotland and its history is of no more than national significance. Allan Macinnes has argued that the most important challenge facing Scottish historians is 'to make a comparative impact internationally'. Of course, the best of them have done exactly that, whether it is Walter Bower in the fifteenth century, John Mair and George Buchanan in the sixteenth century, David Hume and William Robertson in the eighteenth century, or Geoffrey Barrow and Chris Smout in the twentieth century. Scottish chroniclers and historians always have sought to place their subject in relation to the rest of the world. The entire thrust of Scottish humanist and Enlightenment thinking with its mission to explain man in society discouraged antiquarian concerns with the particular, and one might argue that Scottish historians have always been more interested in investigating universal causes and effects than English historians who have, in general, been more concerned with explaining English uniqueness.[37] Indeed the occasionally hectoring tone of those historians today who believe they have discovered the secret to putting Scottish History on the international map is irritating.[38] For Scottish historians there are many means of making that international impact, which certainly does not have to rely on British History, but neither can one adopt the Scotland-in-Europe tactic in order to avoid dealing with England as though Britain and its history was somehow not European.[39]

Besides, British History is too important to be left to English historians. Prime minister John Major's 'thousand years of British History' has been ridiculed by a reborn David Cannadine as a piece of typical English nationalist arrogance that asserted 'the essential Englishness of the United Kingdom, its separateness from the rest of Europe, the long unbroken continuity of its traditions and precedents, and its unique characteristics and institutions'.[40] This is a possible English past, but it can never be a British past, far less a Scottish or Irish one. As for the British millennium, it is worth being reminded of another historian's suggestion that 'Britain is an invented nation not so much older than the United States'.[41] Of course, all nations do some inventing, and both the English and Scottish kingdoms had their medieval and early modern apologists to make absurd claims about their 'ancient' legitimacy.[42] It is not even clear where, in terms of geographic space, this Britain was at different epochs in its history. Does medieval British History include the English possessions in France? Has Orkney, with its Norse heritage, any place in the narrative before it falls into the hands of the Scottish crown in 1472? Should colonial America and Hanover be part of eighteenth-century British History? At this point the debate becomes horrendously complex as Britain stretched its possessions out across the globe. And where Britain went the Scots went too, taking their history with them so that even in the mid-eighteenth century 'the Empire embodied a diffusion of Britishness, which made it a distinctively British empire'.[43] That theme of imperial expansion, of Scotland's contribution to the empire, and of the empire's impact on Scotland needs to be addressed: it must be undertaken within the parameters of British History.

That empire originated as an English empire and with it came varying degrees of Anglicization. Nicholas Canny has suggested that the process of Anglicization and the ideology that undergirded it is 'the central theme' of British History.[44] This is an overstatement driven, perhaps, by Irish experiences that are less appropriate to Scotland. In Ireland, English national consciousness and self interest combined most destructively in an enormous effort to change the laws, government, culture, religion and even the people who lived on that island. But it was not only the English who were enthusiastic colonists as the Scots too poured into Ireland, creating a new set of problems for Dublin. These Protestant settlers were preferable to the English administrators than the native Irish, but their presence posed questions about what the New English colonists were trying to create.[45] Lurking here in the patchwork settlement of Ireland with its Gaelic, Old English, New English and Scottish communities, is the thorny question of national identity for it is too easy to superimpose onto the multiple-monarchy model of the early modern British state the four 'ancient' peoples of Britain.[46] English policies in Ireland displayed national identity at its most brutal and arrogant, but also at its most insecure and unsuccessful. Wales, by contrast, provides a lesson in the slow pace of acculturation, it being the later seventeenth century before Welsh elites might properly be described as Anglicized, some three hundred years after conquest.[47]

What of Scotland where there was no lasting conquest? The ebb and flow of English influences on the kingdom of the Scots created complex and shifting identity patterns. In writing about the effects of the absorption of English Lothian into the kingdom of Scotland in the tenth and eleventh centuries, James Campbell suggested that 'it is almost as if there are two Englands and one of them is called Scotland'.[48] By the early modern period lowland Scots still felt a greater cultural affinity for the English than for the Gaels, considering their highland neighbours to be Irish though subject to the

Scottish crown. Here one again encounters the lowland Scot as ruthless colonist, and it was a Scottish king, James VI (taking his cue from John Mair), who described the highlanders as 'barbarous for the most part'.[49] The Scottish crown had an imperial language of its own that had been thoroughly absorbed by the kingdom's elites long before 1603, and Scots participated creatively in the European debate about empire, largely in response to the Iberian examples. That thinking continued to develop over the course of the seventeenth century without any great need to borrow from England, and was carried into the eighteenth century, particularly in relation to America.[50] Therefore, while in seventeenth-century Ireland, the Scots were militantly British, lowland Scots experimented with those same policies of extermination, colonization and assimilation for the Gaelic highlands. Yet unlike their Gaelic counterparts in Ireland, the Scottish highlanders adjusted to the new British parameters of the seventeenth century, even helping to shape the contours of that world.[51] Possibly the Campbell family grasped the meaning of Britain for practical politics long before any other institution, interest or kin group in the three kingdoms.[52] It was the political misjudgement made by some chiefs in identifying with the exiled Stewarts in the eighteenth century that allowed Scottish lowlanders to complete their conquest of the highlands, eradicating those remnants of Gaelic culture that had survived the previous century of assimilation. With the full backing of the Hanoverian state, the Scottish church, law and education reshaped the region and its culture.[53] For many eighteenth and nineteenth century Scots any association with a Celtic past was spurned in favour of a Teutonic racialism identified with an Anglo-Saxon empire.[54] It took Sir Walter Scott in the nineteenth century to persuade the nation that it was patriotic to dress up as highland rebels, and the tyranny of tartan tomfoolery has tightened its grip on the national psyche ever since.[55] It is worth remembering that for the Gael, as for the Shetlander, the enemy was not the English, but the lowland Scot, the Scottish crown and even Scottish History.

In contrast to Ireland, the English had no interest in Anglicizing Scotland even if English influences did seep into the country. Significantly, it was Elizabeth I's refusal to interfere in Scottish affairs that did most at a political level to nurture the emergence of an Anglo-Scottish Protestant culture in the latter half of the sixteenth century.[56] Indeed, in the early years of the regal union there was among the English political elite concern that the ambitions of their new Scottish king for a British Empire threatened the identity of the English nation.[57] English ignorance of and lack of interest in Scotland did not alter greatly in 1603, a factor that helps to explain the success of the regal union. Conrad Russell tellingly explained English attitudes to James VI and I by suggesting that 'if the king chose to be king of Scots in his spare time, that was nothing to do with them'.[58] Perhaps, but Jenny Wormald has used a background in Scottish history to illuminate much about James VI and I that was never previously understood by English historians writing about James I, a king who appeared out of nowhere in 1603. The thrust of Wormald's argument has been to emphasise the distinctiveness of James's two kingdoms, not to use British History as a means to press the case for a whiggish convergence. In suggesting that James VI and I's British ideology was a means of persuading the English to accept Anglo-Scottish rule she is perhaps taking the argument a stage too far.[59] In any event James failed utterly and the monarchy was progressively Anglicized over the course of the seventeenth century, its early efforts at presenting a British image to the three kingdoms being abandoned.[60] However, Wormald's demolition of the traditional James I of England and her construction of a more complete James VI and I of Great Britain has changed the terrain of the early seventeenth century. The entire nature of the regal union that James brought into being is now in the process of being reinterpreted by historians who have had to engage with a much broader discussion than a single national history would generate.[61]

James VI and I did harbour the wish that his countrymen would conform more to English customs, but although the union of 1603 has been blamed for allowing Anglicizing influences to be released on Scotland, similar developments in state interference at a local level were taking place throughout Britain and were resented as much by Yorkshire gentry as by Scottish elites.[62] The English were content to keep the Scots at arm's length, except briefly and disastrously in the 1630s when archbishop Laud had designs to bring the Scottish church into a measure of conformity. Similarly Sir Thomas Wentworth expressed the desire that the kingdom be subjugated in the same manner as Ireland once the royal administration began to unravel after 1637.[63] Even Charles I himself was not wholly an Anglicized monarch, and it was his failure to act as an English king that accounted in some measure for his failure in that kingdom. As Morrill observes, it was his tendency to approach problems from the British perspective that multiplied the problems before him.[64] Perhaps what is most consistent in English attitudes towards Scotland was pragmatism. Thus in 1643 the English parliament found it useful to invite Scottish assistance in the war against Charles I, but in succeeding years that relationship changed with the political circumstances. Even under the relatively short-lived Commonwealth, initial good will towards the Scots soon gave way to fear and distrust of a presbyterian ideology that threatened the freedoms of English independency and republicanism.[65] The success of the eighteenth-century union also rested on the fact that the English were not interested in Scotland, which remained uniquely outside of England's imperial administration, as long as its meagre taxes were paid to Westminster and the Jacobites were kept under control.[66]

Among the Scottish nobility there is little evidence of Anglicization outside a small circle of courtiers before the late eighteenth century, and insofar as the process did take place between the sixteenth and nineteenth centuries it did so at a glacial pace. Residence at court, an English wife, an English title and an income derived from English sources did not make the third marquis of Hamilton or the second duke of Argyll Englishmen, although they might conceivably be described as Brito-Scottish, just as the first marquis of Antrim or the first duke of Ormonde might be described as Brito-Irish.[67] It is worth considering whether these great court aristocrats were any different from those twelfth century Scottish lords with lands and interests scattered throughout France, England, Ireland and Scotland, but whose national identity was nevertheless relatively strong?[68] Furthermore, courtiers did not, on the whole, exercise much power in Scotland, and the great majority of Scottish nobles remained in Scotland, sitting on the privy council, presiding as judges, and administering their own private courts. There were changes in lifestyles and social behaviour in the seventeenth century, but often what is described as Anglicization, especially in a cultural sense, means nothing more than the transmission to Scotland of European tastes that may have arrived first in the southern kingdom. It was not until the eighteenth century that English modes of thought and expression began to make a significant impact on Scottish elite culture.[69] Undoubtedly there was a problem of national stereotyping which continued to annoy the Scots throughout the eighteenth century, but the racial animosity was less intense than in the case of English attitudes to the Irish.[70] In the end the Scots could shrug and go home to a state in which their own laws and institutions reinforced their national identity, unlike the Irish who had to endure officials who drew distinctions between those who were English by birth and the English by blood who were not considered to be English at all.[71]

While the Stuart crown's ecclesiastical policy in Ireland can meaningfully be described as Anglicization in that it targeted not only Catholics but Scottish Presbyterian colonists, the policy in Scotland fits uncomfortably into such a concept. Of course, there was less need to develop an Anglicizing policy because the Scots were Protestants, and no matter how much Church of England Protestants disapproved of the Church of Scotland, there was a common bond there which set the English and the Scots apart from the Catholics of Ireland. As early as the 1540s it was in Protestantism that a British identity was most likely to be created.[72] Yet too much emphasis has been given to Gordon Donaldson's efforts to demonstrate that in its origins the Protestant Church of Scotland was some kind of Anglican off-shoot, when in fact the Scottish church owed more to continental Calvinism than to England.[73] Sir Robert Gordon referred to the Protestant religion 'which is now settled by the state of Great Britaigne',[74] but in spite of the efforts of James VI and I and Charles I, the gap widened between the two churches in the early seventeenth century. Besides, it is far from clear that Anglicization was the engine driving royal policy rather than a desire for an acceptable level of conformity within the new imperial world brought into being in 1603. Congruity rather than conformity describes the crown's ambition, and there was a superficial similarity in form imposed from above, but apart from some of the failed liturgical innovations there is no evidence of the introduction of peculiarly English ideas to Scotland.[75] As early as the 1560s John Knox crafted a usable past that established clear differences between Scottish and English Protestantism, and while the two kingdoms shared certain attributes of a religious culture, they had distinct political and religious identities. Religion contributed little to the structures of a British state, and the union of 1707 specifically recognised the diversity of the national churches of England and Scotland, although it did help remove some of the obstacles to imagining that state into existence.[76]

Did integration provide an alternative to Anglicization, and is this perhaps what was in the minds of those Scottish nobles who described themselves to Charles I as 'his British subjects', a phrase that echoes John Mair's '*nobiles Britanni*?[77] Perhaps, but this might be nothing more than the equivalent of the contemporary fashion among political elites to describe themselves as 'European'? James VI and I did have a vision of a British imperial king, an aristocracy brought together in a melting-pot court, and parallel churches in which the conflicts between English, Irish and Scots would be replaced by universal peace and concord. A few enthusiasts for these ideas can be found among the

King's Scottish subjects. Sir William Alexander, first Earl of Stirling, the Scot who tutored Prince Charles and helped shape his imperial views was among the most energetic proponents of British ideas. Surprisingly, within the Presbyterian community where royalist ideas about Britain were seen as threatening, being suggestive of a Constantinian church with its attendant corruptions, there evolved a quite different apocalyptic version of Britain.[78] Scottish political thinkers from opposing traditions found it relatively easy to embrace British ideology, but political ideas are over-rated among historians, and one should be suspicious of those who self consciously promoted their British identity during this period. Scottish enthusiasm for federal union during the 1640s had little to do with any commitment to Britain except as a security framework designed to protect Scottish interests within a regal union. The objective of most Covenanting federalists was primarily to tie the hands of the monarch and to restrain the freedom of the English state; creating a Godly Britain as a counterweight to Counter Reformation Europe was less important to Scottish political leaders.[79] By the early 1640s Irish ambitions too were focused on Britain, but as a means of escaping the thraldom of the English Parliament. Here too the purpose was not integrative so much as a means of preserving an Irish identity within a multicultural empire. For the Scots and the Irish the idea of Britain had become a route to subsidiarity; to the English it was an irrelevance and an encumbrance. The recourse to Scottish aid on the part of the English parliament was a strategic not an ideological decision differing little in substance from those Lancastrian leaders who turned to the Scots in the 1450s.

Arguably it is in this period of conflict between the kingdoms and peoples of Britain and Ireland that British History is at its most convincing. No one can explain the mid-century revolutions and wars simply as an English occurrence in which the Irish and Scots have walk-on parts any more than the Thirty Years' War can be understood as nothing more than a German civil war.[80] Here Conrad Russell's brilliantly pioneering work has been a little unfairly received by Scottish and Irish historians (including myself) who think he did not go far enough, or by English historians who would rather leave the English revolution to the English. His quarry always is explaining why the political process broke down in England, and for this the Scots and Irish are very necessary, but his contribution to the creation of a British explanation for the fall of the Stuart kingdoms is immense.[81] John Morrill has offered a more holistic version of the conflicts between Charles I and his peoples, although one wonders if his identifying of British agendas by the king, by royalists like Hamilton and Antrim, or by the covenanters, is anything more than tactical manoeuvring? Four Scottish invasions of England in eleven years followed by intransigent support for Charles II who the Covenanters crowned at Scone in 1651 as 'King of Great Britain, France and Ireland' does look like a militant British agenda, but the British dimension to Scotland's dealings with England from 1603 to 1651 should not be overstated. Similarly, enthusiasm for Charles II in 1649 should not confuse the innate conservation of the Scots towards the rights of the Stuart dynasty with an acceptance of James VI and I's imperial ideology.[82] These observations do not detract from the need to offer a British interpretation of the 1640s, and Martyn Bennett's study of the wars is a creditable attempt to provide a view that encompasses the whole of Charles I's inheritance.[83] It is, perhaps, a matter of debate as to whether England can be left out of British History as a recent examination of the 'Celtic Dimensions' to the British civil wars suggests. Here terminology again proves to be inadequate since the likes of the third marquis of Hamilton, the twelfth earl of Ormond, Samuel Rutherford and the south-west of Scotland were certainly not 'Celtic'.[84] Significantly, the English conquest of Ireland and Scotland that brought the wars to an end did not alter English attitudes to or enthusiasm for Britain which remained distinctly cool. If anything the experiences of the 1640s made the English even more determined to keep the Scots at a distance.[85]

In spite of their reservations about British agendas, there was in Scotland a British thread running through the nation's history that was more persistent than elsewhere in the archipelago. Even in the early sixteenth century, within a few years of the battle of Flodden, John Mair demonstrated that it was possible to be a British unionist and still remain committed to a distinct and traditionally patriotic history, though one shed of its more ludicrous mythological claims.[86] The experiences of the 1540s left Scots with a deep suspicion of any association between union and empire.[87] Yet by the early seventeenth century Scots had learned to wear more than one identity. In 1609 David Murray wrote from court that 'I am a trew Scottisman unchengable for all that I can sie heer and so I think to continew by goddis grace to my lyves end', while describing himself in the title page of his London poems as a 'Scoto Brittaine'. Scottish writers like Robert Pont, John Russell and Sir Thomas Craig were among the most supportive of the king's British ideas in the face of intense English scepticism.[88] A century later, during the Union debates of 1706–7, it was Scots like William Seton of Pitmedden who argued with passion that his country would not only enjoy the economic benefits of union with England, but 'we will have our liberty, property, and religion, secured under . . . one Parliament of Great Britain'.[89] In voicing these views Pitmedden and other unionists were articulating what many of his fellow countrymen thought; he was imagining a future history of his nation that would be British without ceasing to be Scottish. Enthusiasm for Britain did not make these North British Scots any less Scottish, and historians must not permit history to be appropriated by a one-dimensional view of patriotism.[90] In the eighteenth century many more Scots cautiously adopted a British identity, and the experience of colonisation and empire forced the English and Scots to find acceptable means of integrating along with a mutually agreeable vocabulary to describe that process.[91] North Britain was a place of remarkable intellectual and creative energy, Edinburgh was a city of European significance, and figures like David Hume, Adam Smith, Robert Burns and Walter Scott thrust themselves onto the world stage. Here was an age when many informed Scots, cloaked in their Anglo-British identity, turned away from their own history as a serious scholarly pursuit rather than a source of legend and romance because of the association between national freedom and outmoded feudalism. In so far as Scottish History had any utility for the likes of William Robertson it was in providing a contrast to the progressive developments made in society since the parliamentary union of 1707. For those eighteenth-century Scots looking to history to investigate causes and effects, progress and modernity was a product of English History and they pressed on towards an Anglo-British future.[92]

Undoubtedly the present debate has been started and largely conducted by political historians interested in state building and national identity, and we need greater input from economic, social and cultural historians.[93] That emphasis, however, is not surprising, since the British state is less problematic than the British nation. One only need look at the failure rate among other multi-kingdom states of the early modern era to appreciate how durable and peaceful that between England and Scotland has been.[94] The Union is fast approaching its 300th anniversary and in those three centuries that separate us from 1707 not a shot has been fired in anger between the two kingdoms. The tediously picked over Jacobite risings of the eighteenth century were not Anglo-Scottish conflicts, but rebellions against the British state which pitted Scot against Scot.[95] Far more important than the rag-tag army that trudged to Derby with their Italian prince in 1745 is the untold story of the thousands of Scots who crossed into England over the course of the eighteenth century, finding employment and opportunity, being absorbed by their English hosts with remarkably good grace, and enthusiastically participating in the imperial activity that brought into being an empire that was genuinely British.[96] That shared past is self evidently a British past, and part of the story that Scottish historians must tell is of the massive contribution England and the English have made to Scotland's story. For example, Scotland's feudal law derived largely from England, a point conceded by sir Thomas Craig in his *Jus Feudale* in the early seventeenth century. Especially in the sixteenth and seventeenth centuries Scots Law took a separate path to English Common Law, but its foundation in natural law and the law of nations retained an affinity between the two that was recognised in the eighteenth century. Arguably at the time of the union, English subjects enjoyed greater freedom under the law than did the Scots, hence Daniel Defoe's point in 1706 that in a British state the Scots would enjoy all the benefits of free Englishmen.[97] Over many centuries Scotland has been shaped and reshaped through its close contact with England, and Scottish identity is very much tied up with that reciprocal relationship. Scots who went in the opposite direction made an equally important impact, especially in the army, medical profession, education and engineering, and a few like like David Hume, Tobias Smollett, James Boswell and Thomas Carlyle made their own contribution to refining English self awareness and identity.[98]

In conclusion, I find myself less nervous about gift-bearing British historians than I was when I wrote an earlier version of this paper in 1992. To discuss Britain is not to deny the legitimacy of the kingdoms of England, Ireland, Scotland and the principality of Wales any more than a history of Scotland is an affront to the separate but connected histories of the Gaelic highlands or the Scandinavian archipelago north of Cape Wrath. The point can be broadly conceded that these kingdoms, and the peoples who have inhabited them, each possess their own national and even tribal histories. And just as a history of Scotland is a story of shifting frontiers and colonising peoples before anything recognisably like the kingdom of Scotland with a Scottish people emerged, so there is a history of Britain prior to the emergence of a political authority governing all the territories of the British archipelago, or before anything resembling a British people appeared on the scene. The sixteenth to eighteenth centuries saw Scotland move a long way down the road to union with England, and it would be impossible to write an intelligible history that did not give enormous weight to the process by which that pathway was constructed. There was no inevitable progression from the dynastic politics and contiguous religious reformations of the sixteenth century through the regal union and shared revolutions of the seventeenth century to the beginnings of a common imperial adventure in the eighteenth century. On the other hand, an informed view of early modern Britain might legitimately argue that Anglo-Scottish union and Irish subjugation were always likely. To say that is not to betray Scottish History, however much nationalist historians with their tartanised view of the past dislike hearing it. At the same time, Scottish and Irish historians need to go on provoking English historians out of their own complacent and insular form of nationalist history that has for so long got away with either appropriating British History or ignoring it. As a Scottish historian I remain cautious about any embrace from that historiographical tradition, but I am also increasingly encouraged by the current dialogue from which a genuinely British History is slowly and even painfully emerging.

Notes to Chapter 9

1   J.G.A. Pocock, 'British history: a plea for a new subject', *Journal of Modern History* 47 (1975), 601–28; J.G.A. Pocock, 'The limits and divisions of British History: in search of an unknown subject', *American Historical Review* 88 (1982), 311–36. The arrival of the new British History was signalled by a volume of essays on medieval Britain, R.R. Davies ed. *The British Isles 1100–1500. Comparisons, contrasts and connections* (Edinburgh, 1988). Yet even in the late 1980s a debate about the future of British History was carried on with only a passing reference to Scotland or Ireland, D. Cannadine, 'British History: past, present – and future?', *Past and Present* 116 (1987), 169–91, and the replies by P.R. Coss, W. Lamont and N. Evans, 'Debate. British History: past, present – and future?', *Past and Present* 199 (1988), 171–203. Only Evans realised that British History was more than a history of England. The most recent statement of the debate is found in A. Grant and K. Stringer eds. *Uniting the Kingdom? The Making of British History* (London, 1995) where there is evidence that things have moved on substantially in the 1990s.

2   This point has been made by Conrad Russell, 'John Bull's other nations', *Times Literary Supplement*, 12 March 1993, 3–4. Cannadine rightly suggests that historians of the twelfth, thirteenth and seventeenth centuries have been most open to the British argument, 'British History as a 'new subject', in Grant & Stringer (eds), *Uniting the Kingdom?*, 22–23.

3   G. Barrow, *Feudal Britain, 1066–1314* (London, 1956); R. Frame,

'Overlordship and reaction c.1200–c.1450' and K. Stringer 'Scottish foundations: thirteenth century perspectives', in Grant and Stringer eds. *Uniting the Kingdom?*, 65–84, 85–108.

4   This point is explicitly made by Grant who writes that 'the fourteenth and the fifteenth centuries are the least obviously "British" of any in the archipelago's history', 'Scotland's foundations: late medieval contributions', in *ibid.*, 97.

5   Cannadine, 'British History as a 'new subject', 23–24; Evans, 'Englishness and Britishness, c.1790–c.1870', and K. Robbins, 'An imperial and multinational polity. The 'scene from the centre', 1831–1922', *ibid.*, 233–24, 245.

6   Conversation with Kevin Sharpe on 14 December 1994 and see K. Sharpe, *The Personal Rule of Charles I* (New Haven and London, 1992).

7   N. von Maltzahn, *Milton's History of Britain. Republican Historiography in the English Revolution* (Oxford, 1991), especially ch. 4.

8   J.C.D. Clark, 'English history's forgotten context: Scotland, Ireland, Wales', *Historical Journal* (1989), 211–28.

9   In Canny's view British History places undue emphasis on high politics, exaggerates contacts within the two islands of Britain and Ireland at the expense of contacts with Europe, places England at the centre of the story, stresses similarity in place of identifying contrasts, and is beyond the competence of most historians, N. Canny, 'Irish, Scottish and Welsh responses to centralisation, c.1530–c.1640', Grant and Stringer eds. *Uniting the Kingdom?*, 147–69.

10   S.G. Ellis, 'The concept of British history', in S.G. Ellis and S. Barber eds. *Conquest and Union. Fashioning the British State 1485–1725* (London, 1995), 3.

11   S.J. Connolly, 'Varieties of Britishness. Ireland, Scotland and Wales in the Hanoverian state', in Grant and Stringer eds. *Uniting the Kingdom?*, 197.

12   This deficit in Irish History is usefully explored in R.F. Foster, 'History – the Irish question', in *Transactions of the Royal Historical Society* 33 (1983), 169–92. For an effective critique of nationalist Irish History see S.G. Ellis, 'Historiographical debate: representations of the past in Ireland: whose past and whose present?', *Irish Historical Studies* 27 (1991), 289–308.

13   On this point see J. Pocock, 'Conclusion. Contingency, identity, sovereignty', in Grant and Stringer eds. *Uniting the kingdom?*, 295–96. For an excellent example of how Ireland is necessary to British history, and British history to the history of Ireland, see T. Barnard, 'Scotland and Ireland in the later Stewart monarchy', in Ellis and Barber eds. *Conquest and Union*, 250–75.

14   K.M. Brown, 'British History: a sceptical comment', in R.G. Asche ed.

Three Nations – A Common History? England, Scotland, Ireland and British History c. 1600–1920 (Bochum, 1993), 117–28.

15 D. Broun, 'The birth of Scottish history', *SHR* 76 (1997), 4–22.

16 Although this was rarely uncritical and even medieval historians could paint a very unflattering picture, S. Boardman, 'Chronicle propaganda in fourteenth-century Scotland: Robert the Steward, John of Fordun and the 'anonymous chronicle', *SHR* 76 (1997), 23–43.

17 D. Allan, 'This inquisitive age': past and present in the Scottish Enlightenment', *SHR*, 76 (1997), 69–85.

18 P. Wood and F. Payne, *The Knowledge and Attitudes towards Scottish History of S4 Pupils in Scottish Schools* (Social Studies Research Unit, Northern College, 1997).

19 James Young to the editor, *The Herald*, 22 February 1997. See, for example, the letter to the *Scotsman* from a councillor Jim Mitchell of Paisley on 10 January 1997 in which he refers to 'the forced emigration of our people to the far corners of the world, the banning and denigration of the culture and heritage of the Scottish people shortly after England gained control of our country, and our history being consigned to the waste paper bin while a policy of assimilation into a British/English way of life was encouraged', *Scotsman*, 10 January 1997. Both the then Conservative secretary of state for Scotland, Michael Forsyth, and the leader of the Scottish Nationalist Party attempted to exploit the Declaration of Arbroath, *The Herald*, 30 January 1997 and 26 February 1997.

20 Keith Robbins keenly observed that 'we should beware of imputing a deep underlying core of beliefs, attitudes, values, and genes transmitted in uncontaminated form among the English, the Welsh and the Scottish over centuries, even over a thousand years, upon which "Britishness" was superimposed at a particular point in time – only for these "core" cultural features to resume their "natural" course once internal or external facts appear to diminish its utility, ' Robbins, 'An imperial and multinational polity, 1832–1922', in Grant and Stringer eds. *Uniting the Kingdom?*, 249.

21 R. McCreadie, 'Scottish identity and the constitution' in B. Crick ed. *National Identities. The Constitution of the united Kingdom* (Oxford, 1991), 38–56. The degree of popular interest in Scottish History was in evidence at the public conference organised by the *Sunday Times*, 'A Most Historic Nation? The Future of Scotland's Past', on 3 March 1997. In spite of a rail strike over five hundred people attended the meeting at the University of Glasgow.

22 For a review to the early 1970s see B. Lenman, 'The teaching of Scottish history in the Scottish universities', *Scottish Historical Review* 53 (1973), 165–90; More recently see the essays in I. Donnachie and C. Whatley eds. *The Manufacture of Scottish History* (Edinburgh, 1992), and volume

73 (1994) of the *Scottish Historical Review*, T.C. Smout, "Writing Scotland's History': Preface', *SHR* 76 (1997), 3.

23 This legitimate fear is expressed by N. Macdougall in 'Response: at the medieval bedrock', and A. Macinnes, "Early modern Scotland: the current state of play', in *Scottish Historical Review*, 73 (1994), 27–28 and 42–43.

24 For example, see H.R. Trevor-Roper, 'The union of Britain in the seventeenth century', in H.R. Trevor-Roper, *Religion, the Reformation and Social Change* (London, 1967), 445–67; H.R. Trevor-Roper, 'The Scottish Enlightenment', *Studies in Voltaire and the Eighteenth Century* 58 (1967), 1635–58. A useful reply is D. Stevenson, 'Professor Trevor-Roper and the Scottish revolution', *History Today* 30 (1980), 34–40. C. Beveridge and R. Turnbull, *The Eclipse of Scottish Culture. Inferiorism and the Intellectuals* (Edinburgh, 1989) exaggerates the problem, but their case cannot be ignored out of hand.

25 For some insight into this modern invention see M. Chapman, *The Celts. The Construction of a Myth* (Basingstoke, 1992).

26 J. Black, *A History of the British Isles* (Basingstoke, 1997); M. Kishlansky, *A Monarchy Transformed. Britain 1603–1714* (Harmondsworth, 1996). For an infuriating example of this kind of history see L.K.J. Glassey ed, *The Reigns of Charles II and James VII and II* (Basingstoke, 1997) where all the contributors apart from Ronald Hutton treat Scotland with contempt. For example, a chapter on towns does not mention Edinburgh, the second city in Britain.

27 M. Hechter, *Internal Colonialism: the Celtic Fringe in British National Development* (Berkeley, 1975). For an updated interpretation of this model see S. Clark, *State and Status. The Rise of the State and Aristocratic Power in Western Europe* (McGill, 1995).

28 For some discussion of this in relation to medieval Scotland see Stringer, 'Scottish foundations: thirteenth-century perspectives', in Grant and Stringer eds. *Uniting the Kingdom?*, 92–94. T.C. Smout, 'Centre and periphery in history: with some thought on Scotland as a case study', *Journal of Common Market Studies* 18 (1980), 256–71 suggests that Scotland can be viewed as both core and periphery. A more refined restatement of the core-periphery idea is found in J. Robertson, 'Union, state and empire. The Britain of 1707 in its European setting', in L. Stone ed. *An Imperial State at War. Britain from 1689 to 1815* (London, 1994), 224–57. The model is more appropriately applied to the American colonies, J.P. Greene, *Peripheries and Center. Constitutional Development in the Extended Politics of the British Empire and the United States* (Athens, Georgia, 1986). For an alternative model see J. Wormald, 'The creation of Britain: multiple kingdoms or core and colonies', *Transactions of the Royal Historical Society* sixth series 2 (1992), 173–94.

29 D. Stevenson, 'Twilight before night or darkness before dawn? Interpreting seventeenth-century Scotland', in R. Mitchison ed. *Why Scottish History Matters* (Edinburgh, 1991), 37–47. The vitality of Scottish civic life independently of the question of union is apparent in R.L. Emerson, 'Scottish cultural change 1660–1710 and the union of 1707', in J. Robertson ed. *A Union for Empire. Political Thought and the Union of 1707* (Cambridge, 1995), 121–44, and D. Allan, *Virtue, Learning and the Scottish Enlightenment* (Edinburgh, 1993).

30 Ellis, 'The concept of British History' in Ellis and Barber eds. *Conquest and Union*, 4 writes 'British history thus ought properly to refer to the whole process of state building in the archipelago'. He goes on, p. 5, to make a distinction between 'British history as a process of state formation and nationalist history as the making of the nation'.

31 B.P. Levack, *The Formation of the British State. England, Scotland and the Union 1603–1707* (Oxford 1987).

32 J. Morrill, 'The British problem, c.1534–1707', in B. Bradshaw and J. Morrill eds. *The British Problem c.1534–1707. State Formation in the Atlantic Archipelago* (Basingstoke, 1996), 1–38.

33 J. Campbell, 'The united kingdom of England', in Grant and Stringer eds. *Uniting the Kingdom?*, 43–45; E. Evans, 'Englishness and Britishness, c.1790–c.1870', in Grant and Stringer eds. *Uniting the Kingdom?*, 233.

34 R Hutton, The British Republic 1649–1660, (Basingstoke 1990); S.C.A. Pincus, *Protestantism and Patriotism. Ideologies and the Making of English Foreign Policy, 1650–1668* (Cambridge, 1996) draws attention to English awareness of European-wide issues but ignores the theme of Britain in influencing foreign policy. However, see D. Armitage, 'The Cromwellian Protectorate and the language of empire', *Historical Journal* 35 (1993), 531–55; A.H. Williamson, 'Union with England traditional, union with England radical: Sir James Hope and the mid-seventeenth century state', *English Historical Review* 110 (1995), 303–22; D. Stevenson, 'Cromwell, Scotland and Ireland', in J.S. Morrill ed. *Oliver Cromwell and the English Revolution* (London, 1990), 149–80.

35 Robertson, 'Empire and union', in Robertson ed. *A Union for Empire*, 35.

36 Quoted in Dickey, 'Daniel Defoe's political writings 1698–1707', in Robertson ed. *A Union for Empire*, 84.

37 C.J. Berry, *Social Theory and the Enlightenment* (Edinburgh, 1997); Allan, *Virtue, Learning and the Enlightenment.*

38 A. Macinnes, 'Early modern Scotland: the current state of play', quote is on p. 31; R.A. Houston 'Eighteenth-century Scottish studies: out of the laager?', both in *Scottish Historical Review* 74 (1994), 31–46 and 64–81.

39 For some stimulating thoughts on this theme see J.G.A. Pocock, 'History and sovereignty: the historiographical response to Europeanisation in two

British cultures', *Journal of British Studies* 31 (1992), 358–89. Many English historians would also prefer to deal with England's relations with Europe as though Britain did not exist. See the recent R.M. Smuts ed. *The Stuart Court and Europe. Essays in Politics and Political Culture* (Cambridge, 1996) in which there is virtually no sense of this being a British court.

40 D. Cannadine, 'British History as a 'new subject'. Politics, perspectives and prospects', in Grant and Stringer eds., *Uniting the Kingdom?*, 13.

41 Peter Scott, quoted in L. Colley, *Britons. Forging the Nation 1707–1837* (Yale, 1992), 373.

42 For the Scottish inventions see E.J. Cowan, 'Myth and identity in early medieval Scotland', *Scottish Historical Review* 63 (1984), 111–35; R.A. Mason, Scotching the Brut: politics, history and national myth in sixteenth-century Britain', in R.A. Mason ed. *Scotland and England 1286–1815* (Edinburgh, 1987), 60–84. On England, T.D. Kendrick, *British Antiquity* (London, 1950); H.A. Macdougall, *Racial Myth in English History. Trojans, Teutons and Anglo-Saxons* (Montreal, 1982); R. Porter ed. *Myths of the English* (Cambridge, 1993).

43 Marshall, 'A nation defined by empire', 208–22.

44 N. Canny, 'The attempted Anglicization of Ireland in the seventeenth century: an exemplar of British History', in Asche ed. *Three Nations – A Common History?*, 50.

45 N.P. Canny, 'The formation of the Irish mind: religion, politics and Gaelic literature, 1580–1750', *Past and Present* 95 (1982), 96–116; N.P. Canny, 'Identity in Ireland: the emergence of the Anglo-Irish', in N. Canny and A. Pagden eds. *Colonial Identity in the Atlantic World 1500–1800* (1987), 159–213; D. Hayton, 'Anglo-Irish attitudes: changing perceptions of national identity among the Protestant ascendancy, ca. 1690–1750', *Studies in Eighteenth-Century Culture* 17 (1987), 145–57; T.C. Barnard, 'Crisis of identity among Irish Protestants 1641–1685', *Past and Present* 127 (1990), 39–83; J. Smyth, "Like amphibious animals": Irish Protestants, ancient Britons, 1691–1707', *Historical Journal* 36 (1993), 785–97.

46 This is apparent in Kearney, *The British isles: a History of Four Nations* (Cambridge, 1989); see too L. Colley, 'Britishness and otherness: an argument', in *Journal of British Studies* 31 (1992), 311–16.

47 W.O. Williams, 'The survival of the Welsh language after the union of England and Wales: the first phase, 1536–1642', *Welsh Historical Review* (1964), 69–93; P. Jenkins, *A History of Modern Wales, 1536–1990* (London, 1992), 57–77.

48 Campbell, 'The united kingdom of England', in Grant and Stringer eds. *Uniting the Kingdom?*, 47.

49 Gordon Donaldson argued that the 'Scotland which mattered politically and economically was consciously Anglo-Saxon, and would have

indignantly repudiated the suggestion that it was anything else', *Scotland. James V to James VII* (Edinburgh, 1965), 259. J. Sommerville ed. *King James VI and I. Political Writings* (Cambridge, 1994), 24; A.H. Williamson, 'Scots,Indians and empire: the Scottish politics of civilisation, 1519–1609', *Past and Present* 150 (1996), 57–62.

50 A.H. Williamson, 'George Buchanan, civic virtue and commerce: European imperialism and its sixteenth-century critics', *Scottish Historical Review* 75 (1996), 20–37; D. Armitage, 'The Scottish vision of empire: intellectual origins of the Darien venture', in Robertson ed. *Union for Empire* 97–120; D. Armitage, 'Making the empire British. Scotland in the Atlantic world', *Past and Present* 155 (1997), 34–63; N. Landsman, 'The provinces and the empire. Scotland, the American colonies and the development of British provincial identity', in Stone ed. *An Imperial State at War*, 258–87; N. Landsman, 'The legacy of British union for the North American colonies: provincial elites and the problem of imperial union', in Robertson ed, *Union for Empire*, 297–317.

51 A.I. Macinnes, 'Gaelic culture in the seventeenth century: polarization and assimilation', in Ellis and Barber eds. *Conquest and Union*, 162–94; A.I. Macinnes, *Clanship and Commerce and the House of Stuart, 1603–1788* (East Linton, 1996).

52 J. Dawson, 'Two kingdoms or three? Ireland in Anglo-Scottish relations in the middle of the sixteenth century', in Mason ed. *Scotland and England 1286–1815*, 113–38; J. Dawson, 'The fifth earl of Argyle, Gaelic lordship and political power in sixteenth-century Scotland', *Scottish Historical Review* 67 (1988), 1–27; W. Gillies, 'The invention of tradition, highland style', in A.A. MacDonald, M. Lynch, I.B. Cowan eds. *The Renaissance in Scotland. Studies in Literature, Religion, History and Culture Offered to John Durkhan* (Leiden, 1994), 144–56.

53 P. Womack, *Improvement and Romance. Constructing the Myth of the Highlands* (Basingstoke 1989); R. Clyde, *From Rebel to Hero. The Image of the Highlander 1745–1830* (East Linton, 1995).

54 C. Kidd, 'Teutonist ethnology and Scottish nationalist inhibition, 1780–1880', in *Scottish Historical Review* 197 (1995), 45–68.

55 J. Anderson, *Sir Walter Scott and History* (Edinburgh, 1981); M.G.H. Murray-Pittock, *The Invention of Scotland. The Stuart Myth and the Scottish Identity, 1638 to the Present* (London, 1991); M. Ash, *The Strange Death of Scottish History* (Edinburgh, 1980); C. Harvie, 'Scott and the image of Scotland', in R. Samuel ed. *Patriotism: the Making and Unmaking of British National Identity. Volume II Minorities and Outsiders* (3 vols. London, 1989), 173–92. P.D. Garside, 'Scott and the 'Philosophical Historians', *Journal of the History of Ideas* 36 (1975), 497–529 suggests a quite different side to Scott's involvement with history.

56 J. Dawson, 'William Cecil and the British dimension of early Elizabethan foreign policy', *History* 74 (1989), 196–216; J. Dawson, 'Anglo-Scottish protestant culture and integration in sixteenth century Britain', in Ellis and Barber eds. *Conquest and Union*, 87–114.

57 B. Galloway, *The Union of England and Scotland 1603–1608* (Edinburgh, 1986); B.R. Galloway and B.P. Levack eds. *The Jacobean Union. Six Tracts of 1604* (Scottish History Society Fourth Series, 21, Edinburgh, 1985).

58 This is argued effectively in Russell, 'Composite monarchies in early modern Europe. The British and Irish example', in Grant and Stringer eds. *Uniting the Kingdom?*, 133–46. Quote is on p. 146.

59 J. Wormald, 'James VI and I: two kings or one?', *History* 68 (1983), 187–209; Wormald, 'The creation of Britain'; Wormald, 'The high road from Scotland: one king, two kingdoms', in Grant and Stringer eds. *Uniting the kingdom?*, 123–32; J. Wormald, 'James VI, James I and the identity of Britain', in Bradshaw and Morrill eds. *The British Problem c.1534–1707*, 148–71. This last essay is perhaps a case of an argument over-reaching itself.

60 K.M. Brown, 'The vanishing emperor. British kingship and its decline', in Mason ed. *Scots and Britons*, 58–87.

61 For example, see Galloway, *Union of England and Scotland*; N. Cuddy, 'The revival of the entourage: the bedchamber of James VI and I in administration and politics, 1603–1625', in D. Starkey ed. *The English Court from the Wars of the Roses to the Civil War* (Harlow, 1987), 182–225; N. Cuddy, 'Anglo-Scottish union and the court of James I, 1603–1625', in *Transactions of the Royal Historical Society* 39 (1989), 107–24; M. Lee, *Great Britain's Solomon. James VI and I in His Three Kingdoms* (Urbana, 1990). Also see the essays in R.A. Mason ed. *Scots and Britons. Scottish Political Thought and the Union of 1603* (Cambridge, 1994).

62 As John Morrill has argued, 'the Scots were the victims of a Stuart authoritarianism backed up by the threat of English (and Irish) force, there was no grand design by monarchs, let alone by English elites, to incorporate Scotland into a greater English state', J. Morrill, 'Three kingdoms and one commonwealth? The enigma of mid-seventeenth century Britain and Ireland', in Grant and Stringer eds. *Uniting the Kingdom?*, 170–71.

63 The advice Charles I received from Laud and Wentworth is discussed in P. Donald, *An Uncounselled King. Charles I and the Scottish Troubles 1637–1641* (Cambridge, 1990). On the broader issue of Laud's ecclesiastical policies and Scotland see D.G. Mullan, *Episcopacy in Scotland. The History of an Idea 1560–1638* (Edinburgh, 1986), ch. 9, and M. Lee, *The Road to Revolution. Scotland under Charles I 1625–1637* (Urbana, 1985), ch. 6.

64 'What is striking about Charles's policies towards Scotland is not anglicisation but a naked authoritarianism', J. Morrill, 'The Scottish National

Covenant of 1638 in its British context', in J. Morrill ed. *The Scottish National Covenant in its British Context 1638–51* (Edinburgh, 1990), 6.

65 S. Barber, "Scotland and Ireland under the Commonwealth: a question of loyalty', Ellis and Barber eds. *Conquest and Union*, 195–221.

66 This has become progressively obvious in studies of eighteenth-century Scotland. See A. Murdoch, *The People Above. Politics and Administration in Mid-Eighteenth Century Scotland* (Edinburgh, 1980); A.E. Whetstone, *Scottish County Government in the Eighteenth and Nineteenth Centuries* (Edinburgh, 1981); J.S. Shaw, *The Management of Scottish Society 1707–1764* (Edinburgh, 1983); B. Lenman, 'A client society: Scotland between the '15 and the '45' in J. Black ed. *Britain in the Age of Walpole* (London, 1984), 81–93; R.M. Sunter, *Patronage and Politics in Scotland 1707–1832* (Edinburgh, 1986); D. Szechi, 'The Hanoverians and Scotland', in M. Greengrass ed. *Conquest and Coalescence. The Shaping of the State in early Modern Europe* (London, 1991), 116–33; M. Fry, *The Dundas Despotism* (Edinburgh, 1992). In spite of the title, Scotland's administrative distinctiveness is apparent in M.C. Noonkester, 'The third British empire: transplanting the English shire to Wales, Scotland, Ireland and America', *Journal of British History* 36 (1997), 251–84. The extent of that administrative separation needs to be more fully explored in the light of John Brewer's discussion of the eighteenth century English (sic) state, J. Brewer, *The Sinews of Power. War, Money and the English State 1688–1783* (London, 1989).

67 Of these only Antrim has been adequately written about, J.H. Ohlmeyer, *Civil War and Restoration in the Three Stuart Kingdoms. The Career of Randal MacDonnell, Marquis of Antrim, 1609–1689* (Cambridge, 1993).

68 G.W.S. Barrow, *The Anglo-Norman Era in Scottish History* (Oxford, 1980).

69 K.M. Brown, Aristocracy, Anglicisation and the court 1603–37, *Historical Journal* 36 (1993), 543–76; K.M. Brown, 'The origins of a British aristocracy: integration and its limitations before the treaty of Union', in Ellis and Barber eds. *Conquest and Union*, 222–249 argues against any significant Anglicization of Scottish elites before 1707. Allan, *Virtue, Learning and the Scottish Enlightenment,* and K.M. Brown, 'Scottish identity in the seventeenth century' in B. Bradshaw and P. Roberts eds. *British Consciousness and Identity* (Cambridge, 1998), 236–58 stresses the continuity in Scottish culture, while R.B. Sher, *Church and University in the Scottish Enlightenment. The Moderate Literati of Edinburgh* (Edinburgh, 1985) underlines the importance of native institutions. The case for Anglicization in the eighteenth century is made by N. Phillipson, 'Politics, politeness and the Anglicization of early eighteenth-century Scottish culture', in Mason ed. *Scotland and England*, 226–46.

70 Colley, *Britons*, 105–17.

71   Canny, 'The attempted Anglicization of Ireland', 55–6.

72   Dawson, 'Anglo-Scottish Protestant culture', in Ellis and Barber eds.
     Conquest and Union, 87–114; R.A. Mason, 'The Scottish Reformation and
     the origins of Anglo-British imperialism', in Mason ed. *Scots and Britons*,
     161–86; M. Merriman, 'The assured Scots: Scottish collaborators with
     England during the Rough Wooing', in *Scottish Historical Review* 67 (1968),
     10–34.

73   G. Donaldson, *The Scottish Reformation* (Cambridge 1960); J Kirk, The
     Calvinist contribution to the Scottish reformation, in J. Kirk, *Patterns of
     Reform, Continuity and Change in the Reformation Kirk*, Edinburgh 1989,
     70–95.

74   W. Fraser, *The Sutherland Book* (3 vols., Edinburgh, 1892), ii. 337.

75   J. Morrill, 'A British patriarchy? Ecclesiastical imperialism under the early
     Stuarts', in A. Fletcher and P. Roberts eds. *Religion, Culture and Society in
     Early Modern Britain* (Cambridge, 1994), 209–37; Mullan, *Episcopacy in
     Scotland.*

76   R.A. Mason, 'Usable pasts: history and identity in Reformation Scotland',
     SHR, 76 (1997), 54–68; Dawson, 'Anglo-Scottish protestant culture', in
     Ellis and Barber eds. *Conquest and Union*, 88. Dawson concludes, 'Anglo-
     Scottish protestant culture could help to integrate the English and the
     Scots but it could not forge a new multinational state', 114.

77   J. Morrill, 'The Britishness of the English revolution 1640–1660', in Asche
     ed. *Three Nations – A Common History?*, 98; Williamson, 'Scots, Indians
     and empire', 61.

78   A.H. Williamson, 'Scotland, antichrist and the invention of Great Britain',
     in J. Dwyer, R.A. Mason and A. Murdoch eds. *New Perspectives on the Politics
     and Culture of Early Modern Scotland* (Edinburgh, 1980), 34–58;
     Williamson, 'George Buchanan, civic virtue and commerce'; A.H.
     Williamson, 'From the invention of Great Britain to the creation of British
     History', *Journal of British History* 29 (1990), 267–76.

79   D. Stevenson, 'The early Covenanters and the federal union of Britain',
     and E.J. Cowan, 'The Solemn League and Covenant', in Mason ed.
     Scotland and England, 163–81 and 182–202.

80   John Morrill has forcefully and convincingly argued that 'the national
     histories of England, Ireland, Scotland and Wales are necessary but not
     sufficient in explaining why there were wars in all three kingdoms or
     what the dynamics of those wars were', Morrill, 'Three kingdoms and
     one commonwealth?', in Grant and Stringer eds. *Uniting the Kingdom?*,
     190. For a tortuous dissection of definitions and terminology in relation
     to the wars see J.G.A. Pocock, 'The Atlantic archipelago and the war of
     the three kingdoms', in Bradshaw and Morrill eds. *The British Problem
     c.1534–1707*, 172–91.

81 C. Russell, *The Fall of the British Monarchies 1637–1642* (Oxford, 1991).

82 Morrill, 'The Britishness of the English revolution 1640–1660', in Asche ed. *Three Nations – A Common History?*, 102. For Morrill's review of Russell see 'The causes of Britain's civil wars', in J. Morrill ed. *The Nature of the English Revolution* (London, 1993), 252–72.

83 M. Bennett, *The Civil Wars in Britain and Ireland 1638–1651* (Oxford, 1997). Bennett is still too concerned with English affairs, but that is largely due to the relative inequality in the existing historiography, and it is up to Scottish and Irish historians to put that right.

84 J.R. Young ed. *Celtic Dimensions of the British Civil Wars* (Edinburgh, 1997).

85 D. Hirst, 'The English republic and the meaning of Britain', in Bradshaw and Morrill eds. *The British Problem c.1534–1707*, 192–219.

86 R.A. Mason, "Kingship, nobility and Anglo-Scottish union: John Mair's *History of Greater Britain* (1521)', *Innes Review* 61 (1990), 181–222.

87 Mason, 'The Scottish Reformation and the origins of Anglo-British imperialism', in Mason ed. *Scots and Britons*, 161–86.

88 SRO Breadalbane Muniments GD 112/39/21/1; *Poems of Sir David Murray of Gothry* presented by T. Kinnear (Bannatyne Club ii., Edinburgh, 1823); Galloway and Levack eds. *The Jacobean Union*, 1–38, 75–142; T. Craig, *De Unione Regnorum Britanniae Tractatus* ed. and trs. C.S. Terry (Scottish History Society, second edition, 1909).

89 Quoted in Dickey, 'Daniel Defoe's political writings 1698–1707', in Robertson ed. *Union for Empire*, 85. Unionist ideas have received more attention recently but still require elaboration. J. Robertson, 'An elusive sovereignty. The course of the union debate in Scotland 1698–1707', in Robertson ed. *Union for Empire*, 198–227 provides a useful outline of the issues.

90 C. Kidd, 'North Britishness and the nature of eighteenth-century patriotisms', *Historical Journal* 39 (1996), 361–82. Some aspects of early modern English patriotism are explored in L. Colley, 'Radical patriotism in eighteenth-century England', in R. Samuel ed. *Patriotism: the Making and Unmaking of British National Identity* (3 vols. London, 1989), i. 169–83; D. Eastwood, 'Patriotism and the English state in the 1790s' in M. Philp, *The French Revolution and British Popular Politics* (Cambridge, 1991), 146–68; Colley argues that 'the patriotism of the past requires flexible, sensitive and above all, imaginative reconstruction', *Britons*, 372.

91 Colley, *Britons*, 11; Armitage suggests that 'The creation of a "British" empire demanded that the Scots and English alike arrive at mutually acceptable methods of integration', 'Making the empire British', 50.

92 Berry, *Social Theory of the Scottish Enlightenment*; Ash, *The Strange Death of Scottish History*; C. Kidd, *Subverting Scotland's Past: Scottish Historians and the Creation of an Anglo-British Identity, 1689–c.1830* (Cambridge, 1993); C.

Kidd, 'The Strange Death of Scottish History revisited: constructions of the past in Scotland, c.1790–1914', *SHR*, 76 (1997), 86–102; S.J. Brown ed. *William Robertson and the Expansion of Empire* (Cambridge, 1997), especially the essays by N. Phillipson, Karen O'Brien and C. Kidd on his historical writing. Many eighteenth-century British historians continue to write English History, although a few textbooks have begun moving in the right direction. For example, see G. Holmes and D. Szechi, *The Age of Oligarchy. Pre-Industrial Britain 1722–1787* (London, 1993). Aspects of the alienation that was a consequence of this process are explored in K. Simpson, *The Protean Scot. The Crisis of Identity in Eighteenth Century Scottish Literature* (Aberdeen, 1988). Where it led to was the elegant nonsense of Henry Buckle, see his *On Scotland and the Scotch Intellect* (Chicago, 1970).

93   Cannadine points out that 'political history has run far ahead of other, no less essential, ways of looking at the British past', 'British history as a 'new subject', 25. For an important exception see R. Houston, *Literacy and the Scottish Identity 1600–1800* (Cambridge 1985). Some interesting observations are made in K.E. Wrightson, 'Kindred adjoining kingdom: an English perspective on social and economic history of early modern Scotland' in R.A. Houston and I.D. Whyte eds. *Scottish Society 1500–1800* (Cambridge, 1989), 245–60.

94   J.H. Elliot, 'A Europe of composite monarchies', *Past and Present* 137 (1992), 48–71; Russell, 'Composite monarchies in early modern Europe.', in Grant and Stringer eds., *Uniting the Kingdom?*, 133–46.

95   Jacobitism is best understood in a British context, most successfully in B. Lenman, *The Jacobite Risings in Britain 1689–1746* (London, 1980), and D. Szechi, *The Jacobites. Britain and Europe 1688–1788* (Manchester, 1994). However, that bigger British picture requires national investigations, for example Macinnes, *Clanship, Commerce and the House of Stuart* for the Scottish highlands, or P.K. Monod, *Jacobitism and the English People, 1688–1788* (Cambridge, 1989).

96   Colley, *Britons*, 117–32; Colley, 'Britishness and otherness: an argument', 316–26; Armitage, 'Making the empire British', 34–63; N.C. Landsmen, *Scotland and its first American colony* (Princeton, 1985); J. Robertson, 'Empire and union: two concepts of the early modern European order', in Robertson, *Union for empire*, 3.

97   Scots Law was derivative of English feudal law and yet became highly distinctive, H.L. McQueen, *Common Law and Feudal Society in Medieval Scotland* (Edinburgh, 1993); H.L. McQueen, '*Regiam Majestatem*, Scots Law and national identity', *Scottish Historical Review* 74 (1995), 1–25; B.P. Levack, 'Law, sovereignty and the union', in Mason ed. *Scots and Britons*, 213–37; J.W. Cairns, 'Scottish law, Scottish lawyers and the status of the union', in Robertson ed. *Union for Empire*, 213–37; L. Dickey, 'Power,

commerce, and natural law in Daniel Defoe's political writings 1698–1707', in *ibid.*, 81. Although the English treason law was far more draconian, as was the English criminal code.

98 G. Newman, *The Rise of English Nationalism. A Cultural history 1740–1830* (New York, 1987), fails to make adequate distinctions between British and English identity, and ends with Carlyle as a prophet of English nationalism.

CHAPTER 10

Critical Perspectives: The Autonomy of English History?*

Tim Harris

The purpose of this chapter is to consider the shortcomings and limitations of the new British history, specifically from the view of someone interested in understanding the early modern English past. What are the dangers of the British approach? What can it lead us to ignore, and to what extent can British history be seen as providing *the* key to understanding political developments in seventeenth-century England? I must confess at the start, however, to being deeply sympathetic to the enterprise of British history; indeed, I am currently writing a monograph on the revolutions of the later seventeenth century which argues for the necessity of taking a multiple-kingdom approach, and of exploring the interactions of developments within the constituent kingdoms of the Stuart multiple kingdom.[1] Nor do I believe that the new British history poses any threat to the independence of English history. Early modern English historiography is so well developed and has such a long-standing and rich tradition that it is scarcely likely to be undermined by the relatively small number of scholars who have sought to incorporate a British dimension into their own work. Of more concern is the potential threat to the integrity of Scottish and Irish history, since the British approach at times seems to risk marginalizing those aspects of the Scottish or Irish pasts that seem irrelevant from a British or Anglo-imperialist perspective. What is being offered here, therefore, are the critical perspectives of someone who believes in the value of the new British history and is an active practitioner of it himself. There are certainly many scholars

*Research for this essay was supported by a Fellowship from the John Simon Guggenheim Memorial Foundation. I should also like to thank Clare Jackson for comments on an earlier draft.

who are far more sceptical than I, and not a few who believe that English historians have little, if anything, to gain from pursuing a British perspective.

It is important, however, not allow the debate over the merits of the new British history to become polarised. There seems greater likelihood of this happening for the seventeenth than the sixteenth century, because of the way in which an appeal to the British dimension made its initial impact on Stuart historiography. Thus in his important pioneering work, Conrad Russell invoked Scotland and Ireland to explain the outbreak of a civil war which he felt was inexplicable within an English context alone; those who do not share Russell's brand of revisionism, or who feel that the English civil war is perfectly explicable within the domestic context, have tended to remain suspicious of or even hostile to the three-kingdoms approach. Instead of allowing a 'for' or 'against' mentality to develop, we need to reflect critically on what the British or multiple-kingdom perspective both can and cannot offer us, recognising its benefits (without exaggerating them) and discerning its limitations.

This chapter, then, will consider some of the potential problems of the British approach, concentrating on the seventeenth century, and in particular on the later-Stuart period. Some of the objections that have been raised against the British approach – namely, that it works for the early but not the later seventeenth century, or that is only relevant to the discussion of high politics amongst the elite – will be shown to be misplaced. Not only can Restoration scholars gain much from embracing the multiple-kingdom perspective, but they will find it fruitful in helping to shed light on the formation of public opinion and political agitation out-of-doors. However, a number of warnings will be sounded, which all relate to the question of the explanatory force the British approach can carry for the course of historical development within England itself. First, we must not confuse the British dimension with a British problem. That is to say, recognising that the Scottish and Irish contexts are necessary for a full understanding of the outbreak of the English civil war or the causes of the Glorious Revolution, for instance, does not necessarily mean that the Stuart multiple monarchy was inherently unstable or that Scotland and Ireland provide the key to explaining 1642 or 1688. Secondly, a desire to incorporate Scotland and Ireland should not blind us to the need to consider England's relationships with other foreign powers or external forces which may have had equal or even greater impact on the English polity. Finally, we must be careful not to invoke Scotland and Ireland as a way of accounting for developments within

England that really require an internalist explanation. By this I do not simply mean, to take the obvious example, that we should not invoke the prior revolts in Scotland and Ireland as a way to explain the outbreak of civil war in England in 1642, when political and religious developments within England are sufficient by themselves. Rather, my point is that we need to recognise that even when political actors in England appear to have been reacting to developments in Scotland and Ireland, they reacted in ways that were structured by the context of their own historical experience and the distinctive character of English political culture. To put it another way, the reason why Scottish and Irish events could have the impact they did in England requires us to seek an explanation that is ultimately English in nature. Such an insight forces us to acknowledge the ultimate autonomy of English history when it comes to explaining events in England (and likewise of Scottish and Irish history with regard to events in those two kingdoms), and illustrates why the new British history must never be allowed to supplant the separate national histories of the constituent kingdoms of the Britannic archipelago.

Supporters of British history not only recognise that it has come to mean 'different things in different centuries', but would also readily concede that it is far from clear whether it 'can be undertaken for every century of Britain's past with the same degree of plausibility, conviction or success'.[2] There are compelling reasons why the pursuit of a multiple-kingdom perspective seems to make particular sense for the early-Stuart period. When James VI of Scotland came to the English throne in 1603 as James I, he brought with him a strong imperial vision of kingship, and both he and his son, Charles I, sought to promote a greater degree of harmonisation or even convergence between all three kingdoms under their rule. Conrad Russell has brilliantly shown how the pursuit of greater uniformity, especially on the religious front, under Charles I, created problems in Scotland, Ireland and England, producing a billiard ball effect, as developments in one kingdom impinged upon the others with devastating results.[3] Russell's conceptual approach remained self-consciously anglocentric; his desire was to explain the outbreak of a civil war in England, not to get to the root of the tensions and difficulties that bedevilled the Scottish or Irish polities. There are others, however, who believe that a genuinely British history can (and should) be written for the early-Stuart period, pointing to the greater presence of the Scottish and Irish upper classes at the English court or in the English privy council, the beginnings of the emergence of British (rather than separate

English, Scottish, and Irish) organs of government, and perhaps even a process of 'briticization' amongst the nobility (as many wealthy landowners began to intermarry with heirs/heiresses from the other Stuarts kingdoms, acquire titles in more than one realm, and become assimilated into the political and cultural life of more than just the country of their birth). Early Stuart politics can be approached, in other words, from the point of view of a ruling elite who had a British, or at least multiple-kingdom, outlook, who were trying to rule a British polity, and who had to address issues and problems that were often of a distinctively British (or pan-archipelagic) nature.[4]

At first glance it might appear that neither of these approaches is likely to prove particularly fruitful for the period after 1660. Following the break-up of the Cromwellian union in 1660, we see a return to a more fractured British polity; whatever progress had been made towards the emergence of a British ruling elite was halted or even reversed; and Scotland, Ireland and England went largely their own separate ways. Though all three kingdoms, of course, were still ruled by the same king, based in England, neither Charles II, nor his brother, James II (and VII of Scotland), shared the imperial vision of either their grandfather or father. Indeed, it is revealing that Ronald Hutton's recent biography of Charles II, which sees a consideration of the Merry Monarch's rule in Scotland and Ireland as central to its enterprise, nevertheless provides us with three parallel narratives of what was going in the three constituent kingdoms, rather than with an integrated British history. Perhaps there is not much of an integrated story to tell.[5]

While the approaches advocated by early-Stuart historians might not prove readily translatable into the later Stuart context, there nevertheless remain compelling reasons for why those working on the period after 1660 should take the British dimension into consideration. The three crucial landmarks of the later-Stuart historiographical terrain – the Restoration, the Exclusion Crisis, and the so-called Glorious Revolution – appear to be crying out for treatment on a multiple-kingdom level. The restoration of monarchy in 1660 itself was triggered by prior developments in Ireland and Scotland – namely, the coup in Ireland of December 1659 and the seizure of Dublin Castle by more conservative forces within the army, and the intervention in English politics in the new year by General George Monck, commander of the forces in Scotland. Similarly, the Restoration settlement was an attempt to solve, on a multiple-kingdom level, the problems created by the upheavals of the 1640s and 1650s which had been brought about in the first place by what we now recognise to have been a crisis of three kingdoms. The attempt to exclude from the English succession the man who was also heir to the crowns of Scotland and Ireland provoked a crisis which was never simply English in its implications, and which was fed (as we shall see shortly) by perceptions of what was going on in all three of the Stuart kingdoms. The Glorious Revolution was likewise, at a very basic level, a 'British event', since James's 'abdication' in England necessarily provoked simultaneous crises in Scotland and Ireland, even if the revolutions in the three kingdoms ended up taking very different paths.

Yet beyond this, in numerous specific respects, we can detect the operation of the billiard ball effect with regard to Charles II and James II's management of their multiple-kingdom inheritance. For example, many of the problems that developed in Restoration Scotland were the result of the unsatisfactory nature of the post-1660 religious settlement, which saw the imposition of an intolerant episcopalian establishment and the outlawing of Presbyterianism. Yet episcopacy was restored in Scotland not because there was a popular demand for the return of bishops (as there was, to a certain extent, in England), or even because the Scottish ruling elite were necessarily predisposed to favour episcopacy, but because of Charles II's desire to bring the Scottish church into 'better Harmony with the Government of the Churches of England and Ireland'.[6] The roots of political instability in Restoration Scotland, in other words, might be traced back to the pursuit by a royal administration based in England of a British agenda in church affairs which lacked sufficient sensitivity to the distinctive national religious context north of the border. On the other hand, too much sensitivity to the distinctive national context could also create problems, as the example of Ireland illustrates. Whereas in both England and Scotland those outside the established Protestant church were to be subject to extended spells of persecution between the Restoration and the Revolution, in Ireland, where over three-quarters of the population were Roman Catholics, political realism dictated a policy of greater accommodation. Yet the perception that the government was being too soft on the Catholics in Ireland created repeated political difficulties for the crown in England, and heightened concerns about the threat of popery, particularly during the Exclusion Crisis.

Examples of the ways in which developments in the respective constituent kingdoms of the Britannic archipelago impinged upon each other could be extended almost indefinitely. Fears that emerged in England in the later 1670s that Charles was intending to rule with a standing army were in part fuelled by the way the king used military force in Scotland to crush political and religious dissent in his northern kingdom. In turn, the reason why Charles II recalled the Highland Host and the other militia forces raised in the early months of 1678 to suppress Presbyterian disaffection in the Scottish south-west was because he came to appreciate that continuing such a policy 'would be prejudicial to his affaires in England'.[7] James II, who came to the throne in 1685 with the intent of helping his Catholic co-religionists, self-consciously used Scotland as a testing ground for reforms that he wanted to introduce into England. As his daughter, Princess Anne, commented to her sister in June 1688, 'all that has been done there [Scotland], has been but a fore-runner of what in a short time has been done here';[8] she was alluding to the promotion of Catholics to government office, the encouragement of open Catholic worship, and the use of the royal prerogative to dispense with and even to suspend the operation of the test and penal laws. At the same time, there was also a rapid and extensive Catholicisation of the civil and military administration in Ireland. Those in England needed only to look north of the border and across the Irish Sea to discover what was in store for them; it was James's style of government throughout his Britannic kingdoms, in other words, that informed the reactions of his English subjects to the perceived threat, under his rule, of popery and arbitrary government. Although the revolutions in England, Scotland and Ireland took very different paths, the respective settlements were nevertheless influenced by what was going on in the Britannic archipelago as a whole. To give just one, specific example, the reasons for the failure of plans to comprehend Protestant dissenters within a more broadly defined Church in England in 1689 are to be sought in large part in Scotland; the abolition of episcopacy north of the border, and a consequent propaganda campaign by the Scottish episcopalian clergy warning their brethren to the south of the dangers of Presbyterianism, scared off the Anglican clergy, who grew increasingly reluctant to grant any concessions that might conceivably undermine the security of the episcopalian establishment in England.[9]

Yet even if the British approach might be pursued with some merit for the whole of the Stuart century, it nevertheless appears to be one, some would suggest, that is only suited for the study of high politics. It might work fine when we are dealing with kings, privy councillors, MPs, or bishops, but what about people below that level, or those out in the provinces, far removed from the centre of power? Thus both John Morrill and Peter Lake have complained that Russell's account cannot explain the provincial response to the crisis that developed in England from 1640, the intrusion of the crowd (especially in London) in politics, the petitioning campaigns both for and against episcopacy, or the process whereby both king and parliament were able to mobilise the masses to fight for their respective causes – about which we have learnt so much through the work of scholars such as Brian Manning, Anthony Fletcher, and David Underdown. As Lake has put it, in a memorable turn of phrase: 'No doubt much remains to be learned about the London mob, but it seems unlikely that many of the people who flocked from London to Westminster to petition Parliament were Scottish'.[10]

Although Russell might be fairly criticised for his overconcentration on the elite, it would be wrong to suggest that the British dimension is irrelevant to understanding the formation of public opinion or the reaction of those out-of-doors. By this I do not mean that some of the London crowd were indeed Scottish, although we can in fact find Scots, Irish and English involved in collective agitation outside their home country.[11] The more important point is that the British dimension, or at least an awareness of political developments in the three constituent kingdoms of the Stuart multiple monarchy, did intrude in interesting ways into crowd politics at this time. The inhabitants of the Scottish capital during the Exclusion Crisis, for example, were just as concerned about the prospect of a popish successor and the threat of popery and arbitrary government as were Londoners. The decision by the students of Edinburgh University to stage a pope-burning on 25 December 1680 was in self-conscious imitation of the London pope-burnings of 17 November; a group of them had got the idea when they saw a print of the London procession hanging on the wall in an Edinburgh tavern. The main innovation by the Scottish students was to wear blue ribbons in their hats with the motto 'No Pope' printed upon it: the practice was adopted because in the Old Testament (Numbers 15, v. 38–9) God appointed the Israelites to wear blue ribbons, so that they might remember and observe the Commandments, and since Scottish law condemned popery as idolatry, Catholic religious worship was, by this definition, in violation of the Decalogue. This wearing of blue ribbons was soon copied by English crowds, to designate support for the Duke of Monmouth, Charles II's illegitimate though Protestant son, as an alternative successor to the Catholic Duke of York.[12] Perhaps the most striking example of how the multiple kingdom influenced crowd politics at this time is the Irish scare of 1688. The Earl of Tyrconnell's build up of Catholic forces in Ireland in late 1688, and the suspicion that he was planning to use these to invade Scotland on James II's behalf, prompted the circulation of rumours towards the end of December that Irish Catholics had landed in Galloway in the Scottish south-west and were 'Putting all to Fire and Sword'. The local inhabitants armed themselves in self-defence, began rounding up local Catholics, and even stormed the houses of Catholic notables resident in the area.[13] Similarly in England, panic alarms that spread throughout the country following the king's flight on 11 December, that James's recently-disbanded Catholic Irish soldiers were on the loose and 'putting all before 'em to Fire and Sword', prompted Protestant attacks on papists' houses, under pretence of searching for arms, and mob arrests of suspect Catholics.[14]

Nor is the British dimension important only when considering what we might call 'opposition' crowds. We have long since come to appreciate that there was a significant loyalist reaction in England as the Exclusion Crisis unfolded. Following the dissolution of the Oxford Parliament at the end of March 1681 there were a number of demonstrations on behalf of Charles II and the rest of the royal family, including the Duke of York himself, as crowds sought to demonstrate their support for the monarchy, the hereditary succession, and the established church, against the perceived threat of the Whigs and nonconformists.[15] What has not hitherto been recognised is that the first large-scale demonstrations in support of York took place in Scotland, and were widely reported in the London press not only to demonstrate the alleged public support there was in the northern kingdom for York's succession, but also to suggest a model for the English to emulate. Thus when Charles II sent his brother to Scotland in the autumn of 1679, to keep him out of the way whilst the struggle over the succession heated up in England, the Scottish authorities did their best to ensure the Duke a warm reception. The Scottish Chancellor and the leading nobility of the kingdom met York and his wife at the border on 21 November, and escorted them in grand style to the Scottish capital. Their royal highnesses arrived in Edinburgh on 24 November to a rapturous welcome, the streets being lined with 'many thousands of people' shouting 'Long life and Prosperity to the King' and 'Health and Wellcome to the Duke and Duchess', and that evening there were so many bonfires 'that the whole Town seemed one fire'. York himself was delighted, writing a few days later that he 'had as handsome a reception' as he could desire. Moreover, coming just a few days after the huge London pope-burning procession sponsored by the Whig Green Ribbon Club on 17 November, these pro-York demonstrations provided the government newspaper, the *London Gazette*, with an opportunity to publicise the popularity of the heir to the throne.[16] An equally extravagant welcome awaited the Duke in Edinburgh, so we are told, when he returned to Scotland in late October 1680, with 'the whole body of the People' allegedly 'universally shouting with great joy and cheerfulness, "Lord preserve His Majesty, and their Royal Highnesses"'. Not that anything had been left to chance; Charles II had written to his Scottish Council in advance to ask them to ensure that there were suitable 'publick Demonstrations of Joy' when his brother arrived.[17] A few days after York's reception the Scottish Council wrote to the king thanking him for 'sending his royal brother amongst them', and promising they would 'own and assert the lineal succession of the Crown to the utmost', a 'boast' that was made, one contemporary observed, 'to hector the House of Commons, and generality of the English nation, who would have the Duke of York declared incapable, as being a Papist'.[18] In other words, public opinion in Scotland was being held up as a counter to public opinion in England, in order to make an anti-exclusionist point to the English. It was to deflate the impression that 'the whole body of the People' in Scotland were 'universally' behind the Duke of York that the students of Edinburgh University decided to hold their pope-burning the following Christmas day.[19]

Here we are dealing with the representation of public opinion, and the attempts by different political interest groups to lay claim to having public opinion on their side. Much of the struggle over exclusion centred around which side could most plausibly represent itself as the voice of the people.[20] It was a struggle that was conducted on a British (and not purely English) level. In fact, it is impossible to develop a proper understanding of public reactions to the Exclusion Crisis, unless one adopts a multiple-kingdom perspective. Let us take the growing concern about popery and arbitrary government in England in the later 1670s. People were worried not just about what the Duke of York might do should he become king; they were concerned about what Charles II had been doing, in Scotland (where there did seem a marked drift towards arbitrary government) and Ireland (where there was a real threat from popery), since his Restoration. Whig publicists persistently played the British card in their attempts to influence public opinion during the Exclusion Crisis, as the most cursory of surveys of Whig newspapers, pamphlets, and broadsides, and the speeches of leading Whig politicians makes clear. Yet Tory propagandists and opinion-shapers pursued a similar strategy, appealing in particular to developments in Scotland. For example, their claim that the Whigs and their Presbyterian allies were dangerous political and religious subversives carried such conviction, despite the fact that the English Presbyterians were in reality quite moderate, because they were able to point to the activities of the Presbyterians north of the border, and especially the radical Cameronian wing, who published a series of manifestos disowning Charles II and declaring war on the royal brothers. On the other hand, York's spell at the head of the government in Scotland, where he had shown himself to be a keen supporter of the episcopalian interest there, convinced English Anglicans that their church would be safe under a popish successor. In short, Scotland is crucial to helping us understand why many people in England came to feel that a greater threat was posed by the exclusionists than by a popish successor, and hence why they rallied to the crown against exclusion.[21] They were to be disillusioned by James's style of rule once king, and again what he got up to in Scotland and Ireland played a crucial role in alarming public opinion in England.

What has been identified as a shortcoming of the British approach, in other words, is instead only a shortcoming of the particular conceptual approach adopted by certain types of British historian. Far from being incapable of working at any level other than for the elite, or of shedding insight into crowd politics, agitation out-of-doors, or the formation and mobilisation of public opinion, a multiple-kingdom perspective in fact proves essential for understanding all these things, at least for the later-Stuart period (though I suspect also for the early-Stuart period, if in somewhat different respects). What, then, are the limitations of the new British history?

One is the tendency for early modern historians to think in terms of a British *problem* or the *problem* of multiple kingdoms. This encourages the view that the Stuart multiple-kingdom inheritance was intrinsically difficult to manage – or even unmanageable – given the politico-religious expectations of the age. Thus it was because Charles I, as divine-right sovereign, could not conceive of himself as being head of three very different religious establishments in his three kingdoms, that he felt compelled to pursue a policy of greater uniformity, which necessarily antagonised different interest groups in Scotland, Ireland and England in turn. Trying to solve tensions created in one kingdom simply exacerbated the problems in the others: for example, appeasing the Catholics in Ireland antagonised the Presbyterians in Scotland and the Puritans in England; moves to appease Scottish Presbyterians inevitably alarmed Irish Catholics and

English Anglicans. The problem became a circular one, from which there was no escape. In fact, it remains far from clear whether Charles I's problems stemmed predominantly from the difficulties inherent in managing his multiple-kingdom inheritance. Many early Stuart historians would hold that the reign of James VI and I sufficiently demonstrates that such an inheritance could be managed with success. Although once things had begun to fall apart for Charles I the interaction of events in Scotland, Ireland, and England might have created a crisis from which it proved impossible (as a result of the multiple-kingdom dimension) for the crown to extricate itself, the reason why Charles I got into problems in the first place was because he brought difficulties upon himself through the unwise pursuit of inappropriate or misguided policies.[22]

That the Stuart multiple-kingdom inheritance need not have been a problem for the crown can be seen by comparing the reigns of Charles II and James II and VII. Indeed, being king of three separate kingdoms within the Britannic archipelago seems to have worked to Charles II's advantage, since he was able to use Scotland to help stave off the challenge of the exclusionist opposition in England. We have already seen how the government press sought to counter Whig claims to be representative of the voice of the people by pointing to the extensive popular support York appeared to enjoy in the northern kingdom. Scottish support for the Duke proved to be very significant in the long run, since it meant that within the Stuart multiple-kingdom context, a successful attempt by the English to exclude York from the succession would either destroy the regal union or else provoke war with the northern kingdom. In the debates over exclusion in the English House of Commons in May 1679, opponents of the bill pointed out that Scotland 'would never joyn in changeing the Succession' but 'would catch at such an occasion to separate again from England'.[23] In the Commons debate over the second exclusion bill on 2 November 1680, the Tory, Edward Seymour, argued that 'it cannot be imagined, that such a law will bind all here in England, or any in Scotland; and it is disputed whether it will be binding in Ireland: so that in all probability it will not only divide us amongst ourselves, but the three kingdoms one from the other, and occasion a miserable civil war'.[24] A recognition that the ability to play one kingdom against another might prove beneficial to the crown was one reason why plans for political union between England and Scotland came to nothing under Charles II. When such a proposal was considered in 1669, there were many in Scotland who were quick to point out how this would be destructive to the king's interest:

seeing whilst the Kingdoms stood divided, his Majesty had two Parliaments, wherof the one might always be exemplary to the other, and might, by loyal emulation, excite one another to an entire obedience; and, if either should invade the royal prerogative, or oppose unjustly their Prince's just commands, the one might prove a curb to the other's insolence.[25]

Charles pursued precisely this strategy in 1681. At the end of March he dissolved the Oxford Parliament, which had sat for just one week, and fed up with the opposition he had met from his English Parliaments over the last few years decided to call one instead in Scotland that summer, where he felt royal control was stronger. His Scottish advisors had suggested that 'the loyal disposition of the great-est part of the nobilitie and Gentrie' would undoubtedly 'make a Parliament not only contribute to the quiet and advantage of Scotland, but by running counter to that of England, be a check and bar to such violent proceedings as hitherto distracted that Nation'. As one Edinburgh newsletter writer put it: the parliament to be called in Scotland was 'by their good example to mother the English to a bet-ter compliance with the counsel [i.e. council]'.[26] Charles asked his Scottish Parliament, amongst other things, to defend the succession, and Scottish MPs, well aware that they had been called to show his 'other Kingdoms and all the World' that they were prepared to maintain 'the Native Succession', proved true to their trust.[27] One of their first measures was to pass an Act asserting that the Scottish crown was passed by lineal descent 'according to the known degrees of proximitie of blood' and making any attempt to alter or divert the succession treason. At this time (August 1681) Charles could not have known whether he would have to face an English Parliament again. The Act was intended, therefore, to make it impossible for a future English Parliament to contemplate trying to exclude the Duke of York. With the Scots thus tied to the succession, passing an exclusion bill in England could only lead to war between the two kingdoms.[28]

Charles II ultimately was able to manage his multiple-kingdom inheritance to his advantage. Moreover, he was able to do this despite the fact that he had major problems in all three of his kingdoms: a highly volatile religious situation in Scotland; difficulties over both religion and the land settlement in Ireland; and a serious challenge from a powerful and fairly well-organised political and religious opposition in England, both in- and out-of-doors. Charles neverthe-less succeeded in building up the position of the monarchy in the final years of his reign, and when he died in 1685 he left the crown in what was arguably the strongest position it had ever enjoyed – in all three kingdoms – throughout the whole of the Stuart century.[29] That the position deteriorated so quickly under his successor tells us more about the political ineptitude of James II and VII than it does about the difficulties of wearing the English, Scottish and Irish crowns all at once. The crisis that ensued inevitably had multiple-kingdom ramifications because James II had a multiple-kingdom inheritance, and many of the problems that developed can only be fully understood if we take a British perspective; but this does not mean that the multiple-kingdom inheritance created the problems for James II.

A second danger of the British approach is that it can mislead historians into prioritising developments in Scotland and Ireland over other external factors that created difficulties for the English polity. British issues appear to have played very little part in the crisis of the 1620s; instead it was policies such as the pursuit of the Spanish match and the subsequent wars with France and Spain that destabilised English politics at this time.[30] Likewise, no account of the changing political fortunes of the English crown in the late 1630s and in the lead up to the meeting of the Short and Long Parliaments in 1640 can be complete without adequate attention being given to the changing international context. The pro-Spanish alliance after 1638 heightened fears of popery in England, and it was concern that Charles had become embroiled in an international popish conspiracy to subvert Protestantism at home (of which the Irish rebellion was just one aspect) that explains why many who accepted that monarchs ruled by divine right and could not be resisted nevertheless sided with Parliament against Charles I when civil war broke out in 1642.[31]

Likewise, for all the need to recognise that the growing concern in England in the 1670s and early 1680s about the threat of popery and arbitrary government was caused (in part) by a reaction to developments in Scotland and Ireland, we must again be careful not to lose sight of the international context, and the growing alarm about the seeming pretensions of Louis XIV of France to establish himself as universal monarch.[32] The pamphlet and periodical literature of the Exclusion Crisis was more preoccupied with continental European affairs, and especially with what was going on in France, than with Scotland and Ireland. It was not just that exclusionists argued that a popish successor would rule in an arbitrary fashion like Louis XIV; there was also concern about the French threat posed to the security of European Protestants, the fact that Louis had already begun to violate the provisions of the Edict of Nantes by persecuting the Huguenots (many of whom fled to England with lurid tales of their sufferings), and that he was preparing to move into the Spanish

Netherlands, which he could use as a springboard for an attack both on the Protestant Dutch and the Protestant English. Considerable evidence exists to show the extent to which public opinion during the Exclusion Crisis was shaped by anxieties over the French threat. As one diarist summarised the situation towards the beginning of the Exclusion Crisis: 'The two thinges fear'd are the designes of the papists and the power of the French', 'the present Designe' of the French king being 'visibly' to establish 'the Universal Empire (at least of Europe)'.[33] A report in early December 1678 that some 1,000 or 1,500 Frenchmen had landed in the Isle of Purbeck in Dorsetshire prompted the whole country to rise 'immediately in armes', though 'it prov'd a mistake'. Within a week or so it was being 'spreade abroade, that an Army of 40,000 French were landed about Weymouth', and there continued to be similar rumours over the next few years.[34] Reports of a five-year peace 'concluded between our King and the French' in December 1679, together with a deal whereby 'the French King will give our King two thousand pounds to keep the Parliament from sitting', prompted someone to write a paper to the mayor of Bristol complaining how 'our popish And treacherous King hath sould the Kingdomes of England, Scotland, and Ireland . . . To the King of France'.[35] Here we have an individual who thought in pan-archipelagic terms; the *problem*, as far as he was concerned, however, was France. Research has shown that those who had greatest reasons to be suspicious of Charles II's pro-French leanings or concerned about the French threat – whether for political, religious, or economic reasons – were likely to identify particularly strongly with the Exclusionist position. That is why Tory propagandists found it necessary to try to neutralise the Whig appeal to anti-French feeling, by suggesting that the Whigs were playing into the hands of France by sowing discord at home.[36] Likewise, the international context, as has long been recognized, is vitally important to a proper understanding of the Glorious Revolution; we need to pay attention not only to the increasingly aggressive stance being taken by Louis XIV, but also, of course, to what was going on in the United Provinces, so we can appreciate both why William of Orange felt it necessary and how it became possible for him to launch an invasion of England at this juncture.

The most serious danger with the new British history is that it can mislead us into seeking explanations of English events by looking to Scotland and Ireland when they need to be sought within England itself. For some, of course, the very point of invoking the multiple-kingdom perspective is to provide an explanation of English events when the English context by itself does not seem to provide the answer. In Conrad Russell's view, for example, there was not enough combustible material within England itself to cause the English state to self ignite; both fuel and the spark had to be provided from outside. Similarly, for Kevin Sharpe it was 'Scottish propaganda' following on from the Scottish prayer book crisis, designed to persuade the English 'that Scottish struggles were struggles for English liberty too', that managed 'to revolutionize English political thinking'.[37] For both scholars, external and contingent factors are seen as bringing down the monarchy in England.

This is probably going too far, though I am not going to be able to resolve the controversy in the short space available here. Certainly, it is fair to suggest that neither Russell nor Sharpe pay sufficient attention to the disaffection brewing up in England in the 1630s, as a result of the policies pursued by Charles I and Archbishop Laud during the 'personal rule', and to how this helped generate a highly explosive situation in the early 1640s.[38] Furthermore, it was the reaction to the rise of political and religious radicalism within England over the course of 1641, particularly the visible growth of sectarianism at the local level, that explains the loyalist reaction in defence of crown and bishops in 1641–2, and hence also the emergence of a royalist party in England, without which it would have been impossible for Charles I to fight a civil war. In Somerset, for example, disorderly outbreaks in local churches, attacks on the clergy, and the destruction of altar rails and other 'popish' images prompted over 14,000 moderates to petition in defence of episcopacy in 1641. Those who rose to the defence of the bishops in Kent similarly complained that 'the houses of God' were 'profaned and in part defaced; the ministers of Christ . . . condemned and despised . . . the Lord's Prayer vilified; the sacraments of the gospel in some places unduly administered, in other places omitted', whilst a pro-episcopalian petition that circulated in Southwark bemoaned how, in this part of south London, some ministers mocked the prayer book, and how some of the laity abused ministers who conformed to the church rubric.[39] What we have here is surely an English dynamic.

The power of the internalist explanation is perhaps more self evident for the revolution of the later-seventeenth century. Although what James did in Scotland and Ireland created anxieties in England, it was what he did in England – namely, his attack on the Anglican monopoly of worship, power and education through the use of the dispensing and suspending powers – that proved his undoing. James lost the support of the majority of his English subjects, from the traditional ruling elite down to the crowd, and his regime in England had already begun to fall apart from within before William of Orange decided to invade. Orange's invasion proved successful not so much because he came with a large and well-trained, professional fighting force; on paper, the forces at James's disposal were nearly double those of his Dutch nephew. Rather, it was successful because James, in the face of desertions amongst the political elite and also his army, realised he was in no position to fight William. In Ireland, where support for James remained strong, William's invasion force was not to achieve final victory until October 1691! The ultimate cause of the Glorious Revolution in England, in other words, is to be sought not in Scotland or Ireland, nor even in the United Provinces, but in England itself.[40]

Yet the question of whether we need to seek an internalist or externalist explanation of the revolutionary upheavals of the seventeenth century needs to be addressed on a more subtle level than this. Let us take the Irish Rebellion of 1641, for example. This may well be, on some levels, an external and contingent factor: if the Irish had not rebelled, there would have been no militia controversy, and it was the controversy over who was to control the militia needed to put down the Irish rebellion that sparked the civil war in England. Yet as Michael Perceval-Maxwell has pointed out, it was as much the weakness of the government in England as discontent in Ireland that led to the conflict, because that weakness permitted rebellion to become a viable political option.[41] Likewise, we need to ask why the English reacted in the way they did to the Irish Rebellion. Why did a Catholic rebellion by a neighbouring and dependent kingdom provoke division amongst the Protestant English instead of a united front against the foreign, Catholic other? As Ethan Shagan has recently argued, this was because the Irish Rebellion 'was constructed in people's minds in fiercely ideological ways, as part of a struggle [within England] which stretched back for generations'; it was injected 'into an English political discourse which was already radically polarized'. In short, any attempt to understand the impact of the Irish Rebellion forces us ultimately to seek an explanation within the English context.[42]

The point can be further illustrated by considering the impact of Scotland on English public opinion during the Exclusion Crisis. It was argued above that Charles II's style of government north of the border explains why so many people were concerned about the threat of arbitrary government, and that this was something Whig publicists played on in their propaganda. Likewise, it was also suggested that

Tory arguments about the threat posed to Church and State by the alliance of Whigs and dissenters was particularly compelling because they were able to point to the activities of the radical Presbyterians in Scotland. But why should people believe one view rather than the other? Why did the Whig argument make more sense to some English people, and the Tory one to others? The answer to this question needs to be sought within the English context itself. As communications research has demonstrated, people's response to propaganda is largely dependent upon their existing ideological predispositions. Thus during the Exclusion Crisis, for example, we find that those sympathetic to the plight of dissenters tended to identify more readily with Whig ideological constructions, whereas hard-line Anglicans were more likely to swallow the Tory line. What this means is that we have to reconstruct the cultural and ideological worldviews of the people we are studying in order to understand how they reacted to events, whether internal or external. One way in which this might be done has been suggested by David Underdown in his study of popular politics and culture in the first half of the seventeenth century.[43] It is not enough to say, Underdown would contend, that people reacted in the way they did because they were a Puritan or an Anglican, but we have to ask why it was that certain types of people, in certain areas, were attracted to particular religious outlooks; the search for the explanation, in Underdown's account, requires an understanding of local ecological systems, social and demographic regimes, parochial and manorial structures, cultural context, and so on. No-one has yet sought to duplicate an Underdown-type analysis for the Exclusion Crisis or Glorious Revolution, and Underdown himself was not interested in considering how people in early-Stuart England responded to developments in Scotland and Ireland. But if we are to recognise that a British perspective is necessary in order to understand not just the politics of the elite, but also politics out-of-doors, the formation of public opinion, and even the activities of the crowd, making sense of the nature of that public opinion or crowd activity in England – of why certain English people responded to developments in Scotland and Ireland in particular ways – is going to require an appreciation of the appropriate cultural and ideological contexts in specific localities in England, such as Underdown attempted to recreate. In short, it will bring our search for an explanation back to within England itself.

In many respects, this critical reflection on the limitations of the new British history has endorsed the value of the three-kingdoms approach, as applied to the study of political upheavals of the seventeenth century. Indeed, some of the criticisms that have been levelled against British history, such as that it can only work at the level of the elite, have been shown to be unfounded; instead, not only is it possible to write a British history that incorporates the middling and lower sorts, but a strong case can be made for insisting that those who are interested in opinion and action out-of-doors need to adopt a three-kingdoms perspective to understand the whole picture. Yet the logic of the argument pursued here has ultimately served to reemphasise the autonomy of English history. For all the extent to which developments in Scotland and Ireland might have intruded into English politics, and into English political consciousness, understanding the reason why Scotland and Ireland had the impact on England that they did ultimately requires an explanation that is rooted in the English historical experience and the specific English (central and local) political, religious, legal, economic, and cultural contexts. The same would be true if our focus were on Scotland or Ireland rather than England. In other words, although historians of any one country within the Britannic archipelago might find it essential to incorporate the other kingdoms of the Stuart multiple monarchy into their accounts, their explanations of why things transpired in the way they did in their particular area will require an explanation that is rooted in a context that is distinctive to that particular nation (whether England, Scotland or Ireland). This is why we must not let the pursuit of British history subsume or replace the separate national histories of the constituent kingdoms of the British Isles. British history can only advance if we have more, not less, research into the English, Scottish and Irish pasts for their own sakes. The pursuit of separate national histories, rather than being at cross purposes to the British enterprise, is in actual fact essential to it.

Notes on Chapter 10

1   To be published by Penguin under the title *British Revolutions: The Emergence of the Modern State, 1660–1707.*

2   David Cannadine, 'British History as a "New Subject"', in Alexander Grant and Keith J. Stringer (eds), *Uniting the Kingdom? The Making of British History* (London, 1995), pp 22, 24; Conrad Russell, 'John Bull's Other Nations', *Times Literary Supplement,* 12 March 1993, pp 3–4.

3   Conrad Russell, *The Causes of the English Civil War* (Oxford, 1990); Conrad Russell, *The Fall of the British Monarchies 1637–1642* (Oxford, 1991).

4   The keenest advocate of a more thorough-going British history is John
     Morrill. See in particular his 'The Fashioning of Britain', in Steven G.
     Ellis and Sarah Barber (eds), *Conquest and Union: Fashioning a British State,
     1485–1725* (London, 1995), pp 8–39.

5   Ronald Hutton, *Charles II: King of England, Scotland and Ireland* (Oxford,
     1989). Hutton's scepticism of the British approach is brought out in his
     'The Triple-crowned Islands', in Lionel Glassey (ed), *The Reigns of Charles
     II and James VII and II* (Basingstoke, 1997), pp 71–89.

6   Robert Wodrow, *History of the Sufferings of the Church of Scotland, From the
     Restoration to the Revolution* (2 vols, Edinburgh, 1721–2), I, 96–8, and
     Appendix XXV, pp 48–9.

7   N[ational] L[ibrary of] S[cotland], Wodrow MSS Qu. XXX, f 50.

8   Sir John Dalrymple, *Memoirs of Great Britain and Ireland; From the Dissolution
     of the last Parliament of Charles II till the Capture of the French and Spanish Fleets
     at Vigo* (3 vols, London, 1790), II, Part I, Appendix to Book V, p 176.

9   NLS, Wodrow MSS Oct. XXX, fols 34–6.

10   John Morrill, *The Nature of the English Revolution* (London, 1993),
     pp 266–7; Peter Lake, 'Review Article: The Causes of the English Civil
     War; The Fall of the British Monarchies; Unrevolutionary England; by C.
     S. R. Russell', *Huntington Library Quarterly,* 57 (1994), p 194; B. S.
     Manning, *The English People and the English Revolution* (Harmondsworth,
     1978); Anthony Fletcher, *The Outbreak of the English Civil War* (London,
     1981); David Underdown, *Revel, Riot and Rebellion: Popular Politics and
     Culture in England, 1603–1660* (Oxford, 1985).

11   *The Scots Demonstration of their Abhorrence of Popery* [Edinburgh, 1681];
     *Historical Selections from the Manuscripts of Sir John Lauder of Fountainhall.
     Volume First, Historical Observations, 1680–1686* (Edinburgh, 1837)
     [hereafter Fountainhall, *Historical Observations*], p 18; Wodrow, *History,*
     II, 649; Mark Knights, 'London's "Monster" Petition of 1680', *Historical
     Journal,* 36 (1993), p 53.

12   Fountainhall, *Historical Observations,* p 19; Wodrow, *History,* II, 217; *HMC,
     Dartmouth,* I, 42.

13   NLS, Wod. MSS Qu. XXXVIII, fol. 115; *London Mercury,* no. 6, 27–31
     Dec. 1688; *Five Letters from a Gentleman in Scotland* (London, 1689), p 4;
     NLS, MS 7026, fols 89, 90; Dr Williams's Library, Roger Morrice, Ent'ring
     Book [hereafter Morrice] II, 403; [Thomas Morer], *An Account of the
     Present Persecution of the Church in Scotland* (London, 1690), p 15; [Charles
     Leslie], *An Answer to a Book, Intituled, The State of the Protestants in Ireland,*
     (1692), sig. b2.

14   George Hilton Jones, 'The Irish Fright of 1688: Real Violence and
     Imagined Massacre', *Bulletin of the Institute of History Research,* 55 (1982),
     pp 148–53.

15 Tim Harris, *London Crowds in the Reign of Charles II* (Cambridge, 1987); Tim Harris, 'The Parties and the People: The Press, the Crowd and Politics 'Out-of-Doors' in Restoration England' in Glassey (ed), *Reigns of Charles II and James VII and II*, pp 125–51.

16 *London Gazette*, no. 1464, 21 Nov.–1 Dec. 1679, and no. 1465, 1–4 Dec. 1679; *HMC, Dartmouth*, I, 38; J. S. Clarke (ed), *The Life of James II* (2 vols, London, 1816), I, 576; Wodrow, II, 110.

17 *London Gazette*, no. 1561, 1–4. Nov. 1680; *A True Narrative of the Reception of their Royal Highnesses at their Arrival in Scotland* [Edinburgh, London and Dublin, 1680]; Wodrow, *History*, II, 153.

18 Sir John Lauder of Fountainhall, *The Decisions of the Lords of the Council and Session from June 6th, 1678, to July 30th, 1713* (2 vols, Edinburgh, 1759–61), I, 114; Wodrow, *History*, II, Appendix LII, pp 52–3.

19 Fountainhall, *Historical Observations*, pp 18–19; Clarke (ed), *Life of James II*, I, 655.

20 In addition to my own work cited above, see Mark Knights, *Politics and Opinion in Crisis, 1678–81* (Cambridge, 1994).

21 Tim Harris, 'The British Dimension, Religion and the Shaping of Political Identities during the Reign of Charles II', in Tony Claydon and Ian McBride (eds), *Protestantism and National Identity: Britain and Ireland, c. 1650–c.1850* (Cambridge, 1998), pp 131–56.

22 Lake, 'Review of Russell', p 172.

23 Clarke (ed), *Life of James II*, I, 550.

24 *Parliamentary History*, IV, 1185–6; Anchitell Grey, *Debates of the House of Commons, from the year 1667 to the year 1694* (10 vols, 1763), VII, 408; Clarke (ed), *Life of James II*, I, 606. Cf. the Earl of Halifax's speech in the Lords on 15 November 1680: Clarke (ed), *Life of James II*, I, 621.

25 Sir George Mackenzie, *Memoirs of the Affairs of Scotland, from the Restoration of King Charles II*, ed. T. Thomson (Edinburgh, 1821), pp 138–40.

26 Clarke (ed), *Life of James II*, II, 683; NLS, Wod. MSS Qu. XXX, fol 94.

27 *His Majesties Gracious Letter to His Parliament of Scotland: With the Speech of His Royal Highness the Duke, His Majesties High Commissioner, At the Opening of the Parliament at Edinburgh, the 28th Day of July 1681. Together with The Parliaments most Loyal and Dutiful Answer* (London, 1681)

28 *Acts of the Parliaments of Scotland*, VIII, 238; Dalrymple, *Memoirs*, I, Part I, Book I, pp 11–12.

29 See my forthcoming *British Revolutions*.

30 Thomas Cogswell, *The Blessed Revolution: English Politics and the Coming of War, 1621–1624* (Cambridge, 1989).

31 Kevin Sharpe, *The Personal Rule of Charles I* (New Haven, 1992), ch XIV; Caroline Hibbard, *Charles I and the Popish Plot* (Chapel Hill, 1983); William

Lamont, *Richard Baxter and the Millenium: Protestant Imperialism and the English Revolution* (London, 1979), chs 2, 5.

32   Jonathan Scott, 'England's Troubles: Exhuming the Popish Plot', in Tim Harris, Paul Seaward and Mark Goldie (eds), *The Politics of Religion in Restoration England* (Oxford, 1990), pp 107–31; Steven C. A. Pincus, 'From Butterboxes to Wooden Shoes: The Shift in English Popular Sentiment from Anti-Dutch to Anti-French in the 1670s,' *Historical Journal*, 38 (1995): 333–61; Steven C. A. Pincus, 'Republicanism, Absolutism and Universal Monarchy: English Popular Sentiment during the Third Dutch War,' in Gerald MacLean (ed), *Culture and Society in the Stuart Restoration* (Cambridge, 1995), pp 241–66; Steven C. A. Pincus, 'The English Debate over Universal Monarchy,' in John Robertson (ed), *A Union for Empire: Political Thought and the British Union of 1707* (Cambridge, 1995), pp 37–62.

33   Gerald E. Aylmer (ed), *The Diary of William Lawrence, covering periods between 1662 and 1681* (Beaminster, 1961), pp 37–8.

34   Huntington Library, HM 30315, no. 199; Narcissus Luttrell, *A Brief Historical Relation of State Affairs from September, 1678, to April, 1714* (6 vols, Oxford, 1857), I, 5; Somerset Record Office, DD/SF/3074, 21 December 1678, Aldred Seaman to Edward Clarke.

35   Longleat House, Coventry MSS, VI, fol. 199.

36   Harris, *London Crowds*, pp ; Harris, 'Parties and the People', pp 137–8.

37   Sharpe, *Personal Rule*, pp 819, 820.

38   See, in particular: Underdown, *Revel, Riot and Rebellion*; A. J. Fletcher, *A County Community in Peace and War: Sussex, 1600–1660* (London, 1975), ch 4; James S. Hart, *Justice Upon Petition: The House of Lords and the Reformation of Justice 1621–1675* (London, 1991), ch 2.

39   David Underdown, *Somerset in the Civil War and Interregnum* (Newton Abbot, 1973), p 26; Fletcher, *Outbreak*, p 288.

40   See my forthcoming *British Revolutions*.

41   M. Perceval-Maxwell, *The Outbreak of the 1641 Rebellion in Ireland* (London, 1993), p 49.

42   Ethan Howard Shagan, 'Constructing Discord: Ideology, Propaganda, and English Responses to the Irish Rebellion of 1641', *Journal of British Studies*, 36 (1997), 1–34 (quotes on pp 6, 33).

43   Underdown, *Revel, Riot and Rebellion*.

CHAPTER 11

Britain or Europe? The Context of Early Modern English History: Political and Cultural, Economic and Social, Naval and Military*

John Reeve

INTRODUCTION

England is a European society. The offshore islanders, an ingenious and dynamic people, have written great pages in the history of the world. But they have long been a part of European civilisation. Always seeking to improve our judgement as to where to cut history's seamless web, we are increasingly aware of the British context of early modern English history.[1] We are less aware of the need to place early modern England in its European context so as to properly understand it. This essay will argue that while the search for a new British history is admirable, an Anglo-European history – incorporating but moving *beyond* the essentially British context – is indispensable. In adopting a different conceptual focus this approach forms a contrast with the search for an intrinsically British history, new or otherwise, and as such is the renegade element amongst the essays in this book. Its purpose in this is entirely constructive: less to make a case for the prosecution than to give pause and offer an alternative mode of thought. Hopefully the outcome will place the issues in clearer relief. The approach will be mainly thematic, and to some extent narrative, with the central contention that pan-European forces of continuity and change run through seventeenth century English history. The

*Financial support for this work was provided by the Royal Australian Navy under the Osborne Fellowship program at the University of New South Wales, Australian Defence Force Academy.

intention is to suggest a conceptual framework for the pursuit of early modern Anglo-European history. The concentration on the seventeenth century is a matter both of convenience and topicality. A reasonably manageable historical period, it encompasses England's rise as a major power abroad as well as political revolution at home – plenty with which to be going on. Occasional reference will be made to the British context, where appropriate, but the theme is the location of English history within a whole European picture.

It is remarkable how underdeveloped is a substantive Anglo-European history.[2] One could probably count on the fingers of two hands the number of early modern English historical scholars visiting the great Spanish state archive at Simancas during the last hundred years. The pioneers were the great nineteenth century masters, Gardiner and Froude. Others have made the pilgrimage into deepest Castile, publishing the fruits of their labours, in more modern times.[3] There has also been, for example, successful utilisation of Dutch history to illuminate the revolution of 1688.[4] But it is a slender tradition. Historians of the British Celtic frontier have arguably been more progressive in exploring its European connections.[5] English history has been the poorer for this neglect. The brilliantly controversial ideas of Conrad Russell on the causes of the English civil war could be said to boil down to four factors: personal monarchy, religion, war finance, and the problem of multiple kingdoms[6] – all richly paralleled on the continent and intimately linked to its history. Extensive Anglo-European investigation of such themes, for example, could surely shed light on English and British controversies.[7]

We might say that the European picture can enhance our understanding of seventeenth century England in two not unrelated ways: the *comparative* and the *relational*. That is to say, we can often clarify English (or British) historical phenomena by comparing them with wider European. In many cases, moreover, situations and episodes in the British Isles were integrally connected to a European context, signalling clearly the need for us to seek the answers by studying the problems in their entirety. Sometimes both these contextual dimensions are relevant to an issue. In the case of Anglo-Spanish warfare in the 1620s, for example, comparative study of the means of funding war in the participant states helps to measure their relative strengths. This knowledge in turn is valuable in understanding the course of the war. We will employ both comparative and relational perspectives in this essay. This essay, moreover, in outlining themes of change and continuity in seventeenth century English history, does not pretend to offer a comprehensive solution to monumental complexities. The point is to suggest the variety of areas in which a European contextual approach – comparative, relational or both – can help to unlock historical problems. The English seventeenth century is notoriously one of the most complex areas of history – in the words of an elderly, distinguished archaeologist to this writer when a research student: 'Too hard for me. Too many trends'. That complexity is rooted not only in the number of powerful changes contending with the status quo, but in their doing so within a European, not simply an English or British context.

This essay will deal first with certain methodological questions relating to Anglo-European history, as well as anticipating some of the arguments for English distinctiveness. It will then deal thematically with international forces of continuity and change affecting seventeenth century England. A fourth section will offer a concise narrative of what we can term the Anglo-European seventeenth century. This further illustrates the explanatory power of an international contextual approach, as well as balancing the thematic structure. A final section will make some concluding points.

METHODOLOGIES

Is Anglo-European history a valid concept? That is to say, what and where is Europe? Rivers of ink have flowed in seeking to answer this question. Seventeenth century Europeans still largely saw themselves as members of Christendom, the community of Christian believers. The progress of Protestantism and secularism, the decline of the Moslem threat, the expansion of Europe overseas, and the evolution of the idea that princes ruled over territory, rather than over persons, all this contributed to our modern conception of Europe as a geographical expression. While not being particularly applicable to the early modern era, it remains imprecise. 'Where does Europe end in the east?' is an old question. Austrian tradition is that Asia begins in the suburbs of Vienna. The expanding overseas possessions of the early modern western powers gave Europe distant frontiers. Within Europe there were ideological, political, economic, and geographical complexities creating subsidiary worlds: Protestant and Catholic, northern and southern, Mediterranean, Baltic, North Sea, and Atlantic communities. Multiple dynastic and imperial possessions, particularly those of Spain, meant that political power blocs overrode ethnic and cultural demarcations. 'Europe', therefore, is a crude and necessarily flexible expression, referring commonly to the areas west of the Urals and bordering the Mediterranean and the Atlantic. While we can use it thus it is often more realistic to speak of 'international' phenomena, that is those transcending the emerging European nation states or the continental area.

While we sometimes seek to make international comparisons in history, there is no sub-discipline of comparative history to parallel comparative literature. One of the major intellectual tools which we lack in the humanities today is a textbook offering a conceptual framework for comparative history.[8] Certain practical obstacles – including linguistic barriers, distant archives, and professional categories – have contributed to its lack of development. It is also intellectually difficult. The number of historical variables involved is multiplied greatly by international comparisons. But the potential rewards are considerable. Jeremy Black has argued recently that 'analyses of causation take on most value in a comparative dimension'.[9] Christopher Hill once wrote that comparative history is the nearest the historian can come to a laboratory test.[10] Distinguished comparative history was written in the 1980s on political, military, and economic themes.[11] Well controlled, it can be a powerful tool, readily applicable to an era of developing nation states.

Diplomatic history is long established as a genre.[12] Renaissance diplomacy, the distinctly European practice of employing resident ambassadors at foreign courts, was a creature of the new age of government by paper. It provided the sources and much of the framework for the study of early modern interstate relations.[13] Ranke is the nineteenth century ancestor of rigorous diplomatic history. Often caricatured as 'what one foreign office clerk said to another', the narrower study of diplomatic relations has been supplanted in the last twenty-five years by the 'new diplomatic history'. This broader approach seeks to recreate the context in which decisions on foreign policy were made, and potentially takes in mentalities, personalities, power politics, and economic, social, and cultural themes.[14] Largely reinvented, diplomatic history is thus a vehicle for studying the interaction of domestic and wider factors, for overcoming the false distinction between national and international history.

Diplomatic history affords material for, and overlaps with, the study of international relations. Younger as a discipline, with its origins in the early twentieth century, and instinctively theoretical rather than empirical, international relations generally posits models of state interaction in the international sphere. Historians credibly suspect it of ignoring change, the human factor, the historical particular, and narratable events. As a product of twentieth century history it can also be seen as an inappropriate tool for the study of the early modern era. International relations, however, places great emphasis on the seventeenth century, which saw the pioneering by Hugo Grotius of international theory and the role of the Peace of Westphalia (1648) in establishing the international state system. The sophisticated exponents of international relations have things to teach us, not least because they are historically literate. The British school of international relations, with its view of a complex set of relations among states in an international society, its empiricism and relative lack of dogma, is pertinent here.[15] It explores inter alia the roles of transnational ideas and institutions, great powers, war and conflict, order in the international system, and the interconnected internal and external functioning of states – all themes germane to the European seventeenth century.

Finally, the booming field of 'war and society' studies is relevant to any attempt at an international historical perspective, especially upon an era of unremitting warfare. While respectful of the technicalities of military and naval history it seeks to enrich them, and integrate them with wider historical themes, by a broadly contextual approach. It has thus restored war as a major theme in historical literature – a force shaping society as well as being shaped by it: a return to the wisdom of Thucydides.[16] For various reasons, not least the constant interaction of armies with populations, the war and society genre of the last generation has been stronger in military than naval history. Early modern scholarship, however, has exceeded modern in relating sea power to society, notably in the classic strategic-historical writings of Mahan in the late nineteenth century.[17] More recently the story of British sea power has been told in relation to the development of both the British economy and the British state.[18] A war and society perspective illuminating the role of British sea power is of obvious relevance to Anglo-European history. War and society is a theme which obviously facilitates both comparative and relational internationalisation of English history.

BRITAIN OR EUROPE?

It was the Victorian sense of imperial destiny, and the teleology of the Whig historians (including ironically Gardiner – a master of diplomatic history),[19] which more than anything imbued our historical consciousness with a sense of English distinctiveness. In a post imperial age holding out the prospect of English constitutional compromise with Europe, and witnessing the weakening bonds of the British state, we are better placed to perceive the complex interactivity of England and Europe in the past. There is clarity in the long view of history (as Chou En Lai said of the consequences of the French Revolution, it's too early to tell). It is perhaps too the Elizabethan legend, with ideas of providential deliverance from the invader, of seafarers venturing boldly into vast oceans, which still nourishes the sense of English separateness. Briefly, the case for England's essential difference runs as follows. Here was a society which the sea had cut off from the mainland, and which had developed its own particular common law. It implemented a unique form of church settlement in the sixteenth century and in the seventeenth carried out a radical constitutional revolution. Its authority territorially consolidated within the British Isles, it reached out and created the greatest empire in history. It was a nation like no other in Europe – or was it?

The sea unites at least as well as it divides, and the narrow waters between archipelago and continent had been navigable for millennia by the seventeenth century. Wave upon wave of invaders had brought their languages and cultures to England. The medieval centuries had seen Angevin and Lancastrian rule bridging England and much of France. The retreat into the islands by the late fifteenth century was incomplete. English monarchs nursed European territorial and political ambitions for centuries afterwards. Calais, Brill, Flushing, Dunkirk and Gibraltar, not to mention Holland and Hanover, were prized possessions during the early modern period. The continent was an area of necessary strategic intervention until the twentieth century. It was also long an English court of political appeal, for Elizabethan Catholics, king and parliament, exiled royalists, post-restoration republicans, 'glorious' revolutionaries, and Jacobites. The sea is neutral. England was vulnerable to invasion from the continent, to a greater or lesser extent, on many occasions between the sixteenth and eighteenth centuries, and later. In 1688, by collusion, Dutch invasion succeeded. The Low Countries had long been of vital strategic relevance to England and continued to be so, as a potential springboard for the invader.

England's common law of course differed from continental codes, but like them preserved property as the basis of social authority. Renaissance and Reformation ideas of law as human science and of resistance theory also had an influence in England.[20] The English legal system of itself, moreover, is not an overriding historical factor in terms of an argument for English distinctiveness. The English church settlement always differed from the religious histories of

Scotland and Ireland, themselves deeply influenced by continental currents. England, as a former province of the Roman Church, always carried the marks of its tutelage. Protestantism was not an English invention, and the theology of Geneva influenced English culture profoundly. The English constitutional developments of the seventeenth century were largely European in their causes, courses, and consequences, and involved turmoil closely resembling wider European crises. The radical nature of the English regicide would influence Europeans, the French in particular, creating a terrible precedent. England was far from being the only European power to indulge in state-building and overseas imperialism. The technological changes which empowered Europeans intellectually and physically – printing with movable type, the military use of gunpowder, and the means of oceanic travel – were no monopoly of the English, who of course employed them skilfully. These innovations transformed the whole of European civilisation when Europeans gave Oriental knowledge a practical, often ruthless application and in turn transformed the world.[21]

England in the seventeenth century had, of course, an emerging national character and consciousness. In the previous century it had shown national strengths and registered considerable achievements: famously in constitutional development, seafaring, and literature. It was not, however, alone in Europe in developing a national identity: witness France, Spain, and the Dutch republic amongst its neighbours. This made it no less European than these and other continental states and societies. England remained integrally part of the European world in geographical, political, social, and cultural terms, linked to the continent in a multiplicity of complex ways.

II

INTERNATIONAL CONTINUITIES

(i) Cultural trends

Renaissance humanistic influences continued to shape seventeenth century European culture. England drank deeply of this tradition. Since the late fifteenth century cultural luminaries had come to visit, work and teach: notably Torrigiano, Castiglione, Erasmus, Holbein, Rubens, and Van Dyck. English life was inducted into the international language of artistic, learned, and Christian humanism. The development of classical education at home, exposure to the print culture of northern Europe, and, for the well-to-do, the coming of the grand tour all promoted Anglo-European cultural integration. Algernon Sidney, a doyen of the seventeenth century English intellectual world, was inspired by Plato, Aristotle, Livy, and Tacitus, as well as two moderns: Machiavelli and Grotius.[22] The spread of Renaissance diplomacy – whose practitioners were by definition fine linguists – was a significant force for humanistic cultural exchange and integration. England, like other states, sent selected rising, prominent, learned, and educable citizens abroad on foreign missions. Sir Dudley Carleton, for example, had acquired knowledge of antiquities and Venetian painting and made acquisitions for Charles I abroad. Cultural forces could be divisive, but such conflicts in England were manifestations of wider European issues. Charles's aesthetic interests were provocative to puritan piety, but clash between text and image was frequent in the post-Reformation world. Sidney and Locke were seen as dangerous threats to the restored English monarchy, but their radical ideas dealt with European problems and were soon to be influential on the continent and beyond.

(ii) Economic relationships

In economic terms, England had been part of European society for centuries. Development of international capital markets and expansion of international trade only compounded this nexus. The English crown borrowed great sums from continental bankers to fund wars in the sixteenth and seventeenth centuries. The crown's dependence upon customs revenues meant effectively that the constitution increasingly rode upon trade – European and in the seventeenth century global. The long standing dependence of English cloth exports on the Antwerp mart was a vital factor in Elizabethan foreign policy. Trade wars with Spain and the shifting of the cloth staple to Emden and Hamburg highlighted the Anglo-European economic connection. The development of England's Baltic, Levantine, and especially southern European trade by the early seventeenth century further bonded her to the continent. The inhabitants of warmer southern climes appreciated the 'new' lighter English draperies, and the growing English navy needed Baltic products, especially pine wood, to fit out its ships. Overseas the English competed with other European powers for international trade in all manner of commodities. It was England's further integration with the European economy during the

expansion of the 'long' sixteenth century which ensured her importing of the price revolution, as well as her sharing the shock of the
1620s trade slump. When Europe sneezed, England caught economic
flu.

(iii) Monarchy

England was a European monarchy in its broad generic resemblance
to continental models, which of course varied in history and form.
While the English crown was made answerable, and its power finessed,
in the seventeenth century, it stood – like other monarchies – at the
apex of a social hierarchy founded on land and buttressed by a noble
class. Monarchy was, like aristocracy, an international guild. Only
beyond its own frontiers might a supreme political authority seek alliance, proper competition, appropriate communion, and mutual
respect. Cross-dynastic alliances meant frequent cross-inheritances.
England had foreign monarchs from 1603: Scottish (with French
blood), Dutch, and German. James I brought an intellectually
cosmopolitan approach to monarchy, and a strategy for dynastic mar-
riages: German Protestant (achieved) and Catholic Spanish (failed).
Charles I loved a French wife, Spanish royal life, and great Italian art.
He took England to war for the sake of his brother-in-law's lost
German lands. Charles II spent over a decade in exile and was
influenced by his cousin Louis XIV. In his heart a Roman Catholic,
he represented a leaning within the Stuart family towards the religion
of Europe's great kings and emperors. James II also grew up in exile,
fought in continental armies, was a professed Roman Catholic, and
died an exiled pensioner of the French crown. Charles and James
both had continental Catholic wives. William III, Prince of Orange,
was of Anglo-continental stock, made an Anglo-continental marriage,
spoke six languages, and devoted his life to continental politics and
war. Anne had a Danish husband and presided over participation in a
great European war. George I was the Hanoverian grandson of
Elizabeth Stuart, Electress Palatine and Queen of Bohemia, whose
husband Frederick of the Palatinate had triggered the European
conflagration of the Thirty Years War. English royal involvement in
Europe was political and diplomatic, marital and military, intellectual, cultural, and religious – often with momentous consequences
on both sides of the Channel. Foreign policy being a royal prerogative, the crown linked the domestic and foreign workings of the state,
even during the quasi-reign of Oliver Cromwell.

(iv) Multiple kingdoms

Dynastic territorial possession, and the multiple kingdoms it produced, made for an untidy political map. The British kingdoms, we know, were one dimension of a European phenomenon whose persistence complicated the state-building process.[23] Armed revolts against metropolitan regimes, stimulated especially by religious and fiscal pressures, occurred similarly under the British, French, Spanish, and Habsburg monarchies in the seventeenth century. The Stuart succession simplified the British picture in a sense by redefining Scotland as a domestic problem after 1603. Anglo-Scottish troubles and warfare persisted in various forms, however, between the 1630s and the mid-eighteenth century, and Irish troubles persist still. Seventeenth century British problems were not only comparable with those on the continent. They were intimately connected to European events and developments, not least by the sharing of international religious divisions. These in turn encouraged foreign powers to meddle in British affairs, a temptation which in times of crisis was virtually irresistible. Ireland was an Anglo-Spanish theatre of war in the 1590s and an Anglo-French one a century later. Scotland became a focus of the Franco-Jacobite cause. At critical points in mid-century continental events impacted dramatically upon the British Isles. The revolt of Catalonia in 1640 scuttled English plans for Spanish help against the Scots, setting the scene for the Long Parliament. The Franco-Spanish war which continued into the 1650s left Cromwell free to pacify Ireland and Scotland. The British setting underlines the European contextual factor in English history, sometimes acting as an Anglo-European historical bridge.

(v) Permeable frontiers

We should realise that Europe's internal frontiers were permeable throughout this period. It is misleading to conceive of nation states as having static and homogeneous populations. Religious persecution and military service caused noticeable movements of human groups. Over six thousand Irishmen had served in the Spanish army of Flanders by the early seventeenth century. Ten British regiments were serving with the Dutch forces in the 1620s. Almost twenty per cent of the Swedish army in Germany in the early 1630s were Scots. A British brigade fought for Portugal against Spain in the 1660s and a corps for France against the Dutch in the 1670s. The British corps in the

Low Countries in 1697 numbered 56,000. British soldiers fought far to the east in Imperial and Russian service. Mercantile activity and naval service meant contact with continental societies by sea. Many central European Protestants fled to England during the Thirty Years War and over 50,000 French Huguenots after 1685. Cromwell readmitted the Jews to England in 1655. Many English royalists were in exile during the civil wars and interregnum. Migration and diaspora are integral dimensions of crisis and war. There was also widespread emigration into the wider world. Internally, Europe's frontiers were vague and unsettled until well into the eighteenth century.[24]

(vi) The warrior culture

European Christendom was, like Islam, a warrior culture.[25] Since the invention of the stirrup there had been a link between the role of the knightly caste as mounted warriors and their status as social and political authorities. While gunpowder was a democratising influence, and the early modern era saw the rise of the professional soldier, European aristocracies – descended from the knights – were slow to surrender their military function and propensities, especially when nation states coopted their services. War, above all, remained a prerogative of monarchy. The seventeenth century saw virtually continual war in which England was often involved. English monarchs, like others, had personal, domestic, and foreign incentives to enter into external wars. Prosecution of those wars could ignite dangerous issues at home, frequently revolving around war taxation. Monarchical failure in war could also undermine aristocratic loyalty.[26] Disenchantment with Charles I's pursuit of the Protestant cause is notable case. War was thus a force for the domestic-foreign nexus. It also brought international contact at every social level. In this way it influenced political and religious ideas, as well as spread knowledge of military techniques. James II's service in the Spanish and French armies confirmed his admiration for Catholic absolute monarchies. Scots who fought with the Swedes in Germany played significant military roles in the British civil wars. Continuing European warfare, in which England participated, was reflective of an internally competitive civilisation. But it was also a legacy of the warrior culture and thus, paradoxically, evidence of an internationally shared value system. War locked Europeans together, and became an abiding feature of their international state system, part of the anarchical society.[27]

III

INTERNATIONAL CHANGES

(i) Confessional religious conflict

Ideas cross frontiers readily, and it was essential to the subversiveness of the Reformation that it was, particularly after Calvin, a transnational force. By 1600 Europe was divided into Protestant and Catholic worlds. England, and Britain, were party to this division and to a pan-European crisis of wars of religion.[28] While we are increasingly aware of the complexity of English Christianity by the early seventeenth century,[29] the essential irony of the English Reformation holds true. England had enhanced its ecclesiastical independence, but in the sixteenth century progressively replaced one international form of religious doctrine with another. Calvinist ideas – moral, textual, covenanting, and predestinarian – were woven deeply into the English view of the world, persisting into the secular modern age. Thus the role which strategic circumstances forced upon Elizabeth I, that of champion of European Protestantism, invested English engagement in the continental war with a crusading quality which became part of her legend and haunted her early Stuart successors. James I's role in the Synod of Dort, his conclusion of the Palatine marriage, and Charles I's traumatic participation in the Thirty Years War were largely products of this Anglo-European tradition of Protestant engagement. England's mid-century troubles have been credibly termed her wars of religion.[30] Late seventeenth century English political conflicts still had an inflammatory religious dimension which was Anglo-European.[31] International Protestantism changed English life, recast English politics, changed English views of the world, shed English blood, and conditioned English revolutionary issues as well as shaping their ultimate settlement.

(ii) The state building process

The European state building process, of which England and Britain were one dimension, did not begin in the seventeenth century. The Dutch state had its origins in sixteenth century revolt. Sixteenth century France has been well described as a society in crisis.[32] But the seventeenth century saw that process contribute to a pan-European crisis well recognised at the time. It was arguably also the critical era for the shaping of the modern state in a number of countries such as

England and France. The European crisis of the seventeenth century was undoubtedly a phenomenon, although its nature and significance have long been hotly debated.[33] But the centralising ambitions of powerful states, especially in fiscal, religious, and regional terms, were a trigger for resistance, revolt and revolution. That history spared England, and Britain, this agony is a myth, which the human and material cost of the civil wars refutes.[34] England actually acquired a European reputation for violence and disorder lasting well into the eighteenth century. England's constitutional revolution was real and radical, but her experience was not unique. Continental absolutism struck fear into the Dutch, who challenged their own monarchy during this period. The English interregnal regime was measurably similar to the merchant oligarchy of the contemporaneous 'Stadholderless' period in Holland. The English monarchy was ultimately reconciled to the political elite as often happened in Europe in the late seventeenth century. But England's famously 'bloodless' revolution of 1688 was not so bloodless in Scotland and Ireland. Here the British story is more comparable to the violent challenges to some early eighteenth century continental regimes.[35] The broad constitutional issues inherent in the European crisis were not the monopoly of any polity. Wider forces of change racked England, where continental political ideas had their influence.[36]

(iii) Economic warfare and overseas expansion

The development of Europe's trading economy, and the entry of Europeans into the wider world –seeking to discover, trade, plunder and possess – significantly altered the nature of international conflict by the early seventeenth century. Trade became a form of warfare. War, trade, and overseas expansion increasingly merged as western Europeans were locked in a ferocious competition for preponderant power.[37] A global competition, fought out particularly in the Americas and Asia, it was primarily directed towards the enhancement of power at home. Mercantilist ideas provided the mental framework for this Darwinistic new world order. Political economy was perceived as a zero-sum game in a world of limited wealth. Favourable trade balances and monopolistic activity were seen as means of accumulating more treasure, and hence greater power, than one's rivals. While in modern economic terms this was primitive logic, it perceived the fundamental links between economic, military, and political power.

The consummate exponents of economic warfare in the seventeenth century were the Dutch.[38] Their success in an amazing variety of entrepreneurial activities, especially intra-European trade, facilitated their struggle for independence from Spain. It weakened their enemy, funded their standing army, and subsidised their sea power which in turn furthered their trade. The Dutch were not the only successful practitioners, however. England increased her trade, colonies, and naval power between the Elizabethan and late seventeenth century periods.[39] The Anglo-Spanish Atlantic war – both cold and hot – from the 1560s onwards, with its plundering and commercial competition, had the blessing of the queen and set the scene for later developments. England successfully employed economic warfare, including privateering and trade embargo, against Spain in the 1620s, and was a partisan (while officially neutral) part of the Spanish war economy in the 1630s. Anglo-Dutch conflict from the 1650s onwards was largely fuelled by economic rivalry.[40] The Anglo-French wars under William III and Anne involved maritime conflict and trading rivalry, and resulted in valuable colonial gains for England, especially in North America. Success in the European race for global commercial supremacy nourished English imperial power, as did strategic balance between ocean and continent. England was emerging as a great European, not simply an overseas, imperial power.

(iv) Military revolution and grand strategy

The debate on the nature and significance of the early modern military revolution has been lively and important.[41] We can say that between the fourteenth and eighteenth centuries European warfare changed dramatically, and that this had profound implications for European society. The gunpowder revolution altered tactics and strategy on land and sea. The scale of war – the size of armies and navies – increased enormously. European warfare became globalised, with Europeans fighting each other, as well as other peoples, in the wider world. These developments, in conjunction with the price revolution, meant that the financial cost of war was vastly increased. Thus the military revolution was linked to the state-building process. By the late seventeenth century, state power rested on an exclusive ability to fund and control violence. Given these changes, and the long chronological parameters suggested for them, it is tempting to think in terms of 'the military evolution'. Certainly, in considering the effects of the revolution we must think comparatively. Military history implies comparison, for military power is relative rather than absolute.

England adopted the military revolution in a particular way which conditioned the manner in which the English state was made. But neither the military techniques involved nor their English socio-political consequences were unique. England imported the gunpowder revolution in the sixteenth century and in the seventeenth the military methods of (and many of the participants in) the Thirty Years War. The New Model Army was formed on modern Dutch and Swedish lines, and the killing, plunder and destruction inflicted on continental societies appeared in the British Isles, thus 'England turned Germany'.[42] In the 1650s there was financial tension between the cost of a navy required by foreign policy and that of an army required to control discontent. English society reacted against the experience of war and military government, acquiring an antipathy to standing armies as tools of tyranny: a vital theme in late seventeenth century English politics.

The growth of a powerful navy by the late seventeenth century, however, represented a social nexus attractive to the English: a London-based alliance between maritime, commercial, and parliamentary interests which was central to the modern English state and its overseas empire.[43] The navy, while a commercial and strategic investment, was no threat to liberty. Its cost meant financial dependence on parliament, and it could not be used to coerce the population. Its technical nature made it less open to aristocratic use in political power plays, although its political complexion was a sensitive issue in the late seventeenth century. (The army became essentially a limited, amphibious force, a haven of the aristocracy but monitored closely by constitutional interests.) The navy became an anti-invasion guard, a tool of overseas empire, and a bargaining chip in forming alliances with continental powers, such as Prussia, weaker at sea but with military assets useful in preserving a continental balance of power.

England was not alone in adopting the military revolution this way. Dutch society was remarkably similar: maritime and commercial, constitutional and Protestant, and successful in defending itself from Spain by the seventeenth century. The merchant oligarchs of the Dutch Regent party distrusted the army and its aristocratic officers, favouring the navy – no threat to the constitution and the guardian of trade. As in England by the late seventeenth century, this group largely made terms with a monarchy needing its support to fund foreign wars.[44] This comparability assisted the smooth assumption by the Dutch William III of the English throne and his prosecution of the Nine Years War. Dutch strategy, like the emerging English, had long been to polarise Europe against hegemonic power and to balance the continent and overseas empire. The military revolution saw European trends impacting upon English life and a complex English process of response, impacting in turn upon European politics and war. That English response was comparable to the Dutch, and goes far towards explaining the hard fought nature of the Anglo-Dutch wars. We can contrast these societies with more militaristic, absolute monarchies such as France: less commercial and maritime, more autocratic, but potentially vulnerable to Anglo-continental naval and military alliance.[45]

Grand strategy, the deployment of the overall resources of a society for war, has usually been fundamental to military activity.[46] The military revolution greatly enhanced its importance by greatly increasing war's cost. The cooperation of entire social groups, even populations, became necessary to sustain the sinews of war, and England was no exception. The development of a viable system of war finance is a major theme of seventeenth century English history. By the era of William III and Anne, parliament oversaw military strategy, financial support being contingent on plausible planning. A variety of interests and lobby groups was thus involved. Soldiers and sailors making strategy were connected to political clientage networks.[47] Ship construction was largely the work of private contractors. Commercial interests had an intimate stake in naval planning. Thus a whole spectrum of internal concerns became factors in external national policy and its role in international affairs.

(v) The great age of sea power

The era from the late fifteenth to the late nineteenth centuries is often termed the great age of sea power. It began with the European development of the armed, ocean-going sailing ship and ended with the opening of the Eurasian and North American land masses by railways.[48] Sea power, in this era, had a profound and decisive impact on the history of the world. It is an epic which has, to a great extent, never ended. The military revolution at sea increased European potential for mobility and violence, wealth and power, conflict and strategy exponentially. It was the work of a number of European nations on the Atlantic seaboard, both Catholic and Protestant. Europeans during this era learned to conceive of the earth as a globe – covered by connecting seas providing freedom of movement upon it. Sea power was an inherently internationalising force, within Europe and beyond. England played a great, ultimately a dominating, role in this process, but not an exclusive one. English monarchs from the sixteenth century onwards, seeing the sea as part of their majesty, took a personal interest in the Royal Navy which became a vehicle for English contact with the wider world in peace and war. Sea power was a physical link – diplomatic, naval, imperial, economic, and cultural – between the Atlantic archipelago, Europe, and every corner of the globe. A seafaring nation has perforce an international personality.

(vi) Great power relations and the state system

As an interactive system of states emerged in Europe by the seventeenth century it came to be dominated by major or 'great' powers. These competed over extended periods for influence within the system – France and Sweden, for example, being recognised at Westphalia in 1648 as guarantors of the treaty. Ranke defined a great power as one capable of military independence against all others.[49] Now considered an imprecise definition, particularly in relation to the need for alliances, it still sets the scene. Great power rivalry stimulated the search for a 'balance of power' against hegemonic states. This search originated in fifteenth century Italy, was promulgated as an idea in Europe by professional Renaissance diplomats, and was recognised by the Treaty of Utrecht in 1713.[50] It was a concomitant of the growing conception of European politics as a single system. Renaissance diplomacy itself promoted such a system. It employed French to the extent that it became a largely universal European language by the early seventeenth century. It generally assumed that ambassadors had a right to interfere in the affairs of host countries. Above all, it produced a constant and voluminous stream of political reporting from both overt and covert sources. This integrated the domestic politics of every state with the international scene and put Europe in touch with itself in an unprecedented way.

England was increasingly part of this European international system. It was an Englishman, Thomas Hobbes, whose philosophy best summed up the ruthless international rivalry of the seventeenth century.[51] In that dog-eat-dog world a significant state such as England could not remain isolated. London was a major focal point of competitive diplomacy, intelligence gathering, and foreign meddling by the great powers, particularly Spain in the early decades of the century and France after 1660. The Anglo-Spanish agreements of 1630–31 and the Secret Treaty of Dover in 1670 represented policies of enlisting or at least neutralising England in the Hispano-Dutch and Franco-Dutch conflicts respectively. England, for its part, could not opt out.

Despite domestic differences over foreign policy which were largely ideological, it developed a national strategic posture, pioneered by Elizabeth I, to counter the threat of an ambitious continental power. Strategy implies a threat, and the threats – from Spain, the Dutch republic, and France – were real in their different ways. They signify England's inescapable involvement in the struggle for mastery in early modern Europe. England's status in that struggle changed over time. In 1600 a lesser or second rank power, it had evolved into a great power by the 1690s, which by its intervention was transforming the shape of Europe and the world. This was, in broad terms, a movement from the receiving to the delivering end of international relations, while remaining always a part of the European whole. As a great power England revolved just as much around the intersection of its internal and external affairs. The military cutting edge of such a power is utterly bound up with its domestic evolution.[52]

IV

THE ANGLO-EUROPEAN SEVENTEENTH CENTURY

What we can term the Anglo-European seventeenth century was prefaced by the Elizabethan war with Spain. This was a sustained and intensive engagement with European affairs over at least twenty years. The wealth, power, and ambition of Spain cast a long shadow over English history which did not lift until the collapse of the Spanish monarchy in the 1640s.[53] Spanish imperial power in the Atlantic, Spanish naval and military force in Europe, Spanish diplomatic leverage, and Spanish commitment to confessional religious conflict were unavoidable facts for England. The invasion scares of the 1580s and 1590s, as well as the 1620s, testify to this. Spanish statesmen tended to see England as a critical political zone whose role could not be left to chance. On the English side, while an abiding pattern of strategic factors emerged under Elizabeth – naval self defence, the control of the Low Countries, and the balance of power, in the background were domestic issues which continued to condition that strategy: religion, trade, money, and foreign policy as a royal prerogative.

James I was dabbling in European politics before he became king of England. Worried about Spanish interference in the English succession, he courted other Catholic states before 1603.[54] His major ambitions after arriving in England were European. The western European movement towards peace during the first decade of the century was largely his work: the Anglo-Spanish Treaty of London (1604) and the Hispano-Dutch Truce of Antwerp (1609–21). Peace brought trade and customs revenues and relieved the financial pressure on the English crown. Court factions revolved around opposition to or furthering of Spanish influence, James being in the latter camp despite the failure of the attempted Spanish match. The Anglo-Palatine marriage of 1613 linked England to the outbreak of the Thirty Years War. English Protestant religious and younger royal political interests called successfully for military involvement. In the 1620s foreign policy and war strategy became divisive parliamentary issues.

Charles I's sojourn in Spain in the early 1620s influenced him greatly, and he remained an admirer of Castilian civilisation.[55] The Anglo-Spanish war of his youth was an act of pique for the failure of the marriage negotiations. Its mismanagement by the duke of Buckingham led to a grave English constitutional crisis, including the duke's assassination, and eventually to non-parliamentary rule and withdrawal from the war by the early 1630s. Spanish diplomacy had facilitated this breakdown of English state policy in order to isolate the Dutch. The pro-Spanish neutrality of the personal rule was linked to ecclesiastical and court politics, as well as commercial interests. The foreign policy of the 1630s helped generate powerful ideological and political forces critical in the coming of the English civil war. Charles's withdrawal from the Thirty Years War had important European consequences. It was a vital ingredient of an historical phase which saw Spanish decline, the rise of French power, and the settlement of the German war.

We have alluded to the role of events in the Spanish empire in forcing Charles I to face the Long Parliament. Foreign policy was an issue in the English civil war, largely as a function of the religious question, and appeared in parliament's Nineteen Propositions on the eve of the conflict. Despite the desire of the Pym clique for an Atlantic strategy against Spain, the parliamentary war effort in England relied significantly on Spanish silver imports. On the royalist side, Mary Stuart's marriage in 1641 had linked the Stuart cause to the House of Orange, which sent guns and money to Charles I under Dutch naval protection. France and Spain, at war, each manoeuvred to turn the British crisis to their advantage. The risk of foreign intervention, and parliament's dependence on London's shipping and trade, made command of the sea a war-winning factor. European waters, from the Bay of Biscay to the Baltic, were a vital theatre of the British civil wars. Naval conflict connected the British and European wars, privateers taking commissions from continental powers.[56]

Oliver Cromwell rightly saw England's political destiny as bound up with Europe's. Franco-Spanish conflict, we have seen, enabled him to pacify Ireland and Scotland by 1651. It was vital for the survival of the Commonwealth to deny the royalists outlying British bases. Cromwell's targets were always the English royalists, at home and abroad – where their privateers were still active, and the Roman Church. These lay behind his decisions in favour of the French alliance and the Spanish war, and his naval build-up. Cromwell used military and naval power to guard the revolutionary regime and obtain respect for it in Europe. In this sense the first Anglo-Dutch war (1652–54) was a success. Ideological and commercial grievances triggered the conflict, but the Orange-Stuart alliance was also an issue: only the Dutch navy could cover a royalist landing in Britain.[57] Cromwell insisted on breaking the power of the House of Orange and of the royalists in Holland in the terms of the peace. The mixed success of English involvement in the Franco-Spanish war, and the Treaty of the Pyrenees (1659), cleared the way for an unopposed British restoration. Charles II then induced the repeal of the Dutch Act of Seclusion. This restored the Orangists and led eventually to Prince William's assumption of power, indeed indirectly to his ascending the English throne.

Charles II, despite his apparent loyalty to his nephew, William of Orange, was a Francophile more impressed by the power of his cousin Louis XIV. French influence hung over restoration politics much in the way that Spanish power had pervaded the early Stuart court. French absolutism and Catholicism struck fear into Whig political interests, linking domestic and foreign issues, against the background of Franco-Dutch rivalry and warfare. Louis and William battled fiercely for influence in England. The second Anglo-Dutch war (1665–67) was the work of English political and commercial interests and led to the earl of Clarendon's fall. The third war (1672–74) was predicated on Charles's secret alliance with France and his personal agenda in England: the enhancement of royal power by a war of aggression. The fallout from the war was serious constitutional conflict, and reluctance to trust the king with foreign policy or control of a standing army. Charles played out the Exclusion Crisis amidst foreign manoeuvring, ultimately accepting French money in exchange for satellite status abroad.

James II's regime was a casualty of cumulative English political conflicts coinciding with an international crisis. Louis XIV's attack on the Huguenots had already intensified English anti-Catholicism.[58] A Dutch decision – in Dutch interests – to invade England, William's boldness in carrying it out, mutual Anglo-Dutch political interests, and the facts of French strategy all combined to bring about political revolution at the expense of the Anglo-French Stuart line. James fell in failing hopelessly to fight a fourth Anglo-Dutch war. The ramifications – for England, Britain, Europe's balance of power, and the world – were profound.

William III immediately committed Britain to a decade of war with France, in continuation of his lifelong struggle against French domination of Europe. The Protestant succession in Britain was also at stake, the Jacobites having French backing and recognition. The Irish campaign of 1690 was the first of a number of Franco-Jacobite invasion attempts. Dutch political and military leadership, as well as financial skills, were vital in building the English war machine. Various interests competed in parliament, linking domestic, foreign, and strategic issues. The governing classes accepted the fiscal revolution to defend the nation from foreign threat.

The war of the Spanish succession, presided over by Anne, sustained the interconnected national and European causes of the Williamite war. The Treaty of Utrecht (1713) recognised the Protestant succession in Britain. The English political background to the war was fierce factional strife and the fall of the Whigs in 1710–11. The duke of Marlborough, in alliance with his wife Sarah, enjoyed a formidable conjunction of English political and European grand strategic power. With Peter the Great he essentially shaped the western European state system until the French Revolution. He also ensured the defeat of the Jacobite cause which, had it succeeded, would probably have undone the Anglo-Scottish Union of 1707.

V

CONCLUSION

'Inevitable' is one of the strongest words employable in history, but we can fairly use it here. The European – and international – context inevitably enhances our understanding of seventeenth century (and, by extension, early modern) England, subject as it was to very powerful international trends. Even Imperial Spain, a dominant power with an overseas empire, which sought to close its intellectual borders against the tide of new ideas, was buffeted by a variety of international forces. We must therefore conceive of an Anglo-European and Anglo-international seventeenth century history, incorporating both comparative and relational elements. English history is European and international history. There is a dual purpose here: English history contributes to the understanding of the wider context, as well as the reverse. In thus contextualising English history we are recognising the tension between the seamless historical web and the need for coherent investigation. One might object that we need a 'new European history', incorporating English history in proportion: an admirable idea but beyond the scope of this essay to advocate. There is, however, no reason why we cannot pursue Anglo-European history so defined, with the purpose of understanding both England and Europe.

Seventeenth century England is not, of course, utterly of a piece with its European context any more than other European states and societies. It exhibits important and subtle differences which extended essays in contrast can fruitfully identify.[59] By the early eighteenth century England was a relatively constitutional, commercial, and socially mobile society. But international forces had run, and continued to run, deeply within it. England's seventeenth century constitutional revolution contributed greatly to what was an early modern European achievement: the acceptance of the idea of novelty as a positive value.[60] In constitutional terms, the English revolution influenced the wider world in Europe, America, and beyond. Our conception of English history as a distinct national story is arguably a product of modern times: of a nationalistic and imperialistic nineteenth century, and of a twentieth century in which, it has been said, England has been as gratified to remember its recent history as continental countries have been eager to forget theirs. International history is a not inappropriate genre for an age of globalisation. After all, it is often hard to have a brief for nations. Insofar as civilisation has moved up the hill, nations have probably done less to bring this about than great cities, great empires, great religions, and great ideas. Our very conception of nations is open to question: Britain is certainly not a nation, and perhaps neither is England, but that is another story. We *can* say that Anglo-European history will be intellectually enlightening and pedagogically enriching, for it is a step closer to the truth. The English apples have never fallen far from the European tree.

Notes on Chapter 11

1   I use 'British' here in the sense of the three kingdoms of England, Scotland and Ireland. See for example B. Bradshaw and J. Morrill (eds), *The British problem, c.1534–1707* (London, 1996).

2   John Elliott called for it in general terms in 1991. See J.H. Elliott, *National and comparative history. An inaugural lecture delivered before the University of Oxford on 10 May 1991* (Oxford, 1991). See also J. Scott, 'England's troubles 1603–1702' in R.M. Smuts (ed.), *The early Stuart court and Europe. Essays in politics and political culture* (Cambridge, 1996).

3   See for example R. Lockyer, *Buckingham, the life and political career of George Villiers, first duke of Buckingham 1592–1628* (London, 1981); C. Martin and G. Parker, *The Spanish armada* (London, 1988); L.J. Reeve, *Charles I and the road to personal rule* (Cambridge, 1989); and the chapters on foreign relations by S. Adams and J. Reeve in J.Morrill (ed.), *The Oxford illustrated history of Tudor and Stuart Britain* (Oxford, 1996).

4   J.I. Israel (ed.), *The Anglo-Dutch moment. Essays on the Glorious Revolution and its world impact* (Cambridge, 1991). See also S.C.A. Pincus, *Protestantism and patriotism. Ideologies and the making of English foreign policy, 1650–1668* (Cambridge, 1996).

5   See for example H. Morgan, 'British policies before the British state' in Bradshaw and Morrill, *The British problem.*

6   C.Russell, *The causes of the English civil war* (Oxford, 1990).

7   Russell has pursued the comparative agenda to a significant extent. See most recently C. Russell, 'Composite monarchies in early modern Europe: the British and Irish example' in A. Grant and K.J. Stringer (eds), *Uniting the kingdom? The making of British history* (London, 1995).

8   See however Elliott, *National and comparative history,* and J.R. Gillis, 'The future of European history' in *Perspectives. American Historical Association newsletter,* 34, 4, April, 1996, pp. 5–6.

9   J. Black, *Convergence or divergence? Britain and the continent* (London, 1994), p. 2.

10   C. Hill, introduction to T.S. Aston (ed.), *Crisis in Europe 1560–1660* (London, 1965), p. 3.

11   J.H. Elliott, *Richelieu and Olivares* (Cambridge, 1984); P. Kennedy, *The rise and fall of the great powers. Economic change and military conflict from 1500 to 2000* (New York and London, 1987).

12   See the various contributions to 'What is diplomatic history?' in J. Gardiner (ed.), *What is history today?* (London, 1988).

13   See in general M.S. Anderson, *The rise of modern diplomacy 1450–1919* (London, 1993).

14   See for example P. Kennedy, *The rise of the Anglo-German antagonism, 1860–1914* (London, 1980).

15   The classic statement is H. Bull, *The anarchical society. A study of order in world politics* (London, 1977; second edn with an introduction by S. Hoffmann, 1995). Hedley Bull was Montague Burton Professor of International Relations at Oxford until his untimely death in 1985.

16   A classic text is M. Howard, *War in European history* (Oxford, 1976). See also 'What is military history?' in Gardiner, *What is history today?*

17   See in particular A.T. Mahan, *The influence of sea power upon history 1660–1783* (Boston, 1890; repr. London, 1965).

18   See respectively P. Kennedy, *The rise and fall of British naval mastery* (London, 1976) and N.A.M. Rodger, *The safeguard of the sea. A naval history of Britain. Volume one 660–1649* (London, 1997).

19   S.R. Gardiner, *History of England from the accession of James I to the outbreak of the civil war, 1603–1642*, 10 vols (London, 1883–84).

20   C. Brooks, 'A law-abiding and litigious society' in Morrill (ed.), *Oxford illustrated history of Tudor and Stuart Britain*, p. 139.

21   See in general G. Parker, *The military revolution. Military innovation and the rise of the West 1500–1800*, second edn (Cambridge, 1996).

22   J. Scott, *Algernon Sidney and the English republic 1623–1677* (Cambridge, 1988), p. 17: the first part of an outstanding two volume study of Sidney.

23   Note, however, the Quinn-Canny thesis that Anglo-Irish relations were a dimension of English Atlantic colonisation. I would not regard these views as necessarily mutually exclusive. See Bradshaw and Morrill (ed.), *The British problem*, pp. 10ff.

24   Anderson, *Rise of modern diplomacy*, pp. 96ff.

25   For an outstanding recent account of war as a cultural institution see J. Keegan, *A history of warfare* (London, 1993). Keegan's book is also a polemic against the Clausewitzian or statist view of war.

26   M. Knox, 'Conclusion: continuity and revolution in the making of strategy' in W. Murray, M. Knox, and A. Bernstein (eds), *The making of strategy. Rulers, states, and war* (Cambridge, 1994), p. 622.

27   Bull, *Anarchical society*, pp. 18, 39ff.

28   See P. Collinson, 'England and international Calvinism, 1558–1640' in M. Prestwich (ed.), *International Calvinism 1541–1715* (Oxford, 1985).

29   See A. Milton, *Catholic and reformed. The Roman and Protestant churches in English Protestant thought, 1600–1640* (Cambridge, 1995).

30   See J. Morrill, *The nature of the English revolution* (London, 1993).

31   J. Scott, *Algernon Sidney and the restoration crisis, 1677–1683* (Cambridge, 1991), pp. 357–8 et passim.

32   J.H.M. Salmon, *Society in crisis. France in the sixteenth century* (London, 1975). On the complexities of the general state building process see M. Greengrass (ed.), *Conquest and coalescence. The shaping of the state in early modern Europe* (London, 1991).

33   See in particular Aston (ed.), *Crisis in Europe 1560–1660*; G. Parker and L.M. Smith (eds), *The general crisis of the seventeenth century* (London, 1978).

34   On which see Morrill, 'Politics in an age of revolution, 1630–1690' in Morrill (ed.), *Oxford illustrated history of Tudor and Stuart Britain*, p. 367.

35 These late seventeenth and early eighteenth century comparisons are partly indebted to Black, *Convergence or divergence?*, p. 142.

36 See J.H.M. Salmon, *The French religious wars in English political thought* (Oxford, 1959).

37 See the excellent general account in Howard, *War in European history*, pp. 38, 46–8, 52–3.

38 See J.I. Israel, *The Dutch republic and the Hispanic world 1606–1661* (Oxford, 1982).

39 For a concise account see J. Reeve, 'Britain and the world under the Stuarts, 1603–1689' in Morrill (ed.), *Oxford illustrated history of Tudor and Stuart Britain.*

40 See in general J.R. Jones, *The Anglo-Dutch wars of the seventeenth century* (London, 1996).

41 See Parker, *Military revolution*, now the major text, as well as C.J. Rogers (ed.), *The military revolution debate. Readings on the military transformation of early modern Europe* (Boulder, 1995).

42 I. Roy, 'England turned Germany? The aftermath of the civil war in its European context', *Transactions of the Royal Historical Society*, 5th series, 28, 1978.

43 Here I argue similarly to Nicholas Rodger, who has posited the idea of a 'naval revolution' during this period in England and Holland. Cf. *Safeguard of the sea*, pp. 430ff.

44 Jones, *Anglo-Dutch wars*, p. 79 et passim.

45 There is also a contrast with traditional Celtic ways of war and society, surviving into the age of eighteenth century Jacobite rebellion. See J.M. Hill, *Celtic warfare. 1595–1763* (Edinburgh, 1986)

46 See in general P. Kennedy (ed.), *Grand strategies in war and peace* (New Haven, 1991).

47 On these matters see W.S. Maltby, 'The origins of a global strategy: England from 1558 to 1713' in Murray et al. (eds), *Making of strategy*, pp. 162–3.

48 See Parker, *Military revolution*, ch. 3, especially pp. 82–3.

49 Bull, *Anarchical society*, p. 195.

50 The balance of power was an influential concept by the early eighteenth century, such as in the Whig tract *The balance of power* of 1711. J. Black, *A system of ambition? British foreign policy 1660–1793* (London, 1991), pp. 146–7.

51 Bull, *Anarchical society*, pp. 23–4.

52 Paul Kennedy emphasises the economic dimension of the domestic scene. See *Rise and fall of the great powers*, pp. xv-xvi.

53 On Spanish grand strategy in the late sixteenth and early seventeenth centuries see G. Parker, 'The making of strategy in Habsburg Spain:

Philip II's "bid for mastery," 1556–1598' in Murray et al. (eds), *Making of strategy*, and J.H. Elliott, 'Managing decline: Olivares and the grand strategy of Imperial Spain' in Kennedy (ed.), *Grand strategies in war and peace.*

54 S. Adams, 'England and the world under the Tudors, 1485–1603' in Morrill (ed.), *Oxford illustrated history of Tudor and Stuart Britain*, p. 414. On seventeenth century foreign relations see Reeve, 'Britain and the world under the Stuarts' in *ibid.*

55 For an Anglo-European account of the late 1620s and early 1630s see Reeve, *Charles I and the road to personal rule.*

56 On the civil wars at sea see Rodger, *Safeguard of the sea*, pp. 415ff.

57 Jones, *Anglo-Dutch wars*, p. 8.

58 The Edict of Nantes was revoked in 1685.

59 See, for example, Black, *Convergence or divergence?*, passim.

60 See J.H. Elliott, 'Yet another crisis?' in P. Clark (ed.), *The European crisis of the 1590s* (London, 1985), p. 308.

Further Reading

(A) General

Valuable general books that present a British approach are Hugh Kearney, *The British Isles: A History of Four Nations*, (Cambridge, 1989); and John Morrill (ed.), *The Oxford Illustrated History of Tudor and Stuart Britain*, (Oxford, 1996). A fine textbook for the seventeenth century is David L. Smith, *A History of the Modern British Isles 1603–1707: The Double Crown*, (Oxford, 1998). A stimulating Scottish-centred approach is Keith M. Brown, *Kingdom or Province? Scotland and the Regal Union 1603–1715*, (Basingstoke, 1992). Brian Levack surveys thinking about Anglo-Scottish union across the whole of the seventeenth century in *The Formation of the British State: England, Scotland, and the Union 1603–1707*, (Oxford, 1987). But the best introduction to the rapidly developing field of 'British' history is probably provided by a sampling of the work contained in several recent collections of essays that set out to explore the parameters of the subject. Most of these collections are of uniformly high quality. See especially Ronald G. Asch (ed.), *Three Nations – A Common History? England, Scotland, Ireland and British History c.1600–1920*, (Bochum, 1993); Steven Ellis and Sarah Barber (eds), *Conquest and Union: Fashioning a British State, 1485–1725*, (Harlow, 1995); Brendan Bradshaw & John Morrill (eds), *The British Problem, c. 1534–1707: State Formation in the Atlantic Archipelago*, (Basingstoke, 1996); Alexander Grant & Keith I. Stringer, *Uniting the Kingdom? The Making of British History*, (London, 1995); and Brendan Bradshaw & Peter Roberts (eds), *British Consciousness and Identity: The Making of Britain, 1533–1707*, (Cambridge, 1998). Essential reading, too, are the seminal essays of J.G.A. Pocock, 'British History: A Plea for a New Subject', *New Zealand Journal of History*, 8

(1974); reprinted in *Journal of Modern History*, 47 (1975), pp. 601–28; and 'The Limits and Divisions of British History: In Search of the Unknown Subject', *American Historical Review*, 87 (1982), pp. 311–336.

(B) The Regal Union 1603–38

The Jacobean union of crowns (1603) is an obvious starting-point and has been well-discussed. The standard account is Bruce Galloway, *The Union of England and Scotland 1603–1608*, (Edinburgh, 1986). It is supplemented by the relevant portions of Brian P. Levack, *The Formation of the British State: England, Scotland, and the Union 1603–1707*, (Oxford, 1987); and the collection of contemporary opinions in *The Jacobean Union: Six Tracts of 1604*, ed. Galloway & Levack, (Edinburgh, 1985). Important interpretative essays include Conrad Russell, 'The Anglo-Scottish Union 1603–1643: A Success?', in Anthony Fletcher & Peter Roberts (eds), *Religion, Culture and Society in Early Modern Britain: Essays in Honour of Patrick Collinson*, (Cambridge, 1994), ch. 10; Jenny Wormald, 'The Creation of Britain: Multiple Kingdoms or Core and Colonies?', *Transactions of the Royal Historical Society*, 6th series, 2 (1992), pp. 175–94; and Wormald, 'James VI, James I and the Identity of Britain', in Brendan Bradshaw & John Morrill (eds), *The British Problem, c. 1534–1707: State Formation in the Atlantic Archipelago*, (Basingstoke, 1996), ch. 6. For the apocalyptic dimensions of union, see Arthur H. Williamson, 'Scotland, Antichrist, and the Invention of Great Britain', in John Dwyer et al. (eds), *New Perspectives on the Politics and Culture of Early Modern Scotland*, (Edinburgh, 1982), pp. 34–58. On the reign of James VI & I as a whole, see Maurice Lee, Jr, *Great Britain's Solomon: James VI and I in His Three Kingdoms*, (Urbana IL, 1990). Broader still, but important, is Conrad Russell, *The Causes of the English Civil War*, (Oxford, 1990). A valuable collection of work on political thought is Roger A. Mason (ed.), *Scots and Britons: Scottish Political Thought and the Union of 1603*, (Cambridge, 1993). The early part of the reign of Charles I has attracted less attention from 'British' historians (for the period after 1638 see the following section), but a start can be made for Scotland with the early chapters of Allan I. Macinnes, *Charles I and the Making of the Covenanting Movement 1625–1641*, (Edinburgh, 1991); and for Ireland with Hugh Kearney, *Strafford in Ireland 1633–41: A Study in Absolutism*, (Cambridge, rev. ed. 1989); and Julia F. Merritt (ed.), *The Political World of Thomas Wentworth, Earl of Strafford 1621–1641*, (Cambridge, 1996).

(C) The War(s) of the Three Kingdoms 1638–60

For a handy introduction see Peter Gaunt, *The British Wars 1637–1651*, (London, 1997). More ambitious, but perhaps less succesful, is Martyn Bennett, *The Civil Wars in Britain and Ireland 1638–1651*, (Oxford, 1997). The body of work that has done most to foreground the British history of the mid-seventeenth century is contained in three books by Conrad Russell, *The Causes of the English Civil War*, (Oxford, 1990); *The Fall of the British Monarchies, 1637–42*, (Oxford, 1991); and his collected essays, *Unrevolutionary England 1603–1642*, (London, 1990). These should be read alongside John Morrill's critique in Morrill, *The Nature of the English Revolution*, (Harlow, 1993), ch. 13. For Morrill's own view of the period see especially Morrill, 'Three Kingdoms and One Commonwealth? The Enigma of Mid-Seventeenth Century Britain and Ireland', in Alexander Grant & Keith J.Stringer (eds), *Uniting the Kingdom? The Making of British History*, (London, 1995), ch. 10. Another valuable discussion is Arthur H. Williamson, 'Scotland and the British Revolutions', *Scottish Historical Review*, 73 (1994), pp. 117–27. Essays that should prove seminal are (on the 1640s) J.G.A. Pocock, 'The Atlantic Archipelago and the War of the Three Kingdoms'; and (on the 1650s) Derek Hirst, 'The English Republic and the Meaning of Britain'; both in Brendan Bradshaw & John Morrill (eds), *The British Problem, c. 1534–1707: State Formation in the Atlantic Archipelago*, (Basingstoke, 1996), chs 7–8. A stimulating collection of material that escapes the anglocentrism of much discussion is John R. Young, *Celtic Dimensions of the British Civil Wars*, (Edinburgh, 1997). The work of Jane Ohlmeyer provides another model for the writing of British history of this period. See her *Civil War and Restoration in Three Kingdoms: The Career of Randall Macdonell, Marquis of Antrim 1609–1683*, (Cambridge, 1993), and her own contribution to Ohlmeyer (ed.), *Ireland: From Independence to Occupation 1641–1660*, (Cambridge, 1995). Recent work on the pivotal events in Scotland (1638) and Ireland (1641) can be found in Allan I. Macinnes, *Charles I and the Making of the Covenanting Movement 1625–1641*, (Edinburgh, 1991); John Morrill (ed.), *The Scottish National Covenant in its British Context 1638–51*, (Edinburgh, 1990); Brian Mac Cuarta SJ, (ed.), *Ulster 1641: Aspects of the Rising*, (Belfast, 1993, rev. ed. 1997); and Michael Perceval-Maxwell, *The Outbreak of the Irish Rebellion of 1641*, (Montreal, 1994).

(D) Restoration to Revolution: 1660–1690

Recent attempts to adopt a 'three kingdoms' approach to the history of this period include T. Barnard, 'Scotland and Ireland in the later

Stewart monarchy', in S. Ellis and S. Barber eds., *Conquest and Union. Fashioning a British State, 1485–1725*, (Harlow, 1995), pp. 250–75; M. Goldie, 'Divergence and Union. Scotland and England, 1660–1707', in B. Bradshaw and J. Morrill eds., *The British Problem, c. 1534–1707. State Formation in the Atlantic Archipelago*, (Basingstoke, 1996), pp. 220–45; R. Hutton, *Charles II. King of England, Scotland and Ireland*, (Oxford, 1989) and 'The Triple-Crowned Islands', in L. Glassey ed., *The Reigns of Charles II and James VII & II*, (Basingstoke, 1997), pp. 71–81; J. Kelly, 'The origins of the act of union: an examination of unionist opinion in Britain and Ireland, 1650–1800', *Irish Historical Studies*, 25 (1987), pp. 236–63; J. Smyth, 'The Communities of Ireland and the British State, 1660–1707', in Bradshaw and Morrill, *The British Problem*, pp. 246–61; C. Kidd, 'Protestantism, constitutionalism and British identity under the later Stuarts', in B. Bradshaw and P. Roberts (eds), *British consciousness and identity: the making of Britain, 1533–1707*, (Cambridge, 1998), pp. 321–42; J. Smyth, '"No remedy more proper": Anglo-Irish unionism before 1707', in Bradshaw and Roberts (eds), *British Consciousness and Identity*, pp. 301–20; Tim Harris, 'The British Dimension, Religion, and the Shaping of Political Identities in the Reign of Charles II', in Tony Claydon and Ian McBride eds, *Protestantism and National Identity: Britain and Ireland, c. 1650–c. 1850*, (Cambridge, 1998), pp. 131–56; Harris, 'The People, the Law and the Constitution in Scotland and England: A Comparative Approach to the Glorious Revolution', *Journal of British Studies*, 38 (1999), pp. 28–58; and Harris, 'Reluctant Revolutionaries? The Scots and the Revolution of 1688–9', in Howard Nenner ed., *Politics and the Political Imagination in Later Stuart Britain: Essays Presented to Lois Green Schwoerer*, (Rochester NY, 1997), pp. 97–117.

With regard to Restoration politics in the multiple monarchy, see T. Barnard, 'Settling and Unsettling Ireland: The Cromwellian and Williamite Revolutions', in J. Ohlmeyer ed., *Ireland from Independence to Occupation 1641–1660*, (Cambridge, 1995), pp. 265–91; K. Brown, *Kingdom or Province? Scotland and the Regal Union 1603–1714*, (Basingstoke, 1992); and S. Connolly, *Religion, Law and Power. The Making of Protestant Ireland 1660–1760*, (Oxford, 1992). For the reign of James VII and II and the Revolution, see I. Cowan, 'The reluctant revolutionaries: Scotland in 1688', in E. Cruickshanks ed., *By Force or Default? The Revolution of 1688–89*, (Edinburgh, 1989), pp. 65–81 and 'Church and State Reformed? The Revolution of 1688–9 in Scotland', in J. Israel ed., *The Anglo-Dutch Moment*, (Cambridge, 1991), pp. 163–84; D. Hayton, 'The Williamite Revolution in Ireland, 1688–91', in Israel ed., *The Anglo-Dutch Moment*, pp. 185–213; P. Kelly,

'Ireland and the Glorious Revolution: From Kingdom to Colony', in R. Beddard ed., *The Revolutions of 1688*, (Oxford, 1991), pp. 163–90; J. Miller, The Earl of Tyrconnel and James II's Irish Policy 1685–1688', *Historical Journal*, 20 (1977), pp. 802–23 and J. Simms, *Jacobite Ireland 1685–91*, (London, 1969).

(E) Britain and Ireland, 1690–1715

There have been relatively few works taking an integrated 'three kingdoms' approach to the history of Britain and Ireland in the period 1690–1715. The best of the limited field are two articles by David Hayton (either on his own or in collaboration), which concentrate on the problems of coordinating three independently minded legislatures: Daniel Szechi and David Hayton, 'John Bull's other kingdoms: the English government of Scotland and Ireland', in Colin Jones (ed), *Britain in the first age of party, 1680–1750* (London, 1987); David Hayton, 'Constitutional experiments and political expediency', in Ellis and Barber (eds), *Conquest and union: fashioning a British state, 1485–1725* (Harlow, 1995). The most accessible general surveys of Ireland, Scotland and England respectively are provided by the relevant sections of T.W. Moody and W.E. Vaughan (eds), *A new history of Ireland. Volume 4. Eighteenth century Ireland, 1691–1800* (Oxford, 1992); K.M. Brown, *Kingdom or province? Scotland under the regal union, 1603–1715* (London, 1992); Geoffrey Holmes, *The making of a great power: late Stuart and early Georgian Britain, 1660–1722* (Harlow, 1993). Despite their titles, however, these volumes do not always make Anglo-Celtic interaction a central theme.

In contrast to the general area of Anglo-Celtic relations, 1707 has received much attention. Mark Goldie, 'Divergence and union: Scotland and England 1660–1707' in Bradshaw and Morrill (eds), *British problem* is the best short survey and comes with an excellent guide to further reading – not only on the Union but on many aspects of Scots society, economy, religion and identity. Irish identities in the period are covered by: Sean Connolly, *Religion, law and power: the making of protestant Ireland, 1660–1760* (Oxford, 1992); David Hayton, 'Anglo-Irish attitudes: changing perceptions of national identity among the protestant ascendancy in Ireland, c.1670–1750', *Studies in Eighteenth-century Culture*, 17 (1987), 145–157; Toby Barnard, 'Protestantism, ethnicity and Irish identities, 1660–1760' in Tony Claydon and Ian McBride, *Chosen peoples? Protestantism and national identity in Britian and Ireland c.1650–c1850* (Cambridge, forthcoming); Jim Smyth '"Like amphibious animals": Irish patriots, ancient

Britons, 1691–1707', *Historical Journal*, 36 (1993); Jim Smyth, 'The communities of Ireland and the British state, 1660–1707, in Bradshaw and Morrill (eds), *British problem*. The first of these works provides a stimulatingly revisionist account of social relations and self-perceptions, the last provides a guide to further reading. R.F. Foster, *Modern Ireland, 1660–1972* (London, 1988) renders this period of Irish history (as many others) curiously bloodless. For the penal laws, see the works in note 29 of ch. 5 above. For Jacobitism (a pan-British phenomenon somewhat perhaps too much neglected in ch. 5 above) see Bruce Lenman, *The Jacobite risings in Britain, 1689–1746* (London, 1980); Eveline Cruickshanks (ed), *Ideology and conspiracy: aspects of Jacobitism, 1688–1759* (Edinburgh, 1982); Eveline Cruickshanks and Jeremy Black (eds), *The Jacobite challenge* (Edinburgh, 1988) Daniel Szechi, *The Jacobites: Britain and Europe, 1688–1788* (Manchester, 1994). For another neglected theme, the 'British' identity of Wales, see Philip Jenkins, 'The Anglican church and the unity of Britain: the Welsh experience, 1560–1714', in Ellis and Barber (eds), *Conquest and union* and Scott Mandelbrote, 'The bible and national identity, c.1660–c.1760' in Claydon and McBride (eds) *Chosen peoples*. For more on the present author's scepticism about the project of 'British' history as a whole, see Tony Claydon, 'Problems with the British problem', *Parliamentary History*, 16 (1997), 221–7.

(F) Socio-Economic History of Britain

A number of essays or collections of essays have tried to develop comparative analyses between the British kingdoms and Ireland: especially, Keith Wrightson, "Kindred and adjoining kingdoms'; an English perspective on the social and economic history of early modern Scotland', in Robert A. Houston & Ian D. Whyte (eds.) *Scottish Society 1500–1800*, (Cambridge, 1989) pp. 247–8; Thomas M. Devine & David Dickson (eds.) *Ireland and Scotland, 1600–1850*, (Edinburgh,1983); L.M. Cullen, & T. Christopher Smout, (eds.) *Comparative Aspects of Irish and Scottish Economic and Social History 1600–1900*, (Edinburgh, 1977); Rosalind Mitchison &. Peter Roebuck (eds.) *Economy and Society in Scotland and Ireland 1500–1939*, (Edinburgh, 1988); and S.J. Connolly, Robert A. Houston, & Robert J. Morris, *Conflict, Identity and Economic Development. Ireland and Scotland 1600–1939.* (Preston, 1995). These provide the best introduction to the possibilities of a 'British' socio-economic history; and references to specific essays in the collections can be found in the notes to chapter

7. It is worth noting also that economic issues were important in relation to the union of 1707: an introduction to historical controversy on this subject can be found in Christopher A. Whatley, *'Bought and Sold for English Gold'? Explaining the Union of 1707*, (Edinburgh, 1994). Few books have been written that provide holisitc approaches to the socio-economic history of early modern Britain and Ireland; but one on demography is Robert A. Houston, *The Population History of Britain and Ireland 1500–1750*, (Basingstoke, 1992).

(G) British Identity and its Components

Since John Pocock's pioneering essay three decades ago a great deal has been written about British political history and the formation of the British state. However, very little has appeared about the sources of British identity before 1707. The following will provide the most useful beginning point. Jane Dawson, 'Anglo-Scottish Protestant Culture and Integration in Sixteenth Century Britain,' in S.G. Ellis and S. Barber (eds.), *Conquest and Union: Fashioning a British State, 1485–1725* (London, 1995), pp 87–114; Dawson, 'William Cecil and the British Dimension of Early Elizabethan Foreign Policy,' in *History* 74 (1989), pp 196–216; Dawson, 'The Fifth Earl of Argyle, Gaelic Lordship and Political Power in Sixteenth Century Scotland,' in *Scottish Historical Review* 67 (1988), pp 1–27; P.J. McGinnis and A.H. Williamson, *George Buchanan The Political Poetry* (Edinburgh, 1998); John Morrill, 'The Britishness of the English Revolution, 1640–1660,' in R.G. Asch (ed.), *Three Nations – A Common History?* (Bochum, 1992), pp 83–115; Morrill, 'The British Problem, *c.* 1534–1707,' in B. Bradshaw and J. Morrill (eds.), *The British Problem c. 1534–1707: State Formation in the Atlantic Archipelago*, pp 1–38; Conrad Russell, 'Composite Monarchies in Early Modern Europe: the British and Irish Example,' in A. Grant and K.J. Stringer (eds.), *Uniting the Kingdom? The Making of British History* (London, 1995), pp 133–46; Debora Shuger, 'Irishmen, Aristocrats, and Other White Barbarians,' in *Renaissance Quarterly* 50 (1997), pp 494–525; A.H. Williamson, *Scottish National Consciousness in the Age of James VI* (Edinburgh, 1979); Williamson, 'Scots, Indians, and Empire: The Scottish Politics of Civilization, 1519–1609,' in *Past and Present* 150 (February 1996), pp 46–83; Williamson, 'From the Invention of Great Britain to the Creation of British History: A New Historiography,' in *Journal of British Studies* 29 (1990), pp 267–276.

(H) Britain and Europe

Useful books, beyond those cited in the footnotes to chapter 11, include the general accounts of G.M.D. Howat, *Stuart and Cromwellian foreign policy* (London, 1974) and J.R. Jones, *Britain and Europe in the seventeenth century* (London, 1966) and *Britain and the world 1649–1815* (Brighton, 1980), as well as the thematic volumes: D. Chandler and I. Beckett(eds), *The Oxford illustrated history of the British army* (Oxford, 1994), J.R. Hill (ed.), *The Oxford illustrated history of the Royal Navy* (Oxford, 1994), and C. Townshend (ed.), *The Oxford illustrated history of modern war* (Oxford, 1997). At either end of the chronological spectrum are R.B. Wernham, *The making of Elizabethan foreign policy 1558–1603* (Berkeley,1980), J.B. Hattendorf, *England in the war of the Spanish succession: a study of the English view and conduct of grand strategy, 1702–1712* (New York, 1987), and J. Brewer, *The sinews of power. War, money and the English state 1688–1783* (London, 1989). G. Mattingly, *Renaissance diplomacy* (London,1955) and *The defeat of the Spanish armada* (London, 1959) are both classics. H. Butterfield and M. Wight (eds), *Diplomatic investigations* (London, 1966) contains useful perspectives.

INDEX

Entries for concepts central to the book as a whole (e.g. 'British history'; 'multiple monarchy') give references only to explicit discussions of the meaning of the term. Historians' names, especially of those active since about 1960, are indexed very selectively, usually only when they are mentioned as critics or advocates of the new British history. Some terms that appear throughout have not been indexed, in particular 'England', Scotland' and 'Ireland' (but for discussions of the relationship between their particular histories and British history see '"national" histories, etc.'), and the names of their capital cities. Peers are entered under their family names, not their titles. References to relations between the three kingdoms and the European powers are indexed under the name of the other kingdom or state. Topic entries ('commerce', 'ecclesiastical establishments, etc.', 'military history', 'social and economic history') have been used to provide general thematic guidance, and in some cases subsume more precise indexing. The Further Reading sections have not been indexed, and nor, on the whole, have the notes. In general, the index, like the book, is intended to have an historiographical bias, and is not primarily intended for those seeking to locate basic factual information.